Anita Mays, the youngest of four, was born in Nigeria, to Yorkshire parents. She spent a great deal of her upbringing in Africa, while attending boarding school in England where she excelled in sports. At the Universities of Birmingham and Aix-en-Provence she read English and French literature, and attained a combined honours degree. She now lives in Berkshire.

Aeroplanes had always been a seminal part of her childhood. Keen to work in the industry, she applied to become an air hostess, and was subsequently turned down by over 10 airlines. Unable to work in the back, she tried her hand at the front end. She has enjoyed a remarkably colourful career as a pilot, and this book about her experiences, won her a place as a finalist in the national competition 'The People's Author' on TV's Alan Titchmarsh show.

Anita is also a qualified teacher and enjoys teaching English to Foreign students. She travels extensively (recently she backpacked round Colombia), and enjoys cycling, yoga, ceroc dancing and kayaking. She loves history, and reads avidly: novels, science, health, comedy and occasionally nonsense!

Her maxims for a good life: Give yourself time to stand and stare.
                                           Don't take it too seriously.
                                           Most of all....Be Grateful!

FLYGIRL ADVENTURES:

An Autoflyography

I dedicate this book to my mum, for her love, sacrifices, encouragement and generosity. Whose grit, determination and work ethic lifted her out of rations and poverty, and carried her to far flung Africa to face the risks of the unknown, with characteristic courage. For being one of those ladies who'd wear a beautiful white suit with matching hat, gloves and heels when embarking an old BOAC Handley Page Hermes from Lagos, for a two day journey. She'd look a $million but best of all she knocked it up herself on an old Singer sewing machine. For having a song for everything, for being unfailingly elegant and decent and for being my treasured friend.Her words to me as a child were "Aim for the stars and you'll reach the treetops."

Anita Mays

FLYGIRL ADVENTURES:

An Autoflyography

AUSTIN MACAULEY

A CIP catalogue record for this title is available from the British Library.

ISBN 978 1 84963 050 4

www.austinmacauley.com

First Published (2011)
Austin & Macauley Publishers Ltd.
25 Canada Square
Canary Wharf
London
E14 5LB

Printed & Bound in Great Britain

ACKNOWLEDGEMENTS

Gray Joliffe	for the excellent cartoons.
Mike Davis	for teaching me to fly and opening up a special world.
Caroline Davies	for computer assistance and printing out my first copy.
Phil Tomkinson	for love, laughs, and loads of help.
Jack Rose	for worldwide adventures, my first break, and teaching me to land the 727: 'keep her coming down'.
Robbie	my friend and partner in mischief, 'shall we shoot an ILS at Heathrow?'
Mike Woodley	for teaching me so much and for fantastic opportunities, warbirds, air shows, and the seaplane.
My Father	Who flew in Bomber Command in WW2.
FlyPast magazine	For a superb publication.
Virgin Atlantic	For being innovative and progressive, and for some great flights.
Cathy Burnham	For teaching me to be a flight instructor.

All my friends who have 'DANCED THE SKIES ON LAUGHTER SILVERED WINGS' with me at one time or another – they know who they are!

Contents

CHAPTER ONE: Getting Started

A Failed Air Hostess – A Good Start

The sky called again that morning and this time I answered.
"The views are great, come on up!"
"Okay, I'm on my way."

"Clear prop!" the instructor shouted through the little window. The key turned, the prop spun noisily into life, as the nose sunk a couple of inches on its strut.

"Golf Mike Charlie Yankee Oscar radio check and taxi for local."

"Two four left hand, one zero two three," came the reply through the headset (whatever *that* meant). He turned the altimeter knob, opened the throttle, pushed his foot to the floor, which turned us sharply round and off we went. I was expecting him to move the yoke like a steering wheel as we turned the corner.

"Turning is all done with the rudder pedals," he had detected my surprise.

We trundled off like a little duck which moves somewhat awkwardly on the ground yet achieves such grace (as we would) once airborne. He turned into wind by some trees, put the brake on and pushed the throttle to full travel, we rattled and shook like a biscuit tin. He chatted away about the magneto checks, as he went from high to low RPM then aligned his direction indicator with the magnetic compass, dropped his hand between the seats and pulled the flap lever up one notch, then he smiled:

"Ready?"

He had no idea **how** ready I was.

"Oh yes I'm **ready**!"

Would this be the "rabbit-out-of-the-hat" moment that I was waiting for?

We lifted off into a gin-clear November morning. It was the very best autumn could offer – crisp cold air, unlimited visibility and a luminosity and clarity, which made you, glad to be alive. This was my first experience of 'earthshine' and at that moment I lived to appreciate it totally. My heart was cartwheeling.

But – and that's a big '**but**' it had been long journey of disappointment and struggle to arrive at this point.

I had been passionate about getting into aviation because of a lightsome and innocent memory from school days. I would be allowed to leave boarding school at the end of term a night early to catch the BOAC/ British Caledonian flight on a 707 or a DC 10 to Lagos. The excitement was all consuming, joyful anticipation flooded through me. Gatwick was magical in those days, the huge Christmas tree twinkled in the terminal and I'd stand at the gate with my nose pressed against the window, mesmerised by the roaring engines and the flashing lights disappearing into the night sky. Nothing had ever filled me with so much longing.

The association was cemented – planes quite simply meant happiness. Aircraft and airports offered life changing opportunities for adventure; in a matter of hours you could journey into the stratosphere and end up somewhere – *entirely* different. Vast areas that would take all afternoon to drive around could be journeyed across with one glance. "Wow" I used to mutter under my breath if I picked out my home or a village I had *only* known from the ground. It looks so different from up here!

I was fascinated that these huge oversized seemingly cumbersome machines could defy gravity and so gracefully and with such agility, overcome their bulk and ascend, opening up limitless horizons to us, shifting our lives and giving us a whole new vantage point. I'd watch them land – their weight and speed are so cleverly disguised on the approach. How could something that enormous be approaching so slowly without falling to the ground?

Furthermore, airports were wonderful places in those days. It was an age when people didn't need to be told by a robot that they were coming to the end of a walkway or that the doors were opening – yes those Halcyon days when we *knew* to stand clear of the doors because of our own natural instincts. A time when a grown man or woman could be trusted to walk unassisted from a door to a waiting aircraft without slipping falling or suing, getting lost or walking into the engine. An age when the flight would be pleasant dare I say even peaceful – free from the 'pneumatic drill' PA announcements harping on about mind numbing nonsense like scratch cards, special offers, loyalty points, frequent flyers, overhead lockers, smoking, electronic gadgets, what we *can* do, what we *can't* do, vegetarian options, duty free, how to read the magazine, new routes, and their chosen charities. (This all delivered in a voice which could bone herring at twenty fathoms). Yes, just as the Permian period came before the Devonian which was followed by the Cambrian, I hark longingly back to *our* Golden age – the 'Commonsense-ian', which was post 'Getonwithit'era and pre 'Nanny-ian'. Airports and air travel were shining examples of this era.

So, I was determined to become a flight attendant because *that* was the natural way in to the business. It was a job I yearned for. It never occurred to me to become a pilot – yes, I secretly would have loved it but never fancied my chances. It was a distant elitist world full of brainy 'sciencey' people. The only mark I got in my physics O'level was for drawing the white light entering a prism and dispersing into a rainbow and I only got *that* because I had Pink Floyd's 'Dark side of the Moon'. In chemistry, the periodic table was unfathomable, and as for *calculus* – forget it!

So, after graduating I embarked on my first mission – to become a stewardess. Not very challenging some may say but it's what I *wanted!* I applied to all the airlines, large and small and the long and short of it is … that … I got turned down by *every single one.* That was well over ten companies. I was devastated.

Not Another Job Rejection!

"Darling, you've got a letter from British Airways, shall I bring it up?"

Those were the words from my mum who had tried so doggedly to encourage me during the 'year of the job rejection'.

I thought by becoming a hostess, I'd get my foot in the door, start travelling, earn some money, see where the path took me and then, you never know, I might get acquainted with some pilots who would kindly take me along when they used the simulators. Anyway ... I would be happy as a 'hostie' working in the industry, near my beloved aeroplanes learning all about it! Somehow, I believed I would work it out. Sweet reveries!

I managed to achieve something which not *many* people could lay claim to; I *actually* clocked up a dazzling and unprecedented eleven job rejections. That takes some doing! BA, Britannia, British Caledonian, and many others all said 'no thanks'. I was sure it would be a breeze, but what I thought would be an *easy* starter turned into a '*non* starter'.

So that morning whilst standing in my bathroom, my mum handed me the letter, this was my last chance, *every* known airline in the whole of the UK had given me the 'Dear John' treatment. I ripped it open and, as was my custom by then, my eyes shot straight to the bottom. There in print, the by now, familiar words:

"May we take this opportunity to wish you every success in your future career and thank you for your interest in British Airways."

I slowly lifted my weary gaze into the mirror and said sarcastically at my reflection, "The world has more use for an appendix, so do run along, and don't bother us any more, *that's* what they *really* mean."

I was inconsolable, I just slumped and sobbed, my mum tried so hard to rally my spirits. I sputtered through my tears, "We better start a new file for all my job rejections."

"Oh don't be like that darling something will come up, come on cheer up."

The conversation went back and forth over the net like that until mum gave way to her anger in typical maternal style.

"They must be flaming mad, they don't know what they're missing!"

Mums are great aren't they? The only ones who think you are absolutely brilliant and anyone would be darn lucky to have you in their organisation, when, you know in your heart that nothing is further from the truth, in fact, in the evolutionary traffic you are something of a flat tyre. In the animal world, just out of the molecular soup, not even a finned mudskipper at this point.

One which *really* hurt was the rejection from Jersey European, operating from Blackpool to the Isle of Man on a Shorts 360 during which the sum total of the catering service was to hand out a sealed packet of three oatmeal biscuits and pour a cup of tea.

"Why don't you try the RAF and see what *they* say?" mum offered, trying to lift my flagging spirits. Being pre Internet, I found the number in the phone book and call, I did.

"I see my dear, and what exactly is it you are trying to achieve?" came a voice from the other end of the phone. I put a face to it instantly – a blimpish type with a big moustache, grey hair, and specs on the end of the nose who spoke like those bossy wing commanders of old black and white film fame whose favourite words were 'frightful', 'insolence' and 'hup to'. His laugh descended into a patronising spiral until it came to a wheezy stop and he said: "Unless you are of the feathered variety my dear, I'm afraid there's no flying for you here!"

"Thank you *SO MUCH* for your time," I said replacing the receiver.

"Any joy darling?" asked my mum.

"Not unless I am a buzzard."

Enough of the Weight I Need Some Lift

"I've got a three day trip to Nice coming up," was the enviably casual comment from an air hostess I met at a party in town who worked on private executive jets for a company at Heathrow. I was enthralled by this prospect. We swapped numbers. I so wanted her job. I acquired a first aid certificate with St John Ambulance knowing this was a pre requisite and approached them soon after. To no avail, it was the standard 'closed shop' scenario. They only hired their special friends and the network was cosy and nepotistic. Liaisons between the hostesses and the captains or company owners were – shall we say 'close'.

I made it as far as their offices and I recall the very silky, groomed girl who floated around in lots of tumbling baby pink cashmere running her manicured fingers through her long swinging hair. (For someone like me whose hair never moved when I did a handstand, this is an enviable activity!) The phone rang – a guy asking her out I guessed, because she was, much more interested in *that* than this freckly curly haired 'wannabe' in front of her. She giggled and played with her pearls, lowering her chin to nibble on them and running her finger along their length, swivelling around in her leather chair and whispering with a scrunch of her nose, "I'll be with you in a sec." She never did get 'with me' after a sec nor after a month for that matter. As sure as low tide follows high, the letter plopped through my letter box. "We are fully crewed right now, we will keep you on file if anything should come up in the future …"

Yeah yeah yeah I muttered inwardly. I understand *now* that this is how the world works, but it used to hurt.

So … my life was beginning to look like the 'bottom of the parrot's cage', with all the blackballing. I even received a couple of rejections in France, where I tried to take advantage of cross border employment.

'The Careers talk' is a feature of final year at university. We sat in front of the careers officer who politely asked what we were considering.

"Well," I said throwing caution to the wind just to see what she'd say. "What I'd *really* like to do is fly, maybe be a bush pilot in Africa, or just *fly* ... you know ... anywhere."

"I see," she giggled nervously pushing her glasses up her nose and thumbing through her neat piles of paperwork on accountancy, law, medicine, and banking.

"Oh – I actually don't seem to have *a-ny*-thing at all on pilots," she said feigning surprise as though she had just run out.

To earn some money I got a job in a photographic studio (I had a friend there). Photography was a hobby of mine and I fancied being an aerial photographer and combining my two interests. I didn't know much but I experimented with my Canon SLR. I thought the job might teach me about photographic equipment and one day perhaps I'd be heroically hanging out of the side of an aeroplane filming herds of migrating wildebeest for David Attenborough. I ended up stuffing suitcases with foam, sanding gloss paint off huge panels with a Black and Decker and assembling *really* complicated dolls houses and other toys – they were shooting the Argos catalogue. I know we all have to start at the bottom but this was subterranean – I moved on – had to stick with the flying dream. Fun while it lasted – I did a memorable luggage shoot at Brocket Hall where I held a huge light reflector at different angles for six hours. Also met the dashing cad Lord Brockett who showed me the super duper collection of race cars. Wow he's got everything I remember musing inwardly. A few years later he was in jail. This taught me very early on that things are not always as they seem. I've dipped into that little pot of knowledge many times – it was most useful!

I answered an advert for hostesses in a bar/restaurant. A part-time job and a bit of cash were what I needed before the break into aviation came. Having spent some time in the States I thought it would be similar to the bars over there where girls are employed to welcome people, take coats, show customers to the bar, hand over menus then shout down a mike "Mckenzie, party of four, your table is ready".

Not knowing London at all I set off – a little bundle of naivety. Characteristically mum told me to wear a nice suit but my dad said through cigar chomps in his strong Yorkshire accent: "It won't bloody matter what she wears 'cause it's a flaming knockin' shop."

"Don't be silly dad, it will be a really nice place in London and I'll meet new people." (Duh!) I found the address – St James's of course meant nothing to me. So I walked down the cobbled street with thoughts of bars like 'The Rusty Pelican' or 'Carlos Murphy's' full of fun loving, 'bon viveurs' sipping cocktails, feeling sure *this* would be the London equivalent. I hoped my leather suit wouldn't be too racy or inappropriate.

I rang a bell and was shown in. I couldn't believe my eyes, I saw about ten topless girls in stockings and suspenders huddled together round a bar. Breezy Californian cocktail bar it was *not,* however, I had to go through with it – besides I'd never see the inside of one of these joints again so I could learn something. The manageress who, to use an equestrian term looked like she'd been 'ridden hard and put away wet' gave me the brief:

"You need to be able to eat and drink a lot, handle men, and outside these doors you're not our responsibility, you get nothing if you don't get chosen, but it's £25 if a guy chooses to dine with you, then, you can go downstairs and have whatever he buys you to eat and drink ... probably lots of champagne!"

I followed her clunking heels down the wooden staircase. Men were thin on the ground upstairs so I guess most of *those* girls stood around all night topless in high heels, talked amongst themselves then caught the bus home, empty handed.

She sensed I was a bit taken aback – must have been my eyes like organ stops staring at the incongruity of naked boobs flanking a prawn cocktail. So to encourage me she continued:

"We have great cabaret evenings here, a group of girls who have been invited will sit with the guys at this big table and watch a show – something a bit raunchy ya know!"

I glanced over and saw another girl scantily clad having dinner with a cruelly unattractive man.

"Yea I mean look at Susie over there – she's on her second this evening and will probably do another one after this." Susie was quite a girl. He had a few traces of froth in the corners of his mouth and looked like he was on the 'my wife doesn't understand me stories' I caught her looking at her watch discreetly under the table.

I was trying to nod earnestly at her as she described the job.

"Have you done any hostess work before Anita?"

"Well not *exactly* like this," I replied trying to ooze savvy and cool. "I *am* actually trying to become a hostess ... but ... an ... *air* hostess ... and ... well, fly," I said making light of it.

"Well we *certainly* **fly high** in here love," she laughed and flicked the back of her hand against my arm.

"You should start Monday Anita ... I'm telling you, you'd clean up."

Oh well, I thought as I walked back to Green Park tube, at least I've had *one firm job* offer.

"Well?" said my dad when I got home

"Yep, you were right."

"So when d'you start?" he teased

We laughed and he came out with one of his many sayings – never knowing the real Latin he used to make it up.

"Non Illegittimus carburundum love", which was *his* utterly incorrect version of "Don't let the bastards grind you down". He had them in German and French too, all totally incorrect but somehow you knew what they meant! Said with a Yorkshire accent it had me chuckling. I say it to this day when ever things go wrong. Bless him ... he's still making me laugh.

We can smile as we look back, but I keenly remember the gnawing sense of failure and accompanying depression. It is disheartening to find yourself unemployable! My anger was like an icy canal and all I needed was a ship to steer down it. I thought, if I can't work in the back, hey, maybe I'll have a shot at working in the front. I took the phone book and called every flying school in the area and started calmly asking about flying lessons. I had to keep my hopes up. It *was* a gamble! As Churchill said about this life of ours: It is not about the failures, there will *always* be those – what counts is finding the courage to carry on!"

I went first to Blackbush, then on to Fairoaks in Chobham, Surrey. There I met tall lanky Mike who had longish '6ᵗʰ form' hair. He was the slightly geeky, friendly instructor, who was 'a happy soul' passionate about aeroplanes, a competent avionics engineer and could solder or fix any electronic gadgetry no matter how miniscule. He was determined that Fairoaks would be my choice so he did a good sales job. We ended up falling in love of course! From the moment we got airborne on that crisp November morning I knew I *had* to do this. Everything was clear and bright, the world had a glassiness and radiance which filled me with a new elation. The south coast was visible from Guildford, but it wasn't **just** the south coast ... so much more was suddenly visible it was *that* shift in perspective which that little bit of altitude afforded me, – that's what did it. I'd somehow cut the *earthly* tethers which were keeping me chained

We cruised along, he gave me the controls, explaining the basics of attitude and heading in straight and level flight. Then he had a bit of a play, doing lazy 8's and chandelles (a gentle wing over manoeuvre). He could see I was loving it so he climbed a bit higher over Basingstoke and played around with the edges of the clouds. Seeing my 'God this is fantastic' expression, he went the extra yard. We followed the contours of the cumulus clouds just skimming their nebulous edges, dipping into the canyons and valleys, banking sharply round, shooting down the tunnels treating the whole structure like it were solid, yet, magically, the whole playground is illusory, made of vapour. It is liberating to know that if you do knick the edge of a cloud, there is no damage! Some of the cumulus were building and I could see faces and shapes in them, they looked like plump bearded sages chuckling at our games. They were welcoming me here. We cruised and dived around with the speed and grace of a young dolphin around a submerged wreck. There was so much energy all around me both in the billowing clouds and the spinning propeller. Dazzling flashes of sun bounced off the wings as we came cruising out of the spongy corridors of cloud and burst into the full sunlight again.

We descended. Farnborough control released us,

"Nothing known to conflict squawk 2000 call Fairoaks 123.4 – good day."

He talked me through the landing and let me think I had done it (a technique I would learn myself not long after!).

We chatted, and he encouraged me to start. It was indeed because of the kind advocacies of people like him that I found the confidence to proceed and to learn. He made it so 'doable' and was a great support. Shortly after, he gave me the book 'Jonathan Livingston Seagull'. It had a deep effect on me, I loved the words and read it over and over.

"Wants to learn to fly ... you what?" came dad's voice as he dropped his newspaper and looked at mum disbelievingly over the top of his horn rimmed specs.

"There's no bloody future in that – it'll be a waste of money, then she'll want to be a golfer or a windsurfer next month, I mean how can she *ever* make a career of that, girls don't fly *real* planes like airliners – yer daft the pair of you."

He flicked his paper back upright and lifted his head to see through the bifocals, then did his trademark sticking out of lower lip – old habit; and then muttered "bloody nonsense." To be fair he was only trying to be realistic and in time my dad got on board.

"Always have your *own* bit of money darling, this is why." My mum had been left a small amount of money from a deceased relative and now she invested it in my private licence. I was on my way and when Mike my instructor told me that within two years I could be doing *his* job, my goals were set and my tenacity in that pursuit was utterly unflinching. I was an uneasy blend of fragile optimism and creeping doubt. But I just wanted to do this. So much.

As Jonathan said: "Everything that limits us we have to put aside we're free to go where we wish and to be what we are."[1]

Hour Building in USA, West Coast to East Coast

I acquired my private pilot's license in three months. Though tough at times it had been exhilarating. I learnt how to take off, climb, descend, land, come down in a field after an engine failure, land on short runways, and recover from stalls and spins! I must confess I got a little lost on my first solo cross country and had to be rescued by my instructor who set off at lightning speed to find me over Farnborough. It was the final leg back from Pulborough in Sussex, I held the track – adjusted for the wind, watched the timing and was *supposed* to end up over Guildford but I saw a big round gas container.

"That does **not** look like Guildford to me," I whispered to myself as I peered out the window, so I called the home frequency at Fairoaks of 123.42.

"Just fly three sixties," he said, "and don't go **any** further North!" I duly followed orders knowing that to the north lay the Heathrow zone. I know every inch of that landscape *now,* but back then – well it was still unfamiliar. He found me and escorted me back. God, he was my hero after that!

To acquire a commercial pilot's licence in the 1980s you had to have 700 hours. As every student pilot remembers this is tough and you literally take *anything* you can to accumulate those hours. The 'route' for most people was to get a Flying Instructor's rating for which you needed 150 hours, then you'd join some flying school and instruct on little single engine planes, then those hours rolled in! Some people pulled gliders or towed banners, some even borrowed money to buy a share in their own little aircraft.

Having achieved my private licence, I was going for the 150 hours so I could enrol in the Instructor's course at Oxford Air Training School. America attracts British students, hourly rates are lower, the weather is better and this is

[1] Richard D. Bach, *Jonathan Livingston Seagull* (London: Pan Books Ltd, 1973), pp. 76-7.

why you will find a handful of British trainees in nearly every flying school from Florida to California.

I, like so many aviation aspirants went there, determined to accumulate the requisite hours and was fortunate enough to hit a time of favourable dollar rates – it was nearly two to one. I found the nearest airfield to my sister's bedsit (she was a student in San Diego at the time) and asked for a deal on as many hours as they could offer, for ...

"This much cash," and plonked it on the table. My pockets were inside out and empty but I was off. I negotiated a Piper Tomahawk (the teeniest trainer) for something crazy like $35 per hour – less than half the price that I would have paid in England.

Once in the States, I settled in to a routine of flying all day and each afternoon eating all I could at these marvellous venues called Happy Hour buffets where if you buy one beer for a dollar you can help yourself to a smorgasbord of junk food.

"What you mean you don't pay for the food?" I asked my sister incredulously.

"No it's thrown in when you buy a drink."

I couldn't believe my luck because I had no money to eat of course, just to fly.

I happily chomped my way through cubes of cheese dotted with jalapeno peppers, spicy Buffalo wings and plates of nachos with melted cheese and stodgy grey beans on top, fantastic. It is amazing how deft you become at budgeting when you're hour building, the price of everything is always translated into how many minutes flying time. Free junk food was a Godsend!

It got a bit lonely flying solo each day. My sister gets airsick and she wasn't keen, so occasionally I invited people I met in bars or shops or at the beach to come with me. It is easy to strike up a conversation over there since they love the English accent.

"Oh neat" or "Awesuuuum" would be the response, when I told them of my mission to become an instructor, so, if they were keen I'd invite them for a flight up the coast to Laguna Beach. I met all sorts of nice people this way.

I met one rather strange lad who invited me for a drink after we landed. He was a student pilot himself, always hanging around at the airfield.

"C'mon, jump in," he said from the driving seat of his gigantic truck. It was just ridiculously high up. I wondered if he went in for that strange sport of squashing smaller vehicles with his 'monster truck' I've always struggled a bit with that one!

"Let me show you my baby first," and with that he jumped out and opened the back to show me a huge fat snake in a cage. It wasn't a wriggler – it was definitely one of those which kills by squeezing every last gasp of breath out of a grown man. I'd seen enough, I made my excuses and thanked him for his company and jumped smartly into my clapped out Datsun Sunny, which had pieces falling off it each time I closed the door.

Oh well it takes all kinds, I'd clocked up another hour of flight time and who knows, I might have met one of those strange snake handling people who think the Lord protects them from venom. I saw a documentary about them.

Very strange! They talk in tongues that have rather 'alternative' beliefs. But he, and other happy clapping loonies I kept meeting did reinforce my desire for something a bit more varied. I was desperate for a long trip somewhere, well lo and behold, God answered my prayers because 'Ta Daa' my chance came.

A wonderful opportunity cropped up to ferry a Cessna Skyhawk (a light single prop) from San Diego to Long Island New York.

My flying instructor – Mike (now a BA captain) came over to join me, we would do the journey together, *he* also needed the hours for his Commercial Licence. An English friend of ours had bought this plane N758FX and wanted it in the UK. He would change the registration to G-DIVA because his wife was a famous opera singer. If we could get it to the east coast he would crate it up and ship it to England. Fantastic – everyone was happy, we would get about 25 free hours and *he* would get a cheap delivery. We jumped at this with all the enthusiasm of a young Labrador braving a river to retrieve his stick.

Our intended route would be San Diego, Phoenix, Albuquerque, Wichita and then due east across Missouri, Ohio and Pennsylvania to New York. Mike came out a week early and joined me for some 'jollies' from Montgomery field in San Diego. I was so glad of his company, it was great to have a friend *and a* fully qualified instructor with me. I had less than 100 hours, he had a few more but what we lacked in experience we made up for in guts and bravado (actually nearly got ourselves killed but more of that later).

We were two now – we felt brave and chanced our hand at a trip to the Grand Canyon, we were taking on the whole country in a couple of days so this would be a good warm up. Off we went in a piper Cherokee N47508 (that's the beauty of log books!) towards Lake Mead and Boulder City. We naturally ignored all the warnings NOT to go into the canyon because of downdraughts and other dangers like having absolutely nowhere to land in the event of an engine failure. We approached the edge and like mad dogs and Englishmen flew straight over the cliff and into the glorious canyon! It was terrifying and wonderful all at once. The mind boggling size of this awesome red, vertiginous abyss made me feel like one of those tiny spacecraft in a 'sci-fi' movie, dwarfed by the huge wall of a planet as it cruises alongside.

With all the responsible caution of kids playing on a railway track, we descended right into the bottom. After about ten minutes we heard a rather unwelcome bang from the engine. I looked at Mike gripped with panic. Well we were still going along – that was good!

"Think it's the alternator," Mike said as he frowned at the instrument panel. The alternator light was on and the gauge read zero. So there we were miles from home and no electrics – except the small amount in the battery.

"Better drop into Las Vegas," I suggested, looking at the map, "it's only down the road."

We climbed the steep walls of the canyon, up to the valley edges and off we headed for Vegas where we were treated to a priority landing because of our 'injury'. We came down onto the vastness of Vegas Airport, which, with all the cross runways and miles of taxi ways, was a big deal when you only know small provincial airfields! We slowed her up to seventy knots, trimmed, put the flap down and prepared for the landing. The runway was so long we had come to a stop before the first set of runway marker lines! We followed instructions to a parking bay, climbed out and Mike popped open the engine cowling and put his hand in. Out came a 'cat-o'nine-tails' the alternator belt – it was in tatters.

Typical of American hospitality, the guys from the ramp or FBO (fixed base operation) came to assist and greet us.

"You guys need anything? Fuel … oil … chocks … a tie down?" Because we were just passing we didn't need much, but *not* being able to do anything for you sits uncomfortably with an American so they gave us two complimentary baseball hats and a cooler bag with their logo on it, *and* a huge torch which the guy held on his shoulder like a rocket launcher and said, "Its heavy doooty, good for a two hundred yards!"

Only having a limited amount of time on the battery, we didn't want to use up the precious power by starting the engine so we decided to hand swing the prop. A couple of kids hand swinging a prop at Las Vegas International is not a common sight. The airline pilots who were peering down at us from the cockpits of their DC10s and 767s found it most amusing.

Poor Mike, he was puffing and panting trying to start this thing, it's not like a tiger Moth, the direction of rotation means the body is going into the propeller and the compression stroke is at the bottom of the swing so it was awkward. It finally fired up and I was ready on the throttle and mixture levers in the cockpit.

"You guys take care now and have a safe flight," came the voice as we said goodbye to Vegas control and headed West.

We had to save our electrics for the landing back at San Diego, we'd need the radio and some lights so we held off using the battery until we were ten minutes from the field. 'Big Bear' mountain rises to above nine thousand feet and we had to fly over it just as it was getting dark. We were on the home stretch. We contacted Montgomery approach frequency and they vectored us round, downwind. This airfield is smack next door to Miramar of Top Gun fame. The movie had just come out and I was straining to catch a glimpse of 'iceman', 'wingman', or 'anyman' for that matter, but nothing seen.

The twinkling lights of mountain homes and of San Diego in the distance looked enchanting. We slowed up, lowered the nose and came down. The little tyres squeaked onto the tarmac. We were back. I walked in with the shredded alternator belt and started bartering (years living in Africa) for a reduced price on the Cherokee due to the fact that we could have been killed – and they kindly gave me a free hour in a Tomahawk, I was as pleased as punch. Definitely worth putting your life in grave danger if you come out of it with a free hour!

So two days later we set off on our Homeric voyage to the east coast. We had two small bags, (we wanted to be light) a bunch of VFR maps and these hilariously funny 'peeing' devices, which are part of the 'ferry kit'. It helped that we were going out with one another because there's not much turf left untrodden after twenty-five hours shoulder to shoulder in a space smaller than most people's downstairs loo. We would crease ourselves laughing when perched on the back seat trying to pee into the 'relief kit' and the other gave the controls a damn good rocking. Funnier still was when we cruised over vast open cowboy country, dropped down to low level and hopped over telegraph poles giving it a bit of 'yee ha'.

Everything was going swimmingly, we admired the breathtaking 'album cover' views of Arizona and New Mexico. There was such a variety of landscape – mountains, desert, and golden forests of red and ambers (it was November). Unfortunately once we got to Wichita we hit appalling weather and couldn't go any further east, we gave it a full day to see if it would clear but there was no sign of a break so we decided to head south into more clement weather. We set off for Little Rock, Arkansas. Only cruising at about 105 knots we had time enough to admire the new countryside. We'd regularly apply some carburettor heat to prevent icing and we'd keep realigning the direction indicator which, being a gyroscope, suffers from precession and can deviate from the compass. But what occupied us the most was just good old map reading.

After a two and a half hour flight we were ready for a cold beer. Well our luck was out because ... guess what? It was Sunday and we couldn't get a drink on a Sunday! This was a rude introduction to the weirdness that is 'the American bible belt'. The weather followed us south and soon we were ensnared in the same stormy frontal system we'd escaped from in Wichita. The storms cost us two days in which time I learnt *all sorts* of things about country and western culture.

Fortunately there was a happening joint called the Amarillo Grill, and we soon got the knack of the voucher system. It was quite bizarre, no wonder Bill and Hilary headed off to DC. You had to pay for your drinks with a voucher, something to do with God or temperance. It was the first time I saw women who *actually* looked like Dolly Parton and also a beef steak the size of a handbag. I looked over as the waitress was approaching the table and thought I saw a rugby ball slit down the middle and stuffed with cream, 'how nice, I thought, someone who plays rugby is having a birthday and some enterprising mate has organised a cake in the shape of a rugby ball'. Then she put one in front of me and I suddenly became acquainted with the 'Idaho potato'. It was the biggest single expression of a carbohydrate I'd ever seen. It belonged in the world of giant mutant marrows seen at those country fairs where people compete for decades with their neighbours to grow a vegetable that can only be held with two arms outstretched like a forklift. To boot, there must have been a whole tub of sour cream on it, but just in case that wasn't enough for me she left five or six pats of butter. As for the steak I didn't know whether to eat it or climb it. I spent the first five minutes just walking around it like you do an unfamiliar building when you're trying to get in. I kept turning it around on my plate with the massive carving knife and fork they'd given me, battling to find the 'first point of cut'. Bob Cratchit would have fed his whole family if this single piece of meat had been gifted by Ebenezer Scrooge.

The next day the storm raged on, we looked at the weather briefing, it was not good, so we were marooned another night. That evening my cunning plan was to have what looked like the smallest portion on the menu – crab, – a good idea, it would be like those small dressed crabs in the shell you find at the deli in Waitrose, there's never much bulk in a serving of crab, **Wrong!** Next thing I know there are two buxom blondes in miniskirts and tights standing each side of me tying a plastic bib round my neck, placing hammers, mallets, spiked instruments, and a great wooden board in front of me and dropping a bucket by my feet.

"Blimey," I said, "I'm not going to redecorate, I just want to eat a small crab salad."

Well I sat there like Neptune's bride, banging, smashing, gouging, sucking, cracking and scraping whilst busy smiling girls kept rushing past with pens stuck in their hair balancing trays twice the size of the Wimbledon women's trophy high above their heads with one hand, and saying, "You guys doin' ok? – need some more claws?"

She managed, even with her heavy load to pick up our giant jug of beer which we'd just struggled to empty. Five seconds later … 'splosh', down came another full one.

"Excuse me!" I said, "we didn't order another jug of beer."

"Oh aah know honey, but on the pitchers of local beers it's two fer waaan tonight."

I couldn't believe it; suddenly the size of the backsides in Disneyland started to make sense.

We were just discussing our onward flight route to the east coast, when a singer came on the stage; she was slim and pretty and wore jeans, waistcoat and western boots. Guys in cowboy hats were perched on stools, boot heel on the rest bar, lifting the brim with an index finger with that 'I'm cool – and ready for action' type of gesture. She started singing, it was nice music, a few people danced … About halfway through her repertoire she holds the mike with both hands, guitar round her shoulder on a strap and starts talking in that charming southern drawl.

"How's everybardy doin' dernite? Ya'll havin' fuuurn …? Ok, I'm gonna dedicate this next sarng to an ex-boyfriend of maaan, we had great taarms togeether, alotta fuuurn, he met someone else and … well, hey that's life ya know. I was real cutup at the taarm but we're still freends, no hard feelins, I was gonna call it 'Movin on' but I changed ma maand, it's called …'Fuck you, pencil dick'."

The waitresses all cracked up and cheered, there was much 'whoopin' and hollerin' from the bargirls, some men shifted uncomfortably on their barstools. It was a damn good night.

Some great fat American man patted me on the back as he was leaving, "God I'm sure glad I got rid of mine when I see the size of them!" and exploded with laughter as he pointed to my crab.

The next day we finally got the weather to continue, Lexington was our next stop. I will always remember the little statues of jockeys in all their bright, eye catching colours lining the taxi ways. It was a hell of a long flight – 3 hours 30 minutes to be precise from Arkansas, over Tennessee and up to Kentucky. Colossal meandering rivers and thousands of acres of woodland and farms moved slowly beneath us. At least we were back heading north-east. Lil' Rock had taken us way south of track, but it had been worth the experience.

We fuelled up, checked the oils and all the flying surfaces, controls, flaps and lights. We strained the fuel several times until the little bubbles of water in it disappeared, then took to the skies again heading for Charlottesville,

Virginia. We were doing well; from there we could sniff the east coast. We flew over gorgeous mountains, noticing the change in landscape. The 'fall' was firmly established. Compared to the vast open plains near Wichita and the desert areas of New Mexico back west, this was wonderful. We were greeted (the next morning) by a full and brilliant array of toasty, warm colours.

It was getting dark when we landed, we were the last movement on the small airfield that night. There was no time to go downtown and find a hotel, it was late, we wanted an early departure tomorrow so it made sense to stay by the airport. Tony the owner of the plane had told us to be comfortable, but we tried to keep the price down by staying in little inns or motels by the airport which were adequate for our needs.

There was one guy on duty at Charlottesville that evening and he said there was one hotel very near, brand new, just down the road, and he would give us a lift – perfect. He dropped us at the door of what looked like a very 'sprauncy' establishment. If memory serves me, I think it was a Hilton. We walked in to reception, looking pretty bedraggled. Sumptuous oak panelled walls surrounded us. They were adorned with long oil paintings of glamorous, debutantes and heiresses in jodhpurs with riding crops. They wore pearls and diamonds and had immaculate blonde locks tumbling over crisp pink candy striped shirts; they looked like Queen Noor of Jordan. I glanced around and saw more paintings of wealthy smoulderingly handsome men holding polo sticks wearing ten thousand dollar watches with names like Brett Samuel Macintyre Johnson. Then, the tell-tale sign of 'high end'– a symphony of tall exotic flowers in a huge vase on the central table – strelitzias, lilies, curly bamboo, glorious wine red roses gesturing up towards the stucco ceiling. They all whispered glamour and luxury. Oh dear, I sighed internally, we are in the wrong sort of place but we were so tired and so hungry. I looked down at my oily trainers and at Mike's Snoopy sweatshirt which he never took off …
'Damn'.

We did take a room which was beautiful with more wood panelling, humungous towels and logoed robes. We had nothing but jeans and sweaters of which we pulled out the least grubby and went downstairs for a drink. In the bar, sitting on solid mahogany armchair barstools we ordered a beer. The barman in waistcoat and bowtie felt sorry for us and pushed extra peanuts our way.

After a few minutes, a man in a suit approached, leant over and quietly told me they were deeply sorry but we were not dressed appropriately, there was a dress code. I think he was politely informing us not to even *contemplate* the dining room. Totally unoffended, I said, "You know we're sorry not to be able to do justice to these elegant surroundings, but we're two student pilots from England building hours towards a Commercial Licence, we've had this great opportunity to ferry a small Cessna from west to east, so we have to travel light and this was the only hotel around. We've been staying in airport motels and didn't know this was going to be so posh. If it's ok we'll just drink this beer and maybe order a sandwich and take it up."

That was it, he just thought this was the most terrific thing he'd ever heard and he was a dog with five tails.

"John, give these guys anything they want from the bar menu … please allow us to buy you a drink."

He must have been a keen aviator himself because a minute later two Bloody Mary's arrived in chunky cut glass tumblers with a stick of celery like a Scotsman's caber and a generous flotsam of celery salt and fresh limes. It was delicious. The impecunious state of a trainee pilot normally precludes the garnish of such drinks, so it was well appreciated. All the ice-cool, statuesque hotel staff seemed to drop the formality and came over for a chat. What a lovely place.

The next stop was Washington, (not Dulles) but the smaller airport. We spent an exhilarating day at the Smithsonian aviation museum. It was fantastic seeing everything from early bi-planes to rockets and we both had a ball looking at what was by far the best exhibition we'd ever seen.

All the airport staff were helpful and friendly, showing us where to get weather, file flight plans and furnish us with the right maps. They were also keen to hear of our progress

We were feeling pretty brave by now and decided to have a go at a night landing in New York. (*Bad, oh very bad mistake)* N758FX – our little Cessna 172 was serving us well, and our 'Yes, we *can* do this' sort of attitude spurred us on. We planned a departure for 6p.m. that night, it was only a couple of hours away.

So … back to the flight centre and into the VRF flight plans. Mike had what we call an IMC (instrument meteorological conditions) – a basic Instrument rating, so we considered ourselves up to the job of landing in Newark at night. (It's truly cringe worthy isn't it?) God when I think back, our innocence and naiveté makes me look sky ward with a shake of the head. We were the airborne equivalent of those British soldiers going into the battle of Isandhlwana against the Zulus.

Our flight would be VFR (visual flight rules) rather than IFR (instrument) but all the *other* traffic would be IFR so they follow set routes, approach patterns, and waypoints all delineated on their charts. As we approached the busy terminal manoeuvring area around New York – (bear in mind there are three huge international airports and a handful of regional ones) the RT – radio transmissions got faster! The numbers are not necessarily correct but I remember it went something like:

"Continental three cleared down one two zero, change approach one two six point four, Delta four niner descend six zero call tower one one eight point one, so long, Learjet four nine papa bravo expedite climb through flight level niner zero, break United two one eight maintain one six zero on reaching call center on one three four point five."

And so it went on, there was no stopping for breath, it was one long continuous hurried urgent frantic transmission punctuated with the shortest clipped read backs by pilots.

So into this melee we flew, expecting an uncomplicated set of steers to a visual final. My doubts began to swell. There were just lights absolutely **everywhere**, I had been used to the odd "Traffic in your ten o'clock range five miles left to right", but this … this was something entirely different, the night sky was one of those huge rotating disco balls.

A bit of added misfortune was the recent air traffic control strike which meant all the *good* controllers were at home. What *we* had that dreadful night were the less experienced ones, the sort of … 'Dads army' part timers. So it was the one eyed leading the blind. When we checked in with those words "November 758 fox kilo, Cessna 172 with you at five thousand feet VFR" we could feel this woman's despair – like her evening wasn't tough enough. '*You have gotta be joking!*'She must have thought – her gyros toppled! We were ordered to go to point 'zulu' and hold. Oh God, we couldn't find it on the map, there were millions of lights from other aircraft it was looking dangerous, and to make matters worse we had to *ask* her where point zulu was.

"On the two four zero radial, twelve D!" she yelled! This was giving us a radial and distance fix off a VOR. We were physically ducking and rotating our heads around in the cockpit frantically assessing the proximity of the surrounding lights. It was more a case or *which* of the nine lights was a 'head on'– *that* was the one we would attend to first! Things were certainly warming up!

She was diverting planes away from us, screaming instructions like "Do an immediate 360". She suddenly asked us if we were able to accept an IFR clearance. To release us from this pandemonium, Mike blurted "affirmative" which was a bit of a fib, but we were in trouble and it was the right decision. We then followed vectors to the ILS. We had DC10s right behind us, 737 and 727s all around us as we went tearing down the approach, to hell with flaps we *dared not* slow down (always been good at flapless landings since then!). We came in excessively fast but didn't care, it just felt great that reassuring smack (and it was a smack) of the wheels hitting the ground. We were just told in no uncertain terms to call ground on 121.9. They were **so** busy we couldn't squeeze even our call sign out for many minutes.

"Cessna 58 fox kilo go to holding area x-ray," came an exasperated voice. This was a sort of pen for the disobedient. I think we hit a couple of taxi lights on the way, *plus* due unfamiliarity, we had to keep asking instructions. We heard a lot of "Fox X-ray *STANDBY*" which roughly translated means: "Oh do shut up you irritating little English cretin I have big important American airliners here with pilots who know what they're doing – let me deal with *them* first!" But we finally pulled into this area and waited. This was the airport equivalent of medieval stocks for petty offenders, who must be removed from the active areas. That's what it felt like. They sent someone over to us in a truck and we had to sheepishly follow them like admonished children to a park area where we could cause no more trouble!

The best was yet to come, due to the expense of last night's hotel, we decided to just get the cheapest motel advertised on the big lit screen. We called, and they said they'd pick us up. We waited and we waited. An hour later a battered old van with hub caps missing and covered with stickers coughed its way up. A very rotund black guy with his hat on backwards and a huge track suit greeted us and drove us off at breakneck speed picking up various 'brothers and sisters' en route. Mike and I had a serious de brief of *that* flight and decided to celebrate living through another day.

The motel was – well without beating around the bush, a filthy, sleazy, roach ridden, dump, an eyesore of dirt and crime. It was the three layers of bulletproof glass through which you passed your money (cash only) which first aroused our suspicions. They would have been wearing crash helmets I'm sure if it had not been for their turbans. The microphone down which you had to communicate had seen better days, so you only got the odd end or beginning of a word. It was the front for some scurrilous criminal racket I felt sure, it was shouting out 'Tax dodge'.

A rather appealing hand written sign was sellotaped to the wall "$5 extra for adult movie in room". They were running this place as a motel but basically it was a hall of residence for a technical college down the road so ... up to four students per room, and no doubt more on a Friday and Saturday night. Fortunately Mike had the aircraft's crash axe in his overnight bag and we slept with it under the mattress. Noise, shouting and venomous rowing filled the air all night. Doors slammed and arguments raged, most in Ebonics so we couldn't understand the finer details of exactly who had stabbed who. But there were jealous boyfriends, powerful motor bikes and some savage temper loss. "Bitch" was banded around a lot by the guys and "asshole" was a definite favourite amongst the girls but the out and out winner was, without doubt "motherfker" which seemed to have no end of applications.

Needless to say the night was not a restful one.

Next stop Danbury Connecticut. I notice from my log book it was the earliest take off of the trip. Not having undressed or used the rancid bathroom, we left at first light. It was great to see our little plane again, partly because of our attachment to it by now but mostly because it was getting us out of *there*. We had a coffee with the friendly guys from the general aviation terminal and we all laughed about the motel.

"Goddaaam you went *there*? hell that's crazy round there!" said the guy behind the desk and shaking his head.

We fuelled up, fired up, ran our checklist then sat with our little red beacon flashing for many minutes, finger on the transmit button waiting for one free second to get our call in to the ground frequency. The next bit took us quite by surprise and it was probably the highlight of the trip.

"Foxtrot X-ray, do you know where the statue of Liberty is at?"

"Er yes, we can find that."

"Okay you're cleared straight ahead to the statue of liberty."

So, one of the more unusual departure clearances, but that was the unedited truth of it. We took off into a bright chilly morning and flew away from Newark towards the statue of liberty. In those days there was a VFR corridor which took you right beside the world trade towers. We climbed to 2000 feet and Mike asked for onward instructions.

"Confirm I can fly VFR up the Hudson River?" Mike asked incredulously.

"A-firm sir," came the yank voice, "cleared own navigation you can take the river, you all have a good one, so long."

We climbed sunward once again, enjoying the most breathtaking views of New York, it was a real thrill being below the level of the sky scrapers just absorbing all that … 'Big Apple'!

New England was a tapestry of rich colour. We cruised over magnificent stretches of auburn and russet woods. I'd never seen so many shades of red and yellow, it was somehow very elegant and groomed. We made a blissfully uneventful landing in Danbury, where we were received with warmth. The plan was to crate the aircraft up here and ship it to England. It would soon change its name to G-DIVA and be parked on the grass at Fairoaks. I knew Mike would have loved the chance to ferry it across the Atlantic in spite of all the dangers of bad weather and icing.

"C'mon Mike wait 'til you can cross the Atlantic in something decent that goes a bit faster and higher, " was my offering as he nursed his coffee dreaming of a Charles Lindburg type of welcome on the Scottish shores.

Tony the owner, contacted us – he'd found a better deal on the shipping and asked us to do one more leg to Long Island. So after two sublime days in the 'church steeple',' apple pie' haven of New England's suburbia, we flew the final leg to Mac Arthur airfield on Long Island. There followed another scary flight into airspace swarming with aeroplanes. (The New York terminal manoeuvring area is tricky for a beginner!)

So the journey over, we spoke to the shipping guys there who would crate it up, and we busied ourselves with hiring a car to get to the international airport. I was headed back to San Diego from Newark and Mike was BA to London from Kennedy. New York in rush hour was the most terrifying leg of all. The traffic, the bridges, the freeways, the confusion! We were like ants in a concrete labyrinth. I was a complete nervous wreck by the time we found Newark. We hugged like buddies who had been to war together.

"Mike, promise me you won't fly that bloody thing over the Atlantic, I know what you're like, don't sneak back there and fit ferry tanks, I don't want to read about you in the paper being discovered by an Eskimo seal trapper, OK?"

He tightened his lips and looked top left, grinning as though I had really read his mind. Dear Mike there he was in his anorak, jeans, snoopy sweatshirt and tennis shoes, I don't think I've seen him in anything else. He had such unbridled enthusiasm, but he promised me, he'd go straight to Kennedy. The irony of it – he is probably sick to death of crossing the Atlantic now in his 747.

On board the Continental 727 for San Diego, I found myself next to a lookalike rock star all in black leather with dark shades. We were both wannabes of a sort, so we connected there, for a fleeting moment, albeit tangentially.

"Alriiiiight" and "cooooool" were his favoured responses and he seemed perfectly able to sustain an entire conversation with just those two words! I totted up my hours in my little log book, you can't imagine how important this ritual is.

"ONE HUNDRED," I sang triumphantly, that last leg just notched up my one hundredth hour, my God I was on my way. Young Alice Cooper next to me called the hostess over, ordered a mini bottle of champagne and suggested that I be allowed to visit the cockpit with my log book.

The captain congratulated me and unpinned his wings and gave them to me as a memento. I was beyond chuffed, when they said: "We'll be seeing you up here then pretty soon." I returned to my seat, wanting to jog down the aisle with my hands in the air like Rocky.

Alice Cooper clasped the glasses and raised his tray so I could take my window seat. He ordered another round and I joyfully sipped and giggled my way back to San Diego. He told me he was going to write a song about me called 'Seat of her Pants'. I'm sure he never did but he *was* fun.

Just fifty more hours and I could join the Instructor's rating course. I booked it for the coming spring.

Flying Instructor

'For each of them, the most important thing in living was to reach out and touch perfection in that which they most loved to do and that was to fly'.[2]

Richard Bach

Within two years of acquiring my own Private Licence, I was a flying Instructor myself.

One hundred and fifty hours was the prerequisite to sit the course. So after the intense innings of hour building in the States I returned to Oxford to do the Rating. Learning *how* to teach people the skills of flying was a fantastic challenge. Getting to grips with the patter of explanation along with accurate demonstrations was tough but *really* character building.

Seven hundred hours was the magical amount one needed to take the Commercial Licence and become a professional pilot. There were several ways to get there, the quickest being to pay the fifty grand (eighty now!) and do a the full 'ab initio' course at Oxford or Perth in Scotland (now Jerez – Spain), but for most of us who couldn't afford that, the most popular way, was to become a flying instructor.

Isn't it funny – in life, you so often don't realise which are the happiest days until they are gone. We were all so young, driven, fresh faced and keen, and so envious of the BA or Air Europe Captains who frequented our Club. We envied their 757s at Heathrow and stories of high-tech cockpits and faraway places. Derek, a British Airways captain who owned one of the Club's Piper Warriors used to say to us:

"It gets very boring you know, enjoy this while you can because instructing is *fun*".

We would protest and disagree, just like kids do when the holidays are over and they remain unconvinced when their parents say: "I wish I were going back to school; *they* are the best days".

---

[2] Bach, p. 53.

The beauty of those days is that you are all sharing a dream. You are on a journey filled with hope and expectation and with *that* level of enthusiasm, it didn't matter that we earned only £50 per week. We considered ourselves wealthy and fortunate. It was so good not to be paying for the precious hours any more. That was one of the great joys – every hour you flew, someone else was paying and you log it as command time.

When I recall instructing days and the small regional airfields, a scrap book of images float through my mind; the sound of propellers, freshly mown grass, summer evenings, wasps in the beer glass, wicker chairs in the sun, Tiger Moths landing or a small aerobatic planes (my favourite was registered G.FREE) diving and tumbling over the Hogs Back. Piper Archers returning from Jersey, Beech Barons coming back from Deauville, and balloons floating way in the hazy distance over Frensham. People would be studying topographical maps planning a trip to France and enthusiasts in overalls would have their heads in cowlings, devotedly repairing their tail-draggers. At Fairoaks where I taught, Wednesday and Friday were bar nights, this was a great time for everyone to get together – the instructors, students, owners, and engineers, we all indulged in a bit of fun and banter. On fine evenings we'd sit outside in the warm sunshine and enjoy the variety of aircraft coming and going. There was a certain helicopter pilot in his Augusta 109 who, once he saw us gathered there, would put on a little show – go into the hover, move sideways, do a scenic 360, then bow.

I became friendly with the helicopter school who shared the airfield with us. My great friend Jenny was the charter manager there and we had many wonderful days at Silverstone for the British Grand Prix and at Epsom for Derby Day. She'd recruit me as helper and handler. I'd have the passenger manifest and escort people to and from their helicopters, show them to the hospitality tent, get them a drink, etc. Everything went so well at the Derby until I said to Robert Sangster, (had no idea who he was) "Lost money on that last race – that horse should be pulling a milk float!" Jenny's head shot out of the gazebo like Godzilla, her eyes like organ stops.

"Get in here and shut up – don't talk to the passengers – that was *his* horse!"

"Well he asked me if I'd had a good day – any winners, that type of thing ... sorry."

Every single helicopter on the fleet would be engaged on these big days and we fixed wing instructors would get involved. I have an undying memory of Jenny and I following Nigel Mansell with the rest of the celebrating crowds round the track when he'd just won the Grand Prix. But the most beautiful memory – when all the passengers had finally left, we the crew, six of us, all came back in the Augusta 109. I was up front, headset on, with the pilot. We flew in formation with four other helicopters in the early evening sunlight, south from Northamptonshire. We could see the start of the Welsh hills on the right – the visibility was fantastic. All around helicopters were lowering *into* then lifting *from* the gardens of prestigious wisteria covered Jacobean mansions – all five star hotels and restaurants! People were sipping Pimms under umbrellas on rose covered patios, while the Bell Jet Ranger came down to drop more guests off on the stripy 'Wimbledon' type lawn. It was the first time I'd ever seen anything like that – a terrific experience.

Summers were glorious, blue skies sugared with fair weather cumulus and green fields drenched in hours of warm sunshine. All the planes would be booked and often we'd fly until eight o'clock. If all three of us (the instructors) were flying the last outing of the evening we would agree to meet over Guildford cathedral, lark about with a few steep turns around one another and return in formation which was a treat both for us and for the students – a little reprieve after the lesson (what the Americans refer to as 'Miller Time'!).

"If anyone's free and fancies it, I'm off top Compton Abbas," would be a typical shout at the flight center by an aircraft owner seeking a bit of company or another set of hands. Whatever was on offer, we'd all jump at it. 'Fly Aways' were a happy feature of summer when we would take four or five planes over to France, a worthy exercise in navigation and map reading and wine purchasing!

One of the exciting perks for us was the odd trip to Le Touquet in Northern France, famed for great seafood. Business men (and their accountants) needed us to fly them to, but more importantly **back** from Le Touquet after a day of 'fruits de mer' and inordinate amounts of Chablis. I remember one chap – a regular on the Le Touquet run. He turned up in his suit one day holding a child's yellow rubber ring which had a duck's head attached to it.

"Well I was told to bring my own life jacket if possible because there weren't enough spares – at least it's yellow," he grinned. He was quite a card, always laughing, he loved telling me of his past peccadilloes after a boozy lunch.

"I never forget," he said while pacing across the sunny ramp, reaching for his shades to cover his bloodshot eyes, "being in bed with this gorgeous girl in my younger years, and her bloody father came home unexpectedly, being very cognizant of the utter contempt in which he held me, I thought it best to jump out of the window. Unfortunately I couldn't see a bloody thing so in a panic I just grabbed *anything* and scarpered. A few moments later whilst in the headlights of a police car on the main road I realised I had on *her* cotton baby doll nightie … It was a bit difficult explaining that one to the police – looked like a damn pervert!" he said grinning at the memory.

"Never got my brogues back, the old man saw them outside her room and threw them on the bonfire!"

I really enjoyed flying those reprobates back across the channel after their large lunches! Never a dull moment.

Some clients weren't aiming for a licence per se, they just fancied getting airborne. So we'd go on genteel little outings to, say White Waltham, Goodwood, or the Isle of Wight – have a cup of tea and then return, usually via a circuitous route, flying 360s as we looked for their houses and took pictures. At these other airfields, people were also indulging in summertime fun. Aerobatic pilots were practicing their routines, Chipmunks were looping overhead, Students flying round the circuit, the occasional wobbly landing which would bring the odd "whoopsie daisy" from a spectator sat outside enjoying a pot of tea in the sunshine.

There is an extra charm about those airfields such as White Waltham which were unmodernised. The old wartime hangars are still standing. In the 1940s style NAAFI (the cafeteria), old paintings of Mosquitoes and Spitfires hang on the walls. A faded photo of a great hero: the words Wing Commander so and so DFC, BAR, under a handsome, strong face, his uniform immaculate. Everywhere – mugs of tea, bowls of white sugar, and the smell of bacon. The old-fashioned iron-rimmed windows and doors open up onto the lawn. Just the sort of place where you could expect Dougie Bader to stroll in, oxygen mask flopping round his neck saying: "How about a brew?"

Interesting characters frequented our airfield. There was Doctor Joy, (sounds like Mel Brooks character!) he was an eminent heart specialist who owned a Beech Baron, in which he'd occasionally take us for a practise ILS approach into Stansted. Gary Numan the pop singer, had a Harvard painted like a Japanese Zero, he enjoyed a bit of cloud bashing and aerobating on a summer evening and took us up with him occasionally. I was treated to wonderful 'jollies' in a Boeing Stearman and a Beech Staggerwing. One of the most successful charter companies in UK now called Gama Aviation had its humble beginnings at Fairoaks in the eighties – just one small room, one Beech Baron and three people. A good guy friend to all of us – Marwan started it with his mate Steve and now it has big offices, numerous employees and an impressive fleet of jet aircraft.

There were funny, scary and nostalgic moments in the life of a Flying Instructor, as well as many edifying challenges. Here are some snapshots of different students and of fellow instructing colleagues.

First Day Nerves

I was a nervous wreck on my first ever day as a new instructor. It was pouring with rain so we had to do ground school. My student was a six foot six black guy from Gabon in a beige suit and fat shiny tie – he looked like one of the Drifters or The Four Tops.

"Right, we'll go over some met shall we?" I said desperately trying to appear like I knew what I was doing.

"We hav don all dis in di odder place," he said in a strong West African accent. He was on a government grant so apparently he'd done some ground school preparation in Bristol or Staverton prior to coming.

"Okaaay ... shall we go over frontal systems?"

"I have don dis one."

"Right let's talk about icing."

"Yes we did dis icing too."

"Okay what about some weather chart decoding?

"Yes I know dis symbols we learnt it also!"

Feeling pretty exasperated I changed track, gave *him* the coloured pen, pointed to the white board, swapped places and said, "I tell you what Osi, why don't *you* get up there and tell me all you know about … oooo … let's say … advection fog?"

What followed was truly a funny moment, this tall gangly man walked up to the front, holding the green felt pen, looked at the board, looked at me, then at his shoes, drew his hand down the length of his face

"Actchooally, meteorology was not my best subject."

The Young Arab Boy

This poor lad – whose name had an 'al' and a handful of 'bins'– really didn't like flying.

He had obviously been sent down to us by a father or an uncle to improve his education. This was just another of the chores that were the dismal adjuncts of wealth and title.

He must have weighed in at sixteen-stone despite being only a boy. He would arrive every Thursday morning in a big limousine with his driver.

"Ello darlin', alright?" his driver would chirp as he walked through the door in his dark suit with his *Sun* wedged into his armpit, clutching his packet of cigarettes. He was a real cockney, spirited and friendly and had a face utterly robbed of any trace of moisture, dehydrated by years of coffee and cigarettes. I think he used to look forward to coming down to the airfield where he would have mugs of tea and a fry up.

The reluctant cargo would follow him in sheepishly looking forward to it about as much as root-canal work. The lad was so fat he always wore a track suit and on this particular occasion decided on a fry up too because at least it would delay the moment of having to climb into a small plane with me. The chauffeur would love chatting up the big bosomed lady running the café. He'd flirt with her and she gave him extra rashers of bacon.

"Did it 'urt love when you hit the ground?"

"How d'ya mean?"

"Well, when you fell from 'eaven."

"Oh go on with ya, you little devil."

I watched with mild panic as the young Arab boy doggedly polished off all the food on his plate, fried eggs, fatty bacon, beans, the lot. I also noticed the windsock looking rather lively that morning and I didn't like the combination. The chauffeur told him he'd better go for his lesson and he nodded over to me as if to say – "Ok, he's all yours now".

I sat him down for the pre-flight brief – we were doing circuits that day. I explained what our intention was, went over speeds and actions for each of the four legs of the circuit and tried to reassure him, emphasising the fun aspect. It was an uphill struggle.

We took a headset from the drawer for him, I signed us out on the Club's register, and off we went over the apron to the little Piper Cherokee parked on the grass.

I normally sent students on ahead to do the 'walk around' but last time he had taken that literally and just walked round the plane in a big circle – so we went through the checks together, straining the fuel drains, checking the oil and testing the lights and flaps, etc. He heaved himself up onto the wing first and opened the door, the aircraft keeled over as he stepped up.

I enjoyed and looked forward to, at least, *some* banter and chit chat, but this boy never ever spoke, which made things a little uneasy. He *had* to say "I have control" or "You have control" because that was mandatory but I never heard him say anything else. The plane sank on her oleo struts as he flopped into the left seat. The seat belts were expanded to the limits of their travel to get around him.

Even though it was a cold day, he was sweating already. I told him gently to go through the check list, which he did, slowly turning things on, starting with the battery. The mixtures went to rich and he turned the key in the magneto and we sprung into life. I sensed his discomfort so I always reminded him to bring the throttle back immediately after start, because the reduction in noise was calming. He just simply couldn't bring himself to talk on the radio so I offered to do that if, at least, he would do the 'downwind' call, that way he'd get used to pressing the transmit button and saying something even if it was only "Golf Yankee Oscar downwind".

"Yankee Oscar – readability five, runway two four, left hand circuit, QFE one zero zero five," came the voice through the headset.

He set his altimeter, released the brake and we lurched forward. He slammed on the brakes! At least he remembered the check but I was looking for a gentler touch, one which wouldn't put my forehead on the cowling. He always giggled a bit nervously when he got it wrong. So he tried it again and jabbed them on even more fiercely. "That'll do, I think the brakes work," I said and prompted him on his taxi-checks. I noticed the sweat beads gathering in the few dark hairs of his young moustache.

When we check the instruments, compasses, turn slip indicator, etc., we do a small turn to the left then to the right. First, he'd turn the control column as in a car (common reaction during early days), then, when I'd light heartedly say "remember it's the **feet** for turning" he'd suddenly remember and push his foot right to the floor and we'd be in a Ford Cortina sketch out of *'The Sweeney'* – going up on one wheel because for some unfathomable reason, he would always increase the power during this manoeuvre as well.

"Nice and *GENTLY*," I'd say as we careered onto the grass on both sides of the taxiway. His eyes were wide and staring straight ahead.

"Remember what we are checking here?" I asked, and he unconvincingly waved his chubby little hand over all the instruments.

"Needle to the left, ball to the right, numbers decreasing," I suggested slowly and methodically, in a voice which said now *YOU* say it. But his terror choked him. The magneto check at full power was interesting because not having the nimblest of hands, he moved the key all the way round to the OFF position instead of just to the right and left positions. Magnetos don't really like being switched-off while the engines are running at two and a half thousand RPM. He fumbled through the remaining checks, the fuel pump went on and I called for take-off.

"Yankee Oscar – take off at your discretion, wind two six zero, twelve knots."

His nerves were well and truly messed up by now, so I softly reminded him how well he did last time and encouraged him to push the power up keep straight with the rudder and then **ease** it off the runway at seventy knots. Off we went down the runway, he forgot the rudders and when I said, "Just ease in a little bit of right rudder," it was the sledgehammer touch again.

"*JUST* a tad!" I squeaked, trying to keep things smooth. Blimey this was exhausting.

Once airborne we flew the first circuit together so I could release the pressure from him. We went through the downwind checks, which he knew and then I pointed out the big country house where we turned onto base leg, and reminded him of the first stage of flap – "Ok, good; now remember to just look at the picture of the runway and keep that image in the windscreen, fly at seventy knots …"

He came down final approach with the expression of someone on a horse for the first time after it has bolted. But he never actually spoke so it was awkward. He managed to put the aircraft on the ground with only a little ballooning at the last minute. I helped him with the flare, then said much to his despair: "Ok good, now full power and let's do that again."

This went on for about twenty minutes, round and round the circuit we flew. Then I noticed his expression was becoming very blank; he was quite pale and drops of perspiration were gathering on the thin fluff of his upper lip.

"Are you alright?" I asked him with serious concern.

He should have put the 'losing face' issue on the backburner and told me the truth, which was that he felt as sick as a parrot. I noticed that all the windows on his side had steamed up. My left side, that is, the one nearest him, was much warmer than my right. Oh my God – I was sitting next to a human volcano. He wiped his forehead with his hand and that was my cue.

"Ok – I have control," I said, "relax and close your eyes. I am taking you back."

I asked him again if he felt sick and a barely audible, "No, I'm okay," came from his lips that hardly moved.

By now I couldn't actually see out of his window, it was totally misted up. I turned onto base leg very early and told the tower I was coming in on very short finals! I tried my best to avoid sharp turns or changes in pitch, but, alas, my endeavours were too late. His hand came over his mouth and he burped. I put the air blowers on him.

"Just breath slowly and deeply."

But at about three hundred feet, the mightiest and most unpleasant projectile of vomit ever known to man came forth in that little aeroplane. I thought of 'Mr Creosote' from Monty Python, as all my efforts went into getting the aircraft safely down and delivering this poor, retching reluctant back to safe ground.

The three *Macbeth* witches would have had a field day with this one:"Oh, most vile and loathsome stench ... most bilious and yellow livered emunction!"

Poor chap. I taxied in with an open door – he was so embarrassed I really felt for him. I had to escape the smells as soon as possible so I alighted immediately. He followed, looking like he'd been shot; sick all down his tracksuit. Then he disappeared off never to be seen again. Finding someone to help clear that lot up was, as you can imagine, not easy.

I watched him flop disheartened into the black limo, probably back up to Park Lane where he would have to break the news to father that being a fighter pilot in the Royal Saudi Airforce was ... out! I'm sure his minder took him shopping later for a reassuring pair of new bejewelled 'slip ons' from Bond Street.

The Baroness
Her exits and her entrances were unforgettable!

I had the pleasure of meeting an elderly Baroness in her eighties who had a truly balletic presence. She even had her cataracts removed so she wouldn't fail her medical, that is how determined she was to achieve her licence. She was miniscule and fragile, like a Lladro figurine. Her husband, elderly and skinny wore an immaculate cravat and blazer. He had a perfectly round beaming face, huge eye sockets and a 'piano board' set of false teeth. He was like the character 'eyes right' from the old card game. They owned a dazzling Chateau in thousands of acres in France. He always stood with hands clasped behind his back smiling and was most concerned about doing everything correctly and having a debrief with me after her lesson.

Every time I gave her a headset in the flight centre, just before we went out to the plane, she would immediately put it on, in spite of my telling her to wait until we got into the aircraft. This made her go completely – as opposed to partially – deaf. She would beam up at me proudly with her crooked mouth and squint, then hold my hand tightly. We'd walk out together over the apron to our Piper Cherokee. She looked so beautiful and funny in her long skirt, her little hunched shoulders and this great big headset on her tiny head – the flex always trailing behind her with the jack jumping and clacking over the tarmac.

Then we would go through the 'getting her on board' phase for which I would enlist the help of a couple of the ground crew guys. They would bring a stepladder and three cushions for her seat so that she could see over the cowling. They would always watch for me coming back-in so they could help her disembark. We were three instructors and the CFI (chief flying Instructor – the wonderful John Barker) and collectively we knew she would never get the Private License, but we were determined to make it as thrilling and enjoyable as possible. We all admired her guts.

I was often halfway through the pre start checks awaiting her response, which never came because she would be waving to someone out of the window. She reminded me of Margaret Rutherford playing the batty eccentric Madam Arcati from the Noel Coward play. It didn't matter how many times we went over things, by the next lesson it was always like starting from scratch. I would encourage her to taxi-out but remind her to avoid the lights.

"Oh, God yes, those nasty little blue things again," she'd mutter, as we careered along like Herbie the cartoon Volkswagen.

I would let her do the take-off which usually went swimmingly apart from her not actually pulling the plane up aggressively enough to get airborne. I would assist her on the stick and as soon as we got airborne she would look out of the window like an awestruck child.

"Right, let's do some straight and level," I said, "remember how we do that?"

"Oh yes, yes," she'd say, smiling and squinting. "That's that bit out there, looking like that," she said with a shooing gesture towards the landscape. "Then those levelly bits out there", flicking her wrist towards each wing tip. "Then making sure all these agree," she concluded triumphantly as she made a large sweep over the whole instrument panel.

"Good – you have control; let's fly straight and level."

Always the same – we managed about fifteen seconds of level flight then the left wing would drop and into the spiral dive we'd go! I would talk her through the recovery only to repeat the same thing again.

Nonetheless, we had great fun and I let her handle the aircraft as much as possible. She would often make "weheeee" sounds as we came in to land and each time we touched down it was as though we had performed a miracle and her teeth made clacking sounds as she got excited. Even though her seat was fully forward, her little feet with smart Victorian style lace ups could barely reach the rudders.

As we trundled happily back to our parking bay the engineers, bless them, would amble over to assist the Baroness in alighting from her carriage. They would almost lift her out of the seat. Once, John (who always greeted everyone with "Alright?" – and so became known as 'Or-wight John') actually lifted her in his arms, off the wing and placed her on the ground. This amused her no end.

On our little stroll back to the Club house with her headset still on, she would hold my hand and say to me earnestly:"You are a vair, vair clever girl"

"Don't be silly" I'd joke. "I'm just an instructor – it's no big deal"

"No, no, you *are,* you a*re,* I wish I were as clever as you," she'd say in the most beautifully polished voice.

"Yes, well I wish I had a Chateau in France with its own airstrip, so I'll swap you," I winked down at her.

"Yes that's the bally problem, too darn old to enjoy it all now," she chuckled as we went inside to 'take tea' with her adoring husband.

I did do a lot of flying with her and taught her as much as I could. She was a treasure.

When Harry went Solo

There are simply some people who just do not resonate with the environment of flying and others who brim over with confidence from the word go.

One such character was a contemporary of mine, the house building tycoon Charles Church who, on his first solo – which is strictly, just once round the circuit – took off into the local area to look at some houses he was having built in Surrey. I had never heard of such fearlessness on a first solo. Sadly he died in a Spitfire not long after.

Conversely, I had one chap in the seat next to me during a lesson who physically shrunk in front of my very eyes. He just completely withdrew – his arms came up into his jacket sleeves, his neck sunk down into his collar and he was getting smaller. If it hadn't been for his big long shoes, I swear his feet would have disappeared up his trouser legs!

But I taught a real treasure of a chap – Harry – who was a gentle giant; in fact he reminded me of *'Jaws'* of metal-teeth fame from the James Bond movies. Except Harry was utterly benign. All he wanted to do was to fly solo once. It took me weeks to get him up to standard, because every time I would go to open the door and say those dreaded words:

"Right, off you go, once round the circuit, you're ready." He would almost blub and say he didn't want to do it today but he promised he would do it next time. He would grab my arm and look at me with a penetrating glare of an abandoned child that said 'Please, please don't leave me'.

"Harry, you can *DO* this. Don't be scared; you know what to do." But it was no good – he became a six-foot-six jelly.

The weeks rolled by and one day I hatched a cunning plot for our Harry. He was flying well and feeling comfortable in the knowledge that I wouldn't send him solo until he requested it – that was our agreement. Normally the instructor will taxi back to the club house then get out, therefore the student knows that *this* is the moment when they will solo. I didn't do that, I pretended that we had landed long so he should make it a full-stop and I requested a backtrack of the runway. When we were lined up back on the runway centerline, as quick as lightening I opened my door and jumped out. So now he would be left in an aircraft on the runway and he would HAVE to go otherwise he would cause an obstruction.

"Harry, JUST GO FOR IT ok – no more messing around, you can do this so pull your finger out and *get on with it.*"

I slammed the door and banged twice on the roof and I was gone. I stayed at the hold of runway 24 and crouched in the bushes, muttering, "Go on Harry, push the bloody throttles up and get in the air." Nothing happened for about thirty seconds. I hung my head, "Oh God, please make him go."

Then I heard the sweet sound of the throttle going up – Harry was moving off down the runway confronting his fear.

"GREAT!" I said out loud and watched him all the way round like a nervous parent chewing the top off my biro.

He came down final approach making a few too many power excursions with the throttle but he flew right over my head. "That's it Harry – bring it down, fly it level, keep it level, *now* start to pull the nose up." He did a little balloon with an early flare but then put her down handsomely on the centre line.

"Oh thank God!" I exhaled heavily, and clutching my clipboard and pad, I began to walk round the perimeter of the airfield back to the Club. I was watching him carefully, willing him to clear the runway at the end and taxi safely back.

He obviously caught sight of me at the other end, because the next thing I know he had stopped the plane in the middle of the taxiway, got out, and waved triumphantly.

"Christ – what IS he doing?" I asked myself. Then I shouted, "Harry, get back in the plane, go back and taxi in, TAXI THE PLANE BACK TO THE RAMP!"

Back at the flight school; I stood there watched him park then saw this giant form lolloping towards me like some huge inmate just escaped from an institution. He was grinning from ear to ear and waving his arms around.

"Harry, well done!" I yelled.

I walked rapidly towards him:"Go back and make sure you've done all the shutdown checks."

I might as well have been telling a baby grizzly to heel and sit. He came up to me panting heavily from his run, then got both his arms round me and literally threw me high into the air. I couldn't quite believe what was happening. I guess the man was elated.

That was a rather different thank you!

Robbie and the Lance

Although the title might conjure up pictures of a jousting knight from a heroic medieval tale, in fact it is about a great friend called Robert – a fellow flying instructor and his passion for a particular aircraft G-LUNA, which was a Piper Lance. A cut above your average club aeroplane in that it had a super charger *and* a variable pitch propeller. This was *big* stuff for doe-eyed instructors who would gape longingly at anything different or faster to handle. We were so keen that the promise of a free hour in *anything* would launch us into those bounding circles performed by dogs when they see the lead come down off the peg.

The unsuspecting owner had said to Robbie that he could use the Lance only *once* in a while, just to keep it oiled and lubricated. We of course exercised a slightly more elastic interpretation of these terms and conditions. 'Jollies' at least once a week became commonplace.

To break the tedium of teaching straight and level, or climbing and descending, when Robbie flew on his 'jollies' he would always ask for an ILS approach into Gatwick. He became known by the controllers there; heaven knows what they thought but I think his cheek and enthusiasm amused them and they accommodated him whenever possible. You must imagine the eye rolling of the busy air traffic controllers dealing with an endless stream of airliners, getting a call from captain Robbie.

"Golf Lima Uniform November Alpha; PA 32 from Fairoaks at two thousand four hundred feet, requesting vectors to an ILS approach to overshoot, *if* you're not too busy, *please?*"

He actually shot an approach into Heathrow once and I was amazed, it sent us into fits of juvenile hand clapping. He was *very* serious of course and did all the checks and read-backs with the authority of a BA skipper.

"November Alpha; fully established two seven left," and then turned, wide-eyed to me and chortled with laughter as we peeled off left for the overshoot. "Well what did you think of that 'Neets?"

The *really* memorable theft of the plane was one Christmas day when the airfield was closed and deserted. It was a very frosty and ice-cold morning. We had agreed to meet.

Like two truants, we approached the hangar door and pulled it open ourselves. Our breath, forced from the warmth of our lungs, billowed around us in clouds of tiny crystals. Robbie grabbed the prop and I pushed behind the trailing edge of the wing. Fortunately it had lots of fuel and oil. We jumped in and fired her up. A solid throaty rumble as we nudged the throttles up, brought a smile to our faces. We twisted the park brake off and advanced along the frozen taxiway towards the holding point of runway 24. Tiny particles of frost rose into the air behind us as we did our 'run up checks' and advanced the throttles in order to check the magnetos. Powdered diamond dust sparkling in the morning sunlight – perfect!

Such delightful irreverence! Is not the stolen apple always the sweetest? Doing something that was not allowed made it all the better. We were like a couple of wild geese. The low sun shone weakly in a pale slate sky, it was a typical winter day, washed out greys overhead and sparkling silver frost on the earth. Because this was the *one* day when nobody was flying, we didn't have to communicate with anyone, the sky was our very own, it was magical.

I remember being told, when I visited an art gallery in France, that during the war, to safeguard all the precious paintings, they were stored in private farms and little dwellings in the countryside so they wouldn't get destroyed. Those farmhands who guarded masterpieces from the Louvre could sneak down to their cellars and stare at glorious paintings by Caravaggio, Claude or Watteau and pretend just for that one small but sweet moment that they were their own. One day soon they'd have to return them, but for now they belonged to them. In a similar way, I looked at the empty sky and enjoyed the silence knowing that tomorrow the skies would be everybody's once again full of VHF signals carrying endless human chatter.

We flew down to Frensham Ponds and did a low approach and go-around on the grass strip there. We went bombing over Butser Hill near Petersfield, swooped down over the lake in Liss and did low level orbits of the Devil's Punchbowl. We had a romp over Petworth House, had a close inspection of the Shah of Iran's former residence next to the glorious Winkworth Arboretum then made a couple of 360s over Paul Ghetty's splendid pile near Guildford. We looked down at all the houses and wondered how many over indulged kids would be ripping open presents, how many Aunties were knocking back the sherry, how many in-laws were silently smouldering. And thought with appreciated detachment of the panic in the hearts of all those poor mums as they juggled three courses, ten different dishes and the timing of the sprouts!

Oh Lord – how perfectly rhapsodic it was to be in the air.

Thin pockets of morning mist settled in the small valleys, it was spread over the landscape like angel hair. A few Christmas lights twinkled from people's homes. I feel that our winter months are the forgotten relatives in our great family of seasons. Winter's glory is her nudity. It manifests in her ruggedness, resilience and silent splendour – the sparkling winter frosts, the black branches gesturing against pallid skies. The dense cold air is the perfect medium to carry the defiant screeches of the crows, that distinctive clarion call, which trumpets their survival across the land, a sound which has been heard for centuries. That special Christmas morning the earth was like a bulb, stripped bare, but doggedly storing all her goodness, harnessing the energy for next spring when green leaves would once again fill the hedgerows and plump the outlines, when our feisty snowdrops would nudge up through the frozen ground. Life was just ticking over, the landscape in a state of hibernation was conserving just enough energy to make it through. The only movements that glorious morning were the hardy crows hopping around the lumpy farrowed fields and the odd dog walker all wrapped up.

We flew back over Ockham VOR; gave a cursory nod to the old VC10 parked at Brooklands in Surrey, dropped down over the railway line near Byfleet and then banked steeply over onto finals for runway *24*. We lowered the final stage of flap and pushed the props up to fine and did a Christmas cracker of a landing on the frosty runway. With our cup of happiness positively brimming over, we put her back in the hangar and pushed the massive hangar doors along their tracks until they clunked shut.

"Merry Christmas," we 'high fived' laughing out loud, then we snuck away!

Emergency Landing into US. Base- Greenham Common

It's not *really* something you are supposed to do – come barrelling in unannounced in your little single engine Piper to the most politically sensitive and top secret, USAF base arguably in the world. This happened to my own dear flying instructor Mike. I followed him into exactly the same job and took his place two years later. Whilst we were both there in our respective roles as instructor and student, he told me of the day when he was having a 'jolly' as we call it. On his own, building hours, he took off from Booker aerodrome in High Wycombe and had an unexpected incident which resulted in him performing a forced landing into one of the most secure and protected military bases in England, none other than the nuclear warhead itself – Greenham Common near Newbury, Berkshire. It was very much in the news at the time because of all the women camping out around the perimeter protesting about nuclear war.

He told me the story in his own endearing way. Mike was tall, lanky and boyish, he had long straight hair that flopped over his brows, and he smoked Marlboro – he had a 'proper' BBC world Service voice.

"Well," he explained, "I was pootling along and suddenly the bloody throttle linkage came undone, so in effect there was no gas getting to the engine, I had no choice but to get the thing on the ground, I was a glider!"

So with no choice but down, Mike did the right thing and put out a 'Mayday' on 121.5 VHF (international distress frequency) and looked out and saw the nice long runway of Greenham Common beneath him.

You know when people just *can't* do accents? Well that's Mike and his American is worse than his Pakistani. You see he is just far too British. But it didn't stop him trying, bless him, for the impact of this story.

"I was aaased all these queestions bah all these guys in uniform," he carried on bravely attempting the Yankee drawl which made it ten times funnier!

Apparently he was surrounded, and arrested by the military, they roped the aircraft to a jeep and towed him off and put him in a room where he had to fill in forms and have interviews and be visited by various uniformed savants with shiny shoes and epaulettes. He started off in a room covered with maps and diagrams of the airfield, when they realised that he could see the bedrock nay the very nucleus of Americas deepest and most arcane defence information they removed him and put him in the room with the coffee machine!

Much chest thrusting, saluting and "Yes *SIR*" went on all around him. I couldn't help but chuckle thinking of Mike in his Tennis shoes and snoopy sweatshirt and innocent open expression, loving the opportunity to talk about his little aeroplane and then throw in "Anyone got a light?" while phones were ringing in the Pentagon.

"What d'you mean there's bin a *goddam* breach of security…?"

"Well it's like this Mr President…"

The RAF police got involved and there was a fair old brouhaha but the amusing thing was that they didn't *even know* he was on the airfield until West Drayton air traffic control in London (who had received the mayday) phoned to inform them! That is how big the place is! You can just imagine can't you:

"We've got *WHAT* on the airfield …*WHO* …"

Then like an atomic fly swat (i.e. an overkill), teams of jeeps screech up, men armed to the teeth, alight, to see Mike sitting on the wing of Yankee Oscar having a quiet smoke. The entire fire brigade came hurtling down the airfield and when they saw him, eager to jump into action, shouted: "Is there fire. Is there fire?"

"Only from my ciggie," said Mike … Priceless.

Eventually he was picked up by car and a few days later a colleague was dropped at Greenham with an engineer to fix the plane and fly her out.

Funnily enough I had the chance to return to Greenham Common many years later – in 2004. It was fascinating. Totally abandoned, it had that 'tumbleweed rolling down the street' look. Weeds towered through cracks in the aprons, the runway was in poor condition and the whole place looked sad and drab. Something which was fascinating though was the peek I had of the underground command bunkers. They were nuclear proof and pretty impressive if you are into that type of thing. I was struck by both the extensiveness of the underground corridors and rooms, and by the sheer size of the place. There was, it seemed a whole city underground. But it is what I saw *on* those walls which was a bit of a shocker. There was a sketch, done by one of the resident American airmen. In disbelief I drew nearer to a drawing on the wall of a windowless, airless room. It was a picture of a huge Hiroshima type mushroom cloud with a skull and crossbones and the grim reaper underneath and the words 'GLCM we aim to deliver's suppose that is ground launch cruise missile. Oh well I guess if the best salesmen are the ones who believe in the product!

Back outside on one of the many vast manoeuvring areas I was shown the massive drop down steel doors in which the trucks carrying the nuclear missiles were housed. They weighed ninety tons each and looked like they belonged on a Hollywood set of *Star Wars* or *Dune*. They took six seconds to open and fourteen minutes to close. *This* was what the Yanks referred to as 'Heavy Dooty'. I'd never seen steel that thick or bulky.

All around this eerie place ran six sets of fences, barbed wire, there used to be guns, dogs, the whole shebang. Breaching this boundary would have been tricky even for the most fervent anti–nuke happy clapper!

The control tower was solid built in a style typical of the airforce of its time. It was once, I am sure, a hive of communications activity – troughs, peaks, modulated waves, chatter, 'over and outs', and all the rest of the tropospheric scatter! Now it was gutted, smashed and ruined. It was reminiscent of some former African HQ prior to the rebel army advancing. The women protesters had apparently done a 'Luddite' job on all the equipment, once they had finally got in and smashed it to smithereens. Very interesting day out. Mike would have had no problems doing a forced landing on here now. His biggest problem would have been how far he would have to walk to find a pub to call for a taxi! How time can change things.

Mad Robs – An Englishman

Mad Robs – one Robs Lamplough was a maelstrom of a man, always racing cars or flying classic planes with his Biggles helmet on, or jumping out of helicopters onto steep canyons of powder snow in some remote corner of New Zealand. He had bushy white eyebrows a very cheeky grin and was usually clutching the keys to one of his vintage Formula 4 Ferraris or Alphas in which he'd just screamed round the most dangerous terrain in Europe.

During the 'hungry years' of hour building, you will jump at any chance to fly. (Quick insight into the level of my keenness – most Saturday nights in my mid-twenties were spent driving up the M1 to Luton to sit in the back of a Piper Seneca doing a mail run to Manchester just so I could 'be there'. If I was lucky I'd get to press a button on the area navigation box!) I challenge any 'anorak' to beat that!

Whilst I was sitting at Fairoaks one day, he burst through the door in long leather flying coat and asked if I was free to fly him down to Haverford West. He needed to pick up a Pilatus P2 from RAF Brawdy in Wales, he would borrow his mate Mike Woodley's Cherokee 180 which I would fly, then we would come back in formation. This prospect awakened that little known gland in the brain with a long Latin name which is responsible for the secretion of euphoria chemicals. I had just got my Private Licence and was up for it.

Robs was a 'sod the maps, don't need them' kind of pilot. He didn't really care if instruments didn't work, he was very 'seat of the pants'. We took off from runway 24 at Fairoaks on a lovely spring day and headed west talking to Farnborough then Lyneham and Bristol. I chatted to a friendly Welsh controller across Wales then contacted Haverford West in the descent. Robs would go from there by road to Brawdy because they didn't allow civilian planes in there. I would wait on the ground in Haverford until I heard his engines overhead then take-off and join him – very 'war time scramble,' I thought.

The unique 'chugging along' type of enthusiasm of the airfield manager was great. He was making the tea when he heard my first transmission, bounded over to the window, picked up the microphone and told me the wind, then he mounted the lawnmower and finished the grass, he did, it seemed, a bit of everything. He had a droopy sort of 'Deputy Dowg' face and the strongest Welsh accent ever.

"Hello dear, and what kind of craft is this one."

"Cherokee 180."

"Oh lovely, yes, I don't know that one but we haven't had this much traffic down h'year for a long time, you're the second one in today," he said, head down entering me in the visitors book and stroking the cat. "Cup of tea love?"

"Love one," I gratefully accepted.

Whilst waiting for Robs to come roaring overhead, he took me round the hangars and proudly showed me the aircraft which were nearly all gliders.

"D'year d'year," he reminisced as he patted one particular glider wing. "Ever been caught in a downdraught? I remember being in this one h'yur, saw a bird shoot up past my window like it was out of a rocket, I was plummeting I was," he chuckled and scratched his head as he remembered the perilous incident.

Moments later I heard the roar of Robs' Pilatus. I thanked the gentleman and jumped in my Cherokee and took off to join him downwind. We had agreed to talk on VHF123.4. He came with a whoosh down my left hand side over taking me. I could see his cheeky schoolboy grin. He slowed and allowed me to catch up and come alongside. It was incredible, it was the first time I had seen a plane floating and bobbing freely in the sky so close to me. Robs wore his mask and flying hat – a true Biggles. The paint job was camouflage and with the German iron crosses (Nazi style) it was truly a picture. He signalled to me that he would lead the way. I followed at full power. We established communication and Robs being mad said he wanted to buzz his mother's house in Stroud. He spent the next ten minutes swooping in and out of those sleepy Gloucestershire valleys trying to find his mum. I circled above cringing at the thought of the letters of complaint and the punishment such a crime might exact – like a fine, or worse, a ban! I then struggled to dissuade him from flying under the Severn Bridge. He was like a ten month old Rottweiler freshly off the leash and in a park, everything had to be sprayed, sniffed, eaten, climbed or destroyed. We were having some serious fun and it felt *GOOD*.

I lost sight of him shortly after that but heard his crackly transmission telling me to go into Staverton. I glanced at the map and set up a heading which looked good and contacted Staverton on my radio.

"Has a Pilatus just landed?" I asked.

"A-firm," came back the controller.

Great, I thought, and flew on to the dead side of the circuit and descended into downwind.

"QFE one zero one seven, call finals," said the controller.

"Uniform Bravo call final," I replied and went through the downwind checks. I turned at right angles to the runway slowed to eighty knots, lowered the first stage of flap and trimmed, put a touch of carburettor heat on then lowered full flap, and slid down final approach loving the new scenery.

As I taxied in I saw Robs – he had already drawn a crowd! He leant proudly against the plane whilst the re-fueller topped her up. God he looked a sight, long leather coat, old flying helmet with flappy ears and these bushy white eyebrows, and a grin that wouldn't quit! We chatted about progress so far and he suggested jocosely that we 'lob' into High Wycombe airfield so he could check on his Fokker tri-plane. I was beside myself with joy, *what* a day this was turning into! We were sky bound again – 3rd leg. This time Robs did rolls over and under my Cherokee, he closed in then banked sharply away flashing his underside, disappeared for two minutes then popped up on my right side then slid over my head and slowly descended on my left side. I was thrilled to bits.

Robs radioed ahead to Wycombe and asked them to pull his tri-plane out of the hangar. I followed him in on the westerly runway. We alighted and walked over to the hangar. Now here was a little plane you had to fall in love with. Its three wings, tail skid, open cockpit and old slim bicycle style wheels painted a perfect picture of a bygone age. Its bright red paint decorated with German crosses looked stunning against the green grass. Robs marched round it admiringly, proudly pointing out all the beautiful features like the shiny wooden prop and the fabric wings. The prop snapped into life after a few swings and Robs taxied off into the wind. It was quite breezy that day and he just seemed to lift straight up vertically in the headwind and towards the puffy white clouds.

I thought of Baron Von Richthofen and his famous red Fokker tri-plane. (Although as often happens with war heroes, we find that *actually* someone else – in this case Lieutenant Voss, shot down many more enemy aircraft than his more well-known and posthumously rewarded compatriot Richthofen.) It was built to match the British Sopwith Tri-plane which was a famous and agile fighting scout of the First World War. Fascinating concept the three wings – they were narrower (fore to aft) than the biplane wings, but the same length. The thinner wings gave the pilot a better view and the centre of lift on the narrower wings did not move around as much as on the broader wing aircraft. This increased stability during violent manoeuvres. Apparently if one of the British Tri-planes crashed behind enemy lines, the Germans studied it in close detail. The German Air Commander Hoppner is known to have openly eulogised about the British fighter.

"Who says the Germans don't have a sense of humour?"

So, here it was buzzing and diving around over my head and I thought of those intrepid fighter pilots who must have nearly frozen to bloody death in those things. How hugely impressive, that, in what amounts to nano seconds (if you think of the 'time' chart popular in Natural History programmes where we *the humans* appear at five minutes to midnight in the planet's history) we have come up with the supersonic, pinpoint accurate, mega manoeuvrable fighting machine of the modern military. There *really* are some innovative and brainy people out there.

"Here it comes," the engineer said lifting his binoculars. Robs was crabbing down sideways so he could see the strip, he kicked it straight and bounced it down on the grass, she ballooned up again and came back down on one wheel and bumped and rocked her way to a full stop, with a cough and a splutter. It had the endearing clumsiness of a young duck attempting its first landing and the same waddle once on firm ground.

Since we were making good progress, he suggested a trip to the Isle of Wight where his third aircraft, a Harvard AT6 was hangared, and in need of a run out! He was definitely making the most of having someone along who would agree to *anything* to clock a few more hours! As for me, I was delighted, great flying – someone else paying, perfect! We flew off in the Cherokee across Surrey and West Sussex, crossed the Solent and landed at Sandown. Here I had a real treat in store.

The yellow Harvard (tandem seat tail dragger with *big* radial engine – used to train fighter pilots) was in World War Two Canadian markings.

"Cmon ol'girl, jump in we'll take her for a spin eh?"

Fearless and utterly unaware of Rob's reputation as a 'nutter' I found the black non slip strip on the wing, planted my foot on it and pulled myself up and stepped into the back seat and connected the heavy five way harness. The engine sounded rugged and meaty, the nose was high in the air. The levers are interconnected by cables front and back, so although he was moving the levers up front, I could see the cables moving right next to me.

I remembered my stall training, which included what we called the HASEL checks – a mnemonic covering the steps you had to go through before any aerobatic manoeuvre. 'H' was for height, a minimum of 3000 feet. At that moment I glanced at the altimeter which read 2000 feet thinking 'ok we've got a bit to go before he starts' and two seconds after that I was looking at my reflection in the glass – *upside-down!* Suddenly my eyes were bulging and the straps digging in I couldn't lift my hands from my thighs, yes we were, no mistaking, indulging in a bit of 'G' here. I knew Robs was an adrenalin junkie after his stories of pylon racing in Nevada not to mention his exploits during the Paris to Dakar rally. He beat up the field that day despite my reminding him that this was sleepy little Isle of Wight and perhaps it might be a bit indecorous to be ripping it up a low level on a summers afternoon. Not surprisingly some local residents called to complain.

Back to Fairoaks, last leg of this extraordinary day which would have had Indiana Jones putting his feet up! I agreed to pick up the Cherokee the following day with another instructor. Because we were non radio we telephoned Fairoaks to say we were landing in about thirty minutes. I must have lost more face during that drama-packed entry into the Fairoaks circuit than ever before or after. I *assumed* Robs would at least join the circuit over head to give us, and indeed the other aircraft time to check out each other's positions. Oh no, if there's a wall let's, like a tank, just blast on through it!

He careered straight into downwind cutting someone up, hurled it round onto base leg then on final he realised he was dangerously near the aircraft in front, which was probably a good 20 knots slower, so he decided to do a quick 360 to put some distance between us. *Might* have got away with that one had it not been for the aircraft which we'd cut up on downwind which had now turned onto *his* final approach and saw a great big yellow aeroplane coming *towards* him– the turning circle is not exactly tiny and we did use some distance during the turn. Apparently (unbeknownst to us at the time, being non radio equipped) the controller in the tower (whose nickname was already 'Panic') was having a full-blown fit. His voice was a positive squeal.

It was pure *chaos*. The plane we were head on with on finals decided to climb and circle overhead until *we* were on the ground, so we completed our turn and landed. All ended well though, no damage, just a few combative scowls and a justly deserved "What the bloody hell did you think you were doing"! Rob bought drinks all round at the bar and yielded to the idea that a radio might be prudent and won everyone round with his unabashed candour. "So sorry old boy I was a damn fool – didn't mean to mess things up ... drink?" The beers were poured and I drank to a defining day – one which I wouldn't forget in a hurry.

Green and Pleasant Landings
(A Sunny Flight to the West County)

It was the season for equestrian frolics, the Badminton horse trials in Gloucestershire. Though no horse expert myself, I flew down with my friend Carrie (a talented rider) in her single engine plane, a Fuji, from Fairoaks in Surrey. We set off due west across England's glorious countryside on a bright delphinium blue day. Small, flat bottomed cumulus segued away in long lines downwind, carried along by the breeze, way into the distance. It seemed we could see forever.

The south coast stretched out on our left, snaking its way into Dorset then Devon. On our right, the Didcot power station blew columns of smoke into the sky above Oxfordshire. We passed the huge Kingsclere mast near Basingstoke then entered the magical hilly area near Marlborough, flew across Wiltshire countryside and admired the white horse near Pewsey. On such days it's heavenly to lift into the sweet un-trespassed space above the ground and view the warm sun drenched landscape as a soaring bird would!

We chatted to Lyneham (military) on the VHF who gave us a squawk and provided radar Information Service. A C130 Hercules was going round the circuit on the easterly runway. In the merry month of May the rape fields are in full bloom splashing the land with vibrant patches of yellow. We swooped down over 'Country Life' houses and along meandering rivers, saw cricket matches and dog walkers on village greens. We clocked the odd helicopter scudding along below us.

Canal boats brightly painted and without agenda moved slowly along the waterways, which were flanked by graceful drooping willows. It was enchanting. We identified the town of Malmesbury on the right, Hullavington gliding site on the nose, and then the unmistakable high ground just to the east of Bristol. A mass of white tents gleamed in the sun about ten miles on, we approached and saw the cross-country jumps, the dressage ring and the avenues of shops and stalls. We'd found it, after what had been an enjoyable 'nav ex'. Hundreds of cars were parked in the field next to the stately home.

A couple of circles round the site gave us time to see the whole area, the views were stunning. Downwind, we lowered the first stage of flap, then turned onto final approach, put out full flap, steadied the speed at about seventy-five knots, tweaked the trim wheel, and just savoured the moment. It was the best kept grass strip I'd ever seen. Power off, into the flare, and another 'green and pleasant landing'! We vacated the strip into a field of much higher grass, closed the throttle and mixture, then slid our canopy back to savour the fresh breeze. Wheel high in daisies and dandelions, that's how we left our little aeroplane parked in a green meadow buttoned with bright wild flowers.

"Hello hello how nice to see our first aircraft. Good flight?"

"Terrific," said Carrie *really* meaning it!

This, we guessed, was the Duke's groundsman who'd come in his Range Rover to greet us.

I complimented him on the state of the landing strip.

"Oh good … good," he beamed "Well anytime you want to land here you are most welcome just stick a fiver in the box at the end by the hut."

The fact that we had arrived in a plane entitled us to free entry. So we wandered around admiring all the saddles, country jackets, deer stalkers, walking sticks, hip flasks and boots, not forgetting all the wonderful pottery, jewellery and art. I'd never been to an event like it before so it was fascinating seeing the organisations (wildlife hedgerows and shooting to name but a few) which existed to promote and protect the future of our countryside. You have to hand it to the British they'd even erected a "Pig and Whistle" sign outside a temporary pub. There were temptations everywhere, from hog roast, to strawberries and cream.

We watched some impressive dressage, and noticed a few whip wielding dandies striding around with 'Jodhpurd' girls in tow. I welcomed myself to the land of the velvet bow and the low slung riding hat. Eye catching rows of silver and red bunting fluttered in the wind around various stands. More little planes were circling overhead lining up to come in.

The parking arrangements were all arranged by NCP (National Car Parks) and for all of us who've ever parked in one of those, we know how crippling the rates are! The owner's son David was there overseeing the parking, tearing around the place on a quad bike which back then was exceedingly modern and revolutionary! Carrie went for a ride on the back zipping round the fields, it looked like a load of fun so I begged a go too. We were all having a good lark on the quad, until he had to busy himself with his real job of assisting people with their cars in the field. How ironical that nearly twenty years later I should, fly his father Sir Donald Gosling, in a private jet. He is, to this day, one of the nicest passenger I have ever flown. How I've railed about the price of NCP parking but when I finally met the owner it took the sting out of it somehow because *there* is a real gentleman. A wow-it's-a-small-world moment happened when over 20 years later I ran into David in a lovely country pub in Compton where he drinks sometimes with a mate, Stuart Tidy, a lovable rascal. Having learnt I was a pilot, Stuart now says to me every time he sees me, "so... Anita, when are you flying me down to Cuba to buy some cigars, in that private jet...*what?*... that shouldn't cost too much should it?"

The next day we were dropped off by our friends with whom we'd stayed the night. We tossed our bags over the fence, clambered over the gate and walked over to G-KARY. After a quick walk round we fired her up and trundled across the uneven ground to the strip. We slid the throttle up to full power for the 'mag check' which had us momentarily sitting in a 'grass storm' with blades of grass flying everywhere.

"Shall we?"

"Let's do it."

I opened the throttle and accelerated slowly, there is certainly more noise than speed in the early stages of a grass take-off. We bumped across the lumpy terrain. I anticipated those expanded horizons which unfurl in front of you as you lift away from the surface obstructions. I banked sharply over to the left to avoid over flying the horses and cruised off remaining low to find our friend's house, to take some pictures for them.

"There it is!" we found it nestled in the valley, and did a few orbits. Good to pull a little 'G' now and again with a steep turn!

We headed east from Gloucestershire to Wiltshire then Berkshire, spotting the huge runway of Greenham Common (can't miss that one). Eventually the BAT (British American Tobacco) building in Woking – my beacon in the storm, came into view and we descended over Bisley for the circuit at Fairoaks.

When we slid the canopy back we had to smack our hands together with a 'high five'. It had been what flying little planes is all about: good weather, some map reading, a beautiful country strip and best of all – avoiding the traffic on the M4!

Sweetness and Flight
(A summer evening – Frensham Ponds)

This little flight seemed to encapsulate all that is 'green and pleasant' about English summer flying. I had a great friend and fellow flying instructor called William; he was an eccentric, lovable and very handsome Anglo Irishman with longish brown hair and a cheeky smile. He loved his flying and was a great artist and deft craftsman (he had done a few illustrations for Tim Severin the explorer on some of his adventures). He did beautiful soft pencil sketches of sleepy grass airfields – wild flowers and biplanes parked behind old blister hangars, or of hazy Greek mountain sides dotted with olive trees. His favourite saying was "Shlantra (spelt Slainte) mahogany gas pipes" which he would say while raising his beer and shouting in an Irish accent: "More drrrink!" He was one of life's good guys. He was always laughing, drove a battered old car and had battered old luggage. He owned a little plane – a red Jodel tail dragger.

With all the lessons of the day complete, he asked me if I fancied taking a little jaunt out in his Jodel. We pulled it effortlessly out of the hanger – it was wood and fabric and very light. He hand-swung the prop and we sat side by side in the seats; it was like being in a little boat, sort of flimsy and scant on the controls. He glanced over the few gauges checked the Ts and Ps as we call them (temperatures and pressures) then just did a north/south, east/west with the control stick to check 'full and free' and we bumped down towards the hold of runway 24. He pushed up the little throttle and for the first five seconds there was no acceleration at all. We lifted up gently like a little Winnie the Pooh balloon at about sixty knots and flew away over the green fields on a lovely summer evening.

In our headsets we had Pink Floyd's 'Shine on you crazy Diamond' playing. It was magical. The job of instructing involves the 'patter' as we call it, this is nonstop talking and explaining, we had both been at it all day so the music was blissful. We flew slowly around 'tout tranquil' as they say in

France, just enjoying the soft hazy summer scenery. As we popped over the southern side of the Hogs Back near Guildford, we spotted a hot air balloon.

"Let's go and say hello," said Wills.

I raised my thumb. He slowed right down – not that we were doing anything resembling 'speed' anyway. This *is* the sort of aircraft in which if you're in thirty knots of headwind you *will* be overtaken by a heron! But it didn't matter a jot; to quote Richard Bach:

> You will begin to touch heaven, Jonathan, in the moment that you touch perfect speed. And that isn't flying a thousand miles an hour or a million ... because any number is a limit, and perfection doesn't have limits. Perfect speed my son, is being there.[3]

We approached the balloon really slowly so as not to startle them. We moved in close then flew a big circle all around them. We could see they were loving it, from their smiles and waves. It was a one of those 'moments'– quite surreal – a bunch of basket borne people floating idly across the summer sky raising their glasses of champagne while we became just for a few special moments, their own little moon, orbiting around them.

We carried on south-west of Guildford towards Puttenham and Elstead and finally arrived at Frensham Ponds. These are two ponds in Hampshire; a large one and a smaller one, they are nestled in the countryside and have a delightful little grass strip. Wills lowered the nose and lined up for a landing into the evening sun. We descended over the fields, I saw a few mini sails on the water, everything was cool, in my ears David Gilmour (a keen pilot) and his mates were singing passionately and strumming their guitars.

---

[3] Bach, p. 55.

"Remember when you were young ... you shone like the sun ... SHINE on you Craaaazy di-iamond."

The ground came up towards us we flew along the grass, Wills chopped the throttle flew her level for a few seconds until her little wheels finally found the ground and we bobbed and rattled as we decelerated along the green grass. He turned her around in a 'one eighty' increasing the RPM and putting in full rudder and we parked up near the little 'honesty box'. This is a small box nailed to a post where there is a handwritten sign asking you very kindly to deposit your landing fee of five pounds (so British!). We duly did and then we walked down the country lane to the hotel on the lake. We bought a glass of fruit juice and went to sit by the water in a caressing breeze.

The lake was dark and glassy. The surface was broken occasionally by a few grebes who dived down and popped up randomly. Mallards preened themselves on the bank near us and at the far side two swans glided elegantly under the weeping Willows. It was a little piece of heaven. At the water's edge, I noticed millions of tiny gnats, all backlit in the evening sun. They formed a little cloud of staccato dancers, moving jerkily up and down together all in unison as though bouncing on invisible teeny trampolines. It's amazing how they communicate, because they would suddenly *all* move off together, in a split second, to some other place ... heaven only knows.

We finished our cold drinks and walked back to the little red Jodel. It looked so cute and chirpy parked there on the grass. After hand swinging the prop we stepped in and strapped up. We lined up on the grass strip and William opened the throttle, after a modest acceleration, which a child running along beside would have been able to keep up with, Wills lifted the tail and seconds later we just floated off the ground and the wings were flying again. We banked round to the east and headed back up towards Guildford. We kept very low coming down to five hundred feet at times admiring all the lovely homes with stables and tennis courts, the meandering tracks through the ranges, the village greens and church spires and tidy little fields surrounded by miles of hedgerow. We were still being 'crazy diamonds' as we dropped back in to the circuit to land on runway two four at Fairoaks. I helped Wills pull it back into the little hangar and offered to buy him a drink in The Sun pub in Chobham.

It was a very happy evening and I wish I could go back and relive it. But it has gone. You *really* have to make every moment count in this life and *that* one counted for a great deal.

Transition to Commercial Pilot

I have to say for someone who did the 'arts' subjects at college and could barely change a plug, the mental gymnastics required for these new disciplines was considerable. The subjects were fascinating. I spent the best part of six months at the training schools of Oxford and Bournemouth learning all about meteorology, flight planning, navigation, radio aids, as well as electrics, aerodynamics, hydraulics, pressurisation, propeller and jet engines, oil systems, performance and loading. We were certainly kept on our toes. The slightly batty but likeable technical instructor who was actually *called* Ken and *did* remind me of Ken Dodd used to come bursting into the classroom on a Monday morning, smack his long pointer on the desk of some poor 'not quite awake yet' student in the front row and shout, "Electrolyte of a Nicad Battery...? Come on!"

Meteorology lessons were no less entertaining. We had a 'real character'. He had reached the stage where he talked only in abbreviation (there are thousands of them in this industry and 'met' is home to most of them!). He was an 'old school', thumbs under braces type – very clear and precise. He would pace up and down the classroom with his baton under his arm waving it occasionally and in his best British accent talk about fronts:

"As the front approaches surface wind **backs,** pressure **falls,** temp **rises,** cloud **appears**."

Then he'd turn sharply on his heel and march back to the front.

"This will be first CI, (pronounced very roundly as 'see eye') maybe CS, then AS and often ... NS." (These meaning cirrus, cirro stratus, alto and nimbo stratus.)

"In the warm sector we'll get DZ, RA maybe fractured ST even ... (then the voice lowered and slowed as he prepared for the big finale of fog) EFF GEE."

Then he'd pick up the pace again ... "As the cold front passes pressure **rises,** wind **veers,** temperature **drops,** cloud will be heavy – (these were his favourites) CU and CEE BEE." With that he'd give a determined tap with the baton on the picture of the towering Cumulo Nimbus clouds he'd deftly drawn on the board. He loved talking about tropical revolving storms, they involved letters which leant themselves very well to clipped, polished pronunciation – 'TEE ARR ESS'.

The navigation exam was invariably the one which gave the most headaches. It was a staggeringly fusty and tricky old subject. A complicated and intricate circular slide rule along with a crumpled old 'Air Almanac'(circa Flamsteed) were given as tools on day one! The common calculator banned, we waded through problems of kilos pounds and litres; associated specific gravities, not forgetting the true tracks, magnetic tracks and wind/ground speed sums very long windedly on our slide rules lovingly known as the whiz wheel. It has now been gathering dust in the cupboard under the stairs for quite some years.

We had to tackle the subject of mapping the globe – there was Lamberts conformal conic orthomorphic projection (or 'lamberts pornographic erection' as Pete the class comic renamed it). Then Mercator, a Flemish cartographer from the sixteenth century who had a cylindrical projection. Anyway most of us used to sit with chin in hand chewing ends of pencils while staring at the board in total confusion as we read about chart convergency being the 'change in Longitude times the sine of the parallel of Origin'. Then ... there were delightful little facts like: 'the two reference parallels are secant to the globe' ... 'rhumb lines are concave to the nearer pole but convex to the equator'.

Great circles were *curved* on one map but *straight* on the other – all shoulder slumpingly depressing. Then we'd have gristly little problems to work out like:

'On a Mercator, the spacing between two meridians is 14.7 inches, use this information to find the scale of the chart at 53North.'... *"WHAT?"* Didn't matter *how* many times you read the question it never really jumped out at you! More gruesome questions followed which demanded that we 'find'(most unwillingly!) the track angle at 'x' having been told that a line has been drawn from one coordinate 'x' to another coordinate 'y' on a Polar Stereographic across the North Pole. Those ones had us all, unfailingly clasping **both** hands around the ears looking down at the desk ...'condemned'.

Then ... to learn that the Mercator map is utterly unreliable above 70 degrees north – why bother! Furthermore I discovered it was *really* a map for maritime navigation. Of course none of us ever used this 'stuff' again in our aviation careers, it had all been for the purposes of mental exercise. It was, along with the lanes and parabolic curves of Decca and Doppler, thankfully never again mentioned. However, I feel that the more skilled amongst us (myself definitely excluded) could have grabbed their parallel ruler, navigation square, protractor and graticule, swung their cape over their shoulders and been of great assistance to Captain Cooke on the Endeavour as he sailed off to find the Southern Hemisphere! Whoever came up with GPS... I would like to say a BIG thank you.

Solid friendships are cemented at flight school and years down the road when you run into those friends again at some airport in the crew lounge, the connection is a deep one – you went through the battlefield together.

Exams and flight tests done, I sent out the CV. It hardly filled half a side of A4! The Christmas parties were no longer just scenes of drinking and merry making, I used them as hunting grounds to prospect, making a B line for anyone who may be recruiting or could offer advice on companies looking for crew. A couple of interviews followed, I set out hopeful that I'd have the same luck as the topless dining job and once again they'd say, "You can start Monday."

Someone at Gama's Christmas party recommended a company down in Gatwick who flew Citations. I called and went along. We chatted about the exams I had just completed at Oxford and what I was looking for out of a career in aviation, I was doing well, I thought – here comes a job offer perhaps? ... then to finish he leant back in his mastermind chair with both hands pressed together in front of his mouth and said, "What about when you get pregnant and want babies?"

"Well that is not even on the agenda."

"Ah yes but you say that now, but if I invest all this money in your training then you get pregnant where does that leave me?"

I didn't hear back.

A week later I landed an interview with British Aerospace at Hatfield. I sat in front of a rather daunting board of 'pinstripes' and had an interesting conversation. Then the old chestnut popped up.

"What about when you want to have babies?"

"Well it's really not an issue I mean I have not even thought about it and don't think I want them anyway," I answered truthfully.

"But you're **OBVIOUSLY** going to want to get married."

My eyes darted from left to right, my brow furrowed, "Oh … am I?"

People normally pay good money for this sort of clairvoyance and here I was getting it for free! I explained I was just looking for my first break, I was ready to work really hard and tried to convince them that it wouldn't be necessary to train all their crews in airborne midwifery, *and* that I wasn't the mum character out of Monty Pythons 'Catholic' sketch who stands at the sink for fifteen years in an old pinny dropping kids.

I do remember him smiling and shaking my hand at the door saying, "I can see you don't suffer fools lightly Anita, we will be in touch"

I did have a second interview during which I quite unexpectedly had to fly their Jetstream out of Dunsfold. I wished I hadn't worn a tight navy pencil skirt. It was nonetheless great fun once I manoeuvred myself into the seat. I hadn't been up to fifteen thousand feet at the controls before so it was exciting.

Of course I tried British Airways and went to the interview, lo and behold a few weeks later the 'Thank you for your interest …'letter came so I filed it with the cabin crew rejection letter and thought to myself with a smile – well it's not a Royal Flush but at least I got 'A Pair' in this poker game of life. Mind you **that** interview was really revelatory – we all sat round and had to build a big wheel (like you'd find in the funfair) out of a type of metal Lego, while some hobgoblin graduate, with spiky hair and a suit that was too big for him but who had an 'ology' from Leicester in something which was supposed to give him insightful perspicacity, sat and watched us all communicate. It was all a bit too much for the very 'alpha' Buccaneer pilot from Lossiemouth who had seen combat and a lot more, who made his excuses with a few breathy expletives. It was a seminal moment in my exposure to psychometric testing and the strange exercises which accompany it. Fighter pilot from Lossiemouth – you get my vote hands down where ever you may be!

Another interviewed followed with Connect Air at Gatwick and I trotted off hopefully searching for someone who didn't think the sum total of my activities was secretly flicking, doe eyed through Bride magazine and shopping every Saturday for rattles and bibs. In the middle of all this the phone rang one day and it was my friend Mike Woodley from Aces High for whom I had done bits and pieces of work over the last three years as I built my hours.

"I don't know how you are getting along with the job hunting, but I've got something which might interest you."

"Oh yes?"

"Yea LWT are doing a series called 'Piece of Cake' and I'm putting my B25 bomber in it as the camera ship – but it is in the States and needs ferrying back – how do you fancy right seat in that? – you have got the twin rating and you don't need a type rating to sit in the right seat, it would be good experience so if you want to do it …"

I couldn't believe my luck – to ferry a Second World War bomber back over the Atlantic, how could I pass *that* up?

I called the few companies I'd spoken to and explained what had happened. The one I really wanted, a small company called IDS flying business jets out of Heathrow were great:

"Just give us a ring again when you're back and we'll take it from there – good luck."

So off I went to a very unexpected first job, on a war bird!

Ferry of B25 Bomber over Atlantic

A surge of heart-warming nostalgia sweeps over you when you hear the crackling of those huge old radial engines. When they fire up, black smoke and scorching orange flames roar from the exhaust. Such sights and sounds conjure up memories of the war years – you can hear the sirens, the echoes of bombing and the music of the big bands.

The Mitchell bomber, N1042B, bought by Aces High, was built and accepted for use in training units in 1945. It was sold after a gear incident to its first civilian owner in 1958 for $835. In 1962, Tallmantz Aviation bought it converting it into a camera-ship for the many upcoming movie productions. I saw it first in Chino, California, just after it had been purchased by Sherman Aircraft Sales of Florida in 1985. She still had the distinctive nose mount and all her film credits painted on the fuselage – 'Catch 22' and 'Battle of Britain' to name but a few. Never did I think then, that I'd be involved in its delivery to UK for LWTs '*A piece of Cake*' series, made in 1988. Sherman eventually sold it to Consolidated Aviation in Vermont, where we picked it up for Aces High and took her to England.

The first few days were busy, tyres and cylinders were being changed, radios installed, the ferry tank fitted. I just mooched around like a kid in a sweetshop enjoying the wealth of unusual aircraft on the ramps there: Chinese Migs, DC3s and 4s, a Grumman Avenger, a Tracker, Fougar Magisters, seaplanes, biplanes and Navy aircraft. The FAA examiner Vernon Thorpe arrived from Florida to type-rate Alan the English captain.

Vernon was fantastically credentialed – a true 'all-rounder'. At 70 he was a life member of the Confederate Airforce and their Chief check-pilot on many big piston bombers. He had spiky white hair and his baseball hat read: '*I will give up my gun when they prize my cold dead hands from around it*'.

We had a true pro on our hands. He had thousands of hours and numerous Licenses; one of which read 'Types: ALL', 'Restrictions: NONE'. He had done it all in his kaleidoscopic history: gliding, pylon racing, crop spraying, tail draggers, vintage bombers, fighters, Lear Jets, 707s, flying boats – he was just short of Lunar landings!

He would come with us as far as Iceland, so on that leg we would be four: Alan the captain, Vernon, Ray the engineer and myself. I was a new CPL (Commercial Pilot) – both American and English Licenses with the exams behind me but no experience! So it was a plum opportunity to get some right seat hours in something very unusual and of course, 'do the Atlantic crossing'.

With flight tests and paperwork done and the ferry tank secure, we climbed aboard and around 3.00 p.m. on a sunny spring afternoon, went through the start-up drill on the port engine. The props clicked over eight times then as we brought the throttle forward, she coughed and spluttered into life expelling a black cloud from the exhaust. With both engines started without incident we taxied out to runway 33 at Burlington bound for Goose Bay. The last words Dean Martin – a wealthy pilot/owner spoke to me were:

"Ahh hell Aneeda you should go back on the Virgin Atlantic, you'll be sucking pond water in this piece of shit." He'd long since got over the thrill!

I thanked him very much for those reassuring words of comfort as I had climbed up the little ladder on the underside of the belly. All the locals waved us off, including the guy who had taken me aero-bating to his carpeted hangar. Many, who had assisted, were satisfied to see the fruits of all their labour over the last few weeks.

The take-off and climb – my first ever in a war bird, were fantastic. The sounds and smells were all new, as were the handling characteristics, it certainly felt like a tank, rugged and sturdy. At 11,000 feet the views were beautiful and gradually the landscape became more and more bleak as we increased latitude. The four hour flight was noisy and a bit uncomfortable but it didn't detract from the thrill one bit. If Ray needed to go to the aft of the plane he had to slide back along a narrow passage between the front and rear. There was no gloss or luxury here, this was a crude bare metal frame built for dropping bombs. One nice feature was the astrodome in the ceiling from which we could enjoy panoramic views.

It was a relief to be at last hauling her round in the descent for a final approach into Goose Bay, which was hugely impressive for a neophyte like myself, never having landed in semi-arctic landscape before. Bleak and chilly, I had thoughts of Ice Station Zebra. So far, thank God nothing had gone wrong, or so we thought until we opened the bomb-bay doors and saw at least four leaks in the ferry tank. Because of all the electrics in that area we'd have to use the wobble pump from now on instead of the electric pump, to transfer fuel to the main tanks.

Our plan was to rise the following dawn at 3.00 a.m. and depart at 5.00 because Vernon our busy septuagenarian had a flight from Reykjavik to Orlando that afternoon, he was booked to do a check ride for someone. So we filled the main tanks and decided to leave the bomb-bay tank until the following morning. The old Mitchell bomber was definitely a crowd puller. Two Lab Air pilots jumped out of their Twin Otter in heavy leather jackets with the fur collar pulled up to their ears and gave a long admiring whistle as they approached for a closer look. A British HS125 biz-jet from McAlpine Aviation, enroute to Luton, was parked nearby and the crew came over full of curiosity. They touched the old propellers and sauntered round it eulogising about the old plane wishing they could swap places. They *were* going nonstop in a nice warm cockpit though!

The B25 did have a rugged beauty; solid, proud and old-fashioned, as she stood with an almost pterodactyl stance amongst all the F18s, Vulcans and modern jets. Goose Bay in Northern Canada made a lasting impression on me;

a superbly equipped NATO base nestled in a remote, barren, icy landscape. I even saw my first two Eskimos.

After a short night in the local 'Lab Inn', we drove back to the airport on a dark freezing morning under millions of stars and a bright moon. We had to tackle the big problem of refuelling – the nozzle on the end of the hose was too big for our bomb-bay tank. We had a funnel, but not for 250 gallons – it would take hours! This was when I first appreciated the leg pulling that goes on between the Canadians and the 'Newfies'. The refueller was without doubt 'two bricks short of a full load', which didn't help. Vernon pressed him to find another nozzle for the fuel hose, and reminded him of our tight schedule.

"I don't know nuth'n bout other fuel nozzles," he stammered, blinking nervously through his bottle bottom glasses, looking like he'd burst out crying. He wore an old ripped anorak with furry collar, had droopy jowls and watering eyes. In the end Vernon commandeered his truck and sped off towards the fire station to find one himself. When he came back he let the Newfie have it with both barrels, in his good ol' southern drawl.

"There are three types of people in the world: those who *make* things happen, those who *let* things happen and those (and stared at him) who just look around and wonder *what the hell* happened!"

Vernon was quite a character and he made us laugh with his 'doggone's and 'goddam's as we sat on top of the wing to refuel whilst being bludgeoned by the cold arctic wind.

Hoping for the best, we climbed the ladder to the spartan yet familiar cabin – it was mercilessly cold. We closed and locked the belly door, buckled up into our seats and ran the check list – fired the left, then the right and taxied out. We sat at the hold for the extremely noisy engine run-ups (increasing the power and holding on the brakes, whilst props, mixtures and engine instruments are checked). The whole frame shook furiously, with the high RPM then rumbled calmly as we retarded the throttles to slow running.

The sky was just beginning to lighten in the east as our world spun. Tender tones of turquoise and gold whispered softly into an otherwise dark and silent sky. The trees, although hundreds of years old were only about five foot high due to the restricted hours of sunlight – they never made it to 'big tree' world but they gestured like elegant Balinese carvings against the pale light. The moon threw an eerie silvery light on the military hangars in the distance, and our engines looked mighty as they exhausted streams of roaring flame from the pipes. Checks completed, boost and props set, we took off on the southerly then banked steeply to the east, into the breaking dawn and took up a heading for Narsarssuaq, Greenland.

Our small petrol fired heater worked valiantly to keep us warm – good job since we had no coffee (voted against because of the seven hours with no loo). If we wanted to stretch our legs the only way was through the rectangular aperture amidships. Ray went back a few times to check things although on this leg he was busy hand pumping the fuel – we estimated a four gallon per hour loss through the leak.

Established in the cruise and backtracking Goose, we set up the Loran (Long distance navigation equipment). Fortunately, for chitchat and general morale, all the headsets had 'receive' and 'transmit' so we kept each other amused. Vernon with his marathon innings had many a yarn: crazy low level pylon racing in Reno Nevada, sea planes round the Florida Keys, and his student in a Lear simulator who screwed up and went completely out of control.

"He cried out HELP me Vernon help me!" Vernon's eyes watered, he shook his head and said. "I swear to God, that poor sonofabitch thought it was for real."

The first glimpse of Greenland was welcome after the icy monotony of the grey mean Atlantic, which had filled me with many a grim thought: being stranded on a life raft and discovering your emergency locater transmitter is unserviceable. How long could a human survive down there? – a thought which had me glancing with undying appreciation at our chunky engines – two powerful Wright Cyclone radials. I was looking through the cowling imagining all the hot metal in those reciprocating parts, the cylinders, valves and pistons turning and burning furiously. All that 'suck, squeeze, bang, blow' as we called it. I was willing them on, sharply aware that my life depended on their ceaseless rotation.

Greenland rises up to as much as 13,000 feet of ice. In the southern and western parts, there is some breathtaking scenery. Alan the captain shared some fascinating snippets with us, he spoke of the abundant fishing, the Eskimo lifestyle, the wandering polar bears, the wide Danish influence and all the wreckages of aircraft that had turned the wrong way and piled in at Narssarssuaq (a notoriously difficult approach). I also learnt much to my astonishment that venereal disease is rife there. I suppose because immune systems take time to combat new and imported enemies!

It was an apt moment to swing out of the observer's seat from the side of the cabin and enjoy the panorama from the perspex bubble in the roof. It was an awe inspiring landscape of ice: hostile, magnificent and other worldly. Savage winds raged around unstoppable icebergs. There were flat plains, jagged mountains and massive swathes of freezing white and silver. Greenland gradually disappeared under the left wing and we took up a heading of 096 degrees for Reykjavik. We backtracked Prince Christiansund NDB as we started over the second stretch of the cheerless, leaden, ocean.

Having no HF radio we had limited comms. We did hear a passing Lear Jet above us remarking on his smooth ride. We on the other hand were battling along like an industrial ice collector at 8,000 feet. Our only anti-ice was alcohol on the propeller leading edge. I jumped a few times as chunks of ice the size of bricks flew off the props and smashed into the fuselage echoing ominously round the plane.

Our instruments were pretty basic: a wind up ADF, the needle of which just seemed to rotate constantly (antenna iced-up), two VORs which never gave the same readings as each other, a Loran for ever between chains and therefore pretty unreliable, and the little magnetic compass. But most of the instruments could have been museum exhibits at Hendon or Duxford! And *this* mission precluded the luxury of autopilot so we had to stay alert. Anyway thank God for magnetic north, which never shuts down. We had a big old attitude indicator which along with the ball and the airspeed we stared at for hours on end. Everything was from that bygone age – the quilted walls, the heavy five way seat harness and the huge metal rudder pedals, all still going strong and not without their own enduring charm.

We entertained ourselves with stories of other ferry pilots, their successes and mishaps, we talked of the crashed P38s and of the two famous B17s which had gone down during the war and lay intact beneath the ice. Some rescuers managed to drill a hole in the ice and one of the P38s was lifted out in a spectacularly complicated operation many years later. She flew again in the United States and was named 'Glacier Girl'. How cool.

The route maps were fascinating – there's high magnetic variation in those latitudes and instead of the relatively straight lines of variation I was accustomed to on my topographical map, these ones seemed to loop and curve all over the place.

Just before sunset, we picked up Reykjavik approach, copied the weather and tuned in the ILS. Descent checks, pumps, lights, fans, altimeter settings, decision heights, etc., were done and the power came back. The props wailed momentarily out of synch as we threaded in and out of low broken stratus. It is strange the first time you see clouds coming straight for you through the bright lights at breathtaking speed. It's as though you're riding, flat out through a never-ending cobweb.

On first glimpse of the town, I thought – 'model village'. Little 'monopoly' houses, of similar proportion, with coloured roofs, nestled round the harbour. Hundreds of fishing boats bobbed around on the slate water. We heaved her round onto downwind, the hydraulics were noisy as the gear dropped reassuringly into 'locked'. She felt heavy but solid as we thundered onto base-leg hungry for the runway after such a long journey. Everything looked fine, we were cleared to land and at last I smelt the rubber as the tyres screeched on to terra-firma. The new brakes were super sensitive so there was a fair bit of lurching and sticking during the taxi to stand. We cut the mixtures and shut down – the silence was heavenly.

After seven hours of noisy rattling and vibration, the peace was like a neck massage. We snapped open the bottom hatch, climbed down and after a good stretch went to pay landing fees, refuel, and file the next flight plan. Vernon gave us some of his vintage wisdom. Tomorrow, we would be without him, so we listened carefully to his advice and tips about what to look out for on this particular B25 – any what we call 'gottchas'. He wished us luck and disappeared off to catch his flight to Orlando. I was sorry to see him go – he had become a friend. He was a cheeky monkey, but my God, what an instinctive and deep-rooted understanding he had of old aeroplanes. He was the type to who would cup his ear and say "sounds like the non-return valve in the hydraulic line".

The airport hotel was prodigiously expensive but had a welcome abundance of boiling hot sulphur smelling water, not surprising I suppose for an island which makes a feature of its hot mineral springs. The menu was an Atkins dieter's dream, tons of protein in the form of fish, fish and more fish. Salad or green vegetables were rare in these parts. Leaves of rocket were highly prized. I retired to read pages of the flight manual; tomorrow I would be flying. I was very excited.

At dawn I was greeted by a fairytale scene from the window. Everything on the ramp, which I overlooked, had a delicate sprinkling of fine powdery snow that had turned to ice crystals. The B25 looked almost pretty, her hard lines softened by the delicate overlay of hoar frost. I donned the thermals and wool vests followed by ski suit, it was bitter out there.

After breakfast, while flight planning in the foyer, a chap having identified me as a crew member (ski suit, hat, and a North Atlantic air chart in front of me) approached and with a crack of both his knees squatted down in front of me. His cigarette pinched between his teeth he shook my hand squinting as smoke curled upwards.

"You are with de world war two plane hey?"

"Yes that's right," I removed the woolly glove to offer my hand …"Anita."

He introduced himself. He was a Norwegian photographer doing a glamour calendar. He had a team of models wrapped in the latest winter gear – full length sable furs, thigh high black boots, pink mink muffs and khaki cashmere camisoles.

"But you know, I hev a lot of the military gear as well, so the bomber would be really de perfek bekground. Can we do some shots using your plane?"

I consulted the other two crew members, it was perfectly acceptable. I mean, show me two pilots or engineers anywhere in the world who'd object to a group of stunning, 'Scando-babes' with fur coats and stockings climbing all over their vessel!

When we agreed, fingers were snapped, orders shouted and a virtual mobile studio appeared. Gorgeous models (and of course being Scandinavian, some were men, who too, can be sex objects!) started to assume remarkable

71

positions on the wings, holding poses, and smiling for the cameras despite the penetrating cold. The military clothes bore little resemblance to anything I had seen in Iraq, much more appealing I must confess, skintight combat vest matching nix with full length Russian style heavy coat open just enough to reveal gun in garter and so on. We had sexy peaked khaki caps, high heeled combat boots and furry camouflage hand warmers and … lots of cleavage.

It all went swimmingly! They were grateful and thanked us, then models quickly shot off – to get warm! It had certainly been a more entertaining send-off than we expected.

We were three now – we climbed aboard and fired up the engines. I was in the right-hand seat, familiarising myself with all the controls and instruments around me. I would be doing gear, flaps and radios after takeoff, then sharing the flying thereafter. We taxied out under a grey sky, received clearance, lined up and opened the throttles. All six levers fully forward! – we released the brakes at full power and surged forward. The airspeed rose, the temperatures and pressures were all green, then we pulled her up into the freezing morning air. We disappeared immediately into thick low stratus.

"Positive climb gear up," called Alan and I reached for the undercarriage lever and raised it. We retracted the flap and established a suitable heading for this our last leg. Next stop – Stansted. But we would be in cloud until the north coast of Scotland!

In the cruise, we monitored instruments and fuel carefully. Not much to see on the North Atlantic chart just waypoints and coordinates. For the poor relations, like ourselves who were armed with little more than a compass and altimeter, we could no more than hold headings and keep time. What a bubbling pleasure it was to hear the first Scottish voice crackling through on the VHF. He gradually became more readable and his delight was evident when we reconfirmed our type. He made kindly enquiries about our flight and bestowed special attention on us, handing us over to Scottish radar, passing on details such as 'negative transponder' and wished us a safe onward.

All the controllers from then on were just oases of support and cheer, clearly delighted by the idea of a wartime American bomber thundering into their airspace – made a change from vectoring the same 757 BA shuttles from Heathrow.

I kept glancing out, at last the ground was visual! Gosh it was good to see it after so long. The fields and hedgerows of Blighty had never looked so good. We navigated by map and VOR the rest of the way to Stansted. There, we were vectored round for the ILS onto runway 23, had a minor tussle with a crosswind and landed her firmly down the centre-line. We had been grasping that control column for seven hours holding 'straight and level' and by God it was good to release it. We cleared customs and then took off immediately for North Weald, just up the road, ten minutes chock-to-chock. It felt right to be taking her there since it was, after all a battle of Britain airfield. We indulged the waiting crowd with a few low passes before dropping the wheels and landing for the last time. Ray had, throughout managed heroically to control the fuel leak.

A handful of reporters from local papers and aviation magazines clicked enthusiastically and gathered information. Mike Woodley, the owner, greeted us with a bottle of champagne, which we savoured after all the appropriate toasts. As everyone buzzed around and chatted, I stood near her N1042B feeling an uncanny sense of attachment. I could feel the heat radiating from the body and hear the deep cracking and popping as the engines cooled and metal contracted. People were exploring every nook and cranny taking pictures, asking questions. She had all the patience of a pedigree dog, a 'Crufts' winner which stands uncomplainingly while people lift up the tail or the chin for a good inspection and she stands proud and solid.

Ray and I unloaded the bags and the raft from the rear hatch. We put the chocks under and finally left the apron – the daylight was fading. I looked around in the dwindling light thinking about the cameraman who would occupy the rear position soon strapped in and actually hanging out of the back, his lens protruding clear of the airframe. How brutally different it must have been for the rear gunner, desperately defending his ship from unrelenting attack. Those brave boys, they knew the icy hand of fear on their stomachs. Would they ever make it back home?

I looked at her with billowing appreciation in my heart, the same appreciation a jockey would feel for his horse on winning the Gold Cup. I thought of those who had achieved memorable victories with the B25 and other bombers in the war and tried to imagine what had gone through the hearts and minds of the crew. My escapade was a mere dalliance in comparison but nonetheless I knew I had done something I would always remember.

Fairoaks team: (Left-Right) Simon, William, Lisa, John B, me, John H.

Chris Orlebar – Concorde Pilot.

Gary Numan's Harvard, painted like Japanese zero.

Fairoaks flight center, 1980s – bar night.

The flying club gang, birthday party!

The Pitts special aerobat. Sums it up!

Robbie: friend, and Lance Pilot!

Tornado crew, Prestwick – couldn't talk them
into a jolly.

Mad Robs, Lamplough, Playing piano in his flying helmet
with British passport!

Over Greenland on ferry flight of B25

Interior of B25 – no frills here!

Reykjavik, ferry flight: me, Ray, Alan and Vernon.

Mike, friend &instructor – glad to be alive!

CHAPTER TWO: Game, Jet and Match! First Job

Flying the Small Jets

With the adventure of the ferry flight behind me I resumed the job search. After a few more rejections I finally landed a couple of offers. One was from a company at Gatwick flying Shorts 360s for a small airline. *If* I had chosen that it would have put me in mainstream airlines eventually where I would have plodded my way up and had my pension. The job I chose was flying business jets at Heathrow. This probably in the long run is not as lucrative, secure or structured but it was the beginning of a kaleidoscope of different adventures and experiences. It was like opening a secret door at the back of the wardrobe, – I discovered a whole new world. And as Edith Piaf sang, *Je ne regrette rien*!

I trained on the jet itself – a small Cessna Citation 500 with the chief pilot a kind man called Brian who took me 'under his wing' and I was soon off flying the line as we call it. Here are some of the early trips I did as a novice in this brand new world of VIP flying.

Algeria

The aircraft was a Citation and the destination – Algiers. The passengers (all executives from Shell) were picked up from Rotterdam. It was 'early days' for me and my first encounter with non first world air traffic control.

Bearing in mind, this was pre GPS and electronic flight management systems, so, it was somewhat tricky, since DMEs were scant (Distance measuring equipment). If another aircraft reported in, the controller's voice became markedly louder and more panicky. They had no radar in those days, consequently you would hear rather a lot of *"Tango Alpha wot is yorr pozeeshun?!"* I soon learnt that anything south of Milan and Nice was dodgy and once south of Brindisi … well anything could happen.

The weather was appalling! Thick harmattan; visibility down to a couple of kilometres or so. By the time we spotted the airfield we were nearly overhead, only to lose sight of it again once we went downwind. All this whilst the exasperated Algerian in the tower was firing out, machine gun style, the latest met report which was fairly incomprehensible and included upper winds and dew points and other stuff which was of absolutely no use at this stage of the game!

I smiled and remembered Hugh my met teacher at Oxford telling me about his landing in a BOAC 707 in Calcutta when the controller had said, (assume strong Indian accent)"The vind between zero and zero nine zero is nothing, and the wisibility is calm"

I turned the volume knob down and just listened out for 'clear to land'. After an untidy and frankly nerve racking approach and landing (I *was* very inexperienced! and the viz was dreadful), we said goodbye to the passengers and arranged to meet them later at the hotel.

Resplendent though it was, with lofty arches, mosaic floors, pillars and palm trees, the hotel had no rooms for us. There had been a cock-up with the booking but our passengers very kindly offered to double up so I could have a room and Brian my captain would share with the senior executive. I must confess I had never seen two greater opposites. The executive was a mountain of a man, a paunchy grand duke of industry, a loud, authoritative leader – coloured shirt with white collar which he must have had specially made because his neck was the diameter of a small oak! I just couldn't control the laughter at breakfast the next morning when Brian, a slim, quiet, conservative, Rover driving man with 2.4 kids, a dog and a house in leafy Surrey, admitted that he hated sharing rooms:

"But I couldn't believe it – he knelt down at the end of the bed, eyes shut, hands pressed together and said his prayers in his huge pyjamas like Christopher Robin. Then said 'N'night' and snored all bloody night!"

It was an amusing image.

Shell's company policy was to have the crew in easy reach, especially in third world countries. So, we were invited, very kindly to have dinner with them. We went tearing round the back streets in a Peugeot taxi, getting bursts of loud, heady Arabic music 'doppler' style as it came and went through the open window. It was crowded and dusty, a bustling city of high rises and shanty town. Big old Mercedes and scooters cruised along side by side, through the streets full of people, markets, beggars, mangy dogs, exhausted donkeys and scrawny street urchins. We arrived at an authentic couscous restaurant and sampled the delights of the local wine and cuisine. We sat on comfy burgundy cushions, all velvety and tasselled. The lampshades were mirrored and colourful, the smells exotic. The men were a cosmopolitan group, having lived in all corners from Bangalore to Kinshasa. Stories flowed of embassy parties, missing flights, being stranded in the bush, canoes capsizing, lassa fever, robberies, military coups, power cuts, the whole nine yards. Tensions were rinsed away by the ever returning wine bottle and by the voluptuous belly dancer whose rippling bejewelled abdomen brought smiles to their faces.

The next morning the party was decamping to Oran further into the desert, where they would visit gas fields.

Brian and I arrived about six a.m. and got cracking with the usual preparation, flight plan, catering, hot water (which on this occasion Brian thought it a good idea for *me* to go and find). It shouldn't be a problem I thought travelling hopefully, there was always a catering department or an obliging staff member in some cafeteria. I eventually found a cafeteria/bar which was three men deep from one end to the other. Algerian men in long tunics, some in fez hats, were gathered round drinking coffee yabbering loudly with one another, smoking strong cigarettes. It was a tad strange standing in a bar full of Arabic men, being the only female with fair hair, a funny uniform on clutching a small rectangular steel urn. They were all dead friendly and gestured for me to come forward as I held up my urn and said, *"l'eau chaud s'il vous plait."* A few of them started shouting loudly at the barmen as if he were a complete idiot.

"Yalla yalla.... mettez l'eau chaud, dedans, dedans elle veut de l'eau chaud!"

There followed lots of pointing, and grabbing while orders were being barked out.

"Vous etes d'où, vous etes d'où?" asked one man with a huge smile, which pushed his wrinkles right back to his ears and showed his worn brown teeth.

"Okay! Okay no problem, hut wuter coming coming. You take coffee, have cigarette... voila."

Oh well, one day you're having a bacon bap and a mug of steaming tea in a lay-by off the M40 with some chirpy lorry drivers, next you are having strong coffee and a croissant with a gathering of Algerians in an airport café in North Africa. Some, didn't really know what to make of me and glanced strangely, some detected my awkwardness and were friendly. I had a Woody Allen moment, when he imagines himself as different characters in embarrassing situations. I rather liked the one when he turned into the orthodox Jew with ringlets, skullcap and black gown round the dinner table of anti-Semitic New England Socialites.

This airport was disorganised to put it mildly. I met up with Brian but we were unable to get any met or paperwork. However, they did produce the *bill* promptly – funny that isn't it? We abandoned any catering hopes or transport back to the aircraft, so by the time we walked back over, the passengers were on board. (I am sure the airport has improved leaps and bounds since 1989!)

I spoke on the VHF to the guy in the tower, whose strong accent I was getting familiar with –

"Tango Alpha you are clird taxi to holled of runway ..."

The berry red morning sun cast a thick rich glow over the sand as we got airborne for Oran, which seemed to be in the middle of nowhere. Fortunately we were able to do a visual approach (navigation aids were sparse in these necks!).

The Shell passengers left promptly in their minibus for their day's visit to the oil and gas fields which would have their cash tills chinking away happily. We stayed there for a full and should I say *different* sort of day. Three Algerian policemen in 'dress to impress' uniforms, screeched up with lots of 'hello hello welcom welcom' and demanded our passports. Brian, who was a pretty 'reined in' type of guy and enjoyed the telegraph crossword, suggested that I go with them whilst he stay and do the paper work, it would be good experience for me. Off we went to the terminal (if it could be so dignified). It was a bit shabby and fairly deserted and like so many places in Africa, over staffed with police and military who all sport a dazzling array of epaulets, badges and curtain tassels on their shoulders, but who don't actually do much, and who wear of course, the obligatory mirrored sunglasses. Very eighties – but it *was* the eighties!

Next thing, I am filling in forms in triplicate while they all hustled for position nearest me shouting and gesturing, trying to impress and prove that *their* job is the most critical. Our arrival must have been a welcome break from the hum drum of card playing.

"Pliz pliz," they said, arms pointing to a counter where I would "tek coffee". I saw a grubby glass, come crashing down in front of me full of **very** black coffee. The head honcho who had arrogated unto himself the role of 'absolute senior official in charge', then spooned three sugars from a bowl that was home to a small colony of ants. The spoon was standing up in the glass, just to buy some time I asked: *"Is there a toilet please."*

That launched them into another jostling and frenzied shouting match as they all tried to be the one to help me. I should have been flattered really. They told me not to use this near one because "iz very very durty" – I should go upstairs. Well as I entered the one upstairs, I was wondering what on earth the downstairs one must have smelled like. There were two cubicles, with squat basins and broken doors, crazed flies buzzed around and the whole stinky place. I returned to do battle with the coffee. Be nice ... I thought ... *they* have the passports after all.

"You English yes? English?"

"Yes I'm English."

"You like maybe marry Algerian boy ...? Why you no marry Algerian boy?"

They were laughing like a bunch of kids. One, who was examining the contents of his one long nail after a foray up his left nostril, suddenly asked me, having moved on from the disappointment of the marriage proposal if I liked Michael Jackson. He shouted to his mate who disappeared into the office and returned waving a cassette above his head. They clicked it into the player on the counter and with a press of the button I was treated to North Africa's rising star: Michael Jackson's Thriller à la Algerian security guard. I could just hear it:

"Tonight Jeremy, I am going to be ... inshalla ... Michael Jackson!"

God I must **really** bring out the child in a man because I stood there watching an apparently very serious, airport official doing the famous 'monster walk' from 'Thriller' with his hands in front of him like claws swinging from left to right, and the famous slide walk, followed by triple spin, whilst all his Gadaffi look-alike mates stood round in a circle pinching their ciggies in their teeth clapping with undiluted joy and happiness! It was actually wonderfully comical and I laughed out loud with them.

I foolishly thought seven hours would be enough notice for catering. It never came, but they still wanted eight hundred US dollars for it, in advance because it *would* come. We had no cash dollars and they wouldn't have credit card! But the airport bank was closed and only downtown would "shange dollar" it was sounding to me like a 'baksheesh in back pocket' sort of day. I was growing a bit impatient and spoke to the uniformed supervisor who had his own office with a faded picture of the president above his black swivel chair. He was obviously a little embarrassed at the ostensible cock ups of his entire staff, so his token gesture was to pick up the phone, pinch it between his ear and his shoulder so he could wave his arms angrily. His cigarette smoke made him squint – I think he was *trying* to look like Clint Eastwood, he was certainly after a 'fistful of dollars' anyway. He slammed the phone down, nodded reassuringly, his palms facing towards me in a gesture of appeasement saying, "Cat'ring okay, okay no problem okay, cat'ring coming."

He reluctantly agreed to accept our Euro cheques. That put a damper on the evening theft of funds.

Seven of them crowded round a huge desk calculator jabbing buttons trying to work out the exchange rate for our bill. We went back to the plane empty-handed having been royally ripped off and still no catering. Having done a thorough walk round of the aircraft checking the front and rear holds and all their associated gauges, we prepared for departure.

With battery on and beacon rotating and passengers seated, we started up the engine, just then a filthy old truck pulled up belching out diesel smoke. A skinny young lad jumped out and handed over eight airline meals and three bags of brown ice. There were four or five other lads hanging off the top of the truck all grinning, they'd just come along for the ride.

I unfastened my belt, opened the door to the screeching engine noise and quickly took the meals in plastic boxes.

"Here I'll take those," said one of the passengers, so I could get back in my seat and proceed with the taxi check list. $400 for that lot – it was – for those days, very expensive. Still, as Brain pointed out, not likely to make a dent in the profits of an oil company! Being seasoned travellers they knew not to use the ice in drinks so they stabbed a load of beers into it, and drank those en route home!

We checked our brakes and instruments on the way to the hold, set the flaps for take-off, checked the speed brakes, dialled in the transponder code and lined up.

Up came the two thrust levers

"N 1 set" we accelerated smartly down the centre line.

"Eighty knots."

"Check."

"V one rotate."

"Positive rate of climb …

"Gear Up."

We climbed out of the sandy haze gaining altitude.

"…flaps zero … after take-off check list."

Once again we tucked everything in like a bird for high speed flight and set off north across the Mediterranean towards the south of France then up towards Holland.

The Elderly Millionairess

One of our loyal and regular customers (and trust me, these are the sort of regulars you dream of) was the charming, skinny, bejewelled, and scented Mrs

'W'. Hubby had left a considerable pile and she flitted around Europe on a private jet, doing lunch in Paris and weekends in Venice, whilst her money burgeoned beautifully like a tropical cloud, into piles 'un-spendable' by one human. She was elderly and sophisticated, always sported dark "Jackie-O" shades, and 60s style tweed suits by Channel or some designer (who was always a friend). Her brown hair turned up at the bottom, like a child's drawing of a girl. She was well heeled and gracious, and glided around with her little short strapped handbag over her elbow which showed off her tiny hand mottled with liver spots and barnacled with diamonds. She had substantial connections with the Metropolitan museum of Art in New York.

She once chartered us to fly down to Rome, pick her up and take her to Milan. So she paid the hefty sum for an empty leg out and back to London at nearly £2000 per hour, just to do a twenty minute flight. Still, what the heck, she felt comfortable with us. We were those familiar smiling faces who always dealt uncomplainingly with the small platoon of Louis Vuitton cases, from trunk down to hat box.

On this occasion, I was the co-pilot on a flight to Venice where she was waiting to return to London. It was a stiflingly hot summer day. She had told us she'd be with *one* other passenger, so Don the Captain went over to the terminal and I waited on the scorched tarmac with the aircraft to supervise the refuelling. I calculated the weights quickly of 2 passengers and bags and filled up the wings with fuel putting us at maximum take-off weight. A few moments later a baggage trolley trundled passed me laden down with very superior looking bags. Must be headed for the Gulfstream next door I thought to myself (a decidedly bigger biz jet). But then the tousle haired drop dead gorgeous Italian baggage handler pulled up at our little jet.

"Errr, tango alpha for London," came the sexy Italian voice.

"No it can't be!" I protested, knowing with a sinking heart it was probably true. He was grinning and whistling and looking me up and down with that practised expertise known so well to Italian men, as he unloaded the bags. Just then my flustered captain came striding across the apron towards me, shaking his head and announced that she had offered to give another friend a lift back to London, he had to catch Concorde and was running late. You can't exactly say no, can you? Still when you are an elegant, classy millionairess with designer friends and a private jet at your disposal, a bit of capriciousness is acceptable … n'est ce pas?

"But we've got no room Don, we'll be overweight," I protested showing that 'just out of flight school' naivety. He threw me a look – it said … Oh do shut up.

What followed was like a comedy sketch from Laurel and Hardy as the two of us struggled to load far too may bags in the space available. The Citation only has modest baggage space and once we'd filled the back and the nose hold, we were still staring at five more pieces. Scratching our heads, wiping away the sweat, it was like trying to move house with one car!

The suave I'tie baggage handler whistled a love song as he assisted us totally unruffled, he'd seen it all before.

"Eh relax huh? Is cool, is cool," he smiled, shrugging his shoulders when he saw me sweating. For me it was a crisis for Don the Captain just another day at work. With both holds full we put the rest in the cabin, bags piled up against the walls and door in the front and filled the small toilet area at the back. There would be no weeing and no jumping out of an emergency exit on *this* flight. Hot and heavy are the adversaries of aircraft performance – engines love cold air the density produces more thrust and obviously the lighter the aircraft is the better. So there we were on a stinking hot day and boy *we were heavy!*

Don held the aircraft on the brakes for a long time until take-off power was completely up on the N1 (power) gauges. Even when we released the brakes, acceleration was pretty sluggish, when he did rotate (somewhat late!) he pulled the nose off into an extremely shallow angle of climb, fortunately at Venice there are no obstacles and no high ground. The rate of climb could not be described as spectacular but off we went. We enjoyed the views of Venice and the coastline then shortly afterwards the Alps which never fail to bowl you over with their rugged beauty. I felt a lot more relaxed now we had those two chestnuts *speed and altitude* on our side.

Suddenly I smelt a gorgeous expensive perfume, that's not Don I thought, then Ah Mrs 'W' popped her elegantly coiffed head into the cockpit and in that cool New York accent, said, "Could you possibly radio ahead to Heathrow and ask British Air to hold the Concorde for my friend – he doesn't wanna miss it."

God, I thought it must be lovely to live the fairy tale. Don asked for his ticket and said he would try. A bony, very feminine hand resplendent with gems appeared between our shoulders holding a flute of Dom Perignon and a ticket pinched between two perfectly manicured long red nails. I took it from her. The name on the ticket was Mr O de La Renta. I looked up a frequency for the HF (High Frequency) radio which ranges from 3 to 30 megahertz and varies with the time of day and transmitted to Portishead.

"You do it – good practice," said Don.

So, having learnt in flight school about those waves bouncing off the ionosphere and their skip distance, etc., I did my first transmission.

"Portishead radio Portishead radio this is Golf Juliet Echo Tango Alpha on 6636 position Switzerland, over."

I made contact and the message was copied, over and out, Concorde would be held for the perfume man. I wonder if they would have held the Concorde for Percy Sugbeth from Barnsley? I remember an interview with a famous pop star – she said when she had *nothing* she was offered *nothing*, but when she became a millionairess, companies could not load her up with enough freebies; have a Porsche, have a Jag, a Patek Phillipe watch perhaps …

We landed on the long, beautifully lit and unfailingly welcoming runway at Heathrow and then I tuned into ground on 121.9 VHF. They gave us a lengthy taxi instruction directing us to the Concorde. We parked and then rummaged to find his bag amongst what looked like the Harrods suitcase department. He shook our hands disembarked and shot off up the steps of the supersonic. From her seat in the back, looking like Great Garbo, she raised her tiny hand to the window to wave him off. Back at our executive terminal

'Fields' as it was then called, Mrs 'W' climbed carefully down the steps whilst lots of deferential chaps milled around unloading bags and putting them in her limousine. Crisp fifty pound notes were peeled off her wodge and handed out to these grateful chaps. The captain noticed my fascination.

"I know what you're thinking Anita, we are apparently *too* professional for a tip."

"Oh are we?"

"Hey, but look," said Don, "there is one advantage of these trips." He grinned as he picked up the bottle. "She always leaves some Dom Perignon."

I will never forget my first sip that day – it was truly manna from heaven, ice cold and smooth as silk!

My next encounter with Mrs 'W'– I picked her up from Florence. Having just filled both fuel tanks, the airport staff informed me that they only accepted cash or American Express, strange since that is normally the least favoured card. So despite our arsenal of Euro cheques, a Visa and Diners card, they were intransigent. I soon learnt Italian airports are not the best places to get things done. I called our operations back at Heathrow but what could they do? A 'keen to get going' and mildly agitated Mrs W. saw me in the terminal trying to sort it out and approached me lifting her hallmark dark glasses up on to her head.

"What's the problem?"

"They won't accept the cards we have, they want cash or Amex."

"Oh my dear," she said, "if it's just a matter of *money* let's just pay them and go."

She opened her beautiful little designer bag and out came the concertinaed card holder. She let it unfold and it opened like a fiscal accordion. I had not seen that much platinum since I was down a mine outside Pretoria. I was mortified at having to ask a passenger to pay for the fuel it was hugely embarrassing, but thank God she could, it was the only way we were going to get out of there. Still, I suppose when you are buying Titians and Rubens you exact a fair old limit on the card! She removed the platinum Am Ex and I awkwardly stammered out some feeble apology saying our company would be getting in touch to compensate, and meanwhile perhaps some extra peanuts? Even worse was having to go back into the cabin once she was seated with the fuel man's clipboard and the receipt for her to sign. Oh Lord! However. she was gracious enough to know these things happen and she continued to book thousands of pounds worth of flying with us every month. She was a gem.

I regularly flew her to Paris for lunch. It was a luxurious shimmering world she lived in. It was as elegant as a ribboned Louis Quatorze shoe, or an Antique perfume bottle with tasselled atomiser. Flying her was like being dabbed with a big scented powder puff.

Krakov 1989

Pre perestroika Poland – I'm glad we had one trip there before the big 'changes' came. Whilst working for Heathrow based IDS (which stood for the names of the two founding brothers) I flew the England football manager and his entourage to Krakow, the team went in a Caledonian 757. In Poland the winter had taken a firm grip – it was drabber than a grey dishcloth drying on a line in a concrete yard. We landed in freezing mist. Down both sides of the taxiway were huge Antanov 2s – big old lumbering biplanes from the Polish airforce.

It was bitterly cold and we sat in our aircraft noticing that some poor young lad in uniform and long trench coat had been dispatched to stand guard by our plane all day. He just stood motionless with his gun by his side. I offered him some food and coffee but he shook his head staring straight ahead.

We waited over an hour for the fuel bowser to show up even though I saw no other planes. When I went to pay the handling (what handling? – we had unloaded the bags ourselves and our passengers had no transport), it was a staggering $600 and they didn't want zloty's they wanted Uncle Sam's USD. What on earth we were paying for eluded me. Even in superbly equipped modern airports I hadn't been charged like that, maybe they heard it was a football team. I peeled off the dollars to pay him and turned on my heel to leave. Just as I got to the door I heard, "Kssss Kssss."

I turned round and he looked right then left, pulled a little tin from his pocket and said, "Caviar, Russian good good!"

"How much?" I asked

"Twenty-five dollar," came the optimistic reply.

One of my catch phrases at the time because of an American boyfriend who always said it, was 'I'll give you a dollar'(he *had* been raised on Clarke airforce base in Philippines) so it just came to me.

"I'll give you a dollar."

Well blow me down he accepted, it was admittedly a small tin but I took five off him and he seemed pretty pleased. That was good I'd already done a deal before leaving the airport, I felt quite entrepreneurial – I was looking forward to downtown.

After the painfully slow refuelling, we locked the plane and went through a mini 'pantomime'. A man in a decorated uniform, with a huge square head like a block ushered us through. He had one eye looking left and the other looking right, so his stare was a sort of 'ten to two' instead of a twelve o clock experience. He sat at the first desk and was 'Passport control' so we went through all that, he looked purposefully at the picture then stamped the page. Then he disappeared behind the curtain at the back of the cubical and we heard a "please, please…" and he reappeared in the *next* cubicle where he would now be customs. So we slid five feet to the left and did 'customs' and opened our bags. He still had the same granite expression. His humourless austerity seemed unnerving at first but he pursued his craft with the blind unquestioning commitment to the system so typical of Eastern block officials then. Then he disappeared again – by now we had the hang of it and shuffled down obligingly where the same man was now a 'Policeman'.

The next cultural experience was the airport café where we waited for the taxi. The menu on a blackboard was in Polish with broken English descriptions. I chose a stew, hoping it would be warming. It arrived in one of those battered rather flimsy tin dishes full of dents. I stared at it, pinned to the spot. The waitress tried to convince me with a few gestures, tummy rubbing and kissing her fingertips that it was good, but my untrained palate could coax no more out of it than the nauseating aroma of fat. This was meat of very dubious provenance. Big chunks of pig skin (*not* the yummy crackling type) floated in a grey green greasy gravy. I might have tackled it but the big bristly hairs protruding from the skin finally defeated me and I settled for a coffee. We asked for the bill, she shrugged her shoulders, this means 'Whatever you think'. We gave her ten dollars. She smiled broadly and scuttled into the back undoing her pinny, I think she was retiring.

It was no surprise that the taxi drivers all jostled for our business outside. Acquiring dollars was obviously the 'thing' back then. The driver dropped us in the main square – he would wait. The architecture was grand and imposing, the cobbled square quite beautiful and on a generous day I suppose could be likened to the Grand Place in Brussels.

Groups of teenagers were huddled round portable stereos smoking and listening to Wham and other 'bootleg' tapes. One guy clearly showed his clout as a trader because *he* had Levi 501s – very sought after in those days. He was Poland's James Dean. Whenever an 'official' neared the square they would hide everything just like a scene from 'Only Fools and Horses'. These were little bubbles of revolution rising, a great change was sweeping over Eastern Europe fuelled by the indomitable human spirit and its desire for freedom as they discarded the manacles of Communism. I suppose these were the first bubbles of Perestroika. Young people will always be curious about other people's clothes, music and culture. We saw many things on the black market that day. Twelve years later when I returned on the 727, the place was a thriving trendy café society with everything on sale. Horse drawn carriages clip clopped round the squares. The beautiful municipal park was full of people painting and dancing, the same park where a beautiful and most unusual monument to Chopin stands in a vast shallow pond.

In most European cities a three hour cab ride round the city would be well over $100 but when *he* dropped us back at the airport, he, just like the waitress had done, shrugged his shoulders, hoping we would decide on the price. He sheepishly suggested twenty dollars so when I gave him twenty-five he was well pleased and thanked us as least five times.

I haven't kept many mementoes from foreign airports, but the weather report I received that evening in Krakow, I have kept and it is in my log book to this day. Brian my Captain went to pay bills and file the flight plan and I went for the weather. The meteorology office was a portakabin. Inside sat a dumpy lady in a thick green woolly suit and little ankle wellies. She had a tea cosy hat and sat in front of a very old typewriter. Her cat was curled up on top of the electric fire. She spoke no English and I no Polish but she knew I wanted the met otherwise I wouldn't be there. She smiled, nodded grabbed her torch and trotted outside. I peered round the open door out of curiosity. She shone the torch up at the sky then trotted back in purposefully muttering "two tousand" and tipped her outspread hand left and right which meant 'more or less'. I think that was the cloud base done. Then she sat down at her desk with her collection of coloured pencils and started to draw on a piece of paper. It wasn't like the met room in Heathrow that was for sure. Ten minutes later she put her last crayon down, pushed her chair back, stood up and then this little industrious lady turned to me proudly and handed me my met report. I was fascinated; I'd never seen anything like it. When I showed Brian he smiled and said, "Good heavens these were almost obsolete during the war!"

I looked closely, it was a colourful picture; there were blue and red arrows, wind signs, heights in meters, isotherms, isobars and other jolly little pictures of clouds and raindrops. I have treasured it to this day. It is pressed inside my logbook. It belonged to the age of carousels, dolls houses and jigsaws. In the annals of aviation it belonged to the world of old compasses, dead reckoning and Mercator charts!

We walked out to our parked Citation. The long suffering soldier was **still** standing there; he must have been frozen to the bone. He didn't smile back at me. I felt for him, so I offered him my crew meal. He looked nervously at me then at the meal – prawns, roast beef, chocolate cake. He finally let his gun drop and smiled.

"For you, eat it, you have it," I said.

He put it under his coat and walked off.

The footballers returned, the England manager and immediate entourage came with us, the players went on the Caledonian 757. It felt good to press the start button and hear the reassuring whirring of the engine spooling up. With the after start check list complete we taxied past the huge airforce biplanes and took the runway. We lifted into a gloomy night. Before too long we were talking to Berlin – a nice feeling! It was always an education flying to Eastern block countries back then, it made you appreciate the efficiency of our systems and *their* potential once freed from the strangulating bureaucracy. I thought about the Poles during the flight home, how many unsung heroes they must have and particularly about the fact that it was the Poles who were so instrumental in cracking the enigma code during the Second World War. Little did I know during that flight that within twenty years half of them would be living in England!

Farranfore – Ireland

Have you ever been to Ireland? If not … Go! It's an extraordinary place, there's nowhere *quite* like it. This was my first ever sampling of the emerald isle, as a new and inexperienced pilot.

Farranfore, (or Kerry airport as it is called now) was a sleepy little place back in 1988, now it is a thriving commercial airport. I'm glad I experienced it when it was in the 'small and unknown' category. It was a quintessential little country airfield. We flew from Heathrow (yes small jets could afford to be based there in those days!) across the sea to Southern Ireland. We broke out of cloud at about 900 feet.

"There it is" said Dave and positioned nicely for a downwind. The landscape was voluptuous and green! We did a visual approach over pretty little farms and cottages. The Irish have a knack of establishing a drinking venue pretty much anywhere and an airport is no exception. All the 'wee ones' were pushed up against the boundary fence, best coats on, noses and fingers poking through the mesh dutifully obeying their parents' excited instructions to "look at the jet plane". Our passenger, a wealthy American married to an Irish lady thanked us and disappeared off to his country castle, and we were bombarded with "Will yous com 'n have a drink"? After shutting down, and filling in the tech log, we walked over to the bar. My first time in Ireland, I realised at that moment that drinking and Guinness were truly institutions of gargantuan importance. Through the thick blue stinking smoke layer which I bet never left this room, I could make out a regiment of Guinness levers behind the bar. The place reeked of sour beer soaked into worn carpets. I must have been offered four pints, someone would spot that my glass was half-empty and point to it and say "Will y'have another point" and without waiting for an answer it appeared. There was no sign of this being a flying school, then I just caught sight of a tatty hand written sign stuck to the wall with sellotape "Trial lesson – 25 punts".

My Captain, Dave, had been there before so he had a hero's welcome, he was reminiscing with a couple of the locals about the air show they tried to put on during his previous visit.

"Cor blimey," started Dave. "I remember hearing this loud Irish voice booming from a megaphone.'Will de owner of de brown K registered Morris please com to de car park cos it's on fire'.

There were minor explosions of laughter (some of which turned into gut churning attacks of whooping cough) from the one guy.

"Dat's royt dat's royt, jeeesus what a crack dat was; did we manage to get any aircraft up dat day at all?"

"Yea don't you remember," continued Dave, "they were dropping those parachutists out of that aircraft and one of them nearly landed on the prop of the DC3 which was taxiing."

"Yes it was a little disorganised," chuckled one of the men, on his stool, cigarette pinched in right hand as he leant heavily with elbow on right knee like Rodin's thinker. There was not an unbroken capillary left in his face. He told us proudly how half the planes broke down, the radio packed up and everybody got roaring drunk.

During the course of this liquid lunch when I became an expert on the Liffey waters, I met some of the locals including a tiny but feral looking woman named Bernadette. Her front tooth was missing and she chained smoked with a determination I had never seen, great horns of smoke shooting from each nostril as she simultaneously took the next drag with such power, the ciggie nearly caved in. "Focken bastard, focken bastard" was all she muttered as she chewed her nails, and rocked back and forth. The local 'father' filled me in with the details, apparently her live in boyfriend had escaped but the source or her fury was that he had done so on *her* horse!

Everyone insisted we return that evening for a tipple. The local landlady, who was accommodating us, drove us to our B&B. Her four children were waiting, two boys and two girls. The eldest boy, about eight had grazed knees, flaming red hair, blue eyes and a cheeky grin. His brother, about six, had thick dark hair, dark eyes and rosy cheeks covered in freckles. The two girls were beautiful; the eldest had black straight pageboy hair and a round face bubbling with mischief. Her little sister, blonde with a cotton dress all smudged with muddy hand prints wiped her nose on the back of her hand and blew her fringe out of her eyes. They all shook my hand beaming from ear to ear, I felt like Maria from Sound of Music meeting the Von Trapps. Their mother scuttled around telling them to straighten their clothes.

"This is a very important lady," she announced. "She is very very clever, she is a PILOT!!" She knelt down to be at eye contact with them in case they swooned at this information.

"You must treat her very well and not get on her nerves OKAAAAY?"

"Okaaaaaay mam."

I remember many things about that weekend including the fact that they never got my name, I was just "guest". The kids were jubilant because after dropping my bags in the room, I came out to play. They showed me their potato patch and all their vegetables looking up at me to confirm that this strange person who arrived in strange clothes, understood what all this was. They were all bare foot, tearing around leaping and screaming "Guest, look at this", "Guest, watch me jump", "Guest push me on the swing", "Is it relly true dat yous came in a jet?" asked the lad as he spun round laughing, arms out, imitating an aeroplane. We played with cricket bats and Frisbees and inspected tadpoles in the yoghurt pot, and I gave them all piggy backs. Seamus was determined to find the spare Frisbee so he climbed into what looked like a gypsy wagon, it had two central wheels and a door at one end – it was a kind of store shed. He called me for help because he could not find it, so I crawled in to the far end and our combined weights made it tip up, and we tumbled to the back. With that, their mother came running out of the kitchen in apron and slippers smacking the air with her tea towel.

"I'm only after telling you to leave the guest alone, now com'on she's a pilot and she's had enough or you, pilots don't be doin with all this nonsense." I assured her everything was fine.

"Wait til I tell your father," and with that four pairs of feet shuffled in for tea.

We all tucked in to a huge plate of fish paste sandwiches. The girl piped up.

"Mommy can I play with guest after tea?"

"No, guest has had enough of yous now."

With a flash of her eyes she reminded them to offer me more food. God I loved this family. She was up and down filling my teacup chattering away. She asked many questions about my job and no matter what my answer she looked me in the eye, nodding and whispered "Is dat royt?" over and over. Her husband returned, a kind softly spoken man, balding, and weathered, neutral and uncomplaining. It was like being in one of those marvellous 1950s black and white films like Kes. I congratulated him on his wonderful issue, they had all lined up in descending order and he patted them all on the head.

"Yes der like steps of de ladder, God love 'em." he said clasping his pipe between his teeth. Having learnt that our take-off time was not until midday, he said he would take Dave and I out for a drink that evening.

What followed was basically an Irish coffee run through the luscious velvety hills of Kerry. I listened fascinated by their accounts of local life, the 'Rose of Tralee' beauty pageant, Puck fair where tinkers come to find a wife or just have yet another monumental piss up. A huge goat is the town's famous statue and landmark (a good indication of their activities). There were tales of childhood adventures and subsequent summer evenings of inebriation in the Macgillycuddy's Reek mountains. I heard Kerrymen talking about the horse and cattle fair in Killorgin where men would meet women.

"We've been married these twelve years and have fourteen childer!"

They all had an irresistible combination of a deeply entrenched catholic fear and a healthy drunken irreverence. The joke:

"What's the difference between an Irish wake and an Irish wedding …? One less drunk!" started to make sense. I was offering my condolences to a lad in a pub, because Ireland had lost a football match that weekend – something that came up in conversation.

"Och it's okaaay, like 'cos we're shite at everything, it duznt opset us ya know!"

Once a few years later in Castleisland, I was following two men down the staircase of a hotel and I thought they were speaking Russian because their accents were so strong. At the bottom of the stairs I picked up one or two words of English and chuckled to myself and said to them: "I have to tell you I thought you guys were Russian?" to which he instantly replied: "Well you're not too far off because we *are* in a hurry!"

Our landlord and landlady drove us round beautiful countryside, sheep dotted the meadows and uneven stone walls bordered the country lanes, I was in a Kerrygold butter ad! The retreating sun scattered the usual magic in his wake, the sky was just turning pale tangerine at the horizon and hints of amethyst and violet touched the wisps of high cloud. We stopped to admire the ruins of an old castle next to a placid lake, this was too good to be true – like something out of Excalibur! Mallards preened themselves on the banks and coots flew silently across the glassy black surface which was streaked with the softest pastels reflected off the evening sky. The castle cut a striking silhouette, it seemed to have found peace in its retirement. The patina of moss and grime only enhanced its craggy beauty and stillness.

We went into an old cottage inn which had a rickety gift shop integral with the pub, they were selling tea towels with old Irish poems and recipes on them, maps, trinkets, leprechauns and shamrocks. We drank yet more Guinness and Irish coffee and someone sang a song accompanied by an accordion and fiddle player. The lad's voice had a happy lyricism about it, music is certainly engrained in the Celtic soul. All the buildings are strikingly colourful, giving a real feeling of gaiety. It's refreshing to see in one row of houses, the colours, purple, orange, blue, green yellow and red. It is as though you had asked a child to paint them. "Splash the paint on – use every colour!" It's indicative of an unguarded sort of nature, I think, and when a police station is painted bright pink and blue, this is a good sign.

Some of the bed and breakfasts I have since encountered over there, have had truly amazing décor. Among some landladies there is an endearing touch of the Maggie Smith in the film 'Private Function' when she says arms folded:

"I'm not having Beryl and Stanley at number fourteen thinking we can't afford maraschino cherries!"

Once you have got round the white fake Ionic columns in the garden, you enter a dolls house of velour, colour and gadgets. In one room there was gold guilt on everything, nylon nets, pink candlewick counterpane and a carpet – well I hadn't seen anything like this carpet – it was the 'Big Bang' in thread and weave, it was an acid trippers heaven. In one establishment in Tralee the landlady who was almost blind and nearly deaf, was showing all the symptoms of excessive compulsive disorder, hers was a paranoia about cleanliness. She had used every possible bottle of cleaning agent, and sprayed the place as though exorcising a satanic plague. It was like kipping down in a sodium lauryl sulphate factory, and when I ran a bath, there was so much residual chemical agent on the enamel that in five seconds flat it bubbled and foamed into a towering wall of suds which were tinged with lime green – that must have been the new bathroom spray with added citrus! I'm sure if I hadn't turned the taps off the bubbles would have moved inexorably over the bath edge and slithered down the stairs like a giant spongy worm of disinfectant, asphyxiating everything in its way!

But our family home in Farranfore had been a delight and for a first visit it really awakened my interest in Ireland. The next morning our bill was £15 for bed and breakfast. (I must say that on subsequent visits to south-west Ireland I noticed that everything had become ruinously pricey). We said goodbye and climbed into an old banger belonging to the landlord's friend – they would not DREAM of letting us pay for a taxi, even under protest he picked up my case and said, "Yous 'll go in MY VAY-HICKAL!"

Back at the airport all the bibulous rascals were still in the bar, I managed to find the refueller and pull him out. We filled up and made sure catering supplies were plentiful and the interior clean. Our American and his Irish wife arrived. I found the Jeppesen approach plates for Lugano which was our destination.

We set the flaps, and the altimeter, checked rudders, ailerons and elevator for full travel and set up the cockpit for departure. Loads of them waved us off as we accelerated away into the sky once more. I looked down as I held the control column for a last glimpse of Farranfore and its *lovely* residents. Then we slid away into the cloud. *That* was a very good first trip to Ireland I would say.

Those beautiful peninsulas of Southern Ireland which gesture out into the Atlantic like a bear's foot have become home to some of the world's rich and famous. Celebrities, pop stars, actors and businessmen have built havens of paradise along the windswept shores and within the emerald green interior, and it has become a regular destination for us.

Knock – Enter and have a Guinness

Remember that rather atmospheric advert for the Peugeot 205 which featured the car speeding along windswept craggy cliffs, while waves crashed on the rocks to the sound track 'Take my Breath away'(of Top Gun fame?). Well, we flew the film crew who created that off to the west coast of Ireland in search of the perfect rugged scenery. It was December 1989 and we picked them up in the Cessna Citation II from Exeter on a cold wintry evening and flew across the Irish Sea. Somewhere off the coast near Liverpool, I turned to my Captain.

"How come it's getting light in the north, the glow from the recent sunset should, surely be from the west?" It puzzled me because it didn't fade, perhaps it was the city lights glowing from the Liverpool area.

"Oh it must be the Northern Lights!" said Brian. It was my first sighting and although it wasn't exactly an 'Arctic circle' calibre of show, it was exciting – strange shimmery glows and hazy light wafted eerily thousands of miles away in space. I turned round and shouted to the gang in the back who I knew would appreciate *this*.

"Hey guys, Northern Lights out your starboard!"

With that, there were lightening quick snaps, as they all, like clockwork, grabbed their photographic cases and flicked them open, in the same movement attached and screwed lenses on and prepared to 'shoot'. There is something instinctive about photographers, it is built into them, they waste no time because five seconds delay could mean missing that golden opportunity. The whole sky became a gigantic glowing dome of strange light. They took some good shots. It was their first glimpse also.

We prepared for our decent and landing into Knock. I remembered on a previous trip to Ireland, a man had to scare a sheep off the runway. "Sure you can land whichever way you like" was the reply when I asked for the direction of the landing runway, or "Och it looks okaaay" when I asked for the weather. As this place was remote-ish and on the west side I was expecting a similar unsophisticated set-up. But none of it – as we locked on to the ILS (Instrument Landing System) I was startled by the sophistication of it all. It was the strip in Las Vegas. We had every type of dazzling approach light going, rows and columns of red, green and white lights, shooting rabbits, precision approach indicators, the whole 'enchilada' as the Americans would say. We had approach aids of the highest calibre and a runway fit for the space shuttle and something I hadn't seen before – a luminous windsock, it was floating there eerily in the darkness like a ghostly orange stocking. I subsequently learnt that this was the spot where the vision of the Virgin Mary had taken place so this was Ireland's new Mecca. It was a case of 'If you build it, they will come'. Millions of pounds of EC funding poured in to make an airport, which could take the traffic of Chicago on Thanksgiving weekend. Thousands upon thousands of holy happy folk driven by an unshakable faith and fervour would flock to pay homage to 'Our Holy Lady' steadfast in the belief that their 'fay-eth' would be strengthened.

One of the features of holy Catholic sites, is that a bone of a certain Saint is supposed to be buried there. Bones of the same Saint are in the catacombs of numerous churches and cathedrals. The amount of bones some of these sandal wearing itinerants must have had would mean they must have had eight toes on every one of their five feet and enough arms to make every circus juggler weep. Anyway – Knock is indeed an interesting place, there is no faith like the Catholic one, and no crowd like the Irish to ensure a well-attended day out at the very mention of a vision. I was to encounter this again ten years later in the airline when I used to fly a service from Cork to Lourdes – some of these severely crippled people would not order the wheelchair for the return journey obviously convinced they would be skipping down the steps of the aircraft unaided.

Funny thing was though as we taxied in I couldn't actually see any other aircraft, but I could see crowds of jostling happy people in the bar in the terminal building. There was definitely more Guinness sold here than fuel. I was told that a Ryan Air came in here now and again from Luton but business didn't seem to be *that* buoyant. It felt like being alone on the bleachers of Wembley stadium having got the wrong day for the cup final. Just as I was putting the chocks under the wheels I heard a strong Irish voice come booming down from the control tower which was right beside me and looked like something from downtown Seattle – very modern. I looked up and the lights shining down on me were so bright I instantly went blind, but I could make out his head which was sticking out of a window.

"Would yous please com op to the tower when yous have finished."

I climbed about five flights hanging firmly on the rail because I had big floating red spots across my eyes where the light had dazzled me.

"Well hello," said a beaming Irishman as I entered what was really a very well equipped and sophisticated control room

"Welcome to Knock, I'm Mart'n and dats Paddy."

We shook hands. In front of the elderly Paddy was an ashtray stuffed with cigarette ends, (the days *before* health and safety) and the way he looked at me through lifted narrowed eyes I guessed he was a touch short sighted! He finally locked on and gave me a warm handshake and a great smile.

One was the meteorologist and one the controller, Martin explained as he stepped back allowing me to admire the wonders of their work place. What a double act, and what a superb tower and view.

"God lov ya, yous must be tired, would you like a cigarette?" said Paddy opening a new packet.

"Well shall we take dees good people over to the bed and breakfast and be goin' for a wee drink with Siobhan and Patrick?"

They had obviously been waiting for us and now work was wrapped up. Then with unexpected hospitality they drove us down to the guest house. I loved the way they instantly took us in like family. They wouldn't entertain the idea of a taxi. I felt that they'd been waiting for us before the party could properly get under way! They repeated over and over what good 'foyn' people Patrick and Siobhan were and how comfortable we'd be at their B&B.

Formalities done, it was off down the pub, even though it was already ten o'clock. Two rules in Ireland: it's never too late or early for a drink, and there are no opening or closing hours. The tiny village was called Charlestown in County Mayo. Locals were waiting for us and the Guinness was flowing. There were still people arriving at midnight. I was introduced to the Priest (there has to be one doesn't there), he was a Chaucerian sort, his nose ruby, and his voice elastic from alcohol. Everyone loved him though and he was doing a very good job of nodding earnestly at everyone's mini confessions even though he was deaf, he kept smiling. My friend William Stoney who had lived many years in Ireland told me funny little stories about things heard in bars, like the chap who went up to the bar and ordered "Tree pints a Guinness, a packet of Carolls (cigarettes) and sum bread and botter for da missus".

A man with a face like the nodule covered gourds we used to draw in still life art classes at school, introduced me three times to the barman and in between, was having a truly animated conversation with himself.

"Take no notice of him, he's had a stroke and it's made him a bit fonny like," explained the barman. "Real shame like cos he played a fantastic fiddle – doesn't know a 'B' from a 'C' now." A group of wives were gossiping about the 'younguns' and admonishing some poor Dara girl who had got up to no good. The landlord then introduced me very proudly to the town's 'entreprenou-er' knowing that he was the town's star and bound to impress me.

"This is *Michael*, he's an entreprenou-er, Michael here fixes our bicycles." He patted Michael on the back and leant over and whispered, "It's his *own* business you know."

"Can I buy ya a drink?" Michael sang at me. He was a chirpy soul, he told me all about his adventures as a kid when he and his mate Kieran would steal birds' eggs from the nests on the cliffs, they would be hanging on for dear life while the waves crashed below. They would catch fish from the Gulfstream waters using string and home-made hooks and they would sell them.

"We were always pinchin the apples from the nun's orchard like, they could never catch us! I'd get me mam to make jam and I'd sell that too!"

He was definitely a born entrepreneur and went everywhere on his bike – he had always kept his bike in tiptop condition – it was his getaway vehicle, so now he had a thriving business.

In the background, a serious pool player was about to be beaten by a saucy plump redhead and he paced calculatingly round the table chalking the hell out of his cue frowning intently at the balls. There was a young couple, just married only about nineteen and they were teased all night by their elders about when they would have a baby and whether the young lad had it in him.

"What's that pox on your lip for God's sake," I heard the flat capped farmer (whose tractor was outside) ask one of the girls at the bar. She did have a small rash on her top lip and she snapped at him.

"Jeesus will you leave it out, I'm only after waxing me focken moustache this morning and it didn't work out!"

The 'Chaucerian' priest kept asking if the Guinness was to my liking and then suggested I join him in a whisky – when in Rome. His mate sang a little folk song about Ireland for me and then challenged me to a response;

fortunately I could remember a poem about drinking so I dedicated it to the two of them:

> *"The wonderful love of a beautiful maid,*
> *and the love of a staunch true man;*
>
> *The love of a baby, unafraid, have existed since time began.*
>
> *But the greatest love, the love of all loves,*
> *even greater than that of a mother,*
>
> *Is the tender and passionate, infinite love,*
> *of one drunken sod for another!"*

The two of them exploded into chesty laughs and awarded me with two more whiskies. Then one silenced the other with a hand over his mouth, cleared his throat and told me to listen to this one:

> *The Guinness was spilt on the bar room floor*
> *When the bar was closed for the night*
>
> *When out from a hole crept a small brown mouse*
> *And he stood in the pale moonlight*
>
> *As he lapped up that frothy brew from the floor*
> *Then back on his haunches he sat*
>
> *And all night long, to hear him roar*
> *Send out that bar room cat!*

I thought it such a funny little poem I wrote it down, I am glad I kept it. He delivered it with real drama and expression.

I learned all sort of things that night from those happy drunks, such as the six different words for bog (there are words for forming bogs, Atlantic bogs, raised bogs and so on). I learned that 'Fitz' means son in Norman hence all the Fitzpatrick's and Fitzwilliam's who roam the land.

At about half past one in the morning the landlord was well oiled and he showed us the door. "Shhh," he said as he wobbled about grinning, he looked left and right checking it was all clear. This was just to show us he had at least *a little* respect for the law and opening hours. Of course we all knew if the local policeman had been there, he'd have been in for a nightcap. "Goodnight, thanks a million God bless yous, goodnight, thanks a million."

We wandered back through a soup of fog, it hung around like a devilish miasma. There was not a breath of wind. I glanced at the shops. There was a clothes shop, which stopped me in my tracks. I saw a faceless dummy with a cock-eyed nylon wig, she was leaning backwards, no hands, just steel rods poking out from the arms, she had a brownish zip up dress, I hadn't seen anything like it since my tiny mousey Latin teacher at school who was a skinny vegan and extremely strange. In the men's window some big shiny ties and round-toed lace ups. Next was a grocery store, their display was a pyramid of tins and a packet of candles. There was an estate agent in which I don't think I saw a house over £30,000. Finally, a travel agent offering coach tours to Lourdes. Some very faded pictures were pinned to a board – people kneeling and praying, one of the coach, one of pilgrims looking skyward in Lourdes and a faded testimonial of a girl who had discarded her callipers. The small modest display was finished off with a plastic ornament of 'Our Lady' in the corner.

Further along the walk I saw through the mist, the vague outline of the VOR station (this is a VHF direction finding aid on which I had relied so many times in flight), I'd never seen one, it looked like something out of a science fiction film sitting there amongst the peat bogs, its huge round white frame and three hundred and sixty white nodules poking up through the swirling fog, it was strange to see it so close up. It would have been a perfect night to film The Hound of the Baskervilles. I went to have a look round town the next day in the daylight. A huge Kerry farmer with fingers like pork sausages pulled up in his tractor and gave me a lift back to the B&B. His accent was so strong I could barely understand him.

For our departure the next day we had many well-wishers who came to see us off. The airport manager showed us around and offered us tea. He was trying to promote the airport, I was almost expecting him to say "No landing fees next time if you recommend us to a friend". He asked if I'd show the aircraft to some parents and kids, I was only too happy to. One of them looked up and down the cabin then at the cockpit and said, "And where exactly do yous sit?" Another little girl asked me, "Do you see the angels op there in the sky?"

The film crew arrived in the midst of 'jet tours'; they took some shots of the kids in front of the 'plane and promised to send them to the airport. They had had a very successful shoot, good light, good waves they had got what they came for. Whenever I saw the Peugeot ad after that I thought of the charm and friendliness of the place, the Northern Lights, the control tower, the great hospitality, the swirling mists that night walking home, the cracking pub, the ride in the farmer's tractor and of course the feisty characters all bought together by the life giving Guinness, *and* of course the vision of 'Our Lady'!

'Take my breath away!'

Seduction Flight

It was the perfect material for a Jilly Cooper novel. What could be more predictable than a young, blonde 'innocent' from New Zealand and a hardened Arab businessman who was as slippery as a cartload of eels. A well-heeled, finely tuned predator, full of stealth and knavery and razor sharp savvy. The set-up reminded me of some words I once read about one of the Roman emperors; "… his conscience obsequious to his own interest released him from any inconvenient obligation". In plain speak he didn't allow morals or a conscience to get in *his* way!

"Ah … right. You're his new PA?" I said when she introduced herself and her situation with a warm handshake.

"Yis," she said with an innocent nod, "that's what he said, I can do all his admin and office stuff to get some work experience here in UK."

"Oh well that's great, hope you enjoy your trip in the private jet!" I said with a raise of the eyebrows.

"Ah know it's fantastic hey, he took me to Guaglinos and Annabel's as well, I can't believe it."

Oh I can, I thought to myself with an inner nod. She was as green as the hills of Rotarua from whence she came.

I felt the creeping advance of a 'conquest' here.

It was the very same Lebanese businessman I'd flown before who had shared the *then* joyous news that his wife had given birth. Sounded about right, nappies, noise, wife out of shape, yep time for a bit of new prowl, and here was a sweet, silky young girl, just ripe. He was notoriously rakish and promiscuous.

The jet was a Citation and we were off to Samaden in Switzerland; a beautiful mountain airport near the resort of St Moritz. It boasts the highest altitude of any European airport. Captains need a special check out to go in there, and the company thought it would be a nice treat for me as a new First Officer to experience the glories of this spectacular approach and landing. You basically let down visually, fly down the valley and turn in a tight space to line up with the short runway, as mountains tower each side of you. It did have a touch of the 'Where Eagles Dare' about it.

The passenger had a meeting with some bankers and she was accompanying him as his "PA". I went through the safety brief and pointed out the cabinet containing coffee and tea. He said there was no need to come back and check on them they could help themselves to drinks.

She was porcelain like an alabaster statue of Aphrodite.. He was dark suave and leathery with a killer suit, gold watch and enough cologne to leave a trail behind him for five minutes.

Because it was winter she had a short black wool dress on and opaque tights with little black flats. This was probably a disappointment to him when he looked up her skirt which I saw him doing as she stood up and leant into the back to get her bag. Much to my amusement I saw him lean out of his chair and dip his head right down almost to floor level to look up her skirt while her back was turned.

No slot delay, and no tricky air traffic control, just West Drayton, Maastricht, Reims, then Switzerland, this had the makings of a good day. Once we punched through the stubborn layer of stratus which had settled over south-east England, like a crumpled grey duvet, we burst into clear radiant blue. It was a gorgeous day, the winds aloft teased the high wisps of cirrus crystals into combs and fish bones. They formed patterns like those made by a pastry chef when he drags his fork through the vanilla and choccie sauce on the desert plate.

Up at thirty-nine thousand feet I turned round to get a coffee for the Captain and myself from the urn which lodges just aft of the cockpit, then decided against it as I saw the seduction scene going on. These two were definitely 'getting along'. The hand was on the knee, she was giggling and sipping champagne. A neophyte in the new world of business and seduction, no doubt *believing* his words and responding to his practiced flattery. For him I'm sure it was going to be a 'business doing pleasure with her'.

The Alps came into view, magisterial and magnificent, a panorama of snow-capped peaks. Geneva control asked us if we were visual with our descent point. "Affirm," said the Captain confidently.

Then he pointed it out to me. This part was definitely not an exact science. It went something like:

"See the big peak right on the horizon?"

"Yes."

"Well three to the right of that there's a sort of flattish one, well it's between *that* one and the one in front of it."

"Okay," I said impressed with his recognition and memory.

We sailed over the first mountain ridge and descended slowly into a magical 'other planetary' landscape of radiant white. Although I had skied, it was quite different seeing the mountains from this perspective and doing these kind of speeds especially given your proximity to the granite! It was fantastic. *Star Wars* moment.

We crossed at right angles to the runway, disengaged the autopilot and flew across the valley, made our left turn downwind and descended onto base leg. We had dropped below the mountain tops, so we were in a colossal great stony basin of ice and rock flanking us on both sides. The Alps had such a loveliness that day, with their summits draped in snow, gleaming in the sun. I marvelled at the force of those two continental plates and the craggy splendour they unwittingly created when they moved inexorably toward each other and crashed all those millennia ago.

We moved like a little spaceship down the narrow valley towards the miniature runway which is less than six thousand feet long. It was one of those 'best ever' moments.

I read the checklist:

"Fuel crossfeed … off."

"Ignition … on."

"Gear … down three greens."

"Anti-skid … on."

"Flaps … land."

"Landing lights … on."

The tower gave us a wind check and cleared us to land. The Captain demonstrated a short field landing by planting it firmly on the touchdown numbers without a pronounced flare and stood firmly on the brakes for maximum deceleration.

The ramp was a postage stamp. Little did I know *then* that I would come back many years later in a Boeing 727-100 and the Captain (Capn' Jack as he was known) would not only manoeuvre that big plane round that tight valley but actually *back* into the parking spot using the thrust reversers much to the amazement of the airport staff.

The little terminal was typically immaculate and we were greeted by a charming female handling agent who ordered the fuel for us and took care of our two passengers.

Having straightened their clothes, and brushed themselves off, they alighted. She applied some lipstick, thanked us with a lovely smile, shook our hands then stepped into their waiting limo which would whisk them off to St Moritz, where I'm sure she would busy herself with taking down the minutes of the meeting! I retrieved two small bags from the nose section and handed them to the chauffeur who was straight out of *The Godfather*. 'Hey,' I said inwardly, as long as everyone was happy, good luck to them, it beats staying home and feeding the cat. Life is an adventure to be lived not a problem to be solved. I just hoped she wouldn't get hurt. She would undoubtedly learn about life, its many facets and nuances as we are all doing every day!

I climbed up to the tower to pay the bill. Wow what a work place, it had spectacular views all round. Everything was tidy and gleamed with typical Swiss efficiency. I chatted to the meteorologist about the alpine weather systems, he was deeply knowledgeable. He presented me with a big red sticker for my flight case, it had a Lear Jet on it and the words Samedan airport, the highest in Europe, 5,600 feet.

After a cup of coffee, we prepared to depart. It was my leg and we were empty so we could have a bit of fun. We set the squawk, dialled the cleared altitude in, put strobe lights and ignition on and set the flaps. I held the aircraft on the brakes and pushed the throttles up to full power. After the call "V1 rotate" I pulled her up and we climbed out at a considerably steeper tangle than usual, it *was* a buzz. At a safe clearance and altitude I banked steeply round to the right over the snow-capped peaks.

"Golf Bravo Echo contact Geneva on one two five decimal six five, nice flight good day."

So we bid adieu to Samedan and tuned into Geneva who gave us further climb and once again we were on the roof of the world. We headed north-west towards Dijon and Paris.

The skies were just starting to dress for the evening, small delicate capes of pink and peach chiffon draped over the 'shoulders' of the mountains. Little wisps of high cloud –the shape of 'Nike' ticks turned purple against the deep blue and the sun sank to the horizon. The world looked ripe and sweet like a rosy apple. Always worth being aware though, of the odd hidden worm!

Air Ambulance

There is usually an element of tension when you take on an air ambulance flight. It is life and death, it's critical. You throw the uniform on, and scramble – out the door like a speeding bullet. (Always a great excuse to use the hard shoulder!) The first one I ever did was from Heathrow to Manchester in the middle of the night on a Citation. The situation was 'the big one', it was a heart transplant.

There is always the ice box, but this time *not* filled with the usual yummy cold beers and prawns, oh noooh, *this* ice box is carrying a recently extracted slippery human organ, still purple with life's blood. You know some poor person has 'shuffled off his mortal coil' and a part of his innards is wrapped in ice and winging its way at four hundred odd miles per hour to some other poor soul who is hanging on to life by a fraying thread in some operating theatre waiting for that vital part which will give him a chance for a few more exits and entrances!

As we taxied in, a helicopter was waiting; blades slashing through the rain, bright lights lit the millions of rain drops, which flashed on and off like strobes. The downwash created little waves and ripples moving away in all directions from the noisy beast. It stood like a tethered horse just itching to get away and run the race.

Everyone is like a coiled spring. Medics in white coats jump out, clutching the ice box. Greetings were minimal, the situation and the deafening noise keep niceties very thin. The power increased on the helicopter's collective as the door slams shut. He lifted into a hover, the heavy wind knocked him a bit and he bobbed around unevenly near the ground, sending water streaming away in rivulets. He lifted skilfully, the downwash from his rotors and the ear splitting noise from the engines made us slam the door of our jet shut. I watch him lower his nose and 'whoosh' he accelerated away straight across the runway penetrating the darkness and into the night.

I prayed the mission would go well. Some unknown and desperate human being is hanging on to the hope of another day. It was one o'clock in the morning; we managed a bit of shut eye in the small lounge. We drank coffee and waited … and waited.

Unfortunately, luck was not with the team *that* night. At quarter to four on that dark November morning the team came back, they were silent and deflated; it had not been a success. The pressures are immense and the skill involved in these scenarios is unimaginable. Against impossible odds these medical stalwarts, with great courage and resolution, fight time and misfortune in their undaunted efforts to save lives. It is a terrific experience to work with them and contribute in the small way we do, albeit sometimes very sad.

Other Stories: From Colleagues

Although it is not a laughing matter, there are I am afraid just some funny instances in this strange twilight world of ambulance flying. You are very much 'on the edge', operating on that knife edge of life. It's the light and the dark and sometimes very little seems to separate them.

Two colleagues told me of their ambulance flying. The first was from a very experienced British Airways pilot who, way back in his career found himself flying single pilot on a Cherokee six (single engine piston). He was ferrying a corpse back from somewhere in the middle of the night. There was no coffin because of the weight penalty, so the body was just covered by a sheet. He was all alone, at eight thousand feet no sound but the whirring propellers, suddenly he hears a loud belch from the back of the plane and some movement! There is only him and a body. Can you imagine the shock and terror in that moment? Talk about the heebie jeebies.

I had to laugh when he told me he just didn't *dare* turn round; he just ploughed on white knuckled with max power and did a maximum rate descent and literally threw her on the ground and ran from the plane. Apparently (or so went the explanation he received) the pressure difference at altitude can make air expel from the lungs or other parts even after a person is dead. I could not control my laughter when he described his reaction.

"xxxx me! I thought when I heard this bloody thing belching. I could have sworn I heard the bugger sit up, I couldn't turn round, I just wanted to get down and get out."

We shared this fleeting vision of 'Beetlejuice' complete with black lips and scaly skin hopping over the back of the seat and sliding into the co-pilot's position. With the words:

"Phew that was a close one, I thought I'd bought the farm there, so where are we? Shall I do the radios?"

The other rather dark and humorous story involved a friend who was flying back from Barcelona with a dead body. Out of deference to the relatives who were in the cabin and who, for some reason didn't want to sit next to their dead 'erstwhile', the body was put in the front hold. Apparently he had to be, shall we say 'manoeuvred' in because there was not enough room to lay him flat. That was all fine and well but unfortunately because it got rather chilly enroute home, by the time they opened the front hold back in England he looked like that character in the British museum named after the peat bog in which he was discovered three million years after his death. I got the impression he was a bit bent up and his limbs a tad twisted .He was frozen solid in the locker and they had to get heaters to blow on him to thaw the poor chap out! Again (what is it with my imagination!) I had darting flashes of them laying him out on the apron, unmoving like a lump of twisted metal which holds its shape, while bit by bit his arms and legs were straightened out with the help of an industrial sized blow-dryer. (He assured me the rules have changed since then!)

The same colleague told me of the day he left Aldergrove in Northern Ireland with a liver in the ice box. It was a critical transplant flight. Normally the medic present handles any trolley if it has the organ on it. But on *that* occasion the taxi driver who was driving a Renault Espace took it upon himself to be zealous – he was only trying to help, and pushed the trolley which had amongst other things, the liver sitting on ice, in its box.

Unfortunately he mishandled and the trolley hit some rough ground and the ice box went flying. The nurse watched in horror as the liver skidded off across the apron. Don't panic, the organ was well wrapped up in plastic bag, only the *ice* got a bit dirty – honest, he assured me!

I take my hat off to the whole air ambulance concept, especially the helicopter pilots who arrive at a crash scene and airlift the victims out. Those machines are superbly equipped so a medic can start treatment straight away if necessary. The inside of some jets is configured for air ambulance work. On the jet I flew the stretcher and other bits and pieces had to be put in especially for a medical flight, but some planes are dedicated 100% to ambulance work, and they are truly impressive. They sure get busy during ski season!

Many years later, the company I was working for at Luton brought the much loved comedian Mike Reid back from Spain in his coffin.

An Eccles Cake for the England Football Manager

'Cock ups' are an integral part of life, and private aviation is no exception.

The 'cock up' is that single little incident or series of incidents that can turn your day into a downward spiral, at the end of which you give that withered look, that wan smile of hopelessness as you feebly offer one last apology. I remember taking Bobby Robson (the then England football manager) down to Cagliari in Sardinia; he was doing a rekkie to find suitable lodgings for his team, during some up and coming international event in the football world.

The first mistake was the aircraft. The company's Citation 2 had incurred a technical problem so they put Mr Robson's trip onto the Citation 1 – a smaller and slower plane. Really the trip should be sub-chartered out or at least the client should be told that they are on a donkey rather than Desert Orchid. But as always in this business, you don't turn work away.

The route was Heathrow – Glasgow – Rotterdam night stop, and the next day to Cagliari, Sardinia (where we spent two days), and then back to Liverpool where he had an *important* football match to attend. The rot set in when we had to stop in Nice on the way down to Sardinia, because we could not make it in one hop. He was understandably peeved about this, though we did manage to refuel and turn around with the same comparative speed as a Ferrari pit crew – twenty minutes on the ground at Nice is pretty impressive!

It was December and Sardinia was a very pleasant eighteen degrees and the sun was shining. The England manager busied himself with trying to find accommodation for his squad, and we enjoyed the poolside at the hotel. Amongst the entourage was a chubby 'Chris Biggins'-type. He was like a telly tubby dressed for Henley. I think he was a reporter for one of the tabloids. He had loud flamboyant clothes and big bright garish spectacles and regaled us with stories in his best *Brummie* accent of celebs and their various peccadilloes.

It was along the lines of "… and they were caught red'anded in the guys boat in Port Solent. Oh chroist it was bustin'."

Then a huge chuckle would set his enormous fat shoulders off up and down under his stripy blazer. "… don't know what his missus 'ad to say!"

There was also in the crowd a little man, he looked Spanish or Greek, a property tycoon I believe, He loved football and he was rather fond of himself as well. At dinner he talked of all his money and conquests and then told me he had his own private jet in Spain. When I asked him what he had he replied with a hint of a 'Stavros' accent.

"I don't 'ave a dog and bark myself."'

I took this to mean that he didn't bother himself with minor details like *what type* of plane he had, he left that to the staff, he just flew in it. Mmm I sniffed just a soupcon of faecal matter from the 'toro'.

Everyone got roaring drunk and threw one another in the pool. My uniform jacket ended up on the short Spaniard as he hurled himself into the pool. I had a nightcap and coffee with some Dutch men who were actually very pleasant and chatty. I learnt afterwards that this had been frowned upon because they were from an opposing team. One mustn't have divided loyalties!

The journey back to Liverpool was fraught because Mr Robson had a very important match to attend in the city that day. I had asked the hotel to prepare us a few kebabs thinking they would prepare chunks of meat and fish on skewers. They had misunderstood, first cock up of the day – they thought I meant kebab as in that lump of putrefaction that spins slowly on a skewer in Kiosks around Soho. It came in pitas which just crumbled – I couldn't serve them those! So you can imagine the news of the second and more pressing cock up – that we had to go to Bordeaux to refuel. That was as welcome as a car clamping at the end of a long day.

The winds just were not on our side which didn't help. To really bring up the shine on this black eye of a trip, we gave the two coffee flasks to the handling agent in Bordeaux and said, "Fill these please with black coffee and bring them back as quickly as possible." – Well that was the last we ever saw of those! We refuelled quickly but sat waiting with finger tapping frustration for the girl to return with our flasks. She was obviously 'très peesed off' at having to work on the night before Christmas Eve. Mr Robson, who was now inspecting the two pull out tray tables which had broken between the two rear seats, just told us in no uncertain terms to forget the 'bleep bleep' coffee and get going. He was rightly and understandably annoyed.

We launched late and with no hot drinks or catering. We got as much oomph out of those little engines as we possibly could without blowing them up. Two hours and fifteen minutes later we landed at Liverpool. Ever since crossing the *'enemy coast'* Northern France, as it's fondly known amongst crew, I had been desperately trying to raise Service Air on their VHF frequency to make sure there was someone to meet our passengers and transport was ready to take them to the match. Raising Service Air is a feat at the best of times but on Sunday in Liverpool at Christmas... there was absolutely no chance. I heard a distant voice crackling through the ether but it was someone asking for toilet service at Teeside. I transmitted to ask if they could call their colleagues at Liverpool, but no luck.

So...after doing the quickest, 'pull her round sharpish' type of approach and landing on the Westerly runway, we taxied in to a deserted ramp.

"Where the hell is everybody?" somebody blasted from the back.

"I've had no luck raising anyone on the VHF," I offered feebly, rolling my eyes to myself.

Anyway, they jumped out, throwing overcoats round shoulders, and holding the huge brick mobile phones to ears (it was 1989!) and charged off to the terminal.

"I have to try and make this up to Bobby Robson somehow," I moaned to Dave the Captain. He agreed, but after finishing the tech log, he picked up the Sunday papers with that "don't bother me with it" kind of look.

So, I okayed it by phone with our Operations that I should buy some nice champagne, some first class canapés and some luxury sandwiches for their way home, just as a little apology for the cock ups. So next came the humungous challenge of finding *that* at *this* airport. I entered the building; it was practically deserted, no one at information or car hire!

I pushed open swing doors, and left them flapping behind me as I paced determinedly down corridors, turned corners finding nothing but toilets and locked offices. "Damn! Surely VIPs come to Liverpool don't they," I muttered to myself. Eventually after unsuccessful trawling of depressing corridors festooned with notice boards advertising the company Christmas do, I bumped into a young Service Air girl coming out of an office with a walkie-talkie. Thank God.

"Oh hi, I'm the crew from Golf Juliet Echo Tango Echo ..." I didn't continue, the look on her face meant that I might as well have said, "mwa pudu neh neh imtak embwoto kinonlo ah!" Some really loud voice came ripping through her radio and she jumped, looked at it in horror and failed to find the volume button. I turned it down for her.

"Oh thanks," she said, "only this is me first week like and I'm not sure of everything quite yet ..."

My heart sank, *she* bless her was not going to be able to lead me to the land of first class catering opportunities.

"Oh hi, I'm Anita, the crew off that little jet out there, and I need some really nice catering for the way home, can you help me?"

"Cay-tring?" she said slowly in the loveliest of 'scouser' accents.

"Yea, you know some nice food, champagne, and I need to buy a couple of thermos flasks."

That was it; I saw a deer caught in the headlights, everything aft of the cornea just shut down.

Normally in these sorts of situations a good handling agent if unable to provide catering on sight, comes up with an encouraging little suggestions like: "Well I can run you into town, there's a nice deli, or the Marriott hotel which does good food ..."

106

"Er … actually I haven't been told about any cay-tring but I think I've heard me other colleagues mention the cay-tring upstairs, you can hava look if ya like, I don't know if they'll be open today being Christmas an all, but all as you do, is go up a floor and they're at the end … I think?"

"Okay thanks I'll have a try, meanwhile could you just go and see the Captain and order some fuel and see if he needs anything else, he's on the plane."

"Oh yea right," she said nervously glad to see the back of me. Poor thing I bet all the colleagues wouldn't work the Christmas period and she, being new pulled the short straw.

I padded across yards of lino and found nothing. Everyone had gone home, I peered through the glass panels in doors, empty desks. I tried the last corridor at the top and right at the end was something which looked like airport services. Great there was someone in there, I entered.

"Hi, I'm a crew member off that little Citation out there, and we've got Bobby Robson on board and it's all been a bit of a screw up, and I need some really nice first class canapés and some nice Champagne maybe some luxury sandwiches …"

The heavily booted feet swung down from the table, and the 'Sun' was folded tidily away as he looked at me with a grin. He had such a strong Liverpool accent:

"Owzabout a coupla flamin' dancin' bears to go with it eh?"

"Oh, right … it's going to be difficult then?"

"No offence love and 'xcuse me French like but this isn't Saint Tro-f***** pay, it's Liverpool on a Sunday before Christmas and I'm on me own and knockin' off at four – I can probably sort you out some ham sarnies and some Eccles cake and some cans of beer."

I just burst out laughing, I loved it, images of hooking my little finger through the plastic rings atop a nice warm six pack of John Smiths bitter, two of which had been drunk, was just too funny, and the Eccles cake … it was priceless, what could I say.

We both laughed. He pulled a packet of Embassy out of his top pocket.

"Fag luv?"

The amount of time it would have taken for a cab to get to me into town on a search for gourmet catering and champagne made us decide against it, what with all the football traffic as well. The last thing we needed was for the crew to be absent when the passengers arrived. So I guess it was ham sarnies on white and an Eccles cake for Mr Robson.

A trivial though strangely related footnote: Years later my friend Mark from Wigan the flight engineer on the 727– told me of a strike at Liverpool Airport. His mate Bill was working there at the time. A well-known TV personality, a bit dry and haughty but feted for intellectual penetration – I *think* it might have been Jeremy Paxman, had got caught in these delays and was absolutely desperate to get out and back to London. After wrangling and fruitless toing and froing he was at an impasse.

"My mate Bill the big fat Scouser bastard was approached by Jeremy who said, "You must have *some* sort of advice…I mean there must be some way out of this."

"The only advice I have for you Jeremy is when you go through them doors to the bar drink the bottle beer 'cos the draught's SHITE."

I laughed out loud with him, remembering my little experience up in the office with a similarly cheeky scouser.

I understood why the 'Fab Four' composed 'HELP'.

Ferry of Brand New Citation –And Emergency Descent

The aircraft G-BSVL was a brand new Cessna Citation V bought from the factory in Wichita Kansas. Cornish pasties and savoury pies had paid for this sassy little jet, because the proud owners were two brothers from Cardiff who'd made millions from the sale of their hugely successful food business. Three of us went through the training course at the American flight school, these are very professional, easy going, laid back places full of 'good ole' boys', who invariably have hundreds of stories to tell…Like "I remember one time flying from Lubbock to Boise Idaho …there was a helluva storm cooking...". And so it goes on. Fresh doughnuts and endless coffee refills are major features of these establishments.

In the simulator there is always that same smell, that same atmosphere, in those days the graphics were set for night time so everything was dark. All the control panels and instruments shine with various colours. Through the windscreen a mock up of – say Chicago airport lies before you complete with tower and blue taxiway lights. It is only when you taxi round a corner and you get the distortion of the lights as they fold away round the side of the Perspex. When you're hurling down the runway, however, and you get an engine failure on take-off it is all too real! Nothing worse than just having rotated and you feel that yaw over to one side.

"Engine failure number one."

"Positive climb gear up."

Then a boot full of rudder into the live engine, control the yaw and climb away at V2 – our best single engine climb speed.

Up we go to our acceleration altitude, lower the nose to pick up speed then "Flaps up!"

Then we accelerate to our best en route speed and go into the checklist. If there has been a fire we perform the fire drill, closing the thrust lever of effected engine and pulling the associated fire handle.

We were forever shutting down engines: Throttle off, Ignition off, Generator off. Electrical load reduce, Fuel cross-feed as required, etc. Then we'd attempt a restart *or* land with that old familiar one engine inoperative check list increasing our Reference speed over the threshold by ten knots. Emergency after emergency – excellent for those with dangerously low blood pressure. It's a fiesta of failures and the pressure increases. We covered many scenarios –'hydraulic failure', 'loss of both generators', 'inadvertent deployment of thrust reversers in flight', and our old favourite – electrical smoke or fire.

So after the roller coaster ride, complete with horns, bells and flashing lights in an airless black box filled with a gazillion LEDs, and buzzing screens, you eventually get into the real aircraft and do a normal take-off in a fully functional machine unhampered by failures, overheats, fires, or jammed controls, and it really is refreshingly peaceful!

However, on *that* particular occasion we were rather grateful for the emergency descent training because we ended up doing one for real, *at night* in the middle of Illinois.

Having changed the stall warning system (mandatory CAA requirement – it *had* to go off one millionth of a 'nose up' degree sooner!) and one or two other things which they insisted upon if it was to have UK register, we had our last doughnut and coffee and said 'so long' to all the 'good ole boys'(who were still telling their near death stories) and set off late on the 27th November 1990 from Witchita Kansas bound for Sept Isles in north-east Canada.

Not long after we reached our cruising level we heard a strange bang which startled us. Eyes instantly scan the instruments and dials. I saw that the *cabin* altitude was climbing – not rapidly but nonetheless it was on its way up which meant we were losing cabin pressure. So, on went the oxygen masks, we flipped the comms switch to 'oxy mask' and communications were established. We closed the throttles and put the nose down and flipped the speed brakes out for a quicker rate of descent and as Delboy would say headed back to 'Terracotta'. I spoke to ATC through the mask and asked for radar vectors to somewhere with an ILS and a good maintenance facility – preferably Cessna. Thank God we were in the United States, I was certainly thankful not to be over, say, Chad at that point.

Fortunately the decompression was not explosive it was just a slow leak so it was just 'minor to mediocre' panic, as opposed to wide-eyed terror when something blows out and you lose all your pressurisation instantly and will be a useless, drooling, blue lipped collection of limbs slouched over the controls like a bonfire night 'guy' before you can say "OMYGO...".

We ended up in a small place called Peoria in Illinois.(No I'd never heard of it either.) We were not carrying the entire set of USA charts so the very helpful controller vectored us round and gave us all the ILS frequencies and inbound tracks and everything else we needed. The oxygen masks came off at ten thousand feet, the pressurisation was under control so we completed the approach and landing checklist and put the little jet safely on the ground.

Some poor engineer had been called at home, had got out of his warm snugly bed, thrown his jeans on, fired up his truck and come into the airport to help a bunch of nuisance English who'd decided to have a damn failure over his patch. *And* tomorrow was his day off.

They were so good to us. The popcorn machine went on, as did the coffee and after hearing our account of the problem he told us to rest while he flicked through the manual.

It turned out to be just a bit of 'Friday night maintenance' – the 'S' pipe which brings conditioned air from the air cycle machine into the cabin. It appears it had not been tightened sufficiently and had popped off somewhere behind the rear bulkhead, which in effect means no more air was being pumped into the cabin.

We slept for an hour on some sofas while this young curly haired engineer fixed it and sent us on our way with that standard American phrase "You're all set".

Off we went intrepidly into the night headed for Sept Isles which lies on the north side of the St Lawrence River in Quebec, north-east Canada where we would sleep and refuel. I looked at the latest weather. Temperature was minus eleven degrees Celsius and there were accompanying snow showers blowing in on quite a hefty wind. Mmm. I thought … hope all the anti ice-systems are 'tickety boo'.

Bleak is the word, it sure was cold and dark out there and this was very new territory. Familiar names such as Toronto and North Bay gradually gave way to Chicoutmi and Chibougamau and Natashquan. I had visions of wiry little Indians riding bareback with feathers in their headbands who could throw an axe four hundred yards and split an acorn. My God the landscape looked like a textbook picture of the 'Pleistocene epoch' and its associated ice age. We brought our jet down through the freezing air to land at Sept Isles in Canada's frozen north-east. When I opened the door a thousand whirring snowflakes, like crazy white gnats came straight into the cabin – it was what you might call a blizzard greeting. I stepped out and promptly went flat on my face, it was like an ice rink. A huge guy helped me up, he wore a gortex anorak whose fur lined hood was so deep, his face sat back in it some nine inches, I almost had to peer in to say thank you. We chocked the nose wheel, put the covers on and headed off into the small terminal.

We snuggled down for the night at the local motel which had elk heads on every available wall, and offered lovely warm soup and great slabs of meat. The colour scheme was yellow ochre it was everywhere – funny what you remember. Everyone was big and hardy and wore flannel shirts. The night was short, we took off for Reykjavik the next morning.

After refuelling in Iceland we headed off for Bournemouth on the south coast of England. The flight was just over three hours, it was a huge relief when the wheels touched down on that welcoming runway on the edge of the New Forest. It had been decidedly more comfortable than the B25 bomber!

The flying which followed on this aircraft was of the 'fun and games nature'. It belonged to two millionaire Welsh brothers who filled it full of their champagne swilling naughty boy mates (very naughty boys I might add).More about them later in "Please Meet the Passengers!"

Inverness to Teeside
(The alternative way)

We said goodbye to the passengers – a lively group of larger- than-life Americans who were indulging their passion for bird shooting and salmon fishing in Scotland. Beefy handshakes and sincere thanks were exchanged as business cards were pulled from wallets with the words "If you guys are ever in San Francisco..." Then they walked up to their waiting limos clutching braces of game birds, gun cases and bags which clinked with Lagavullen and Glenmorangie.

We sat in the aircraft enjoying a cup of tea and catching up on the paperwork. Outside a benign autumn evening was arriving like a welcome guest. A pale water colour sky stretched out above us, it was cool and tranquil, the bumpy underside of the cloud was touched with faint hints of pink. My Captain Robin and I discussed the final leg from Inverness to Teeside. He had just left the RAF after many years on Phantoms in the Oman and had a great predilection for low level fast flying. Coincidentally, we had both spent our childhoods in Africa, and I detected in him just a touch of the 'old colonial'. I could see him in shorts and sandals enjoying a 'grin and frolic'(as G&T was known) under a rotating ceiling fan in some lodge. He was bright, sporty and chatty, and had a touch of 'rascal' about him. Last time we flew together we went to Cannes and had attempted wind surfing, we spent all day falling off the board– and long after I retired he kept pulling up that sail he was no quitter. He was a robust "I say old chap" type, with a zest for life and a touch of that English eccentricity.

"How do you fancy something a bit different on the way back?" he said with a cheeky grin.

"Like what Robin?" I enquired instantly perking up at the thought of strafing Loch Ness at ten feet in search of the monster. "I'm up for anything, but I don't do inverted."

Rubbing his hands conspiratorially, he suggested cancelling the IFR plan (Instrument Flight Rules) which keeps us in the airways system and under positive radar control, and filing VFR (Visual) instead. So we dispensed with the upper airway charts and found the low level topographical map – the one pilots use for cross countries or 'jollies' as we call them.

"Inverness, from Golf Delta Bravo India India, we would like to cancel our Flight plan and go to Teeside VFR."

"Rog-gerr, umm confirm that's India India the Citation," came back the incredulous voice from the tower.

"That's affirm sir."

"Okaaay ... any particular reason?"

"Tell him fun and games!" chuckled out Robin not lifting his head from the map on his lap.

"No particular reason sir, just want to brush up on a bit of nav exercise," I offered, trying to disguise our hooligan intentions.

"Roger that's understood double India," came a serious voice, but one which failed to conceal a cheeky smile!

"Err, I assume you are empty to Teeside?"

"That's affirmative sir," I said. They knew we were going to have some fun.

With the checks complete, Robin informed me that we'd do some 'valley flying' like the training done for mountainous terrain. And, by the way we would do an engine failure at V1 (take off speed) just for practice. Yep, I was strapped in beside the adrenalin man. The chap in the tower wished us a good flight (wishing he was coming with!) and off we went. Having dealt with the simulated engine failure, controlled the yaw, and raised the gear we climbed up to fifteen hundred feet.

"Right, let's get down to a sensible height, I get altitude sickness up here!" chuckled Robin in his best 'Red Leader' voice. He took the yoke and pushed the nose down and started the antics. We headed at two hundred knots straight for the mountain range started some military style low level exploration of the valleys. Robin was absorbed, inhabiting the role, he was definitely 'back there'. Out came the best RAF patois used by the fighter pilots when warning each other of "Jerries on their tail" or the "Hun in their four o'clock".

"Now there is always danger of enemy aircraft, so you must be vigilant, keep low avoid the radar, and when you fly down the valleys you must remember the inertia as you carve your path and turn a little early."

He demonstrated then gave me control so I could have a go. I turned for the opposite wall of the valley while the plane continued her previous direction for a few seconds, we were describing a smooth rhythmic 'S' pattern. It was like carving a sort of grand slalom track. We were weaving down a landscape of interlocking spurs, carving elliptical zig zags, it was *really* thrilling. I was loving the old and the new – our little jet with its suite of modern instruments, speeding over the black glassy surface of this deep and ancient loch. The sides rose steeply into dramatic jagged shapes, weathered by the ice and the wind over thousands of centuries. The loch was motionless and silent, the jet fast and noisy; one mysterious and secret, the other flashy and loud.

My eyes were wide, and my grip tight, the adrenalin was coursing. You only appreciate the feeling of speed in a jet when you are near the ground and have reference. It was marvellously silent in the cockpit and we were in our own little spacecraft skimming along the surface like a pelican, harmonising with everything around, moulding our path into the contours, and profiles of this spectacular scenery. It was unspeakably beautiful. It felt as though we'd climbed up onto the spine of the wind, like a child on to a dolphin, we were there on its back riding fast and free.

Back over the land, the heather created lovely shades of purple as it spread out unhindered over the vast craggy moors. I saw wild mountain streams. There was little activity just a few sheep and grouse running for cover as the noise of our engines frightened them. Undulating, and untrodden, the hills rolled away in all directions dotted by the odd abandoned croft. Above us the sky was vast and clear. Scotland on such a day is gorgeous – I thought of the scene from *The Thirty Nine Steps* when Robert Powell pads across the boggy moors and finds the shooting party. The wintry high pressure system gave us excellent visibility, about forty miles ... it was perfect. Here and there a cottage was tucked away by a river or loch. Then (just as in the movie) we spotted a party of grouse shooters stalking over the hills. Their Land Rovers were parked nearby. We banked steeply around and circled them once as though we were filming and gave them a bit of a show. They waved and lifted their sticks into the air, rotating on the spot to follow us. We straightened up again and we were gone.

Glancing outside I saw the shadow of our little plane encircled in a halo, you can see this sometimes and it is a neat sight, an image of the jet in miniature within a circle racing alongside, rippling over the humps and bumps in the uneven landscape.

As we approached Durham, we climbed up and enjoyed the expansive views of the city, its cathedral and river. The North Sea glinted in the distance. Teeside was not far away now and we checked in with tower and Robin asked if they'd like a quick fly past – he could not get enough! They were not too busy and said that would be fine. Robin was off in the war zone again.

"You see you're a sitting duck when you come back into the circuit and this is good avoiding action against being shot down by the enemy."

I was getting the picture, then whoosh my hands became glued to my legs and my cheeks fell a few inches, Robin was pulling some 'G'. We were in a sixty degree angle of bank when I heard, "Ok all yours, you land it!" So rather like a cat righting itself in midair during a fall to ensure a feet first landing, I closed the throttles and levelled the wings, got the speed under control then lowered flap and gear. I did a passable landing, heard the familiar squeak of the rubber hitting the ground then deployed the thrust reversers which crescendoed as we rapidly decelerated, I stowed the reversers and peace returned to the cockpit. We trundled in along the taxiway. If aeroplanes had faces or expressions, this one would have been grinning from ear to ear. She must have felt like a horse who, after months of being harnessed to a cart is given the freedom of a mountainside to gallop around.

Once we'd shut down, I smiled sideways at him, blew my fringe up with a deep satisfied sigh, and nodded slowly in appreciation of the intensity of the last half hour. We looked at each other laughing, he raised his eyebrows.

"How about that then?"

"Thanks … thanks so much for that!"

Motley Crue Concert – Edinburgh

November 1989. Checking the week's up and coming flights in the ops room I noticed my initials against a flight on Thursday evening:

Heathrow – Edinburgh – Rtn.
Client: Motley Crew

I was tidying up some paperwork in the office the day before when the phone rang:

"Can I speak to the pilot of the jet taking the band tomorrow please?"

"Speaking … can I help you?"

"Er yeah, I'd like there to be no alcohol on board, just remove it if you have a bar, probably be best."

"Certainly sir we can do that, any other special requirements?" Then John Cleese from Fawlty Towers crept into my head – chains, muzzles perhaps?

We ended our chat on a positive note, he was polite and grateful and wished us a pleasant journey.

I headed over to the executive terminal, (then called Fields) showed my pass and went out to the aircraft. Maybe they were teetering on the cusp of recovery and needed no temptation. I removed all the booze into a couple of boxes. I wondered what I could give them instead. Rummaging through the dry stores, nothing jumped out as appropriate – ginger snaps, dry roasted peanuts, mmm they'll probably have a few of their own 'condiments' anyway so they won't be hungry. I felt like a Aunty Mavis doing a high tea for some ex-cons. Muesli bars? God no, that was like leaving an endive salad out for the fox.

"These are party animals, Dave, you know, – heavy rock, tattoos, sex drugs rock and roll, fast and nasty!" I explained a little desperately to my Captain when he said, "Motley who? What the hell is that…? can't they drink tea like everyone else."

He had slender knowledge of heavy metal.

"Well they better not make a mess; we've just had the suede done in Bravo Echo."

On that afternoon we filed the flight plan, listened in to the ATIS (recorded weather) and got our clearance from Air Traffic, then waited on the aircraft. Unfamiliar with these types, my Captain was endearingly curious. The ground handler arrived in his mini bus and out jumped the 'Crue'. Spotting the long hair, the sprayed on black leather hipsters with criss-cross sides and pointy steel-tipped boots, Dave removed his specs.

"Ah these must be our passengers."

He had seen 'Grease' so he was used to the black leather trousers. The first band member leapt out like a wild thing, clad in a long kaftan coat, the fur blowing in the wind. He took a series of quick pictures with his camera.

"Awesome ... bitchin!" he enthused. The Sultan of Oman's jet was there, Robert Maxwell's Gulfstream, various Caymen registered Falcons, the odd Lear and the usual array of United Arab Emirates private jets. Since it was a high security and strictly 'no cameras' area, he was politely restrained by one of the ground staff. Two girls tottered on board behind him, fabulous petite bodies, impossibly high heeled stiletto boots, spectacular boobs and lots of leopard skin, furry jackets and long hair. Another couple of skinny long haired guys dressed in black, climbed on, when they were all aboard I closed the door and launched into my excruciatingly embarrassing spiel pointing out the hot water, tea bags and biscuits. Somehow so witheringly inappropriate to the out and out 'Enfants Terribles' of heavy rock. However ... I did it, and it was quite funny – they were so nice and somehow excitable, anyone would think it was their first outing! I realised later it *probably* wasn't due to the goodies from *our* 'Alpha' airport catering but more likely the goodies from *their* Pablo Escobar catering!

We were dwarfed as usual by the jumbos and Tristars as we taxied out to runway 27 right at Heathrow. We waited behind one like a mouse queuing behind an elephant, as one of them nudges up in sequence and adds a little power, we have to hold on to our control surfaces so we don't get shaken around by their exhaust – and that's just idle power!

We took off and headed due north towards Pole Hill near Manchester. I had levelled off at flight level 180 (18,000 ft) and was talking to London ATC when a voice with just a hint of anarchy about it chirped up from the back:

"Hey c'mon let's do a barrel roll!" that brought much cheering from fellow rockers.

"Let's roll this mother!"

My frightfully straight Captain stiffened in his seat, his eyes suddenly widening. He politely explained with a smile that it would be a tad indecorous if our radar blip started dancing around 'Etchosketch' style on the controller's screen at West Drayton air Traffic.

"Oh man that's too bad, we did one coming out of Salt Lake last year in a Lear – it was awesome!"

We made it to Edinburgh avoiding aerobatic manoeuvres. It was a dark beautiful evening, a navy velvet sky was dotted with little diamante stars. The engines made the familiar descending whirr as I retarded the throttles and lowered the nose, the lights of Edinburgh were beautiful. I dimmed the cockpit lights and prepared to shoot the approach down the ILS. I was fully established and just about to land when one of the guys stuck his head into the cockpit and took a photo with a super powerful flash. I was completely blinded by the white light, huge floating planets were cruising across my eyeballs.

"You have control Dave, I can't see a thing."

"Christ I don't think I can either, no you better have it."

We went back and forth and in the end it was a bit of a joint effort, and we, half-blinded managed to get it on the ground safely. A bit angry, I did point out the seat belt signs, in spite of looking like a rebellious savage, he was actually respectfully apologetic. He was a very likeable 'enfant terrible'.

The stretched limo pulled up and they piled in. Then one band member still in his shades with one boot on the door rim, holding a much awaited cigarette turned to us just before disappearing into the sumptuous leather interior.

"Hey, d'you guys wanna come to the show? If you do I'll send the wheels back for you."

Before Dave could decline I jumped in and accepted. It had to be more fun than sitting in the general aviation terminal drinking coffee and picking at the CM2s (the fond abbreviation for cold meal 2) an uninspiring collection of cold meats, tasteless tomatoes and limp lettuce.

"Alright, cool, we'll send the car back to get you guys."

An hour later we were climbing in the limo and heading for Princes Street downtown. The chauffeur was a jolly Scotsman who entertained us with pithy, no-nonsense banter – lots of och's and eye's.

"I don't know what the concert'll be like," he said, clocking the Captain in his rear view, "They were talking a lot about pissin' and shaggin' like on the way down, so I don't reckon it'll be too ref-eyend, you know what I min?"

The distant thumping of the music was audible from way down the high street. It was fun watching people trying to peer into the limo to see if we were famous, they took one look at me and got right back to their kebabs. I looked bad enough but the captain looked positively cuboid – hardly heavy rock entourage. The driver dropped us round the back, and we rang a bell by the stage door. A few moments later the door opened and there stood what I can only, at my most charitable describe as a sun-deprived, malnourished, filthy, etiolated, 'toxed' out freak.

"Yeah?" he managed to drone, drawing heavily on his roll-up.

"Oh hi," I said trying to sound slouchy and cool but feeling decidedly like Julie Andrews.

"We are the pilots who flew the band up, they invited us to the show."

He confirmed this on his walkie-talkie in a voice so elastic he made Keith Richards sound like Brian Blessed doing King Lear. He wore a sleeveless T-shirt with some Gothic axe wielder on the front, his arms were so white and thin I saw not even a suggestion of a bicep. He had not been within five hundred miles of a photon for years. I'd seen more tissue density on my neighbour's greyhound.

"Yeah, it's me downstairs, I've got a couple of cats here say they bought the band up or sumfink. Is it cool yeah?" He looked us up and down through his fringe and said in a nasally groan, "Yeah ok it's a rap," and signalled us through the door with a jerk of his head. His hair fell straight down over his eyes, perhaps he found his way in life by echolocation.

The music got louder and louder as we climbed the stairs, through each fire door it thumped further into my chest, God we still had two flights and a long corridor to go! We had seats effectively in the royal box (though I doubted 'her maj' would be putting a show in this evening). Decibels rose with each swing door, I was biting my lip with laughter eyeing the Captain who was looking uneasy – nervous whistling, always a telltale sign. We opened the door at the back of the box, and, voila, the living, writhing Hieronymus Bosch party. Inches from the box, stood a nine storey stack of speakers and down below armies of long haired rockers were screaming and shouting punching their fists in the air and thrashing their heads in a ghoulish frenzy. They were like things possessed.

"What extraordinary behaviour," shouted the Captain in my ear in his best British accent. We were actually watching the support group who, if my memory serves me rightly were called 'The Scum' or something equally tasty. After finishing the song, a band member thanked the audience and shouted at the front of the stage, "I want you all to say after me ... F*** YOU! Come on I can't hear ya ..."

This finished poor old Dave off, his expression was one of total and utter mystification. He sat down embarrassed and brushed some imaginary dust off his uniform. Some of the kids caught sight of us and stopped rolling their joints and slugging from their drink bags thinking we were cops. The band was whipping them up into a throbbing orgiastic melee and boy they were loving it.

The main band came on amid cheers and screams and fists going wild. There followed lots of screeching guitars, gyrating hips, rotating heads (that really must give them a headache). The backup girls were driving everyone crazy with their peaked caps, spilling cleavages, studded collars and high heels. One of the group approached the front of the stage and nearly kicked some poor bugger smartly in the face because he was not standing up like everybody else, he was on his feet before you could say f*** you.

We left after two tracks, with a heavy dose of tinnitus and laughed our way down the corridors and back outside. The vampire bat was not there to bid us adieu, but funnily enough the limo driver had judged the brevity of our innings and had waited for us.

"Aye, I thought it might not be yur thing like, bit loud eh?"

I could sense the palpable relief of my Captain as he picked up the Telegraph and folded it reassuringly as he had done so many times. We were through at least two sets of lights before the music finally faded.

The band turned up at the airport about eleven thirty buzzing from the performance, it had gone very well and they were in high spirits.

"Hey did ya like the show?" one of them asked me.

"You know I'm a bit of a George Benson girl myself, but it was great – a new experience." I tried diplomatically. Actually I had had fun and thanked them for their invite. We flew them safely back to Heathrow where their limo was waiting. They all bounced about and got into the car rather untidily and haphazardly, you would never get a crazy wild musician just easing himself quietly into the back seat and folding his coat on his knees and placing his brolly on the floor. They have to sort of leap and skip about, and walk round the car a couple of times or lean on the bonnet and have a smoke before they actually get in. Great fun. One of them shook my hand and nudged my shoulder with his fist saying "Cool, thanks a lot man" and off they rocked to the next party.

We had a drink together, filled in the paperwork, and through the open door of the little jet, watched the line of landing lights as planes descended heedfully towards 'terra firma' at Heathrow. Some of those on board may have breakfasted far away in Singapore. I glanced at my work roster for the rest of the week. I certainly couldn't complain about lack of variety, the next day I was flying a Saudi princess, talk about two extremes. We'd be swapping the black leather catsuits for the black yashmak.

The Sixpence and the Private Jet

Golf Delta Bravo India India was her name. Double India to us, and David Brown, (the second) I guess, was its owner. A wonderful new addition to the fleet not only because she had bright orange stripes, but she was a Citation 560 not a 550 so had more updated avionics and a rather plush interior and went faster! We had in our fleet G-JETA, G-JETB, and G-JETC, but along came a completely new registration and because it was the owners initials (David Brown) it certainly wasn't going to be G-JETD!

The North of England was the stomping ground for this plane, that's where this very successful family empire was based. Inside the hangar at Teeside was a company Land Rover, which could be used for towing the aircraft around if necessary.

Bill, my Captain, who loved a bit of a 'Clarkson' type lark about, put his own interpretation on this and one wintry afternoon after a flight, he said, "Fancy a ride in the Land Rover?"

"Sure, why not."

Come to think of it he did look like a cross between Martin Shaw of 'The Professionals' and Jeremy Clarkson. Of course the trip to the hotel was, what you could call 'the circuitous route' which meant a half-hour 'burn up' on the scraggy heather covered moors. We climbed up steep hillsides in the high traction mode, clambered over rocks and went bombing downhill bouncing over tufts of gorse and heather.

"I didn't know you did rally driving on the side!" I grinned as my head hit the ceiling and my flight bag flew off the back seat.

The late, low sun leaked just a touch of pink and mauve into an otherwise grey sky and the wind was driving the clouds across it. It was chilly and clear and from the top we had a superb view of the River Tees and the town of Middlesborough. Everything was going swimmingly until, an irate man in another Land Rover wearing a tweed cap came bouncing up and down towards

118

us shaking his fist and told us to clear off the land was private. So we did but Bill made sure he got a good 'getaway' ride down the hill to the road.

I flew 'double India' on several occasions, once I came back from Reims in France where some passengers had done the famous champagne tour. I was describing this and details of David Brown's aeroplane to my mum that evening and she told me a story which I rather cherished.

"Oh yes, I remember the original David Brown very well, he was the founder of David Brown and Sons in Park Works, Lockwood near Huddersfield, they used to manufacture huge worm gears, they were the same generation as my grandparents."

She explained how he had three sons David, Frank and Percy.

"My dad worked in the factory, he forgot his tea one day, so, aged about eight, I went up to the factory gates where he was working nights. Percy who was dressed like the proper Victorian gentleman in a grey suit with a flower in his buttonhole saw me at the gates clutching a bag containing my dad's supper."

"Hello love, what's your name?"

"Joan."

"And what can I do for you love?"

"This is my dad's tea, my mum sent me to give it to him."

"You're a lovely little girl aren't you? I'll go and find him."

"Thank you."

Before he went he put his hand through the iron gates and patted her on the head affectionately and gave her a shiny new sixpence. That was a huge sum for a child in the early thirties and she absolutely treasured it.

How ironical that now I should be flying the private jet belonging to the next generation. But talk about full circle, she then told me that when my brother was at boarding school, she dropped him off at the beginning of term and he asked mum for an extra pound so he could give it to his 'fag' as they were called. It was a tradition that the younger boys did odd chores (shoe polishing, etc.) for the seniors. The young lad who did odd jobs for my brother was none other than David Brown the great-great-grandson of the original founder. So the sixpence came back!

The chap whose plane I was crewing was known to my mum's generation as 'young David' back in the Yorkshire days. She went on:

"He had a super red MG sports car in the early thirties and always had pretty girls around. He was a bit of a playboy, and the company started a tractor manufacturing business for him to manage at Meltham to give him some purpose. He made a real success of it and eventually received a knighthood."

He ended up buying Aston Martin I believe, I guess that's where 'DB9' comes from, those famous initials again!

I was actually in Cannes in the South of France flying an eccentric wealthy American treasure hunter (one who dives for treasures on wrecked ships), when I heard the sad news of Sir David Brown's death. He was in the South of France when he died. What a great Northern family, I was so pleased to have flown their jet briefly and happy that my mum could fill me in on those interesting details of their beginnings.

Sorry about nicking the Land Rover, it was fun though!

Impounded in Siberia

Our flight plan looked innocuous enough: first two nights: Kiev, second night: Stavropol then on to Izhevsk in Siberia. The client was in the oil business – a wealthy Dutchman and we were in a British aircraft, the HS125, or "Ha-kerr" as the Americans call it. It had belonged to the Nigerian president so we were mindful of its previous life – bullet holes in the wing etc! We took off from Stansted and cruised across the skies of Europe experiencing the gradual decline in air traffic control as we went east. The American voices controlling Berlin give you that safe feeling, but once you say goodbye to them, you are off into the multiplying unknown where heavy Slavic accents shout out heights in meters ("mare-tus") instead of feet and transmissions can be very muffled. Some of those controllers sound as though they have buckets on their heads!

We landed safely on a frozen December morning into a bleak Kiev. The only movement on the barren landscape was the up and down of the hares as they padded resiliently across the fields, somehow steeled against the 'knife edge' wind. The ear shattering emissions of the taxiing Ilyushin and Tupolov aircraft just feet away didn't seem to bother the denizens of this airfield– these were hardy hares indeed.

We secured the aircraft, carefully putting all the external covers on, and took a taxi to the hotel. The driver tore around at breakneck speed, slowing only to point out where we could buy caviar and Russian dolls, he was probably on commission. The hotel had a retro grandeur, a seriously impressive entrance with pillars and flags. The doormen were dressed like courtiers of a bygone age, white feather plumes and lots of gold braid.

The rooms were a staggering $200 per night which for 1994 was plenty and when I saw the room it went from plenty to daylight robbery. The registration was slow and archaic, forms in triplicate, town of father's birth, other ridiculous detail. We were presented with a key with a brass bowling ball on the end, there would be no pinching them! The room was standard 'Eastern Bloc' for *that* time – small and dark, the water from the tap dribbled out in a beer brown cascade into a huge stained bath, the bath mat was wooden strips, and the supplies were spartan. A dim bulb hung from the ceiling, giving it a rather gloomy feel. The wallpaper was parting company with the wall and the bed was a bit creaky. I must say having been back to Kiev in 2007 it is an entirely different place, contemporary, buzzing cosmopolitan and filled with beautiful high end hotels.

I tried to make a phone call. It involved a decoding sheet – if your room number was between one and two hundred then you dial *this*; if you were between two and four hundred, you dial *that*. This was just for local calls, for international you needed to have done a season at Bletchley Park. I called the lobby – all international lines were down anyway, they said. So like every pilot on a night stop, I headed for the bar.

"Twenty dollars!" I exclaimed as I saw the tab for a beer, still this was cheap compared to the $45 they wanted for the spaghetti bolognaise. It is incredible how these countries are all primed to fleece every hard currency guest. The leap from communism to capitalism has certainly created opportunity for a bit of 'ripping off' here and there! A pair of tights was $25 in the hotel shop.

Just before midnight we saw our passenger alight from a big Mercedes and enter the foyer. He told us he had ordered a tour guide for the following day to show us round the city. I accepted gratefully, he expressed his wish for us to enjoy the city because the places we were going to after this were "somewhat less comfortable". A sense of foreboding came over me, visions of frozen grey landscapes, food shortages, and the smell of Chernobyl. I am glad I did not know *then*, how bad this trip was going to become.

After the $30 breakfast, I went to meet my guide. She was a rotund rosy cheeked lady with a long purple scarf and matching hat, she wore big furry boots, a long coat had raven black hair, and a ring squeezed onto each of her little fat fingers. Here was the living babushka doll. The Captain declined so off the two of us went to explore the wonders of Kiev, a city rich in culture and history. Beautiful monuments, museums and churches resplendent with gilt offered welcome colour under the drab December sky. She recited her 'blurb' on the history of Kievan-Rus, of its founding brothers, the migration of Slavic people, the glory of past eras in this, the mother of the Eastern cities.

The medieval glory of monuments such as the Byzantine cathedral of St Sophia and the stunning Baroque churches of the eighteenth century contrasted sharply to the austere 'battleship' grey constructions built in the style she called Stalinist classicism – perfect style and proportion but lacking warmth and passion, (a bit like the mass murderer himself I suppose) they looked cheerless and grim in the slanting rain, not a Baroque blunder or a Rococo riddle anywhere to soften the hard lines.

Back at the hotel I met Alain the Captain to discuss tomorrow's details. We'd leave at eight o'clock for Stavropol, he'd contacted our handling agent, everything was set. Of course you always have to add what we affectionately call 'buggeration factor' when operating in these parts so we agreed to meet two hours early. The morning brought nothing new weather wise. An angry, bruised sky frowned down on us, thick, rain-filled stratus cloud scudded along just above our heads. Freezing drizzle fell, it was grim. We refuelled, signed for the catering and ordered the de-icing (which cost an amazing $1000) making the total bill for two nights into something resembling a phone number.

The passengers arrived, their spirits up, the oil business was obviously buoyant. We read the check list, buckled up and called for taxi. I looked at the Jeppeson charts, these are what help us to navigate the world. They are huge flimsy maps folded up to diary size, covered with thousands of routes, airways, beacons, reporting points, airports and anything else that helps to furnish us with our situational awareness and confer reference on the ever changing landscape below.

The flight went well, though the 'comms' sounded like gobbledygook at times. When we were cleared for descent, Alain retarded the throttles and lowered the nose into the gloom. The outside air temperature was minus twenty, they had no recorded weather information but we knew what to expect. The navigation beacons were the old NDBs – non directional beacons as opposed to the more accurate VORs which is a VHF omni range. Fortunately we had a hand held sat nav. The cloud base was about five hundred feet, we descended on the instrument landing system and touched down onto an exceptionally rough and snow covered airfield dotted with old abandoned Russian aircraft and a 1930s style tower. I'd tried repeatedly to contact the handling agent, but my transmissions went unanswered. The purpose of a handling agent is to ensure limousines are awaiting the passengers, to handle customs and immigration, do all the paperwork and provide all the ancillary services. After a long wait a couple of fearsome men marched up in sweeping grey coats and standard Russian mink hats, guns slung over shoulders and handed us a thick wodge of paperwork. The archaic, dinosaur style bureaucracy which slows these places down is really depressing. The papers, which felt just like the old school loo paper had to be filled out in triplicate. No one could move until they were done.

The general idea in, shall we say, more 'civilised' airports is that the passengers are met by a well groomed multilingual girl in a smart suit with a nice smile who cannot do enough for them, they are then whisked away speedily, their bags loaded. *We,* however, were all bundled into a rusty clapped out mini bus and driven (in first gear all the way) to a dilapidated concrete building. When they could finally find no more paperwork for us, we were released. Fortunately the boss and his colleagues had come here many times, knew the ropes and took it all in their stride. This attitude is a godsend for the pilots who are frequently blamed for the cockups.

A Russian navigator named Sergei would accompany us on the next leg of our journey to a place called Izhevsk where nobody would speak English and for which we had no approach plates…we were to meet him in the hotel. We motored precariously over snow covered roads, skidding and sliding. The de-fog blower despite its loud noise, managed only two half-moons of clear screen at the bottom which had our driver cocking his head at a right angle to see out. The snow now came at us horizontally and we were defended nobly by two frantic windscreen wipers. I cleared a patch on the window with the back of my hand which turned black. There was nothing to see in the lifeless monochrome landscape. We met Sergei and had dinner with him at the hotel (God if we had known just *how* much we were going to need this guy!). The place was quite a bit worse than last night, towel and soap getting smaller, and now a linoleum floor with iron framed bed. There was no décor apart from a faded picture of the Virgin Mary. I was grateful for seven years of boarding school in the 1970s – it was a good grounding for all this.

I heard the encouraging sound of a band as I walked through the foyer, then on entering the dining room I saw three guys on a stage wearing blue velvet suits, ruffle shirts and gigantic bowties which matched their cummerbunds. The lady wore a blue velvet suit and shiny pink blouse and blue patent zip up boots. Her hair, so utterly fatigued from years of bleach just did not move, her chest and waist were somehow one, and this merry ensemble were chirping out Spanish Eyes. What topped it all was the bucket in the middle of the dance floor to catch the drips from the leaking ceiling. Mmmm wonder what the menu is going to be like! As it happened I did not need to worry because there wasn't one. They brought you food and that was that. It was the 'keep it simple philosophy'.

The band were now encouraged by the arrival of the fourth guest and launched into a medley of cheesy popular songs, 'Please release me' was amongst them, funny – that one stuck in my memory. Resigning himself to the fact that he wouldn't be sipping 'Saint Emillion' tonight, Alain ordered 'the' wine – there was only one type. I am not fussy and I was ready for a drink, but this truly made my eyes water. The waiter returned, and with an apologetic gesture lowered a plate in front of us the contents of which bore a remarkable resemblance to the stuff you scrape off the barbecue before it goes into the garage for the winter. We tucked into the bread and the thick skinned tomatoes which sat on a cushion of the brightest oiliest mayonnaise I had ever seen. The band was grooving along now, still no dancers though – maybe the bucket was a deterrent.

Sergei briefed us during this feast – he'd do all the radio work and translate instructions. He had all appropriate charts, etc. He brought out some pictures of his wife and kids. It seemed he had the sort of wife who made a few days in sub-zero Siberian hell holes, a not altogether unpleasant break. Then he showed us some shots of the plane he flew. I had never seen anything like it. The navigator sits in a room downstairs form the cockpit, there was a desk and a curved window rather like a small bed and breakfast; and then a horrifying array of ancient instruments and slide rules. I was waiting for the sextant. We exchanged stories planned an eight o'clock meet then went to bed – the band had that cocked head, raised eyebrow plea on their faces which said 'please don't go'.

A quite savage day awaited us, huge snowfalls overnight dumped great piles on the tree branches which drooped and bowed under the weight. Once in the taxi, we trundled down the treacherous road back to the airport. The inefficiency was absolutely staggering. Although we paid a hefty bill for handling services, there was no transport, we all had to drag our own bags across half a mile of treacherous icy taxiway in a brutal and biting wind to get to our aircraft. How grateful I was for my ski boots and thermals. An Aeroflot 727-ski as we call them taxied past creating great swirling clouds of snow almost blinding me. You would never be this exposed on a ramp in Europe. I could not dispel the caterwauling strains of a Gene Pitney voice from my head. Chorusing "Oh Mis-ery, Mis-er-eeee".

We reached the HS125 aircraft which was covered with ice. Defiant stalactites hung like daggers from the leading edge of the wing. With frozen hands, Alain the Captain, put the key in the lock of the door – frozen solid. We did the trusty Zippo lighter trick and held the flame to thaw the lock. We opened the door and climbed in. Our breath issued out in little clouds of fog, the remnants of some coffee had frozen in a cup. The first task on taking over a dead aircraft is to start up the APU (Auxiliary power unit). This is a small jet engine with a generator which provides electrical and pneumatic power on the ground so you can have wonderful things like radios, lighting and more importantly – *HEAT*.

That frozen, godforsaken morning in Stravropol was the first time I'd ever known the APU not start, due to cold! A little door on top of the aircraft has to open to allow induction air in and it was frozen solid. There followed a 'Monty Python' sketch in which Alain had to give me a leg up onto the wing, which was like an ice rink. I had so many layers on, I slid around like a fat skittle. Rather than flick-flacking up there like Spiderman I was more like a penguin, arms flapping, sliding along on my tummy unable to find stability anywhere, I climbed onto the engine nacelle by placing one foot on the intake and heaving myself most unceremoniously onto the slippery round engine. Alain was encouraging me with fine chatter like you'd give to a colleague caught on a cliff face as you talk them into the harness. Once on top I could reach over with my Swiss army knife and smash the ice away from the intake door. I descended precariously and 'de-winged' backwards tumbling back onto the snow. After several attempts, the APU coughed complainingly into life.

Banging our hands together to keep circulation, we tried to contact the agent to order the de-icing equipment. Not a soul was out there. Sergei spoke to the tower frequency, they shunned all responsibility for ground activities – *we* would have to find ground staff. Easier said than done as in these temperatures they are not exactly milling around to see if everything is ok. They are huddled in a portakabin jostling for position round the fire, flicking dreamily through brochures of Cypriot beaches.

Sergei went to find the de-icing. Meanwhile we thought it wise to try and start an engine. Up on to the wing again and with my head and half my body disappearing into the tunnel of the intake, I scraped the loose snow off the fan blades at the front of the compressor. Back in the cockpit we attempted a start – nothing, no rotation – engines were frozen. A tired old truck of wartime vintage, with bulbous wheel arches and round headlamps trundled up and two men alighted – their heavy wool hats had the flaps *down*. They unravelled yards of canvas hosing. This was the heater to thaw our engines. Alain hauled himself onto the wing and held the end of this hosing into the engine mouth. It took almost an hour to raise the temperature enough to initiate a start. We took turns to hold this 'elephant trunk' heating tube. Finally we got the engines turning and burning and turned our attentions back to the more sinister problem of aircraft ice.

Amidst all this adversity, I must say Alain my Captain never lost his sense of humour. He's an independently wealthy English/Lebanese guy (who lives in Nice and London), he smokes cigars, likes the good life and he flies because he loves it. His runway line up checks were; "full tanks, ray-bans on!" God he made me laugh because he had Italian leather shoes on with thin socks! For fun we spoke Pidgin English because we'd both lived in Nigeria. The catchphrase of that trip became "We are havin' de time of our lives". He never

124

let things get him down. He took frequent cigar breaks during which he would wander off into the blizzard as if he were Captain Oats about to say those famous last words – "I may be some time"– only to stand behind some tractor or blast fence, and savour the aroma of his Cuban cigar. It was one of the funniest things I had ever seen because by the end of the smoke the snow would have advanced up to his knees and his nose was the colour of a tomato. I was not surprised when one of his friends told me that during a ski trip in Val d'Isere he had fallen while off piste and when they found him three hours later buried up to his neck, he was – yes – smoking a cigar quite calmly.

The de-icing mixture was about as useful as an ashtray on a motorbike. It was actually freezing on flow back. The next thing in this ghastly nightmare, the passengers turned up, and we were far from ready. They were just happy to sit there in a warm aircraft and drink coffee. Fortunately we had jumbo supplies of Marks and Spencer's instant cappuccino. After a couple of hours of pathetic and futile de-icing, the light faded. The ice stuck determinedly to the wings and windows. Our navigator shouted tirades of undecipherable Slavic at the ground crew but it was all in vain. The blizzard just kept dumping more snow on the super cooled surfaces and freezing into another layer of ice. We had no choice but to abandon the flight and return to the hotel. The only way to secure a take-off the next morning was to get the plane into a hangar and keep her warm. We were told there was no room, naturally all hangarage was kept for Aeroflot aircraft – I could feel some Yankee dollars exchanging hands shortly. It always amazes me how the 'Uncle Sams' especially in neatly wrapped up bundles can thaw the most icy of demeanours and elicit nods and activity from previously unhelpful officials, to say nothing of miraculously creating space in hangars that were full five minutes ago.

The passengers left and Alain and I prepared to taxi the plane to a hangar. We pushed the throttles way up above normal RPM then realised the wheels were frozen to the concrete, so we stepped out into an arctic wind and crazy whirring snowflakes and tried to dig the snow and ice away from the wheels. By now we were both frozen to the bone, no feeling in my feet, poor Alain must have felt he was walking on stumps. No wonder Napoleon, Hitler and whomever else, had got a well-deserved hiding when they attempted to take this place. Russia is not for wimps! If you were a woolly mammoth then maybe ok! After applying a huge surge of power we moved carefully forward over the frozen tarmac. *Clunk* went the wheel down a pothole. We used differential thrust on the engines to try and free ourselves.

"Could you get out and marshal me in, it's a bit tight?" Alain asked, so I jumped out and ran into the hangar. It was quite a sight, the exhaust whipped up the snow and it swirled around violently in two huge tunnels resembling small horizontal tornadoes. I gave Alain the hand signals and he crept into the hangar, it was excruciatingly noisy – what a relief when he chopped those engines. A couple of mechanics were eating pickled eggs and drinking vodka at the back of the hangar. They nodded and cocked their heads as if to say 'relax it will be ok here'. There was of course no transport so we trudged, heads down, back to the terminal building – a flattering name for the concrete block from which wire cables protruded. We climbed a filthy slushy stairwell to find Sergie who'd gone to file the flight plan for tomorrow.

There he was at a desk pouring over maps doing everything by hand using slide rules and a straight edge. Grey computers the size of filing cabinets stood in the corners. My mind drifted off to the operation room at Zurich where you stand in front of an electronic world map, touch any area and with that reassuring high speed k-shhh k-shhh sound of the laser printer, out comes your weather report. The agent then produces your computer flight plan in seconds with all the frequencies, beacons waypoints, fuel burns and everything else your heart desires on it! It is handed to you by the immaculately dressed Carl with shiny gold cufflinks and just the right amount of pure white shirt sleeve showing below the creaseless navy suit and, of course the perfect Swiss watch – probably an atomic watch guaranteed to lose no more than a nanosecond per Millennium. On this perfect pile of paperwork is a Swiss chocolate with the Matterhorn on it– with compliments.

I looked around, no it wasn't Switzerland – we waited patiently while he ploughed through what looked like the original navigation exam set by the Civil Aviation Authority at flight school and with which every pilot will be sorely familiar. It was not *quite* 'half earth convergency times the sine of the parallel of origin'… but it was nonetheless bloody long winded whatever it was he was doing. He was extracting sunset and sunrise information from old almanacs, like an eighteenth century savant from the Royal Greenwich observatory. Two burly pilots chatted in the corner and I heard lots of "schnitzens, neeyets and pooshka" type of words, not an unpleasant sounding language, in fact very attractive and earthy. They drew heavily on cigarettes, had thick moustaches and wore full length wool coats and fur hats. Probably wondered what the hell I was doing there … for that matter *I* was wondering the same thing!

Another night there brought nothing new, the band hadn't changed their repertoire but after a bottle of the chateau sputnik they actually sounded quite good and I was tapping my feet. The trusty bucket still stood isolated in the middle of the floor, catching the water plops.

Next day, same weather. We agreed to be completely ready to taxi before moving from the hangar, that way we would not turn into an ice sculpture. I was dispatched to pay the bill. As I marched head down through the blizzard, I was muttering that *THEY* should be paying *us* for this godforsaken stay. The next scene was more withering inefficiency. There was one tiny window around which thirty or so people pushed and shoved, some trying to elicit information others trying to buy tickets, all were shouting and all getting nowhere. I unfortunately had to wait in this queue. I went upstairs to try and find *anyone* official but there was just the miserable empty ops room from last night where Sergie had worked. At this point I was cursing everything Soviet, Yuri Gregarin, Lenin, Rasputin; even Olga Korbut got a derisory mutter.

I stood for ages inching my way forward, tempers were fraying. When it was my turn I presented her with the aircraft registration and asked for the bill. She looked at the paper, then looked at me with total and utter vacancy then drew her shoulders up to her ears and put two hands up in the air. She shouted to the back for help. The three thousand US dollars in my bag made me a bit furtive. Out came a comrade from the back, his face like he had just sucked a lemon. He tossed my papers back at me and mouthed exaggeratedly as though I were deaf.

"Priv-ayte flight, upstair!" I protested loudly back to him that there was no one 'upstair' I *must* pay, we were waiting to take-off, and if they did not help me NOW I was leaving without paying. Since there was no liaison, maybe I should have just left, it would have gone unnoticed. He gestured me to follow him, up the slushy stairwell we climbed, past the mangy cat – poor beast, no food here, even the mice would throw themselves on the traps.

In the pokey little office he asked me what services we had had.

"Hangarage, one night, and de-icing which did not work," I returned. He jabbed at his calculator.

"Three thousand dollars," I knew it was dodgy so I tossed my head back, folded my arms and stared at him. He read that correctly – international body language for 'do you think I'm stupid'.

"Sorry sorry one moment please..." He jabbed earnestly at the calculator trying to convince me he was using some sort of formula to work out the bill. "Ok ok three hundred dollars! Is ok, is ok" It reminded me of haggling over Polo shirts in Bangkok. I peeled off three crisp notes and placed them on his desk, he was well pleased.

I hurried back to the aircraft, brushed the snow off my coat and took my seat, it was cozy, Sergei was in the jump seat. After the checks and a thorough brief we lined up. Alain advanced the throttles, I called eighty knots (a good moment) then 'V1' (take-off speed) a very good moment. We lost sight of the ground at two hundred feet. The fuselage gathered in all her extremities, the wheel tucked up into the belly, the flaps slid back into the wing, the machine tightened up ready for high speed flight. We were all unaware then that the place we had left was a veritable Shangri-La compared to the little treasure of Siberia we were headed for.

Sergei took care of all radio transmissions; we certainly could not have managed without him. I tuned in frequencies, read check lists and kept the plog and finally gave flaps and undercarriage according to Alain's request, while he, glued to the instruments, flew the plane. With normal levels of pandemonium we landed off a Non Directional Beacon approach (NDB). These are not renowned for their pinpoint accuracy, even when the needles are reading spot on, it is not unusual to break cloud and see the runway in your two o'clock, so swift alignment manoeuvres are necessary. Mmmm this runway made the last one look like a billiard table. So here we were in Izhevsk, to me that sounded like Slavic for 'Grim'. It was a numbingly depressing barren landscape – the sort of place which you would come to if you had six months to live because it would seem like six years. Here was a place of inconceivable hideousness. (See picture of airport loo.)

Unbeknown to us, there had been a rather serious screw up in the paperwork by our handling agent at Stansted in the UK. Normally all airports and all FIRs (Flight Information Region) must be informed (by fax) of all the details – time and purpose of flight, over flight times, points of entry and exit into *that* particular airspace and permission to use that airport. (I have found that the grottier the destination the more demanding and difficult they are – as if they think we actually *enjoyed* going to these hell holes.)

The handling agent in UK had inadvertently omitted Izhevsk from the list of 'must contact' mistaking it for some Belarus airport – maybe the four letter identifier code was similar. So some Belarus airport now had all our details and *this* place had nothing on us! Izhevsk was politically sensitive being the home of the Kalashnikov rifle and utterly unused to 'G' registered planes. They had no record of our coming nor had they given permission. The increased volume in Sergie's voice told me he was getting hassled. Then he ran out of rebuttals. He went from aggressor to victim in five short minutes. He slipped off the headset, looked at us like a condemned man and said slowly, "They say you hev no owthority to be in zis place."

"Hey no problem," I chirped, "we don't want to offend anyone, let's leave."

Unfortunately it was not that simple. Hefty guards glad to relieve months of boredom approached eager to exercise their rusting authority. They climbed on board and a heated debate followed featuring lots of 'shnitz-ing and neeyetkov-ing' once again. The boss, very perplexed because of upcoming meetings told us he was taking an Aeroflot flight out of there and we should stay and sort it out.

The plane was impounded, we were stuck there. Boris a tall Russian who spoke very little English was our 'man', he tried to help us but proved ineffectual against the powers that be. There was no telephone service and the mobile could not reach England. We were left with just the HF radio (High Frequency) with which, if you are lucky it is possible to obtain a phone patch via one of the stations – Portishead in England or Stockholm in Sweden. We tried fruitlessly to reach anybody who could help us, but we were well and truly…buggered!

The thin watery light of day faded – night fell. Turning to Boris, we enquired about a hotel, he looked at us with pity.

"Zer is not so good hotel in Izhevsk," was his apologetic summary of the situation. Alain tried to console me with comforting allusions to hot bath, nice meal and bottle of wine. We wrapped up like ice mummies, cut the APU, locked her up and trudged miserably over to a friend of Boris's who had a waiting car. There was simply no call for hotels in a place like this, it would be like planting attractive flower beds round a rubbish tip. They were trawling their minds for somewhere to take us. At least they were trying to help. The car was knackered, loads of pendulous junk swung from the mirror. But at least we were in a car.

The town was a faceless, devastatingly depressing collection of grey concrete buildings all uniform in height and shape. In their broken English (which was far superior to our broken Russian) they said we should try the mental hospital which would probably be the only place to receive us. There was a pervading sense of doom. After a little uneasy shifting in my seat I asked timidly if there was any plan B at all. I had images of emaciated pyjamad nutters with shaved heads and staring eyeballs grasping their heads as in

Munchs's painting 'The Scream'. The severely disturbed wandering around on lino floors while blood curdling screams came from tormented souls locked in icy attics. Images of straightjackets and injections drifted past and I shivered. God I would never again deride Hiltons for being 'all the same wherever you go'. Sensing our ill ease, the car suddenly swung off the road and headed out of town.

Poor old Sergei had stayed at the airport under instructions, I was beginning to wonder if he'd got the better deal. The picture was starting to take on a Beckettian absurdity. There we were hurling around the frozen wilderness of Siberia, a Captain from Nice – female co-pilot from Ascot – clutching bottle of Nuits St George just in case it is last drink ever; Boris the bold whose hat must have seen off an entire mink farm (and who, I have been told since writing this has been shot by the mafia); then his friend who drove like a maniac whilst chain smoking, and finally the driver's son who turned to us in the back, and stared at us continuously like he had been abducted by aliens. Occasional chuckles of pidgin came from Alain, my Lagos buddy.

"We are havin' de time of our lives – no be so?"

The car screeched to a halt.

"This can't be it?" I laughed nervously.

"Be ready for anything," was Alain's reply.

"But we're in the middle of a bloody wood."

With that the door was flung open and Boris's friend was removing our bags. So this was our hotel for the night, a shack in the woods. I stood knee deep in snow. The wind was so strong, the moon was positively cantering across the sky behind the clouds. Then dogs began to bark and snarl. I glanced furtively around, the dogs/wolves were standing in the snow between us and the front door. Boris told me *not* to look straight at them and it would be ok. Well, I thought, here I am in a *real* life Grimms fairy tale. I should have worn my Red cape!

I started wading through the snow muttering ridiculous things like "There's a good boy" in an unconvincing whimper as their top lips curled back revealing impressive canines. I am no vet but *that* particular expression is 'beast-speak' for "I want to eat you" isn't it? They barked at us with hostility giving me that 'being in the thick of things' feeling. I had to see the funny side of tramping through a Siberian forest being howled at by wolves under a full moon dragging a Delsey suitcase with heated rollers and a full complement of aromatherapy bath oils in it – when what I *really* needed was a gun, an axe and a small bottle of suicide pills. It's *always* tricky knowing what to pack.

Our driver exchanged some pleading words with the warmly wrapped chubby lady who was obviously running the place – whatever it was – digs for wood choppers maybe. She then took us up some stairs, there were two small corridors of about five rooms separated by a common room which had one of those folding football tables. I was almost joyous at the thought of at least playing a bit of table football, then noticed both plastic goals were missing. It was like the smallest grottiest student common room in the worst polytechnic imaginable. Alain lit a cigar and said, "Ok, maybe we take a rain check on the meal, wine and hot bath!"

Wondering if there was a loo or a basin we ventured downstairs where the hefty lady – of many aprons and no English – gestured toward the toilet, just one, which needed a coin. Since we only had $100 dollar bills, she kindly gave us an advance. The only water was a cold faucet in a huge white ceramic sink. With a bit of sign language we asked if there might be anything to eat. She waddled in front of us with a rocking gate signalling us to follow. In the 'dining room' there were four Formica tables with wooden stools. Two rugged labourers sat at a table ripping apart giant crusts of bread with battered red hands the size of spades and washed it down with tumblers of vodka which they poured from a bottle. The label on the bottle was by now familiar – Cyrillic writing, black triangles and back to front R's and K's. They slammed the glasses down, and dragged their wrists over their mouths as they refilled, one of them blowing his cheeks out to suppress a belch. They nodded acknowledgment at us, one smiled, he was missing a front tooth. We must have been a puzzle to them. By now everyone involved in this 'Hotel California', her daughter and a handyman had gathered to come and see us. They were very friendly and I was grateful for that basic humanity which resides deep within most of us. She put a bottle of Vodka in front of us and a serious knuckle of bread with some fatty salami. We made merry, and after three of those vodkas I was in a chalet in the Italian Alps having antipasta and the two woodchoppers were gorgeous; downhill ski champion Alberto Tomba and swarthy friend.

Piling on every piece of clothing I had, I snuggled down in the child size bed, which felt like one of those remedial boards you sleep on after a slipped disc. Snow fell in outsize flakes and the wind howled and whistled, but the wolves seemed to have padded off elsewhere. I slept.

Boris came for us in the morning and drove us to the airport. Our aircraft now was just a big mound of snow.

"We are going to need a spade," I moaned.

"Get your Visa card out and start digging, we don't have a spade," joked Alain, this was followed by another "Time of my life".

The bureaucracy – a vestige of the old regime, is quite simply crippling. No matter how enthusiastic and resourceful you are, reaching the 'powers that be' is impossible even if you have the negotiating skills of Condoliza Rice. Apologies, explanations, pleading – it was all futile. I spent that entire day on the HF radio trying to acquire a phone patch to our operations in the UK to ask for help. We drank endless cups of coffee or chocolate and used the loo in the airport building which was so utterly disgusting it looked like a murder scene. I recoiled in horror with my hand over my mouth when I first saw this festering toilet. A cubical with no door, a black rancid hole in the floor the edges of which were rotten, putrid and covered with mould and slime. A broom was propped up against the wall, and strips of torn up newspaper in a brown plastic bin. The stench hit you like a boxing glove and the whole place was under a shallow layer of liquid – god only knows what.

"Oh don't exaggerate Anita!" I knew people would say, so I took pictures (please check out the photo!).

Desperation was upon us. It was becoming dark and grisly. I did not find out this next snippet of rather interesting information until many months later back in England, but Gillian (Alain's wife) was really going through hell, this is what she told me a long time after... This incident had been *very* serious indeed to the point where she was expecting to read it in the Sunday papers.

She was dealing with a Russian called Cherkasov who was responsible for permits and clearances. He was furious. The Russians were extremely sensitive about breaches of security after Mathias Russt, an adventurous German, managed to get past security and land bang in the middle of Red Square in a light aircraft. When Inflight at Stansted had requested our exit permit, he and his team had said words to the effect of "Exit permit? hang on, where is the *Entry* permit"? And that's when trouble began.

Nobody wanted to take responsibility, so therefore each person was desperately giving their excuses exonerating themselves in order to avoid a sacking! Alas not even the British Embassy would help her, least of all a Squadron Leader Wheelbarrow (no joke) the resident military attaché.

This was before mobile phones and Gillian had sleepless nights trying to help us escape. With HF and phone patch as the only means of communication you had to go through the "over" and "go ahead" stuff which made it clumsy that is ... if you could get though at all! On top of this was the time difference to think about. Cherkasov called us brigands and pirates and apparently got very nasty. In the end after lengthy machinations with border defence and aerospace heavyweights, Cherkovsky suddenly decided we could go, *only* to Moscow for fuel and then leave immediately and never return... Sounded like a super plan to me!

Our passenger was naturally concerned for our welfare in Siberia and his expensive private jet, it was he who had dispatched Boris the English speaker with some blankets and food! The reason Sergei our navigator had been 'dismissed' was because he was Ukrainian and the Russian authorities at Izhevsk took a dim view. They didn't like each other so he had to leave – not a cheery prospect when impounded in Siberia and your English speaking navigator is waving at you in from the back window as he is driven away to 'destinations unknown' with an apologetic look on his face.

The times of the day effect the heights of the ionosphere (the layer of atmosphere off which our radio waves bounce) so transmission is not always successful. Hour after frustrating hour trudged past as I sat with the headphones on trying to make contact. I was tuned in on 11306 Megahertz when suddenly Speedbird (British Airways) came crackling in calling Stockholm. There followed five minutes of chat at readability one (weak reception). Stockholm suggested 10291. Readability strength goes to three. My heart quickens like a crash victim's in the mountains when hearing the first thrashing of helicopter blades. Then I listened to the most extraordinary conversation, Speedbird pilot had requested phone patch and had got through. A little piping Scottish female voice, like a lark comes on the air.

"Hallo love."

"Hello, just to let you know I'm in Russia." (Oh good I thought he's out here too– misery seeks company!)

"I'll be on the six o'clock shuttle hopefully," continued Speedbird.

"Och that's gree-t, will you pick up Ian and Eileen then and bring them round on your way home?"

"Yep I'll do that no problem, everything OK love?"

"Aye everything's just fiyne love, look forward to seeing ya later for dinner!"

"OK see you tonight … Stockholm from Speedbird thanks for your help, over and out."

Visions flew around my head. The husband picking up friends and returning full of anticipation to his wee lassie. Single malt being spun in cut glass tumblers, honeyed by the leaping flames in the grate, laughter, kilts, haggis steaming on the table with neeps and tatties. Wee bairns creeping downstairs in fluffy flannel pyjamas to kiss the guests. Warm tartan blankets thrown over comfy sofas. The men retiring to nurse balloons of brandy after supper. My head slumped against the glare shield, as I pictured more rancid toilets, icy water, granite beds, fatty cold meats, warm vodka – the type made from Bulgarian potato peelings, and all this lived out in a giant deep freeze.

We did finally contact Gillian who was trying hard to help us, but alas it was too late to achieve anything that day. The British embassy would not help us. Completely disheartened, we once again had to abandon the aircraft. Boris took us to a large austere building near the airport; it had all the welcoming charm of an abattoir. The foyer was simply enormous and bare, but for one tiny kiosk in the far corner, like an old ticket office in a provincial cinema. There were no keys because there were no locks. Good old Boris had pleaded our case with the strange woman in a kiosk. The woman who had no teeth, and a thick head scarf showed us up a staircase to a long linoleum corridor, with damp patches, and a flickering fluorescent light.

The door to my room was already open – a dog skulked out unhappily after she clapped her hands and hissed at it. I noticed a weeping sore on its hind leg. It had been having a well-earned rest on my bed, which now of course had become a giant flea colony. Being very allergic to animal hair, I could feel the hives itching already. Maybe it was too cold for fleas? Then I remembered from Biology O'level that they can survive for years in ice cubes and then burst into the most exuberant fiesta of life when the cube melts and spring off at the speed of light as though nothing had happened.

Alain and I drank a bottle of wine from the aircraft.

"We have to get out of here tomorrow, it's the last bottle," he laughed as he lit a cigar. There were no curtains to draw so we just looked out the window as the grey dish water sky of day turned unspectacularly into the blackness of night. We ate a few dry crackers off the aircraft and enjoyed the luxuries of an en suite bathroom. The big cracked tiles had dirty brown grout, the loo had no seat or lid and there were exposed pipes everywhere, there was just cold water and no soap or towel but having been in Siberia for what seemed like a year now this was beginning to clock up a few stars! Fortunately the sub-zero temperatures precluded the stench from this plumbing which I'm sure would otherwise have been face crumpling.

The next morning I looked outside and saw an old lady thrashing some rugs against the ground, I guessed she was the housekeeping service. Clouds of choking dust rose like a small bomb exploding with each pounding. Fortunately it *was* the last night, Alain's wife Gillian managed to negotiate with someone in authority who allowed us to take-off the next day. Because we were in the dog house, we were given permission to land at Moscow *just* to get fuel then we had to leave the country – they could have beaten me and made me do lines, anything just as long as I could get OUT. We will confess to our sins as long as we can head 270 degrees! V1 (point at which there is no abandoning the take-off) that next morning from Izhevsk was undiluted joy. We picked up our passenger from Sheremetyevo in Moscow and started for the long journey home. We shared stories en route, the passenger too had been through a few adventures! We all agreed it is amazing what *one* tiny slip up in the paperwork can cause.

I *did* return to Russia – the following year on a private Boeing 727, how different that was to be. We stayed in the Grand Kempinski near Red Square, enjoyed a sophisticated piano bar, ate caviar and slept in a five hundred tog goose down duvet. The towelling dressing gown was so fluffy it sat almost two feet high when folded, *with* its matching slippers. It was beautiful, and very different from my jaunt in the Siberian outback. Fortunately they didn't check my name on the PNG (persona non grata) list! I heard a couple of years later that Boris had been shot.

"Na zdorovje!"

Mike Woodley with Oscar winning actress Halle Berry on set of James Bond

Stavropol Russia – Alan trying to defrost the engine intake in savage weather.

Me in cockpit of B25 bomber.

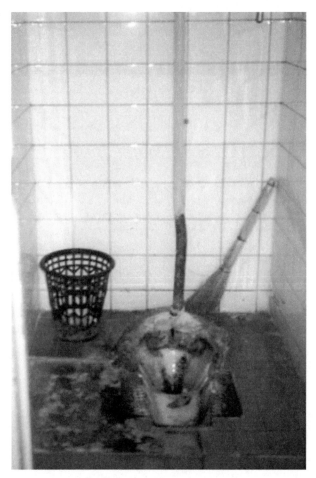

Airport toilet in Izhevsk, Russia.

Ensuite in "hotel" - Siberia.

1st job on Cessna Citation Heathrow. Looks like the 'L' is for Learner!

CHAPTER THREE: Lift is a Gift but Thrust is a Must

Flying the Heavier Stuff – Boeing 727

If there was ever a 'sliding doors' moment, this was it because I so nearly went out for groceries, but because the sun was shining I stayed in the garden to read ... I would have missed this phone call (being *just* pre mobile) and subsequently this opportunity which led to many wonderful things.

My friend Pete from Oxford flying school called one afternoon.

"Yannie (as was his name for me), I don't know if you're interested in doing a hostie job out of Heathrow tomorrow, it's on a Boeing 727 for Banque National de Paris going to Luxemburg. They are looking for another cabin crew – I know you are between jobs right now…?"

Jobs can be scarce so I was always ready to snap up an offer of work, you never know who you'll meet!

I accepted and was soon dusting off the overnight bag. The safety training is compatible between front and back. We have all demonstrated use of emergency exits, life vests evacuation procedures, etc., so, I was 'checked out' so to speak. The other girl was a senior British Airways purser so she would lead, I'd just help her. It was a job and I was happy! I stayed in the galley, until she got busy at one point and I came on to the trolley to assist with a few drinks. It was a short flight, I recall throwing plates and glasses into any available cupboard or drawer when the captain said "five minutes to landing", in order to secure the cabin.

Sometimes in life you just have to take the ball and run with it. It was on this flight that I met the freelance American Captain who was looking for continued work in Europe. Through a few contacts, namely Pete (of earlier phone call) and his acquaintance – a Pakistani 727 Captain who was looking for another Captain to job share, I found him work on a private 727 and in return he gave me a job in the right hand seat about a year later (no type rating needed for right seat on a private plane). It was a terrific break! Soon I was accompanying him to Kuala Lumpur to pick up an executive Boeing 727 from the Sultan of Pahang and ferry it back to London.

Here are some of the times on that fantastic Boeing 727 starting with the initial type rating which I did in flight school in California.

Initial Type Rating
Check Ride Boeing 727-200

With the ground school completed it was off to the simulator for two gruelling weeks! The flight school in California was the toughest challenge so far. Every detail in the simulator (and many were late at night when you are not at your sharpest) was full of emergencies. It's a nightmare of gremlins in the shape of bells, horns, flashing lights and a myriad of horrors and multiple failures which make you wish you were having root canal surgery. Once that's over and you have completed the arduous test during which you've put out fires, landed with two engines out, lost all your hydraulics, lowered the gear manually and sat with goggles and oxygen masks on while the cockpit fills with smoke; then struggled against raging crosswinds to land with asymmetric flap … (phew) … you generally ring your shirt out, physically unfold your white knuckled fingers which have locked into an eagle's claw after hours of gripping the yoke, and head off with fellow students for some cold beers!

A couple of days later you go through what is innocuously known as the aural. Sounds like a friendly light-hearted chat eh? But it is in fact a finger knotting experience with the FAA in Los Angeles where you sit in front of three very important and well informed men who will to do their best over the next two hours to dismantle you with questions. Golden rule if you are not sure, *don't* dig a hole for yourself because as sure as the pope has a big hat, *they will* throw you in it and bury you. I'll always remember my first question, it went something like…

"So Aneeda, werall coming outta say, Salt Lake one evening and there's a helluva storm cookin' and as soon as we get airborne we have a nine light trip on our electrical panel; what will be the status of the AC transfer bus at this point?"

Try to look cool and calm. Heart's thumping, I swallow hard and I think of the electrical schematic, yes there it is … the AC transfer over on the far right hand side linked to AC Bus three *and* the battery charger, yes there's my clue. I answered him correctly and sighed a huge internal 'phew'.

"What's the difference between a phase imbalance and a differential fault?"

"Tell me about the CSD disconnect switch?"

"What's the procedure for dumping fuel?"

"What are the power sources for all eight boost pumps?

"In hydraulic system B, what if we had zero on the pressure gauge but no low pressure light on?"

And so it went on for two hours; questions about the oxygen system, brakes, gear, pack cooling fans, flaps, pneumatics, pressurisation problems, leading edge devices, fire fighting and so on. I got some wrong and they corrected me in a constructive way – I benefited from their vast knowledge of systems. I was like a puppy with five tails when it was all over.

The **final** part of this type rating (which was a Captain's rating and therefore quite a bit tougher) was the three circuits and landings, which had to be performed in the aircraft, *not* in the simulator. The school was using a TWA 727-200 (the bigger one) over in Kansas City, Missouri. They sent us over in pairs or threes whenever the airline could fit us in. We had to wait for a) the training Captain to be available, b) the FAA examiner to be available, and c) the aircraft to be free and not flying a revenue flight. Progress was slow and I was one of the last to go.

I hoped for the best, there were just two small problems. They 'buddied' me up with a Saudi who was checking out as flight engineer. Kill two birds with one stone, he would work the engineer's panel and get assessed while I fly the detail and also get assessed. The only trouble was this trainee engineer – Mohammed, simply became unglued at the thought of working with a woman. It just finished him off totally and reduced him to acts of muppetry and impenetrable silence. He lost his nerve, his tongue and it seemed absolutely all his knowledge. I really felt for him actually. The other small problem was that the biggest bone shaking thunderstorm to hit KC (as they affectionately called the place) in ten years, happened to go through *that* evening at *exactly the* time of my check ride.

We met at nine p.m. in the airline's operations room within the airport. I introduced myself to the TWA chief training Captain and also to one Captain Gann who was the senior FAA examiner. I got the impression they didn't relish these check rides with students from the flight schools – all a bit of a strain and a tad complicated, they would much rather be knocking off! We went through the rigmarole of checking licences, paperwork and logbooks. I asked a couple of questions such as: "Would you like me to leave the flaps at fifteen degrees since we are staying in the circuit?" The TWA man seemed to think that a reasonable idea, though the two Captains were much more concerned about the weather at this point because the forecast was hideous and the pressure was dropping rapidly. I had a fleeting vision of being sucked up into the eye of a tornado like one of those cheap 1970s movies of airliners which are *so* obviously models being bounced around against the painted background. It is an image I quickly drove out of my head. There we all were, strangers, a motley crew and we had to get the exercise done.

So, the rather unnatural situation *is,* that, the training Captain sits in the right hand seat playing rookie first officer, I sit in the left seat playing Captain in charge of the flight (yet I am the least experience of all), the poor Saudi engineer who has all the promise of a small faun caught in the headlights, is perched uncomfortably at the panel behind the co-pilot, and the head honcho Dan was standing behind me checking *everybody* out. I understand that I am supposed to be showing leadership qualities so I initiate things such as the checklist.

We have no ground crew so we don't have to bother with push backs and disconnects. The red beacon light is on and I call for start on number one. My 'co-pilot' holds the start switch to 'ground' on the overhead panel and when the N2 rotation reaches 20% I eased the start lever forward to idle and observed the fuel flow. I call EGT (exhaust gas temperature) rising which indicates light up in the engine. I should have had a call from the engineer of "Packs closed, 40 psi" prior to start but I didn't, so I turned round over my right shoulder and confirmed it myself so my examiners would see I hadn't overlooked that. The disconcerting thing – I'm getting nothing from the engineer's seat, no calls, no familiar and reassuring little ditties like "Start valve open" no comforting words that I long to hear like "oil pressure". Mmm it is testing my reactions. Just my luck on my first 727 flight **ever** in the left seat in command and I have lost my flight engineer the linchpin of the whole operation. Oh well I mustn't let it worry me, I must carry on and do my best.

His lips are moving slowly, I think he was begging Allah to come and sort it. Examiner Gann was trying to encourage Mohammed to come back into the programme.

"Okay Mahoomed," he is saying, "we got one and two started, let's check Hydraulic system A."

I turn to confirm with him that engine two bleed switches are closed and that he's done the electrical power changeover and all the generators have had volts and frequency checks and are in parallel. "Essential power on number three?" I prompt him realising now I'm going to get nothing out of him.

"That's okay Aneeda, I got it," said Mr FAA setting up the panel realising that I needed to turn my attentions to *my* job.

It was indeed a bizarre situation, and it all started to feel surreal. The whole airport was being suddenly lit as if by football stadium lights, just for a split second, as bolts of lightning forked menacingly from wicked black clouds. Cracks of thunder exploded from a riotous night sky and the rain came down – the sort of rain which causes poorly built houses to detach from their foundations and bob down the river. I ask Mohammed another question about brakes and hydraulics and he mutters something at which point Dan pipes up with something really quite comical.

"It's no good praying to Aarla now Mahoomed, we ain't in Sordi now my friend, he ain't going to help ya, see *she* is the Captain and you gotta do what the Missie says see."

I really had to stifle laughter at that one. Lord how did I get myself into *this?* We taxi across the wet airport towards the hold. The TWA guy guides me with rights and lefts, so I don't have to bother with the ground chart. Discussions are now heating up about the weather. Dan picks up the mike from the jump seat and talks to the tower who answer him:

"Yea, looks like the eye of the storm should be passing over head in about twenty minutes. You all might have time to get the three patterns in before the worst hits."

It is getting late and people are tired. "What d'you think Dan?" says the TWA guy looking out intently through all the cockpit windows obviously wanting to bin it.

"I dunno buddy we might just be okay and if it gets real bad we'll just come right back and land," says Dan wanting to get it over and done with – a sentiment I am sharing, the plane is busy tomorrow and I don't want to hang around for days.

"Yea it's really closin' in though."

"Yea it's pretty horrible out there."

And so the exchanges go on. Meanwhile Mohammed is now just staring into the panel focusing about two feet behind it, we've lost him and he has failed his check ride before we even get airborne, poor guy.

With my right hand on the throttles and left on the steering tiller and tightly strapped in I decide just to break the ice a bit and have a little joke. I remember some moustache twiddling RAF guy I met once at an airshow who used to fly Wellingtons or Stirlings in the war telling me that all the night missions were left to the English, the Americans couldn't do the night flights. (How true that was I had no idea!) But I thought I might pull their legs a bit since our situation was pretty grim.

"Oh come on you lot," I said, "don't let a bit of nightfall and a spot of rain throw you, it's typical, just like in the war eh? You didn't like night sorties *then*, that's why you left them to us Brits."

It was either going to get a laugh or it was going to be *really* inappropriate and fall like a lead ball and take me with it through the cockpit floor. Dan laughed out loud, patted my shoulder and said, "I tell you what Aneeda ... you're alright."

We decided to get airborne, so here in this filthy storm over Kansas I'd do my first circuit in the 727-200 which had a maximum takeoff weight of 200,000 pounds (about ninety-one tons). The conditions were far from perfect I was nervous. I did my safety brief:

"Left seat take-off from runway two nine, full power wet runway, anti-ice on, packs on, any malfunctions before 80 knots anyone call stop, between 80 and V1 which is 115 knots, we will call stop for significant loss of engine power, fire or failure, if I abandon the take-off I will close the throttles apply maximum, braking and deploy the thrust reversers and speed brake. If the malfunction is after V1 I will continue the take-off, advise me of the failure and I will call for the appropriate action and ..." Then came a welcome interruption.

"Okay Aneeda, that's alright I'm sure you know it ... now let's get outta Dodge." (Which I assume means Dodge City in mid-western speak.) Good! As I lined up, a flash of lightning illuminated the whole place so I got a quick impression of the entire layout. Here goes.

"Window heat ... high/ignition ... on/antiskid ... on/strobes ... on/transponder ... on."

Dan came in reassuringly with Mohammed's checks: the boost pumps check and the CSD oil cooler ground off check, then auto pack trip normal – all engineers items.

On the runway I stood the throttles up and said, "Three stable." I pushed them forward and felt just an immense surge of power. Fantastic.

"Eighty knots ... check."

"V1 rotate."

I pulled her up into the night sky calling for "gear up". The wheels lifted and clunked solidly into their wells in the belly and nose. I climbed at the 'V2 'speed plus ten knots to 1,500 feet, levelled off, the acceleration was monumental, it would be at 350 knots before you could say knife so I pulled the throttles way back. I was instructed to turn almost immediately crosswind and to keep the turn going into downwind.

"After take-off checks," I called and asked for the flap to remain at fifteen degrees.

It was turbulent but I steadied her out at 150 knots. Abeam the threshold, gear down, turn the corner, flaps 25, ease her down at about 700 feet per minute rate of descent, I looked for the approach lights, judge the descent, call for flaps 30, landing checklist, it's looking pretty good, I am nervous though. I ask for the reference speed for landing and bug that and also bug plus ten knots on my air speed indicator. I came down the approach; the examiners don't seem to be too terrified they're letting me get on with it. My scan is rapid, speed, horizon, fuel flows, back to speed, out the window, check the profile, looking good nicely on approach speed. The wind buffets me a bit, it's a first and it feels exciting.

"Okay Aneeda looking good, bit of wind from your right."

Into wind aileron down, opposite rudder I mantra to myself in anticipation of the crosswind. I am keeping it tightly in the bars of the flight director coming down, there is often a tendency to level off too high with inexperienced pilots – it's a sort of fear of the ground, so I chant to myself "keep her coming down."

I get near the ground, the lights are coming up at me, speed is good, ease off the throttle, not too much. I am ready to flare, power levers off, oops a bit early right aileron down smidge of left rudder, where's the ground, I have flared a bit high, we are a bit spongy, still no ground, V ref minus 10, a bit untidy, then clunk there it is. Oops a small bounce, but I quickly remember the rule – 'hold or re-establish normal landing attitude, add a little thrust if necessary'. It wasn't necessary – the bounce wasn't too high. DO NOT whatever you do push the control wheel over, this could lead to damaged nose gear and a touch of the old Barnes Wallaces! Quiet a hard second landing not brilliant.

'Hold the nose wheel off keep straight,' I mutter.

"Okay," chirps up my 'co-pilot'. "I got the power, I'll set that for ya." He pushes the EPRs up to about 1.4, moves the flap lever through the gates from 30 back to 15 degrees and calls V1, we are off again. Phew I am relieved – I have one under my belt. I think momentarily of Chris my ATPL instructor from American Flyers Fort Lauderdale. He was a bit of a 'bacci' chewing, gun wielding, red neck who drove a pick-up and liked shooting wild turkeys.

"Don't ever be intimidated by an airplane Aneeda," he used to say, "just strap the bitch to your ass and *fly her* ... don't ever let her fly *you.*"

Not exactly the "Sterling job old boy, but a bit more positive on the power perhaps" debriefs enjoyed by our RAF boys but I did, however, in this lonely moment, appreciate his angle.

The tower transmitted, warning us that the eye of the storm was moving very close, he suggested we maintain runway heading and go out towards Topeka in Kansas and fly around there until it went through. So off we went, we climbed up to 8,000 feet, My TWA guy talked to the controllers and we just followed their instruction for a while flying headings. It gave me a welcome break.

"Go ahead and engage the autopilot Aneeda, you can relax a bit." So we enjoyed an unplanned night cross-country watching the sky change colour and shape as fearsome explosions of positive and negative charges fought it out in the heavens.

The 'Fed' used this calm time to try to bring poor old 'Mahoomed' as he called him, back into the programme. I overheard him asking a few questions about the fuel and the environmental systems but there was no joy. He had lost face and, death, I am told is the more favoured option in that culture. He had shut up shop and gone for the night. Anyway I just had to concentrate on completing my detail successfully, one landing down, two to go. We were vectored back by the tower, it seemed the worst was over. We turned back east and dropped down to three thousand feet. I slowed her up and we joined downwind. Under 200 knots, I called for flap two, then five, then started muttering to myself which always helps my concentration.

"Level off, that's it power set for 150 knots, hold it steady ..."

I asked for gear down and turned onto base leg and then on to final approach.

The TWA 'co-pilot' was feeling quite relaxed and was feeding me some useful bits of information about attitude and fuel flows and so on. I was feeling good, feeling strong. Down the approach, still a bit of wind, stabilise the speed at Ref plus ten knots ... keep her coming down, full flap that's it, now fly level power off, back wheels give a little screech as they touch the runway, hold the nose gear off, let it lower, gently bently.

"Nice jab," came the reassuring words from the head honcho behind me.

And so I went round for the last time and completed my three circuits. As we taxied in we could still make out the distant bolts of lightning which had moved off to the west, the rain still fell. Squally gusts made ripples across the puddles which shone under the bright ramp lights. I savoured the moment moving this great hulking mass of metal slowly down the taxiways, waiting until the nose had long overshot the turning (because of the aft position of the nose wheel) then moving her round with the small wheel, feeling all that weight following through. Such a small wheel for such a large object. It was so quiet inside, unlike outside where a couple of ground crew stood with their fingers in their ears.

We went through the shut downs. Dan did the engineers panel, I closed the throttles and moved the start levers to 'cut off' watching the EGT fall. Park brake on, ignition off, anti-ice off, probe and window heat off …emergency lights and radar. The ground engineer signalled to me that the chocks were in place. We unstrapped and walked out of the front exit down some steps which the ground crew had wheeled into place.

Back in the office. "Well congratulations Aneeda, that was alright, let's get ya all signed up here …"

Then the paperwork – forms needed filling, logbooks signing and so on. The night shift employees were already busy in the office preparing for tomorrow's flights. A nice girl in operations knew I was on test and asked me how I got on.

"Alriiiiiight congratulations, that's awesome…"

They are so friendly the Americans aren't they?

"I got some coffee on would you like some? Sure wish I could offer you a cocktail."

Dan stamped all the papers and gave me the appropriate FAA forms, then walked me to the terminal.

"Aneeda, you did a good job, and that wasn't easy with Mahoomed and all and the damn weather but you hung in there … if you ever need a reference, here's my card, I'd be happy to…"

"Thanks very much," I said, really meaning it.

"You okay for a ride?"

"Yes I have to call the hotel and they'll come for me."

"Okay, you got a dime?, the phones are over there."

I thanked him, shook his hand and walked through the deserted terminal. It doesn't sound much but completing your first major left seat check ride on a big aeroplane is as big as your first solo. I was elated and shattered. I wanted to party and celebrate, but with a hotel bar that shut hours ago at ten o'clock and a teetotal Saudi Arabian as a colleague, I think there was more likelihood of running into Elvis. I called the hotel bus and a young lad from Wisconsin obligingly picked me up. I would love to have been going to a humdinger of a party to celebrate with friends, but I was somehow in the twilight zone, alone, in a storm, at night, in … 'East Jesus'. I bounced along in a hotel bus with a youth in a green bus boy's uniform towards the airport Ramada. We chatted and though I was longing to talk shop, and relive my experience, I, instead learnt all about the Green Bay Packers, his home town of Kinosha, how people from his state are called 'Cheeseheads.' He offered me a beef jerky which is air dried meat in a stick. He was a nice lad and it was all a bit surreal and unconnected!

He knew I'd just done a flight test. Bless him, he knocked at the door twenty minutes later with a bottle of unchilled Michelob Light on a tray.

"All the liquor's locked up but I found this one in the kitchen."

"Oh you're a star, thanks so much."

"Congratulations on your test," he smiled and he turned on his heel in his fez hat and gold epaulettes and was gone.

Fortunately I had a bottle opener on my Swiss army knife (pre 911). I sipped the beer as I peered out of the rain lashed window across unfamiliar territory. What a weird feeling, all other accomplishments along the way during the years of training and testing, we celebrated in the bar at Oxford or at Fairoaks with much animated debriefing, but here I was celebrating on my own. I wished I'd had company.

I know ... I'll call the only person in the world who would truly be delighted to hear from me at this ungodly hour of the morning ... my mum. They must be the only ones who are able to tolerate a disturbance of this magnitude (from stage four slumber to bolt upright) without the minutest trace of annoyance. She even managed squeals of delight and lots of "Oh darling that's wonderful" even though she didn't have the faintest idea what I was on about. Dear mums.

Back in the UK I ended up flying a rather special 727. It used to belong to billionaire Malcolm Forbes and it was painted money green and money gold with the huge words "Capitalist Tool" on the tail. Nothing if not understated!(see picture) I loved it, it had huge cream leather swivel seats and sofas inside, an en suite bedroom and a special pulley at the back where he used to load all his Harley Davison bikes. This man had a profound grasp on FUN. It had now been bought by a man from the Middle East and I along with two other Americans ferried it back over the Atlantic, in rather shorter time than the B25!

The Magic and Mystery (and Money) of the Middle East

The Middle East certainly plays a premium on the senses. There are so many 'firsts' awaiting you – the hubbly bubbly pipes, the gold, the mosaics and minarets, the aromas of perfumes and oils, the exotic beats of the music, voluptuous veiled belly dancers and the tea pourers in the market. I recall clearly on a balmy evening in the Damascus souk the pinpoint accuracy of the boy pouring the amber coloured tea from his pot, his arm at full stretch above his head, into a tinted egg cup, and didn't miss a drop.

Because of the cultural differences, little things make a lasting impression such as the woman dressed head to toe in black with a small metal visor round her nose, trying to eat noodles in the hotel in Kuwait. A women peering through the little mesh window in their headdress checking out the price of kitchen cleaners in the supermarket. Then the boys and men in the crisp white dish dash, walking along the promenade swinging worry beads and stopping at cafes to take coffee. The lamb being carved from the skewer and served with pita and chilli on the roadside at midnight.

We, as crew make many trips there, so here's a photo album type glance at some of the memories.

The private Boeing 727-100 I was crewing was equipped with auxiliary fuel tanks in the forward cargo which gave us extra range, although we couldn't quite make it in one hop to Dubai so we would land in Larnaca on the island of Cyprus to refuel. It was always a pleasure hearing the chirpy Greek voice on Nicosia radar.

"Calimera Bravo echo, descend flight level nine zero …"

"Five Bravo, yassos cleared to land runway tutu (22)… wind two four zero five knots."

I never tired of that scenic approach – cruising out to Dekelia power station then turning back along the beach front and down to the runway immediately adjacent to the sparkling blue sea.

After refuelling, off we'd head east towards Lebanon, then depending on the destination turn on track accordingly, sometimes Damascus, other times over to Kuwait, Abu Dhabi or Dubai.

After the first Iraq/Kuwait war, there was of course extensive damage. Naval bases, military installations and huge swathes of land had to be rebuilt. We all know there is nothing like a war or its clear up to provide excellent money making opportunities. There was much fat to be picked off the carcass of *that* war. We flew a Middle Eastern man around who was doing particularly meaty deals which yielded him astronomical commissions. I soon realised how adept they became at evading enquiry, if ever someone asked him what he did, his reply was "I do my best".

His best was good – millions of dollars every month in commission. Kuwait was rebuilding its military with what seemed like unlimited funds, so you can imagine the fierce competition to sell equipment there. He was a deeply religious man and there were icons of Mary and Jesus along with crucifixes and engraved prayers all over the aircraft – we even had one in the cockpit. He was a committed *Christian* (that was the only reason I was there for a start – don't think I'd have been employed by a Muslim). He was always very fair with me. This deep religious conviction didn't stop him sitting round gambling tables losing and winning hundreds of thousands in a blink, or discussing the buying and selling of arms. The light-hearted chit chat of parabolic trajectories, explosive warheads and intermediate ballistic missiles tripped off the tongue with the same consummate ease as 'Our Father who art in heaven'…

He had, I believe convinced them to buy Russian equipment, to rebuild the naval base. So many journeys were made between Moscow and Kuwait. It was impressive hearing a senior Russian speak fluent Arabic. At 35,000 feet over Iran one day he came into the cockpit and asked exactly where we were.

"We are between Esfahan and Tehran sir," I answered.

"My God don't let us get engine failure here and go down, they will kill me!" So I surmised he'd made a few enemies here and there. (Years later after I had lost touch, I was told two London businessmen were after him for an obscene amount of debt he'd run up in their casinos – I would imagine *they* were *not* the sort of boys to cross. They had his plane impounded at Bournemouth!) Later I read he was suing a casino for extending him credit!

I had a bit of a soft spot for the Fat Man as he was known. He invited me and my boyfriend to be his guests at Les Ambassadors club in Mayfair. He put his arm round the head waiter and said in that delightful Arabic accent: "She can have all what she want – it is her birthday!"

I will never forget the champagne flute which was nine inches high and so delicate, when you pinged the rim with your finger it had a resonance so sweet, it was like a humming bird tightrope walking across a piano string. He threw 2 chips down – £100 each and told me to enjoy a gamble upstairs after dinner. I did and I won, my Yorkshire genes kicked in and I quit while I was ahead. Result!

He was a big... no, wait, he was...an absolutely **gigantic** gambler, often hours late for departure because of his addiction. Once I saw him lose six hundred thousand in minutes. His mood was often determined by his luck on the tables. He always stayed at the Noga Hilton on Lake Geneva, he had a private suite on the whole of the top floor with his own elevator. The Captain once got a frantic phone call to bring more MONEY at ridiculous o'clock in the morning so he could continue at some casino, near Lausanne. Boy he couldn't help himself.

Approaching Kuwait, flying around the famous 'golf ball' tower as we called it, is an experience in itself. The modern buildings and the glittering waters of the gulf give a powerful impression of their wealth. The airport is immaculate but *HOT?* Even though I was raised in Africa, I had never felt heat like that. When I opened the front door, there was a wind blowing and it was like standing in front of an industrial size hair dryer on 'max hot' setting.

There are lots of contradictions about the place. We joined the boss and his business colleagues for lunch in a hotel.

I *do* remember the resident English catering manager with whom I had a long chat. He prepared the food for the aircraft for our onward journey. He was from the North of England and quite happy to be chatting to some Brits – he was looking forward to coming home. I gave him a peck on the cheek as I shook his hand. Oops I was in trouble.

"You **can't** do that ... it is just *not* done," murmured the hostess in low tones squeezing my wrist. She had lived in Saudi and was more au fait with the rules than I! I found the segregation and draconian moral rules strange at first especially given the alleged reports (whether they're true or not?) of the lustful defiling of young boys. It was somewhat disproportionate that an innocent peck on the cheek could cause such consternation, still, when in Rome...

We had the chairman or a similar ranking member of Taylor Woodrow on board, bound for Abu Dhabi. After the arrogant, demanding types from the sultanate of 'Givme' he, with his John Mills-ish face and manner, was rather a breath of fresh air. He was a cashmere V-neck/suede brogues sort, polite, modest and intelligent. In fact a jewel of courtesy; he came into the cockpit, interested in our activities and he chatted at length and with probing insight about the Middle East. Our boss *told* us to buy shares in Taylor Woodrow – I was a fool not to ... they soared!

Abu Dhabi was, I thought a really stunning place, very aesthetically presented with its elegant corniche. We landed in forty-eight degrees – owch! Thank god for the flight engineer who had to do the walk around and put the gear pins in and pump the rear air stair up. We could have wrung him out afterwards. However, like everywhere in the Middle East the air conditioning is simply glacial. All I know is – to turn ambient air into the refrigerated air that streams out of those units, something, somewhere is working hard. Let's hear it for freon and expansion chambers! When we returned to the aircraft after a couple of days the apples in the fruit bowl had actually **baked** – you could have put your finger through them.

"Salaam alaykum," chirped the men in dish dash in the airport who came to greet us. We sat in a beautifully cooled room which had all the chairs round the periphery in a big circle rather than clusters of four here and there. A man bought round tea on a large brass try and we drank it from little coloured glass cups decorated with gold filigree. It was pepperminty with a hint of herbs – delicious.

"Shuckran" – one of my very few words of Arabic!

Not quite as crowded as crazy neighbour Dubai, the place is still lively but in a somehow more low key way. At the Meridian pool in Abu Dhabi, I met a most extraordinary man. He was a South American mercenary. He was a **big** boy, dark skinned and wore a bandana. He had more scars on him than a manatee round Key West, Florida. He'd done Angola, Mozambique and all sorts of nasty wars which had left him looking rather 'harpooned'. He had one scar, the size of a fried egg but was very forthcoming in explaining the science of it all! In his strong Hispanic accent:

"Sometimes eet better to be shot really close range cos de bullet ... he just pass through but when it is some distance ... den it cause much damage eet tear the flesh more ..."

And so it went on, I only came up to the bar for a pina colada and left with a crash course in bullet wounds, different knives and how to rip someone's throat out with your bare hands. It was a fascinating insight into the life of a mercenary, and his nocturnal tactics. I imagined his card 'Name' and then 'No war too small'.

"What are you doing here?" I asked.

He explained he'd really landed on his feet as bodyguard to one of the Sheiks rich sons who had a huge boat which it was his duty to guard. He had a zippy sports car and accommodation and was enjoying himself thoroughly. They had met at the gym in Los Angeles and that was that. Just looking after the rich boy and his gin palace instead of sleeping rough, must have been a nice change.

"But... I kinda miss the thrill you know!" he said with a wry smile.

All a bit tame for him I suppose poncing around in a red Ferrari with no daily fix of skinning a porcupine then ripping out someone's oesophagus. Apparently many of the bodyguards out there are men like him.

Next stop was Damascus – the boss's home country. This has got to be one of the most fascinating cities in the Middle East and mercifully free of all the Kentucky fried and McDonald's which blot the Emirates. (Nothing against fast food though, I have never really fancied anything that gets served in a 'bucket'.) The city boasts many stages in its evolution and is reputedly the oldest continuously occupied city in the world. There was a city here before Abraham! Egyptians, Hittites, Israelites and Assyrians have all settled there and it has been part of the Persian, Roman and Byzantine Empires. In town there are Aramean and Roman ruins and beautiful dwellings called hammans which had lovely architecture and courtyards. The souks were lively colourful and aromatic, filled with music and exotic artefacts – silver cups, mother of pearl inlaid furniture, goblets, jewellery, and carpets. Inside the city we visited the famous place where Paul was lowered in a basket over a city wall to escape persecution having converted to Christianity. The city eventually became Islamic and as a result there is the most splendid mosque.

The streets are narrow and ancient but alive with freshly squeezed orange juice stalls and funnily enough – wedding dress shops. I had never seen so many white meringue dresses in one place before. Damascus is a rich and intoxicating city, splendid and mysterious. It groaned a bit like an old horse when the saddle is thrown over its back every morning, but somehow it trotted on. I have a lovely picture of my dear friend Susie (the flight attendant) and I dressed in long dark robes with our heads covered before going into one of the holy places. There is a special beauty there, you know you are touching at least the hem of the garment in which 'history' itself is clothed. With a bit of imagination I was back in ancient days amongst elegant women bearing amphoras of water on their heads swaying up dusty streets while traders came from Asia with spices and silk. Olives, music, camels, palm fringed oases in the desert, I saw it all. In reality it was probably a fly blown dump full of iniquity, violence and disease but … I like to be a 'glass half full' person.

Dubai – well what can one say about the place, it has grown beyond all recognition now. When we first went we stayed downtown and went to the revolving restaurant on top of the Forte hotel. Jumeira was not built, there was little traffic and things were cheap! What a stunning approach to Dubai airport, the view from our cockpit is truly amazing. When you land from the sea towards the land you are treated to a view right along the coast, from Bur Dubai, the creek, along from town to Jumeira then off into the distance(which used to be relatively bare). I would enjoy the changes, which were fast and inexorable, every time I returned. It only had to be weeks then the big sail of Jumeira beach was going up, then the palm island started, and bit by bit, fronds would be added. Then the marina went up with all its sky rises making the place look like Manhattan. You know when it takes you 45 minutes to get to an *airport* hotel, there is a traffic problem!

Dubai duty free was a favourite stop for us. I was mooching around once in my uniform buying some goods and I noticed an Egypt Air pilot in uniform sort of following me around and staring at me. I ignored him at first but he was so concerned and baffled by my appearance, it was obviously causing him great concern. The idea that I might, be up there, doing the same job as him, in the same sky! "Al hund du allah" he was praying now. He plucked up the courage:

"You are crew no?"

"Yes I am," I said courteously.

"But er, but you are cabin crew no?"

"No, I'm a pilot same as you." I smiled not feeling any resentment whatsoever, he was just acting from within his own frame of reference.

"Ooh I see," he nodded pretending to get it and I went back to looking at the baklava.

We parted momentarily and then ran into each other at the perfumes, he was still floundering on the rocks of incredulity.

"But, you don fly the plane – I mean ... you not controlling thee plane?" and he made driving actions with his hands.

"Yes I do I fly the plane from the front just like you."

"Ah...Oh... okay, this is very good, very nice, congratoo-lashun!" he gave a smile so big his faced inflated like a balloon, he shook my hand repeatedly and really looked as though he'd made a ground breaking discovery.

The 727 being an ex-airliner seating more than one hundred and sixty passengers had a very generous baggage hold. We certainly made full use of this – the engineer kept his golf clubs in there; the Captain, his scuba diving gear and *all of us* filled it with goods we purchased in various countries but especially when we went to the Middle East. It was nice to know if you wanted to buy *anything,* a mountain bike or a television, complete music system – even furniture and carpets – there was ample room to ferry it back to Luton!

Sometimes if my colleague was busy at the aircraft, I'd remain in the handling agents' office. There I would sign all the papers, and pay the bills. It was entertaining watching their faces when I got the credit card out to pay – that was too much – a girl flying, *and* handling money. Inshala no! It has I am sure, changed now. (Let's hope!)

I have to mention one of the more unusual 'post flight' check list items. After landing in Jeddah, I was told I had to go promptly to the handling agents' office – Jet Aviation and put on the full black Burka in order to leave the airport. It was a strange, doing the post flight walk round, putting the gear pins in the undercarriage, etc., dressed in flowing black robes which flapped in the hot wind. I just couldn't help making Darth Vader sounds as I swooped around the wing tips and secured the cargo hold door! Julie the flight attendant and I were wrapped up head to toe in our black gowns, having a seriously good laugh, she used to be a dancer so she did a little routine in hers which had me doubled up! It's a strange old game – but, once again, when in Rome...

En route home from the Middle East we cruise over great swathes of deserted scorched sands in Saudi Arabia making you realise how big the place is and how hardy those Bedouins must have been moving about on camels searching for the next bit of shade or drop of water. You can look down for hours onto an empty baked wilderness. Lawrence did well out there! The Middle East, particularly the Emirates, will always be a big destination for private jets – so you leave the sun block in the overnight bag!

"Salaam alaykum!"

149

The Party Plane – Forbes Private 727
"Everything in moderation, including moderation!"

It was undoubtedly the paint scheme of the century. Yes Malcolm Forbes, American billionaire certainly had a wry sense of humour. This beautiful executive jet was a statement. The saying 'if you've got it, flaunt it' had never been so bracingly exemplified. A gold coloured front and wings ahead of a dark green tail, the green paint coming forward into the gold in a big 'V'. N60FM was its registration, it was a show stopper. Then in true reflection of the entrepreneurial spirit that is America, and in honour of our friend uncle Sam the subtle words "FORBES Capitalist Tool" were painted on the tail – marvellous! By the summer of 1996 our boss had decided he wanted his second 727 so I was sent over to the States with Captain Jack to ferry it back with the engineer who'd been flying on it for quite some time, that was good, he would know the plane well.

I know Mr Forbes, one of the richest men in the world had used this plane (amongst many others) to ferry his friends to Morocco for his final birthday bash, which took place over several days and I am told was the shindig of the century. We first saw it *prior* to the removal of the Forbes belongings, my God this plane had seen some serious 'action'. Life aboard had been a nonstop 'thrill fest'.

He had a specially unique ramp up the back stairwell to haul his Harley Davidson bikes up, he enjoyed cruising around on his Harley once he got to destination. There were pictures strewn everywhere of famous people – the Reagans, Casper Weinberger, Elizabeth Taylor, senators, ambassadors, heads of state, movie stars, singers and actors. It was *thee* party ship, complete with thick carpets, bar, televisions, pale leather seats all with max swivel and recline and the flashy bedroom with en suite (could *that* suite have told a thousand tales!).

As always with these aircraft deals there is endless paperwork and ours was particularly complicated because the plane was over a certain weight and was being exported – it could fall into the wrong hands. The FAA looks *very* carefully at this and we had to have *this* Certificate of Deviation and *that* Certificate of some other thing. We were ramp checked in Newark on Super Bowl day. (BIG game in America!) They (the Feds) found something they didn't like and we were grounded to sort out 'red tape' issues. During this time we had become friendly with the English pilot from Sussex called Toby, he was Malcolm Forbes's helicopter pilot who was hired to land on the back of his boat. He was only a little guy and looked so young, but he was highly qualified. He knew we were waiting, so he kindly offered to take me up in the Forbes helicopter, a beautiful Augusta 109 in exactly the same paint scheme as the Boeing 727.

The captain said, "You might as well go for it, the paperwork isn't quite ready yet, go and have a nice day out, I doubt anything will happen today."

So off we went in this wonderful helicopter flying all over the magnificent houses of the Hamptons and the Catskills swooping down over tennis clubs and beautiful parkland. En route back to Newark, Toby's mobile phone rang, it was Jack.

"We're ready to go, finally got the paperwork sorted. The FAA has released us – get back here when you can."

"Okay," said Toby, "we are on our way."

The next half-hour was like something from a movie, we flew right along the glistening Hudson river, a wall of skyscrapers running alongside us, I was looking *up* at the buildings. I took a picture of the trade towers, something which gives me an eerie feeling whenever I look at the photograph after 911.

He asked for clearance and we flew low level right over the runway at Newark, I was **loving** it! He raised the nose pulling back on the cyclic at which point his hands and feet are in a tightly coordinated dance, just small but accurate movements lowering the collective and concentrating! He brought the mighty machine into a hover and slowly put us down squarely right at the back of the matching 727. I opened the door, the noise was intense. The wind blew all around me as I shouted my thanks to him, shook his hand and closed the door. It looked damned impressive to have the jet and the helicopter in the same livery, I ran up the back stairs of the 727, pulled the lever to raise them, the door clunked heavily behind me and I was in the quiet cool luxury of the executive interior. I walked into the cockpit where the engines were turning and we were ready to go. The helicopter hovered in front of us nodded his goodbyes then flew off to the west.

We taxied out.

"Boost pumps ... on."

"Hydraulic pressure ... check."

"Door warning lights ... check"

"Three stable ... thrust set ... eighty knots ... V1 ... rotate!"

We were off. The views of New York were fabulous. But the joy didn't last. We were airborne only minutes when the engineer discovered a problem with the fuel dump nozzle valve system. We ended up coming back into Newark where we stayed for another night until the problem was fixed. Some engineers came to assist and the problem was sorted ... I was beginning to think this plane would never make it back to the UK. But we eventually did, after a long trek straight over the Atlantic.

We finally touched down at Luton, and the aircraft went straight into Service for its new boss for whom we flew it all over the Middle East where its flamboyant paint created a lot of interest. We carried dignitaries, arms dealers and heads of State. I think Mr Forbes would have been pleased that his toy was still on the circuit! Even if the new passengers were not quite the 'party animals' *his* crowd had been, we, the crew certainly kept the tradition alive and didn't let him down!

Flying High

The old Boeing 727 makes a terrific business jet and it's in *this* role that many of them end their days after their airline role. Malcolm Forbes, Donald Trump, Wafiq Zaid, Prince Bandar, Andre Agassi and various sheiks and Sultans are just a few among those who have enjoyed the luxuries of this plane. (Wafiq was the first person to carry a defibrillator on board.) Although heavy on the fuel, they are cheaper to buy and offer the passenger a beautifully spacious cabin, complete with en suite bedroom, dining room lounge and kitchen. I flew a couple of 'exec' 727s in 1995 and 1996 and again in 2003. Here are a few memories of some ... eye opening times.

Monte Carlo Grand Prix

On the ramp at Luton, it was a sunny breezy afternoon in mid-summer and we were doing what we knew best ...**waiting!** We were off with some 'players' down to Nice for the Grand Prix in Monaco. Pre-flights include loading the GPS, getting the correct maps and charts and setting up our departure with headings bugged and radials set on our instruments (all analogue!). I listened to the latest met report and worked out our take-off speeds. The APU (auxiliary power unit) is the little jet engine in the belly providing us with electrics and pneumatics, keeping us in pleasant air conditioning and subtle cabin lighting.

My bit done, I'd help the two cabin crew. We'd have to vacuum the whole plane, run a light sponge along the suede ceilings and walls to ensure an even nap, polish all the wood and generally make it shine like a crown jewel. Tasks would vary – I would roll up little white towels and place them in an iced tray, or maybe fill all the cut glass bowls with every type of exotic nut and dried fruit imaginable.

The CD player would be thumping out something jazzy and the smell of fresh flowers filled the air. In the master bedroom fresh crisp sheets and exquisite bedspreads covered the bed, and plump silk pillows were scattered. The en suite bathroom boasted a dazzling array of gold taps and expensive toiletries. A padded leather lid covered the loo and matching towels were folded perfectly over gold holders. It was opulence at its best, resplendent with expensive aftershaves perfumes and soaps, every last detail was observed down to the silk slippers tucked under the bed.

Beautiful dried flowers sat on polished TV tops, and priceless ornaments, discreetly lit, adorned various corners of the cabin. And, of course we had enough champagne on board to see us through a Royal Ascot week. Trays of mouth-watering nasturtium adorned delicacies were brought in by the catering company. The main courses of fish, steak, lamb and chicken were slid into the storage space in the galley along with beautiful salads; the olives and meze would be put out on some surfaces. The best bit of course was that we would eat the leftovers!

The first Bentley, was it an Azure or a Continental? pulls up right at the aircraft steps and a dark skinned man alights, pulls a couple of leather bags from the boot then tosses the keys to the handling agent. A few minutes pass and another Bentley purrs up to the aircraft steps, two men step out with that practiced nonchalance, they have expressions, which say, 'Yep … I'm cool'. They climb the stairs, I see big smiles, firm handshakes, creased linen, dark shades, general chutzpah. Then shortly afterward, Batman arrived in his 'batmobile', a famous British pop star. He pulls up in one of his jaw dropping, futuristic cars, complete with gull wing doors. It *is* actual aero dynamism *itself*. All the handling staff gathered round to have a good look at what was certainly an expensive toy. He is a speed freak and spent the whole journey to Nice in the cockpit entertaining me with stories of speeding fines and ongoing run-ins with various constabularies, but the cops couldn't catch him in this particular car because it's too fast. What an excellent chap. If I recall, one of his plans for the New Year was to go to Russia and fly faster than the speed of sound in a Sukhoi jet fighter.

Two more players in this game of 'dolce vita' arrived in a huge black Mercedes. I see sockless feet in loafers, linen jackets, narrow dark sunglasses and lots of gold. Hands run through hair as they climb the steps slowly and deliberately. This is starting to look like a 'boys tour' of pulsating proportions. Drinks are being poured in the back, ice cubes are chinking against cut glass, handfuls of nuts grabbed from bowls are being shaken into tilted back mouths. Gold lighters flick open and shut, the smell of cigarette smoke mingles cordially with that of aftershave.

I entered the cockpit, put my headset on to listen for any updates in airfield data, through the window I see a limousine pulling up. Ah here come the girls. Out step beautiful young things. I see a bright pink *extremely* tight crop top, a nut-brown belly adorned with sparkling gem, dangerously high heeled open toe clogs, spray on jeans with a few strategic tears in them, and an arsenal of designer bags. One wore daringly low black hipsters secured by sparkling diamante belt slung through the hoops, and an even lower black T-shirt. There was cleavage EV-erywhere, or as our 18th century chums would have said: "an apple dumpling shop". They are laughing and giggling, as they climb aboard, I greet them at the top of the stairs. As they enter the cabin they smile beautiful bright smiles and toss their long shiny hair and we shake hands. I recall Eastern European and Swedish accents and exotic unusual names. They walk down the corridor carefully in their high heels whispering to each other clutching their designer handbags and went to join the party in the main cabin. Because there is a bedroom with ensuite on board immediately aft of the cockpit, this creates a small corridor between the front and the main cabin area. It now smelt like the Harrods' perfumery.

Eventually we're "all aboard", a charming trendy Indian gentleman came into the cockpit, he was learning to fly so he was keen to be in our 'space'. He was Mr Asian cool, tall and statuesque with a ponytail, black leather jacket, dark shades, and dazzling white teeth. He was a pop singer; I asked what kind of music – he said "Punjabi funk" which I thought sounded 'different', I instantly thought of Hollywood musicals where ranks of dancers leap and twirl about, in colourful costumes, heads going from side to side and some man with a haunted agonised expression, is singing and dancing his way through the pains of unrequited love.

He gave me a quick rendition – his head tilted and his arms outstretched then his fingers stabbing downwards a few times with a knee coming up.

"O-*KAAY*." I thanked with raised eyebrows and a slow nod.

"It's very dancey, you'll like it," he assured me, "I'll be playing on the boat."

"I shall look forward to it," I smiled.

We eventually took off, the lively *English* pop singer, having made roads into the drinks cabinet was with us in the cockpit, drink in hand, and was in fine voice. We were only five minutes out of Luton, enjoying the serenading, when one of the party came bursting into the cockpit and said, "We've forgotten Costas, we'll have to go back, he's got the *money*."

They were so busy partying that nobody had noticed his absence. Someone managed while still in phone range to get him on the mobile, he was on the M1 and only minutes away. I think there would have been no U turn if it had been just Costas without his attaché case! Small eddies of excitement stirred in me as I thought perhaps we might *get paid*. (To be one or two months in arrears is quite normal on some of these private jets.) But alas the dosh was just gambling and fun money for them. The trip would preclude the sweetener of that darned inconvenient thing which we kept asking for … salary.

"London radar Delta Bravo Echo request return to Luton."

This is **not** a usual request unless you're on fire, they assumed we had a major problem and asked if I was declaring an emergency.

"Negative," I replied. (Well it's a sort of emergency leaving the case of cash behind.) Naturally they assumed we were in danger.

I won't horrify you with the costs involved in returning to land followed by another take-off, it is prodigious – there are landing and handling fees, ramp charges, not to mention the **fuel!** I explained that our missing passenger should be arriving any second so I requested to stop on the taxiway, engines running and wait, we could drop the rear stair for him. I really should know better by now – 10 minutes away always means 30 minutes.

Then a voice from the tower:

"I'm afraid Bravo Echo you are going to have to pull onto stand and shut down, you're blocking the taxiway there." We parked and shut down.

Everyone was laughing, I thought to myself the laughter might be a little more subdued when the bill arrived. Eventually a flustered Costas arrived armed with a big bag and huge smile and off we went.

Nice was outrageously busy, special published approaches were in operation – a little more long winded than usual. We dropped down over the mountains near Montelimar, flew out to sea round the Cap D'Antibes (mandatory for noise abatement). You must fly a circuitous route into Nice so as not to disturb the residents, who all want to *get* there by private jet but don't want to *hear* one once they are sipping martinis on the floating pink 'cadi' in the pool! I flew in towards the beach and turned right onto final approach to see the familiar parallel runways of 04 left and right jutting out into the blue

Mediterranean, it is a beautiful setting. The mountains were clear in the distance. The views were fantastic, huge speed boats bounced along the water leaving trails of white foam, there were water skiers, swimmers, and jet skis, in this – the ultimate playground. Boats the sizes of palaces were moored out at sea off my starboard. The beach was dotted with cheerful umbrellas, fun seekers, topless beauties and bat and ball players. Brightly coloured parachutes were being dragged behind boats, people strapped in the harness, legs dangling. The sea was deep azure fading to whitish blue near the shore, big sparkles of sunlight bounced off its surface everywhere and over this whole scene, the dome of undisturbed blue sky.

I called for the landing checklist.

"Antiskid … five releases."

"Ignition … On."

"No Smoking … On." (And if you think *that's* going to make a difference…)

"Gear … down 3 greens."

"Flaps … thirty thirty green light."

"Hydraulics … pressure and quantity normal."

At this point on short finals you are only feet above the windsurfers! The pop star in his crazy hat, gave a running commentary as I came down the ILS as though it were a space invaders game.

"Yeah, nice one, correcting left, intercepting the localiser … alright were on the numbers now girl, yeah, wheels comin' down, nailed it, nice one kicking off the drift … into the flare and … beee youtiful."

It was a nice change to have someone taking an interest!

All our passengers shot off to Monte Carlo to the best hotel in town, we stayed in Nice but the hosts very kindly invited us on the boat the next night to join the party. I had a good friendship with the flight attendant so she and I coordinated dresses the next night and decided to go and have a *thoroughly* great time.

Six of us (two of the crew had relatives with them) piled into the mini bus taxi. We were a merry crowd laughing and joking, "Just think we're getting paid for this," then laughing even harder when we realised that we in fact *hadn't* been paid. The driver was abusing every other car:

"Eh bas, qu'est ce qu'il fait ce conard …? Ah merde!!" he moaned as he leant on the horn with one hand and twiddled his moustache with the other. Then he waved his hands, lifted his shoulders to his ears, and pointed at his bonnet and the gap they were inviting him to squeeze through. "Tu es fou ou quoi?" All very Nicoise!

He dropped us at a very swish looking hotel in the center of Monte Carlo. Photographers were at the ready to snap stars as they alighted from cars, their lenses went up, I was all in white and Anna all in black and for a moment they thought we might be celebs, then they tutted disdainfully at the stench of our commonality, lowered their lenses and lit another Gauloise.

The walk along the harbour towards the boat was quite simply a reverie. I'd never seen so much glitz and opulence crammed into so tiny a space. All along the quayside, diners were tucking into lobsters and champagne, waiters scurried about serving hundreds of bottles of wine and on the water people were settling into the serious business of 'mega posing' on the backs of their gleaming white boats, some the size of small ships. Girls in 'can't go any lower' backless dresses with diamante straps showed off their tanned backs. Guys in tuxedos with the bowties casually undone held champagne flutes and lowered their shades to get a better look at the passing bevy of beauties. There should have been a sign up at the entrance to the place: "ALL those NOT going to Gordon Brown's party please enter here!" Live music and heady perfume wafted through the air. It was like walking into a dream, a million bulbs twinkled in the crepuscular light around the harbour, fairy lights adorned the decks and were strung across all the awnings of the bars and restaurants. Fireworks exploded filling the dark sky with kaleidoscopic fountains over the distant hills and the whole scene was reflected in the still waters of the harbour.

We found our boss's boat – it was a cracker, a full crew all in their whites waited to greet us as we walked along the gangplank and onto the spotless wooden deck.

"Good evening," said the immaculate Captain with outstretched hand. We were asked to remove our shoes to save the wood, then we climbed up to the main deck – a beckoningly spacious area where food and champagne were being served amongst mingling people. It was polyglot humanity – so many different nationalities. I spotted the beautiful girls who had been our passengers, and I noticed to my surprise that they hadn't taken their high heels off so had that luxury of those extra few inches.

The Jacuzzi was bubbling away at the very front of the top deck, next to it our Indian 'funk man' was pounding out the Punjabi funk. We were all dancing around the deck which was a hoot – especially since I had a real northern comedian right behind me and he wanted to sing along but didn't know the words so just chanted 'pop-pop padum' and 'mango chutney' and anything else he could remember off an Indian menu; he was very tuneful and kept good time, I have to give him that.

Some of the guys made trips to nearby boats to touch base with their fellow Indians and Middle Eastern mates. There were some 'heavy weights' in from Saudi, their boat was actually out at sea, little tenders were moving back and forth. The boat became more and more crowded as the night went on, the pink champagne tumbled endlessly from bottle to outstretched glass, and spirits were high. Some were keeping clear heads, dishing out business cards selling everything from mobile handsets to Gulfstream Five jets.

My mate from the north (who'd missed his vocation as a stand-up comedian) came up to me at one point and said, "See that woman over there Neets, the one in the goldie top?"

"Yes."

"Apparently I've just heard that she's offering a grand if someone'll shag 'er."

I had to swallow quickly before I burst out laughing. It was the *way* he said it (in that northern 'wukkin' men's club way) and the fact that he'd even *found* that information out.

156

"Oh well I see you have all the latest boat gossip, nice work."

"She's lucky 'cause the way the booze is flowing on this boat, she's in with a fair old chance."

I threw him a 'don't be mean' smirk and we went off to tour the cabins. The bedrooms were pure Ivana Trump, jade statues, bijou ornaments tons of gold, and about three million mirrors. The white carpets throughout were deep enough to sink your toes into. All the bathrooms were gleaming and the wooden doors so polished you could see your reflection. A woman came out of one of the toilets in an eye blinkingly scarlet dress and we engaged in a little conversation. I was actually looking into a face which didn't move a single muscle as she talked. Speech came from the mouth miraculously because the face was set like stone, not a lip curled up, not an eyebrow lifted, not a cheek budged even a millimetre, the only movement was the eyeball itself. I guessed this was platinum package offered by the beauty clinic, Botox: buy five get one free after fifty sets of false nails.

One of our hosts suggested going to a night club called Jimmy's.

"But it's five in the morning?" I said.

"That's a great time to go, everyone will be arriving now," he replied. "Hey this is Monte Carlo Anita, it never stops." Just then I noticed one of the girls we'd flown down who'd been dancing and sipping champers all night and had a luck changing blow – a savage one I'd say. I saw some furtive mouth to ear negotiations going on between two men, next thing she was taken by the elbow and handed over to a greasy fat dodgy looking bloke, with dark skin, a white suit and two earrings. "Eki thump" I said to myself "keep drinking girl".

Reassuring images of duvets and pillows and nurturing thoughts of my Novotel bedroom which had been tiptoeing playfully round my mind, were banished as I toughened up for 'second wind'. A small crowd of us walked to a taxi rank near the port, and to my surprise there were hoards and platoons of people from all nations waiting for cabs to go on to this famous night club. I must say it was well organised because, taxis from normal cars to mini coaches were cruising up constantly. There were even gloved guys there to slide open the doors of the Renault Espace for you. I sat opposite a very inebriated Swedish guy whose eyes rolled around his head and who mumbled and sang – it was a sort of medley of incomprehensible Scandinavian. Then he sat bolt upright shouted something at me in ancient Norse with wide staring eyes, laughed manically then slumped in the chair and was out.

The night club was quite simply unbelievable. People were queuing up outside at dawn. We decided collectively that I should try and get past the bouncer by mentioning the names of our clients, and bring one of them out to assist our ingress! Fortunately it worked and I padded down a long dark tunnel into the club. It was a nightmare of decibels and human beings, you couldn't move. The human sardine factory. I had never seen so many surly looking girls crammed together on a dance floor glancing from left to right to see if any one better was around.

People could barely move their shoulders on the dance floor let alone show off their swing moves. There were noses in the air, lips pouting. The words 'get over yourselves' came to mind. We are a funny old lot aren't we?

We long to go to clubs where a drink, *ANY* drink be it a glass of champagne or mineral water cost one hundred Euros, where you can't even if you have vocal chords like a QE2 tethering rope make yourself heard. I managed to spot one of our crowd and waved, he came over. He was pretty short and almost scrambled over people's heads.

I explained that we were all outside and since amongst the Bentleys, Ferraris, Aston Martins there were models, racing drivers and crowned princes of Europe with their billionaire mates, the chances of a couple of lads from 'oop North and two girls based in Luton being chosen by the all-powerful bouncer were, well, slim to say the least.

Once we were all inside the volume precluded any chance of conversation but thankfully, the boss bought a few bottles of champagne, for simply colossal amounts of money. The dear flight engineer from South Africa, such a nice chap, skinny as a rake and I suspect not *that* worldly, he found it all terrifically amusing, like a kid in a sweetshop.

"Chroyst I could buy a small place in Transvaal for what this lot costs you know," he shouted in thick Afrikaans accent. And he made some 'Emperor's clothes' type of comments such as, "Not really that many people smiling hey?"

Fair dues, he stayed out until lunchtime the next day. Being so small he managed to scale up one of the trees or pillars inside the place, for I remember him perched up there like a little gibbon looking down on the heaving mass of humanity. I saw a strange creature, could have been male or female, not unlike Prince, white suit, heels, bling, bum fluff moustache and side burns, I just caught snippets of his conversation going on right next to me with the crowned prince of 'Sleazaria'.

"What you want? I can get anything, you want girl? boy? two girls? three boys ..."

I felt like chirping in 'goat? sheep? horns, shorn or hairy'?

There was not a square inch anywhere to sit, even standing became difficult, you had to keep raising your glass way above your head to allow passing traffic. The bar was ten people deep all trying to order drinks. Skeletal models from Uzbekistan wearing no more than a sequin handkerchief with lips like pink grapefruit segments perched on fountain edges whilst flotillas of adoring shade wearing aspirants got splashed and shoved trying to procure a drink for them. Talk about the ceaseless litany of materialism, it was a handbags, glad rags, and most definitely rutting season. Some people had just given up all hope of finding the loo or their friends or any purpose whatsoever and they had just slumped 'in situ' holding their shoes, yawning with their brows on their folded arms. These were like the weaker or injured. I could hear David Attenborough in sotto voce saying:

"And these poor creatures ... exhausted by the fierce competition ... will not mate this time ..."

Cabs were becoming scarcer by seven thirty in the morning, however, our chap had his flagging interest reawakened when we said 'Nice' because he knew he could charge us like an injured bull and he duly did. Whilst waiting for the cab in the watery light of morning, we saw three policemen absolutely kicking the living daylights out of some poor bloke on the ground, God knows what he had done but he was certainly paying for it now. Unusual to see in Monte Carlo, much more likely at a football match, maybe someone had tipped the police off that there was an English football fan in town.

Nice airport was awash with the world's finest and most impressive private jets; from the crew bus which took us to our 727 we trundled passed thousands of millions of dollars of gleaming hardware. They came from all over: Italy, Germany, Switzerland, Caymans, USA, United Arab Emirates, Russia and beyond. We did two shuttles back to Luton, the most memorable for me being the second one. The moon was a baby's fingernail that evening and the sky a perfect blue. It was my departure, and we had the gregarious English pop star with flamboyant hat, in the cockpit with us again.

I lined up on the runway. I pointed out the moon just before I pushed the throttles up to 'three stable', and he broke out into a perfect rendition of "Fly me to the Moon".

"Eighty knots."

"Check."

"V1 rotate."

"And let me play among the stars."

"Positive climb ... Gear up."

"Let me know what spring is like on Jupiter and Mars ... in other words."

"Flap five."

"Speed checked ... flap five."

"...darling kiss me ... Fill my heart with song ..."

"Flaps two."

"Speed check, flaps two."

"And let me sing forever more ..."

"Flaps up, climb power, after take-off checklist."

"Fly me to the moon and let me play among the stars ..."

As I banked her round through west after the take-off climb and on to a northerly heading we all savoured the most spectacular unobstructed view of the coast. Lights twinkled on the promenade, boats were lit on the calm water, and the mountains rose up in the distance behind Nice and Cannes. Our flying enthusiast pop star was by now stood in the cockpit in his crazy hat, drink in hand, sliding and grooving around gesturing at the moon as he sang. Yes ... it was a nice one. (This WAS a private flight!) We climbed up and headed towards Dijon, the VHF communication frequencies were absolutely saturated with aircraft all departing Nice. Flecks and feathers of faraway cirrus sat high up in the atmosphere catching the evening light.

At Luton, everyone said their goodbyes and thank yous. The Bentleys and Mercedes were brought to the aircraft and bags were loaded. The last to leave was our pop star who jumped into his gull-wing door racing car along with one of the bevy of pretty girls. I hoped she was ready for a hundred and twenty miles per hour because I think that is what he had in mind. He sank into his super low bucket seat and floored the accelerator and was gone in a mighty roar. We all retired to the luxury of the cabin to finish off all the delicious catering and have a drink. Whilst relaxing after a flight the handling agents or refuellers are milling in and out doing their jobs, it is customary to invite them to enjoy a drink and any leftovers. Those were the moments when stories would be shared about the passengers and the trips. The agonies and the ecstasies of various journeys. Many a laugh was had. Then I heard a real eye opener. One of the funniest. Our male flight attendant told us a blinding story of his previous trip.

Sounds like the Mile High Club

"I kid you not mate, there was just bodies shagging all over the bloody place."

These were the bluntly honest words of our friend, a male flight attendant from up north and blessed therefore with that dry delivery and razor sharp humour. (I saw him pick up the microphone once in the bar of the Intercontinental in Delhi and do the most perfect imitation of a compere of a northern club.)

"Ladies and gentlemen don't go away there'll be more music from the band after their short break and we've still got the raffle to come, and plenty more dancing."

The silver hair and the tan meant he looked quite the part.

He told us about the orgy on his previous trip on the same Boeing 727, during which every guy on board was having sex (or was 'plugged in' to coin a phrase). "I had wondered why they'd requested 'no female crew on board'– front or back. Then … it made sense," he said with a cheeky grin.

"I was walking down the middle of the cabin and all the flamin' lights were off right so I was shinin' me torch on the floor to see where I was going, I was trying to get to the bar at the back. I kept the torch down so I wouldn't disturb them, and all I could see were just arses moving up and down. That sofa had six of 'em on it and in the big armchair here was a blonde with huge knockers just bouncing up and down. I swear I just couldn't believe my bloody eyes, and there were four of 'em in the bedroom. It was unreal."

We were killing ourselves laughing at the thought of all this and we were positively crinkled when he then told us that as he was going into the toilet to afford them some privacy, one of the girls, concerned he didn't feel left out, offered him some 'fun' as well! What a sweetheart!

"I have to say at that point I thought … well beats the hell out of workin' in an office! Here I am in the middle of a flamin' orgy at thirty-five thousand feet." He of course was giving updates to the cockpit who were doing their best to find pockets of turbulence!

My friend continued:

"At one point this Eastern European girl came up to me in tears and said she'd had enough like, she wanted to get off, she didn't want anything from them they were just too bloody rough for her, she'd made a mistake. Poor girl…but, what the hell could I do? I think she was a bit intimidated by it all obviously not very experienced."

I agreed, saying it's a bit difficult to pull over and drop someone off at thirty-five thousand feet. It wasn't the syrupy fantasy she'd entertained. If she was expecting to step into a scene from 'The Bridges of Madison County' make tender passionate love with someone who stroked her hair, told her she was beautiful and wanted to stay by her side, buy her a cottage and a puppy, she was a bit off target. These guys (and I've worked for a few of them) have a diet of pornography, Marlboro reds and Johnny Walker. Sex with them is, I would imagine, pretty dirty, hard and nasty and probably not particularly conventional! Without being declamatory or judgmental, most of them are, hard, promiscuous, pleasure seeking, libertines and you play by their rules if you go into their world. Beware before you jump into these pools for a swim, sharks circle and waters can be murky. It was all too much for this young Uzbeki girl. But hopefully this would be a lesson in the darker more debauched byways of humanity. As Guy de Maupassant and some of his nineteenth century contemporaries showed us ... There's as much to be gleaned from the sleazy back street brothels as from the glittering 'pompadour' salons!

The clients had requested that no female crew should be on board, so my mate had the whole experience to himself but was also left with the task of clearing up which he described as nothing short of ghastly!

After the laughter we had a few grimaces and an "Oh perleeease." when he described the condoms left all over the cabin!

"I mean, fair dos, have your fun but clean up after yourselves for heaven's sake!"

It reminded me of my friend's dad (a Yorkshire man) grumbling after her mammoth 21st party. During the 'rekkie' of the damage, he said, "I don't care about the couple having it off in the bushes, but I do object to underwear being discarded on my herbaceous border."

They should have cleared up after themselves I mean it's just not cricket!

This little yarn prompted a story from my friend – a hostess whose plane was parked next door. She used to work on Saudia Royal Flight, and was talking about the shenanigans that went on there. Girls were chosen to go onto the 747. There were obviously tiers of employment and depending on how 'hard' you worked the more you earned. (This is a plane with lots of what they call 'mejilese' or low comfy lounging sofas.) They all lived in compounds in Saudi Arabia, but a few of them did, when repatriating end up with flats in London, diamond rings and convertible sports cars. I myself remember flying Saudi women who would be covered head to toe in Black when they boarded, no sooner were the wheels in the wheel well and "ker-pow" it was Channel suits with miniskirts, perfume make-up and large cocktails! Well as Cindy Lauper says: "Girls just want to have fun".

The Far East and Back

Whilst on the subject I told my story of a free-lance trip, I flew on a private Middle Eastern executive Boeing 727 in 1996. The boss – well what can one say? Egomaniacal just does not come close. A captious and deeply unpleasant individual he loved to bark and bully. We started at Southend in England of all places and flew to Paris then Bahrain then Dakar. We had the shortest rest I can remember – that would be the kind when, on waking, you feel as though a thimble full of sand is in each eye. We pushed on to Borneo for one day then it was the most gargantuan and never-ending journey back. In one day we flew from Borneo to Paris via Taipei, Kuala Lumpar, and Bahrain.

There are three things I remember about this Homeric voyage. One was the tale told by the two English flight attendants. Apparently the boss would return to his jet dressed in his suit after a meeting, then summon the girls to his private bedroom with en suite and expect to be dressed in his Arabic robes so he could relax. Apparently he would stand, arms outstretched like the Christ figure on the hill in Rio being adorned in his exotic gold and green silks along with matching slippers.

The second, was, not being allowed *any* hot food at all on this twenty-six hour journey because *he* didn't like the smell of hot food from the galley. So we were restricted to a tray of sandwiches whose edges curled up like autumn leaves thirty minutes into the flight. This was as teeth grindingly irritating as was his temper, which could fire clay. When he boarded the aircraft in Borneo the outside temperature was about forty degrees C. The packs (air conditioning packs) have to be **off** for engine start so that maximum bleed air is directed to the engines to start them. Although we had had the air conditioning on it was not man enough against these punishing temperatures.

He burst into the cockpit hissing and popping like a chip pan. The aircraft should be cool, why hadn't we got the air conditioning on and so on. The Captain was French and of gnomic stature in every way and simply didn't say anything. I reached for the Boeing check list and was about to show him the start procedure which clearly states:

Beacon ... on, Galley power ... off, Packs ... off, but I was given a combative scowl from the left seat so I dipped into my pool of hard won self-control and tossed it back on the cowling. This poor guy had to fly this megalomaniac around all his miserable life, *I*, on the other hand was just free-lancing for this one trip. With tongue in cheek the engineer expressed his surprise that given he spends so much time in the sandy arid wastes, he should feel the heat at all.

The most lasting memory was during the cruise when I got up to stretch my legs in the small area just aft of the cockpit where there was a coffee machine for us. He had some dignitaries on board from Malaysia, I didn't know *exactly* who but there were some profitable liaisons occurring – daughters marrying Sultans and so on. There were big businessmen/minor royalty ... certainly 'heavy hitters'.

From their lounge, they saw me standing there just outside the cockpit, and they called me in to speak to them. They were polite and friendly and we engaged in conversation for half an hour. The subject was aircraft because they were thinking about a Challenger 601 (a beautiful Canadian built jet) they were very inquisitive about the Boeing and were obviously enjoying the space, so we discussed costs. I made the point that the Boeing costs only about four or five million to purchase but was very heavy on the fuel, and restrictive on the noise. The Challenger and Gulfstreams were well over thirty million to buy but were lighter on fuel, plus the 727 had old technology in the cockpit as opposed to the high tech electronic flight displays (EFIS) and Flight management systems of modern jets.

We compared the enormous space you get in an airliner size biz jet and that in the slimmer narrower, but infinitely more modern jets. Then one of them showed great perspicacity:

"What about if you put the modern glass cockpit into the old Boeing then you have the space and comfort *and* the hi-tech side?"

I said it has been done – it is costly, but you end up with a very desirable aircraft!

"You'd have something like a 757 (Bill Gate's friend had one at the time) which would be incredible."

We talked animatedly, they asked me how I got started then passed me a couple of business cards. We shook hands, I returned to the cockpit.

A short while later the young lackey knocked on the cockpit door and sheepishly said that the boss would like to see 'the girl'. I looked around and concluded that that must mean me. I went aft to his private office. When I entered I had to suppress a chortle because it was so ... well ... 'James Bondish', he was Doctor Evil in the chair with the cat (only the cat was missing).

"Why did you talk to my passengers?"

"Because they called me in, wanting a chat about aviation, it would be rude to ignore them."

"I see."

I clocked the room whilst I was there. I had a feeling since this was tea and no biscuits, I probably wouldn't be in here again, it was a beautiful room. There were breathtaking artefacts and carvings, they looked somehow Maori. A world of inky opulence. I looked straight at him and raised my eyebrows prompting the obvious forthcoming bollocking.

"It seems you are quite the expert on aeroplanes," he sneered as he flicked imaginary dust of his clothes.

"Oh thank you very much," I fired straight back over the net determined not to give him the satisfaction of intimidation, which was clearly the aim here.

"So, er tell me, what has 757 got that my aircraft has *not* got?"

'Okaaay' I said to myself, doing a high speed appraisal of the situation. He was hurt because passengers have mentioned interesting chat they had re aircraft, new versus old, big versus small. They probably mentioned updating a 727 cockpit and *that* being a winning combo – it'd be like a 757. Oh dear, toys were now being thrown from pram here because audacious girl had suggested there might be something better out there, therefore he *isn't* king of the castle.

"Well," I drew out slowly and determinedly, "Are we talking avionics, nav. systems, fuel burn, climb rate, range, noise restrictions, space, **size** (saved that one 'til last) ... because we could go a long way with this?"

With that I was expecting a hand to go under the polished table, press a button and the floor to open revealing a gyroscopically stabilised pool crammed full of starving piranha with the odd gold Rolex lying on the bottom. But instead I got the flick of the hand which meant piss off and be quick about it.

That journey home was a long and exhausting slog. I sat for hours over the sea between Singapore and India having to listen to the HF radio and because we had no Selcal (when the controller can call you so you can remove the headsets) I had the hissing of interference in my ears the whole time. The stops were short and for fuel only. Having said that fuel stops can be painfully long – on a trip on a different 727 that same year it took us half an hour to find the refueller in Lahore Pakistan. It was the middle of the night and I finally found him asleep on top of an old lorry. So you can never be too certain of an expeditious fuel stop.

We pressed on to Paris. We had left Taiwan on the twelfth – my birthday, by the time we arrived it was no longer my birthday I had spent it schlepping across the world for "Dr Evil". Still no worries we had a bottle of champagne and headed off to the Crazy Horse Saloon and the Champs Elysees. We were so exhausted, we thought 'pah' what's another few hours, let's party.

I knew I wouldn't work for this man again and without doubt, *he* wouldn't be calling *me* anytime soon! It was the last trip I did before joining the airlines at Gatwick, I had had enough of the disregard for crew duty hours on these so-called 'private flights' and I was tired of it. I thought I'd have a change, try the airlines and work to a roster. It was a character building experience and useful learning curve during which I made some really good friends.

Flying for an Airline – Feline Pilot!

Nothing could be further from private jet charter than 'bucket and spade' Airlines. I enjoyed the contrast and lived through some real 'moments' during the three years of flying Boeing 727s for a Gatwick and Stansted based charter airline taking holiday makers all round Europe. I made some great friends. Most of the engineers ('ginger beers' as they were fondly known!) were ex Dan Air, therefore seasoned 'been around the block' types; who loved a beer, a smoke, told loads of dirty jokes and could fix anything. My chief pilot – dear Tony, a lifelong friend was an eccentric character whom we nicknamed Bilbo Baggins, due to his extraordinary likeness to the lovable gnomic scatterbrain from Lord of the Rings. On our first encounter – my training flight, he arrived two minutes before departure (rather than the customary two hours) and had one trouser leg tucked into his sock, the other out, and great clumps of grass stuck to his shoes. His buttons were askew and he'd lost his mobile.

"So sorry Anita … overslept." He did have legendary bags under his eyes, was partially deaf and was always losing his expensive hearing aids. You always knew when Tony was with the previous crew because slipped down the side of his station there would invariably be a hotel key with a big plastic tag attached the size of a cheque book with '**Copthorne Hotel** please return if found' written on it. Some days you'd even find his house and car keys. Eventually he got so tired of losing his mobile he just left it at home.

"That way I always know where it is!"

He was deeply intelligent just a bit lateral! I loved him!

Another funny character was Captain 'Ray'. It was trendy at the time for names like 'Kevin' and 'Sharon' to appear on car windscreens. So he stuck our names Ray and Neeta to the windscreen of the Boeing as we pushed back from stand 11 at Gatwick going to Corfu. An amused handling agent took a picture of this and sent it to us.

We did Europe and sometimes beyond. Rowdy passengers were often a problem. The trouble normally started at the bar in the terminal. Long check in times and delayed departures compounded the problem. Groups of lads, in festive spirit would head for the bar to see who could pour the most pints of lager down their necks before boarding. Some of them managed a staggering four or five *even* at five thirty in the morning. A group were climbing the stairs onto the aircraft one morning when one lad caught sight of me in the cockpit shouted to his mate, "Oi Darren there's a f***ing *BIRD* in there, look!"

"Naah?"

The cockpit door was open and as they boarded, his mate stuck his head in the cockpit and said, "Bet they don't let ya park it love!!"

Guffaws of laughter followed, which I must admit had me chuckling.

There were happy drunks whose biggest beef was the queue for the toilets, and the refusal of more alcohol, but occasionally we got some nasty ones like the boxer with a gold tooth and long black leather coat and dark shades who obviously could kill with his bare hands; he ended up picking up one of the stewards by the neck, *that one* was a tad nasty. I don't think that flight attendant has ever been the same since. One of his party smoked in the toilet (probably not just tobacco), another threw an empty drinks tin at the cabin crew. We handed him over to the 'professionals' on landing at Gatwick. There was a chap – a *big* chap who was trained and indeed was a trainer himself in anti-terrorism and 'security' commonly known as 'agro'. He would be waiting for us on the gate and come straight into the cockpit.

"What seat number?"

"Thirty-one A."

Whoosh, he was off, quick as a flash down the back. He'd ask the person to come with him and if they refused (which was usually the case!) he'd handcuff them and lead them off the plane. I saw him once throw a guy to the ground and put his knee in his back in the aisle! This usually brought cheers and rounds of applause from the other passengers.

It was a comfort to know that service existed, it was better to get the problem inbound to the UK because if it happened outbound to, say Tenerife, we'd get little to no help at all from the security services at *that* end. The Gatwick boys were 'no messing about' sorts, swift in their assistance – proper 'Sweeneys'. Fortunately it didn't happen very often. I have a lasting memory of one guy in a scruffy old anorak being led off down the ramp yelling and screaming, "I'll see the lot of you tossers in court!"

A less serious incident was the day the purser came bursting in to the flight deck: "There are three guys at the back, they're pissed and blowing up life vests."

The Captain was a tiny, bald, slip of a man. 'B' the flight engineer was a bit overweight so he puffed and panted after the smallest of tasks. Climbing the aircraft stairs had him swooning and wheezing. I was fond of 'B' a lovely man, he got so breathless that he could never quite finish a sentence, the last couple of words would be mumbles and a sort of hum. All his kids seemed to be constantly backpacking round the world and phoning up to ask him to send more money.

Whenever I flew with *both* Adrian (big lad) and 'B' together Adrian would tell me to bring a pot of grease and a crowbar so I could squeeze around them in the cockpit!

On this occasion the small Captain and 'B' both looked at me and said, "Go on Neets you go and have a word, they'll listen to *you*!"

I went back. The idea (as taught in our security class) is to start nicely and calmly, appealing to their sense of reason.

"I know you're on holiday guys and you all want some fun – I understand but unfortunately tampering with any safety equipment is an offence and you will be fined." They really were like little school boys nudging and laughing.

"Watch out here comes the bird in uniform!"

"I bet you want to blow one too don't you?"

Explosions of congratulatory giggles from the two mates for *that* gag! They apologised but I said one of our cabin attendants would take their details and they would be hearing from us because that is the policy.

"Well it's only fair if we take *your* number as well …" his mate chirped in, "just in case you lot lose ours then we'll call *you* to make sure that you punish us correctly!!"

His mate considered this line such a blinder that he spurted his mouthful of beer all over the headrest of the seat in front which was the final straw for the long suffering occupant, a woman in a turquoise tracksuit and a head of bleached permed curls who rose out of her chair like a magician's poodle from a top hat. Furious, she turned round, planted the hands barnacled with 'bling' and sporting long square manicured nails firmly on her hips and glowered at them. Her mouth was tight like a sutured cut – her red lipstick bleeding up and down the lines.

"I think you should arrest the bloody lot of them!"

She had obviously been camping on the sunbed for the last month because she had a face like fried red cabbage.

When one of our hosties asked her to please sit down and fasten her seat belt, she started pointing her finger and waving her head which sent her dangly earrings flying around like glockenspiel keys. Then a secondary scene erupted, the mad, poodle perm lady thought she'd let me know just what she thought of this 'poxy bleedin' airline'. When asked to sit down again she launched:

"I'll have you bloody know, my Derek and I go on *THREE*' olidays a yeeya, we're not bleedin' paupers ya know and I ain't used to being treated like *this*. Call this a bleedin' aeroplane, it's a bloody disgrace, I've seen better interiors in public bogs! The seats are falling apart it smells and you've got no bloody entertainment, I mean we must be on the only plane in the whole bloody world which doesn't have any entertainment!" (She *did* have a point.)

Obviously this lady's family were used to this, the husband raised his paper a bit higher, the son whose baggy trousers had slipped round his thighs, pulled his woolly cap a bit lower, kept his shades on and kicked his feet in laceless oversized trainers while he upped the volume in his headphones and continued his spiritless munching of Pringles. The daughter who took gormlessness to quite another level just looked at her mum with no expression whatsoever and then went back to twiddling her (I would guess) brand new belly button ring which had turned septic and was bright red.

Then the life vest lads started to join in and tell her to shut her gob and so it went on. I did apologise for the lack of entertainment explaining that the 727 *was* an old aircraft which is why the seats were worn.

"OLD!!" she splurted before I could finish. "It should be in the bleedin' knackers yard, it's the antiques flamin' roadshow this is!"

The incident like many others ended safely and everyone calmed down, but there were times (and I experienced two of them) when we had to call upon the services of our friendly flying squad as we nicknamed them.

It would be unfair *not* to sympathise with irate passengers, God knows I've been one myself trying to go on holiday! They are often uninformed, no one tells them what's going on, and they endure dispiriting delays, then (only in the case of our airline) sit for hours in a seat with no movie. The more modern jets of course had the entertainment system. It can be a *bad* start to a holiday. (Funnily enough despite the 'high mileage' interior of our 727, Princess Margaret was a passenger once or twice and I saw her sitting in the front row sipping a scotch.)

I cringe when I think of the unceremonial dumping, at Gatwick, of a plane load of holiday makers who were bound for Manchester. This meant they incurred a long coach journey. The reason was that there was a backlog of delays and we needed *that* aircraft for the next flight which departed out of *Gatwick.* That is rotten. How our company rep could stand there on the ramp seeing the passengers off and give out orders as to their coaches – it was shameful!

Due to extensive delays one summer night at Gatwick we took off for the Greek island of Kos and we were out of duty hours to do the return journey (we are allowed to do, say thirteen hours but if we go over this we *have* to take rest, it is a CAA rule). Unfortunately the passengers who were all waiting eagerly in Kos to return home were met with the unwelcome news that the crew had to night stop and we would be leaving tomorrow at eight a.m.

Next morning, when we all marched in to the little terminal wheeling our bags behind us, our long suffering passengers gave a standing ovation and shouted: "All right loves, had your beauty sleep have you, yea don't worry about us we'll just sit in this bloody terminal another 24 hours no problem." I totally understood that frustration, but unfortunately we were bound by the rules.

There were some quite 'revelatory' moments working for an airline, where else would I have acquired such detailed knowledge of the S and M gay scene in Brighton? With all those gay flight attendants around me who simply *could not wait* for an opportunity to gush and tell, I had a crash course in gay-athons and fetish parties. There was one particular guy who played host to a permanent colony of cold sores round his mouth and could hardly hold himself back on a Monday morning to fill us all in (whether we liked it or not) on his lurid gang banging weekends, the bondage and whipping, the manacles and shackles, the rubber and truncheons. He was great for my diet because I never accepted a scrap of food from him when he was looking after the cockpit. We would all politely decline anything that was offered. God we heard some stories. We got truckers in women's clothing the lot! – I will never look at lay-bys on the M1 in quite the same light again.

We had one 'good ole boy' Captain from the deep south of the USA. Well 'listen up folks' this Cap'n L (said with real southern drawl) didn't take too kindly to gays, and he certainly didn't "wanna hear that s**t". He tried hard to fathom it out and show a modicum of acceptance. Pete the flight engineer and I tried to be neutral and non-judgemental to diffuse the situation.

"Hey it's just their preference, each to their own, as long as they do their jobs well ..." We offered to keep things 'sweet'.

'L' just said, "Ah guess so," and looked out of his window pensively with his coffee. I thought the conversation had reached closure, but he turned back a good ten minutes later and said, "But you know what I have a real hard time with?" obviously having been unable to dismiss it.

"Oh are we still on *that?* ...What is it?" I asked.

"They all might be nice guys 'n all, but at the end of the day ... they have to find some guy's big hairy butt attractive, and *thay-at* is what I personally have kinda a hard time with!"

Pete and I were crumpled, it *was* funny! We were forever smoothing things over.

We had one flight attendant, very sweet but who'd barely ventured out of Essex. Her boyfriend was a body piercer and she had a stud in her tongue (she had to remove it for work).

"Doesn't it get in the way of your food?" I asked once.

"No not really I get the odd noodle wrapped around it but vats about it."

One day in Nice we were all sitting round a table and she said, "Neets, what's salad Nick-o-I-see."

"It's a salad with tuna and egg and olives."

"I fink I'll have the burger."

She, was absolutely without pretence or guile and became a friend.

Duty time cards were something every crew member had to keep and she could never quite get the hang of local time and GMT (which we call zulu) and between which there is an hour's difference in summer. When European time was one or two hours *ahead*, again, it got more confusing. Having finished late after an exhausting multisector day, we ended up in a hotel in Bournemouth. The Captain, Adrian, arranged for the bar to stay open so we could all have a nightcap. We all agreed to meet downstairs in half an hour. As we dragged our bags up the stairs she said, "Is that half an hour local or half an hour zulu?"

"I'll just knock on your door when I'm going down hey?"

"Ah thanks."

December was a festive roster with fun filled flights to various European Christmas markets. One day, it was Vienna. The whole crew went off to eat KFC. Don't want to be stand offish but intensely reared foul, deep fried, isn't really my culinary paradigm so I said I'd wander round the Christmas market (splendid in Vienna!) and enjoy the, hot choccie and Viennese pastries.

"I fink I'll go with Neets, she can show me all the culture and all them nice markets."

She really appreciated what little snippets of information I could remember about Franz Joseph, Maria Theresa and their happy band of Hapsburgs and their glorious Austro-Hungarian Empire. We had fun that afternoon amongst the wooden cabins and sparkling lights; bought some lovely home-made Austrian bread and gingerbread men with smartie eyes.

Christmas time! – the airline became busy with flights to Lapland (during which we would all wear our red Santa hats). I'll never forget landing on a clear and steaming runway in minus thirteen degrees while all around the airport perimeter the snow was twenty feet deep! Those Scandinavians have bad weather procedures well and truly 'down'! The Germans might do heated car seats, but those Fins, they do heated runways! One bad memory was departing for Northern Finland, the plane had just come out of a big maintenance check during which all the seats had come out. Unfortunately the engineers had put the seats back in row by row from the front – but three seats were left out. (There are different ratchets in the floor rails so left rows aren't necessarily dead opposite the right rows.) The configuration looked perfect but we were actually one row of three short! Try explaining to a family of three who are standing there holding there boarding passes as the purser does a head count for the fifth time believing she is going *bonkers!* That was dreadful, not being able to understand for the life of you why the plane has less seats than last week, yet looks the same!

We did get some sideways glances from the passengers at times. On one flight I had to wear ridiculously unsuitable lycra hipsters (with silver rings round the waistband!) because I forgot to pack my uniform trousers – I got distracted by the phone mid packing and they never went in the case, so all I had was what I travelled up to Manchester in (for the night stop and early start) – thankfully they weren't the pink ones. I did look like a ninny though!

I managed to upset everyone by smelling of cow dung one day after we'd night stopped in Teeside and went to the Stainton Arms for the evening. Peter the engineer, who loves his 'Scottish wine' said, "C'mon it's pretty late, let's go as we are and get some food and drink." So we just threw a fleece on over uniform trousers.

Walking back down the country roads to the hotel in the pitch black I thought it a good idea to cut across the field, seeing neither the bull nor the carpet of cow pats. I ended up running then tripping into a load of them. I went to bed to be greeted the next day by the revolting sight of my trousers caked in dung, frantic scrubbing in the sink followed, but a faint acrid redolence, from my foot well wafted throughout the cockpit for the next few sectors! We discouraged cockpit visits on the next sector for fear the passengers might think it really was a manger!

As the summer progressed you could count on strikes down route. An old favourite is the baggage handlers strike around August when the whole world is on holiday. Ah yes, memories of Heraklion at two a.m. and not an **inch** of

169

parking space. There were planes… everywhere! A landing aircraft could not even proceed to a stand because even the taxiways were clogged with aircraft. We were not allowed to unload bags ourselves, (so insisted the baggage handlers) but I remember distinctly, three of us *INN* the baggage hold, and two cabin crew down below, making a chain to offload bags. We weren't exactly singing "hi-ho, hi-ho, it's off to work we go" … but it **did** work. In other corners of the ramp, British World, LTU, and Air 2000 were doing exactly the same. The few Greek staff on the ground were powerless against six angry, determined crew members all emptying their baggage holds! It was a fight. Often we'd have to hang around until three or four in the morning before the authorities would release us for the five hour flight back to Gatwick, and that *blinding* morning sun which was brutal on the eyes! But the most tiring bit was then sitting in the 'Road to Hell' morning rush hour to get home. I used to walk in at 8am. looking like roadkill– my family thought I was taking holiday makers not taking part in the Greek and Trojan wars!

The Football Flight

Santiago, Barcelona, Turin, these were just some of the European capitals where important football matches took place. Not being an aficionado of the sport (I thought UEFA was something you stuck in an ice cream) I don't know the difference between leagues, European championships, FA championships, cups, divisions or anything else! Here is a sport which never seems to boast a single 'local' in any team. Madrid is full of guys from England, Dutch teams are full of guys with dreadlocks, 'Van De' somebody's playing for distinctly un-Dutch teams, and French sounding chaps playing for Germany and you're hard pressed to find a single molecule of Mancunian DNA in Manchester United. Anyway I am a self-confessed zero when it comes to football.

We had, however, a lucrative contract taking fans down to see these matches – a memorable one was Turin. We could enjoy an eight hour day stop in the town during which time we could stroll, shop and have lunch. Our gay flight attendants went into frenzies over the Italian designer gear and spent fortunes on sunglasses which were knocked up in China for a fiver. Similarly a hostie who probably earned no more than ten thousand a year, spent a good portion of it on a Louis Vuitton handbag. It was, I thought just red, plain and ordinary.

"Why are you spending so much on a bag, can't you see that it is a rip off."

"But I really really want it."

"Wait 'til one of your mates goes to Dubai and get exactly the same thing for twenty dollars," I urged her, feeling so deeply grateful that I didn't fall victim to the ruinously expensive designer accessory band wagon. But she bought it and surprisingly enough didn't turn into Victoria Beckham, or any other model in a glossy magazine, no, she still looked like good old short, red headed freckly Sarah from Manchester clutching a bag which could have come from anywhere. I learnt much from my cabin crew about the justifications of being ripped off; I am to this day, still unconvinced.

In Turin, life continued as normal except for the thousands of Carabinieri (policemen), ambulances, steel railings, cones, police horses, and mean looking guys from the military with microphones. Isn't it strange that whenever English footballers go anywhere, the town becomes a fortification. I was ready to see grandfathers coming out of their homes with pitchforks, grandmothers wielding saucepans. I shamefully can't remember who was playing, but apparently it was a riveting match packed with all the drama we have come to expect – long haired guys rolling around screeching in agony clutching their ankle as they writhe and weep because someone kicked him in the shin. Then staggering painfully to their feet, making a few phoney limps and suddenly sprinting off with the speed of a greyhound. Quick recovery is a wonderful thing isn't it?

Back at the airport, all the planes were lined up, Airtours, Monarch, Air 2000, British World and many others. We all await, jockeying for position, eager to board the passengers and get out! Everyone knows what lies ahead – Bedlam. There were guys staggering around everywhere, people boarding the wrong aircraft, cabin crew directing them to their rightful planes. On the radios, the pilots were all chatting to the tower on VHF eager for their clearances. The unlucky ones (of which we were in the number) had late passengers which, of course delayed the departure. Fifteen minutes grace was all they'd get *that night* – because who knows how long they could be.

We were missing two; I sat in the cockpit watching British World, Monarch, and Airtours taxiing out to the hold. Sabre, our airline was of course the last one. The ambulance services were taking 'no more'! They were packing up for the night, so any Brit left now was on his own. Fiona our purser did the head count, entered the cockpit and said there was a guy who was so sick she didn't want to take him, his condition was just too dangerous, he was unconscious, and his mate was hardly George Clooney in ER. We called the agents to get an ambulance, their reluctance was apparent, they were *really* hoping to get shot of the Inglesi, but they did assist him off the plane and into an ambulance, his mate stayed with him. At that very moment when we were just about to close the doors for the second time I saw two guys with their jackets tied round their waists running across the tarmac towards the plane.

"Think we might have some late comers here."

"Okay," said the Captain, "we do have two seats 'cos of the off loads, I'll see how Fiona feels about taking them."

They had arrived in a drunken panic and asked if there were *any* seats left going *anywhere* in England. Obviously the Italian handling agent had pointed to us.

"*Andate!! …in fretta!*" she shouted pointing the aerial of her radio towards us. They made a run for it. **'Clunk'** went the big red handle as Fiona reopened the door and a ground crew pushed the stairs up to the door. It was clear the Italians didn't want them on *their* soil that night. They hadn't flown out with us and having missed their booked flight (the Airtours Captain had departed without them) they were trying anything just to get home.

Luckily for them we were still there and they bounded up the stairs two at a time and said, "Quality! … cheers mate, nice one guys thank you!" he winked and waved his tin of Carlsberg special brew at me then bounced his way down the cabin crashing into every other row on both sides. I guess the relief at not being stranded in a Turin bus shelter for the night had reawakened his enthusiasm.

"Hey if you're happy with them we'll take them … your call."

"Yea what the hell," replied Fiona "they are not going to get home otherwise and they are no more drunk than everybody else."

(This was 1998 – the world has tightened up **considerably** since!)

Well, this was a flight during which every sick bag was used! The flight was a series of frantic visits into the cockpit by the cabin crew giving us updates of inebriation.

"Ask him exactly what he's had?" I suggested to one of our poor inexperienced juniors who was finding it hard to cope. "Then at least I can get him medical help at Gatwick, if it's serious."

She was more Lancashire than flat capped Fred Dibnah this girl, the strongest northern accent I'd ever heard. We all loved her announcements after landing at Rhodes.

"Laaaydies and Gentlemen, on behalf of Saaybur erwaaays welcome ta Rhooorrds."

She came bursting into the cockpit, her usually sweet nature being tested.

"I can't oonderstand a flamin' wud they're sayin' these lads."

"How bad are they?" I asked.

"One of 'ems out sparko, and his maaate is mutterin sumit about three eeez and gramarcharlie, I don't know whether they've left a maate behind called Charlie if he wants his grandma or whaaat!!"

"Just leave them and check occasionally in case they need the therapeutic oxygen."

"Right okay then," she replied

"Well you're certainly in at the deep end on this one?" I laughed trying to cheer her up a bit.

"God you're not kiddin, place stinks like flamin' brewery, I've never seen so many people being sick!" It was during the clean up at Gatwick later that night whilst on her hands and knees that one hostie, when asked by the engineer what she was doing, shouted, head down, marigolds on, 'lookin' for the flamin' glamour!'

The airspace over northern France was busy that night and Paris control were handing us over to our appropriate London ATC frequencies. Those headed for Manchester were routed to Daventry, those for Gatwick to Mayfield, and those for Stansted up towards Barkway. Descent began, thank God. Anti-ice, altimeters, go around EPRs and reference speeds were set for landing; the hydraulics, pressurisation and circuit breakers, checked – we were number five in traffic and routed downwind for runway 26. We turned final and saw the electric carpet, those welcoming orderly dazzling lights of Gatwick's ground. The landing gear clunked into position, the flap motors ran to full travel at thirty degrees and down we came.

"Three greens, thirty thirty green light, cleared to land, landing lights on," sang out the engineer.

There are no words to describe the chaos of the cabin. Some just segued away quietly totally out of energy. Others woke up wondering where they were, some came round with the words "any chance of another bevvie"?

We managed to finally disembark them all. There were two at the back passed out in their seats. Someone's T-shirt read: "A woman's place is on my face!" The other one's T-shirt read: "Give me head 'til I'm dead!" each tasty caption accompanied by an appropriate and equally tasteful cartoon. The cabin crew stood there looking at them with their hands over their mouths just giggling. One had his head back, mouth open and was snoring loudly.

"He'll be flamin' lucky to get any girl to go near that *bloody* ugly face with *that* dribble runnin' down it, I'd rather sit on a flamin' cheese grater," said Miss 'Fed up' from Crawley.

The flight engineer finally trowelled them out of their seats and told them they must leave the aircraft now. I swear they had no idea where they were, as they walked down the cabin one said to the other as he fumbled in his jeans pockets.

"Hey you've got the car keys mate haven't you?"

"No I haven't got them mate, you said you'd look after them."

I knew it was going to be a long night for *those two*. I have witnessed the 'disappearing car syndrome' in airport car parks. It's amazing that birds with a brain the size of a mung bean can find their way back after a three thousand mile journey to a nest in a roof of *a certain* house in a *certain* street, after six months away, yet people after a few drinks can stand in a car park, utterly unable to recognise a*nything* a mere eight hours later.

"I'm sure it was *this* row, no no I remember this blue jeep ... wasn't it near that bus shelter-y type thingie?"

"There's bus shelter-y type thingies all over the bloody car park!" snarls unhelpful mate. And so it goes on as they march up and down hands on foreheads trawling their battered memories for clues.

Meanwhile the long suffering industrial cleaners arrived to reconstruct the cabin and try to eliminate the stench of vomit. Amongst the rubbish was even a pair of shoes – explain that one to me, I hope he wasn't walking home. We filled a whole bin liner with sick bags and *that* about sums up your average football flight.

(Just a tiny 'sermon on the mount' before leaving the pitch.) I do think the fans are very loyal and the recent announcement of ticket price rises is grossly unfair.

"But we have to pay all the wages and the running costs ..." say the pundits. Is it fair that the cost gets passed down to a working class dad who wants to take his two lads out for the day? Could they *possibly* contemplate for the sake of humanity and right and wrong, the reduction of the player's wage. Ok he can kick a ball accurately, probably balance it in the nape of his neck, and run very fast but wouldn't it be a tad fairer to trim a smidge off the quarter of a million a week he earns? I'm sure he'll still survive. Yup I know ... it will *never* happen, along with cheap fuel ... dream on!

What did Alexander Pope say? ... "Hope springs eternal in the human breast."

Samara, Russia

In the winter of 2002 our boss picked up a lucrative contract flying Italian engineers out to Russia, to a place well east of Moscow called Samara. One crew would pick them up from Milan and fly to Gatwick, the second crew would take them on to Samara. Then a local carrier took them to their final destination – Kazakhstan. It was a lengthy journey and if we had a headwind we would be twitching around about Berlin as to whether to come down for fuel because this place was right on the edge of our performance envelope in terms of distance. There wouldn't exactly be oceans of fuel sloshing around on landing! It was grim, cold, and pretty depressing. Lines of Ilyushin, Antanov and Yak aircraft were parked on the grey icy ramps. After the usual nausea of forms in triplicate, visas, passports, birth certificates, disclosures and references we would be ferried off in a bus from the Bolshevik revolution to what was generously termed a 'hotel'. The unfamiliar Cyrillic writing was everywhere amongst the grey concrete.

Because this was considered a 'hardship post' our boss had most benevolently agreed that the bar on arrival would be 'comped' or free! When you consider nine crew members, this shows the rather lucrative returns he must have been getting on this contract. So on arrival which was always roughly 2 am, we'd go to the bar for a nightcap. A few things stick in my mind about this hotel. The rooms though obviously very basic, did have the same radiators as the old schools. Massive great units of corrugated iron which could heat an assembly hall. In the corridor walking toward the lift I thought it a bit breezy. I walked to the end of the corridor, passed four dead plants in plastic buckets and pulled back the yellowed net curtain. I was rather glad I hadn't stepped any further because there was no window in it, it was the latest thing in air conditioning – a forty foot drop onto a pile of gravel. I opted for the stairs rather than the lift and found the bar at the end of the first floor. Having glanced around I cast my expectations for a good evening fairly low. But I was pleasantly surprised. I entered the bar, there were two Russian girls asleep, one on a bench and one on a chair with her feet up. God these poor girls, they had obviously been told to serve the crew who would be coming late!

They were both gorgeous creatures in that retro Russian way – dyed burgundy hair, miniskirts, boots and tons of make-up. I apologised for waking them but they sprang into life and applied lipstick. On went all the strip lights, then the wall mounted telly, all hissing and crackling. On went the stereo, good, a touch of Russian folk music for ambience, I mused, when suddenly at a thousand decibels came Kool and the Gang shrieking "Oh yes it's ladies night and the feeling's right ..."

Funny isn't it what they think *we're* going to like, just a lamp and some ethnic Russian ballads would have been nice.

But here we were inside a loud fluorescent biscuit tin of a bar with distorted sound bombarding us from all angles. Gradually everyone came down having changed out of uniform. Out came the vodka from the freezer, no label, and it was poured into tumblers. It was more like mescaline. After one of those my colleague thought he had one eye in the middle of his head, had somehow found solutions to all his problems and felt as though he was on a high speed train – one of those ones which uses magnetism and has no contact with the rails. The engineers were enjoying themselves immensely – well, free beer and lovely girls in miniskirts, it was worth the five hour flight! The menu came out – it was two pages of just single words in a list. There weren't meals per se, it said: perch, egg, tomato, cucumber, potato, all as single items. Oh well at least it made it simple. We all ate and drank and did our best to communicate with the handling agent and the two girls who rather enjoyed the party in the end. Many of the local girls coveted this job once they heard about all the Italian engineers who would be frequenting the place.

We slept until midday, then returned to London with a different bunch of Italians who had done their two weeks in Kazakhstan, they looked decidedly chirpier than the ones going out.

I returned to Russia many times – it's not my favourite place. It's strange how Russia, so keen to be doing business with the West now is still a quagmire of inefficiency. Corruption is like a woodworm.

We flew many extraordinarily wealthy people in and out of there all having a slice of the pie. I was stopped one afternoon, having visited the Kremlin, on the Russian equivalent of the Champs Elysees by two aggressive cops who were trying it on.

"Excuse me can I see your passport please?"

"Well I don't carry it, it's back at the hotel."

"We have to fine you four hundred Euros."

"No you don't – just come with me to the Marriott which is up the road and you can see it."

"No it is O-ffence to not hev passport on person."

These guys know visitors like us have foreign currency so they try because occasionally they get a hit, but they chose the wrong person that day, I was brought up amongst Nigerians. I knew as soon as they started to reduce the fine to 200 euros, they were having me on.

"I didn't know the rules, sorry, but as I said please come back to the Hotel and I'll show you all my ID."

"Ve can put people in jail for not heving peppers."

"Okay well let's go then and I'll explain to your superiors in the police station what has happened," and I made a gesture for 'handcuff me'.

They tried one more go at 100 Euros but when I just smiled politely, looked them in the eye and shook my head, they cleared off to try someone else but not without hissing at me in Russian. Cajoling surly corrupt officials has become second nature.

As I moved off I saw a 'New Bond Street' type of shop window which was simply enormous. It had a huge cut out of a skinny super model in a fancy leopard skin bra trimmed with fur. The square footage of the shop was staggering, it could have been a car showroom. There were just a few exclusive pieces of luxury lingerie in there hanging on little individual silk padded hangers. I saw a bra which cost two hundred and twenty Euros. Up a sweeping staircase some little lace panties adorned the three shelves on the top floor. Outside this shop, an old lady, worn out, shrunken and bent wearing about four overcoats and a headscarf was pulling one of those dilapidated carts that would normally be attached to a donkey. With fingerless gloves she rooted through a dustbin. There are some sad sights out there. I am no sabre rattling socialist but the iniquity there is hard to stomach.

Certainly for me, it's more a case of 'From Russia *without* much Love'.

Lourdes

Ireland became a common destination after we picked up a contract to fly the sick and disabled hopefuls to Lourdes to be cured of their illnesses. This is when I first saw the deep and blind faith which burns in the Catholic soul. We'd fly from Dublin, or Shannon down to Lourdes with some very unwell people. Sometimes up to a quarter of them needed wheelchairs, some were in callipers, some on breathing apparatus, others bent with arthritis, some completely crippled. They believed that they would be cured by a visit to the sacred place where the vision of the Holy mother was seen. Being somewhat of a humanist/atheist, this unshakable belief in the power of our lady was astonishing.

"How come there are only four wheelchair requests for the return and over fifteen on the outbound?" I queried looking over the passenger manifest in my seat. My Captain feted for his sarci sense of humour and a 'seeing is believing' attitude, looked over his bifocals and said in his best 'oirish' accent.

"Because the Lord is going to make me legs wuurk again, so he is." Yes it was true many of them only ordered wheelchairs for the outbound, so convinced they were of the miracles to come. One splash of the holy water and they would be doing a Van Morrison 'skippin and a jumpin'. I quietly told the man at Serviceair to have a few more standing by 'just in case'.

I did notice with a touch of amusement how the priests (all very able bodied) who were accompanying these pilgrims would make sure they plonked themselves in the best seats with the most leg room and wasted no time diving into the Jameson. I have to say some of those passengers touched my heart profoundly. I went back into the cabin to help with the long disembarking procedure. I held the hand of one elderly lady who stopped me, wanting to talk. Her hands, although old and wrinkly, had the softest of skin, her palms were like silk. She had pancreatic cancer and was frail, but she laughed and smiled refusing to indulge in her own misfortunes.

"What a clever girl you are, you're lovely," she said putting my hand to her cheek. There were others in so much pain their friendliness and optimism were *really* humbling. I squatted down to be at eye level with them trying my best to make them laugh and be a good listener. I discovered on those flights a little part of myself – a part that loved helping people and the fact that a laugh from a handicapped person gives more reward than a new car. People's feelings are more important than 'things' or objects. It was rewarding to play a tiny part in their joy, some had saved up for years to do this trip.

We invariably needed all the wheelchairs again to disembark in Ireland, having said that, I will always remember that unflinching faith. I found myself wanting to be a 'happy clapper'. I felt leaden booted, cynical and a victim of my 'if that's true I'll eat my hat' attitude, so bound up with logic and proof which can be somewhat juiceless. I didn't 'convert' as such, but they did show me something – quite profound about the power of hope.

The Honey Bucket

This is just a bit of toilet talk, but nonetheless quite humorous. The contents of the toilets all go into a holding tank. On the Boeing 727 there are forward and aft toilets, which are electrically flushed into this holding tank, which is primed with three gallons of disinfectant, dye and a deodorising solution. There is a timed flusher and rotating filter and the holding tank does its job perfectly. The truck complete with hose and pump which empties this at airports throughout the world is affectionately known by us, as 'the honey bucket'. At all airports (well so I thought until a brief visit to SierraLeone) this is a very efficient means of emptying. Along comes the man (be careful to call him the hygiene engineer) who unscrews the big filler cap, attaches the hose and 'Bob's your uncle' the contents are sucked out into *his* holding tank on the truck, he refills you with water and blue disinfectant – job done.

In Sierra Leone, when they came to the aircraft, we said we would like the toilets servicing, and asked if they had the honey bucket.

"No no no – not hee-ar – we doon need dis machine we can do it ourself."

"Okay this should be interesting."

Then two Africans approached with a couple of black bin liners one inside the other and proceeded to search for the door housing the filler cap into the plumbing of the waste lines, so they could hold the bags below and "catch de content inside de bag". Well that was certainly a first. I wonder if the writers of the systems manual at Boeing in Seattle would now insert an amendment into the toilet servicing chapter – 'Can also be emptied manually'. I think perhaps not.

On this subject of the toilets – a quick deviation. When I was doing my Boeing 727 type rating in California, the ground school teacher who was a tubby, piggy faced cynic with the most sarcastic sense of humour told us about the big blue ice ball that was hanging from the toilet drain on the underside of a passenger 727 – there was a leak or the drain heaters were not working in the toilet (something like that) and the effluence was escaping, but due to the temperature of minus fifty-six degrees it just remained in a great big ice ball, it was *blue* because of the chemicals. In his words:

"Anyhow, this godamn ball o' blue ice full of all kindsa piss and crap in suspension finally breaks off and falls to earth. As luck would have it, fell on some one horse town in Iowa, so you can imagine George and Marge in overalls and apron eating their cornbread on the porch, never been further than the end of the road, suddenly see this blue ice ball falling from the heavens, so they think it's some kinda f******'sign from outa space and they've been singled out for a journey to another dimension. Then they were kinda bummed when four hours later it's melted and they got a yard full of goddam airline turds."

He was wiping away the tears as he told this story!

Back in West Africa when Adrian, the Captain went to pay the airport fees, there were bullet holes in the building big enough for him to get his fist through. Of course he was utterly ripped off – but you expect this in Africa. (Like the time they paid 4 US dollars per gallon in Ougadougou having just paid 1 US dollar at Stansted.)

When our 727 landed in Sierra Leone during the troubles in 2002, the crew were whisked off in a massive great Russian helicopter out of harm's way (that means *away* from the bit where they were physically **firing** on foreign aircraft and off into the jungle part where we'd hopefully be in a compound and have to grapple with less pressing threats like bandits, cannibals and tribal killings). The helicopter was crewed by three and went low level at night with no lights, which was a tad non-conformist. But there is much Russian hardware down there – tanks, helicopters and all sorts of equipment which arrives in the massive Ilyushin 86.

The hotel was fine. Under the balmy African skies the crew went to the pool later that evening and against the background of screeching cicadas and other sounds of the night, they went swimming. They left their belongings on chairs around the pool and – strange, but the contents of their wallets seemed to diminish considerably. 'Teef man' as they are known in West Africa move deftly in these parts.

Something amusing or terrifying usually happens in this part of the world. Adrian my colleague and the Captain on the Sierra Leone trip told me of his previous visit to Monrovia in Liberia to collect Charles Taylor (Chuck as we called him), well famed for genocide and butchery. The airport 'Roberts International' was so completely decimated and wrecked, when he requested temperature and QNH (pressure setting for the altimeter) he got:

"Sorry, please everyting is broken, we don have any equip-ment!" Adrian had to fly out over the sea and use the Radio Altimeter to get a height readout, you only hope it's reading the surface and *not* the seabed! When he landed there was no fuel so he had to fly fifteen minutes north to Spriggs Payne which is about the size of Redhill (small for a 727) and reverse taxi down a narrow rough track with sheep and goats everywhere; he said he must have done the equivalent of ten landings in tyre wear!

Back at Roberts International in Monrovia, old Chuck wouldn't board via the rear stair which is part of the plane, an integral piece of Boeing structure, therefore …SAFE! No, no no, he came up the **front** even though there was no staircase there!

"Why?"

"Because he's de **Pres**," said Adrian sarcastically.

He was actually the former president of Liberia who sponsored the Revolutionary United Front in order to destabilise Sierra Leone, the country which was preventing him from taking the Liberian capital.

"So …" in propa African style, he brokered the deal with Burkino Faso for the supply of mercenaries with payment in diamonds to be made in Sierra Leone.

"Eh heh … sweet." You can just picture the interview can't you?

"I have always don de best for mah peoples, and I will fight corrop-shon where ever it is!"

The trouble was *that* day, all that was available at the airport was a rickety old wooden ladder like a window cleaner would use, they propped that on the side of the front fuselage and he climbed up that and into the entry door. "Because propa airstair no deh!"

'But it deedan matter because he was entering at de front and not de back – ees betta'. That appealed to his sense of rank, better to climb up the front than use the proper sturdy metal staircase made by Boeing because that was at the *back*.

Never a dull moment in 'dis beautiful Africaa'!

Just a closing mention whilst on the subject of the airports in Africa. A few years later when back on the private jets I landed at Dar Es Salaam, as I taxied in I noticed a party going on under some gazebos *right* in the middle of the parking area. In Europe the airside parking and taxi areas are **very** highly protected and policed. You **can't** go on them without appropriate passes. Movements are strictly controlled by ground frequencies and *nobody* apart from authorised staff is allowed. But here was a party with people dancing, a couple of dogs running around, a barbeque smoking away and everyone enjoying beer and some women in colourful African headdress waving their hands above their heads.

"What's going on over there?" I asked the African handling agent after we'd shut down.

"Oh dats a patt-ee."

"A party!" I said, "what *on* the actual ramp with aircraft taxiing all around!"

"Yes som big bank I tink HSBC have jost paid for a new extension to the airside, today it is opening so dey are celebrating!"

Different world, I thought to myself. Why not? They trust themselves not to cause any problems. It would, I felt sure run smoothly and without incident, but it *was* a funny sight. I just somehow couldn't imagine pulling in at Luton and seeing a few guys throwing some sausages on a barbeque and a bit of Karaoke going on in the middle of Stand sixteen outside the Britannia hangars!

Freight ... or is that... 'Fright'

It was my 'bête noire' the least enjoyable flying I ever did. I remember so vividly the great shards of freezing rain lit up under the huge fierce stadium spotlights. It was bleak. Under these Gestapo lights, men in all weather gear would be running around like workers out of an Orwellian nightmare. Guys in what looked like fallout suits had microphones attached to their mouths and were shouting instructions at one another. They wore dark boiler suits and gloves. They moved quickly in an atmosphere of panic and hard labour. Handheld radios on full volume shrieked out instructions.

Goods would be loaded into hug steel igloos which, once on board would be pushed back by our gloved men in their 'nuclear' suits. The floor of the freight hold (which was the entire back of the plane – a huge space) was covered with little castor wheels and the igloos would slide across them and go crashing to the back. They would continue shoving them down one after the other, until we were full, from port to starboard and up to the ceiling. It was like being in a rather sinister, science fiction movie full of menace and clatter. And it was always so horribly cold – I didn't survive long enough to experience the summer months, I am sure they were much more pleasant! It was a hideous unreal scene – a collection of steel conveyor belts, huge steel containers and grumpy people who understandably wanted to be home in bed. If the scene had an expression in celluloid it would be dark David Lynch's Eraserhead. It had all the ingredients: struggle, oppressive industrial environment, mutants, screaming and sleeplessness. I'm sure Ingmar Bergman could have got involved.

The load sheets were vast complicated things the size of a broadsheet newspaper. It really was the first time I felt I didn't belong and I had no desire to belong. Vast quantities of, sometimes, decidedly unsavoury 'stuff' would be loaded. We had to look at the contents – these were astonishingly unpalatable at times, and the Captain would then sign the acceptance form. Some nights we carried Hepatitis B, (what form *that* takes I don't know but I saw those words!). There were vaccines, strange bacteria and other sinister things– I assumed they were going to some laboratory for research. In my short time there we carried radioactive material, toxic and infectious substances and all manner of hazardous concoctions. Normally I am glad of my imagination that can, at times, fizz like two huge alka seltzer in a glass of champagne, but on *those* flights I could have done without it! I would be cruising along through the starry night skies of Europe and have visions of the 'Alien'. I'd see small but deadly bacteria escaping from the rivets in the igloos and multiplying in a frenzy of self-replication. The Captain would have a heart attack, the flight engineer after having trodden on his only pair of specs was rendered blind, so I would have to do the Sigourney Weaver bit, grab the crash axe and go into the fetid ochre coloured air contaminated by escaping miasmas and engage in hacking off slimy tendrils as they fought their way out of their cold steely cages. Fortunately and perhaps not surprisingly this never happened! Such imaginings sure helped to keep me awake though!

Because freight flying is invariably at night, you have to learn to adjust your body clock. At the base in Liege, which was the European hub for TNT Federal Express and many others, they provided a crew room where you could rest. One night, in dire need of some shut eye I went in – it had six big reclining leather chairs down each side and it was dark, full of snoring exhausted men and it stank of cheesy feet. I lay in one of those chairs wrapped in my huge anorak one night thinking 'Nah this is NOT for me'. Glad I experienced it but it really was just too bloke-ish and too hard. Utterly grim is the word actually. Once you had got your voucher and had your free meal downstairs in the dungeon canteen, you could have a snooze until you were woken by some kind ops staff. I was so deeply asleep one night and had to be shaken out of my recliner. Then you faced the very depressing prospect of two legs, say to Lisbon and Seville with a bunch of chemicals in a plane without a loo flying through night storms. It was a cheerless prospect. I met some cracking engineers though, especially Peter Shaw, who saved the day in Orebro (north Sweden) with his 'Scottish wine'. You could never get your comforting pre sleep beer out of the 'rule book' Swedes. Peter would always treat us to a tot of his Scotch!

When you got to destination at about seven a.m. you would breakfast on meatballs and herring (in Sweden), then go off to the room, snap your curtains closed, put earplugs in and try to sleep while hoovers went off in next door rooms. Later that afternoon, you would rise and prepare to do it all again. I take my hat off to guys who can do this every night because I found it the most dispiriting and depressing activity. I only did it because the airline I was with picked up a lucrative freight contract and we all had to take it in turns to rotate out to Belgium and do a week of night freight. I found it tough and didn't last long.

It was a fascinating insight to a world which is so tightly and efficiently run. The logistics of getting goods, commodities and parcels (and the odd nasty!) all over the world takes a hell of a lot of organisation and staff. We were only one small part. It involves the delivery *to* airports, loading, unloading *then* distribution *from* airports at the other end. All the time it is followed and tracked. It is undeniably an impressive and complex network involving many professionals.

Interior of executive 727

Executive lounge on board.

Master bedroom & ensuite bathroom
on board.

Our lovely hostie dusting the
cockpit after a flight.

Hosties Susie & Donna singing Celine Dione
into wash-up brush mikes!

The Forbes 727 – The most beautiful je
I ever flew.

Me in the middle of 727 crew, Lapland, N. Finland – note spectacular paint job of the Cougar!

Airline days.Crew going for lunch – Santiago Spain.

Pushing back from stand at Gatwick, our names Neeta and Ray on windscreen (Ford Escort style) a good practical joker that captain.

CHAPTER FOUR: Farewell 727 – Moving On

Set to Jet

The noise became an issue with the beautiful but loud, gas guzzling 727, so owners started to trade them in for more modern vessels. Due to noise restriction they were excluded from landing at many airports such as Geneva and Brussels. It was time to make the move from analogue, time to leave those lovely Pan Am 'Catch me if you Can' sort of days and fly something more modern. We had yet another sliding doors situation. I was owed a load of money from salary in arrears on the 727 (not unusual) and went up to Luton to collect it from the Captain. Whilst there I bumped into an old friend who was flying Lear Jets for Gold Air. I asked him who was hiring … having been out of the loop, I was unsure. He recommended a company in the South of England who flew many different types including Citations – perfect. I applied, went for an interview and got accepted. I flew the Citation for a while then moved on to the bigger, more luxurious and decidedly more expensive Embraer Legacy. This landed me in a different league of passenger. Here's a little compendium of events while flying for *two* executive jet charter companies.

Skibo Castle for 'The Apprentice'

Following on from the huge successes of Donald Trump's 'Apprentice' in the States, BBC2 jumped on the bandwagon and made an equally successful series in the UK with Sir Alan Sugar. People were glued each week as some poor struggling aspirant got the merciless finger pointed in their face and heard the words "You're fired" as they were slaughtered on the corporate slab.

We are a funny lot aren't we? Relishing the sight of someone struggling then being admonished and abandoned. We are hooked on argument, confrontation, misery and failure. Call me old-fashioned but since when did businesses *really* thrive and succeed when its workforce were all actively encouraged to point the finger, stab in the back, sneak on their pals and be consumed by self-aggrandisement? Answer: all the time actually – so *enough* of my principles, 'Vive le show' I say, for I had the most wonderful experience because of it. Two of the contestants (James and Sirah) were treated, as a reward for their successes so far, to a night up in the magnificent Skibo Castle in Northern Scotland, and the private jet chartered to take them up there, happened, fortuitously to be the one I was flying for a company in Oxfordshire.

The little seven seat Citation Ultra, G-OGRG, was parked at Luton and we were briefed that the film crew from 'Talk Back Thames' would be arriving to do some pre-flight footage – shots of the plane, the two contestants being welcomed, boarding the aircraft and celebrating with the champagne. They filmed us in the cockpit going through the check lists, footage which ended up on the cutting room floor – that was the end of the movie star career!

"Romeo Golf, taxi Alpha one holding point runway 26, QNH 1008," came the voice from the tower. Off we went, with James and Sirah who were relaxed, and sipping champers. Sirah had become known as the 'gobby one' but had also proved to be very engaging and certainly not short of backbone. Not surprisingly she has gone on to carve out a successful career for herself (without Alan Sugar!) and I've seen her make many TV appearances.

We advanced the throttles and sped off down the runway.

"Positive climb, gear up … acceleration altitude … flaps up …"

Luton: "Romeo Golf squawk ident and climb five thousand feet."

A few moments later we set 'standard' on the altimeter of 1013 millibars and climbed away from the London Terminal area.

"After take-off check list."

We set course towards Daventry, Trent and Manchester, or Pole Hill as it's known to us. It was a beautiful September day and we all enjoyed the resplendent views of the Peak District and the Yorkshire Dales. Great swathes of gold, copper and rose spread out around the huge conurbations of Sheffield and Manchester then up beyond Leeds. The scenery grew more beautiful and rugged as we flew north across Hadrian's Wall and up towards Glasgow. This is one of the rare sights in England when you can see both the coasts together, Carlisle on the west and Newcastle in the east. We cruised across the Highlands and made our descent for Inverness.

I was sure we would be in an Airport Holiday Inn Express "like what we normal do" (so says my mate from Devon). But one of the greatest treats of my life was about to befall me, we, yes WE were invited to stay in Skibo Castle with the guests. How lucky!

Two gleaming Range Rovers (green of course) straight from the pages of 'Country Life' were waiting for us on the apron. The guests went off in one and we two pilots were invited to climb into the other. This is a courtesy which Skibo extends to all its guests. The driver – a jolly Scotsman who'd lived up there all his life, wore plus fours and a green tweed jacket with patched elbows. I sat in the front and listened with interest to his stories, both old and new, of life at Skibo Castle the most famous and luxurious castle in Scotland.

The drive was spectacular, around the Black Isle, through charming and 'new to me' places with nice names like Culbokie and Invergordon. Ah … **this** is where Cromarty is, good old Cromarty of BBC's shipping forecast fame. He pointed out the Glenmorangie distillery, which, so he said, had the tallest distilling towers of any in Scotland, so creating the smooth honeyed taste of the pale gold malt whisky. On we pressed up the A9, to Dornoch. It is hard to capture in words how strikingly beautiful the approach to the castle is. It was getting dark and warm red lights glowed from the windows.

185

A large rotunda of grass lay in front of the imposing, pillared entrance. A low balustrade stone wall ran along the left of the circular drive and beyond that lay the fabulous mulberry and green coloured hills undulating away into the far distance. As soon as you enter the great hall with its carved banisters, great staircase and stags heads, a short, beaming, plump butler is standing, with a tray of sherry and fine malt whisky.

One of the most unusual (and refreshing) things about this place was the absence of keys and of check in! In fact no money seemed to change hands at all. It's like going to a friend's house for the weekend. That is a hard feeling to create and they have done it perfectly.

The welcome is warm, you simply take a pew on the comfy sofa by the roaring fire and a smiling lady sits down next to you knowing full well who you are, introduces herself and informs you about your room, where you'll be dining and what's on the fun and games agenda the following day – archery, riding, clay pigeon shooting and so on. She gives you a map of the grounds and details of activities and then invites you to have another drink if you so wish then climb aboard your very own golf cart and be shown to your exquisitely appointed suite of unparalleled luxury.

The rooms in the main house were of the massive four-poster variety but even so, mine, being one of the cabins in the woods, was still the epitome of taste and comfort! They all had huge fluffy down duvets, tartan throws and pillows of incomparable goose feather softness. For someone who would normally be plumping up her single foam filled pillow in the local Holiday Inn Express this was a joyous treat. The bathroom was gleaming, and a fully equipped living area complete with, TV, CDs and DVDs, a roaring fire, fully stocked kitchen and bar, meant you could indulge in everything from a cuppa with toast and marmalade to the finest malts. Barbours, hats, wellies, scarves and walking sticks were by the front door – you simply wanted for nothing.

What a man that Andrew Carnegie must have been. The son of a weaver he emigrated to Pittsburg in the mid 19th century age twelve and created a huge steel empire. But instead of the greed and egomania which is the hallmark of so many of these tycoons, he was a great philanthropist, fascinated by many things – education, the arts, peace, international trade and the betterment of the human race. His heart always returned to the Highlands and in the calm and tranquillity there, he thought up the magic which is Skibo. He entertained lavishly, his guests included great writers, kings, politicians, musicians and other distinguished benefactors. His aim was to bring together like minded people from different nations and walks of life and indulge in stimulating conversation, outdoor pursuits and enjoy the spirit of good will and amity in the most elegant and comfortable surroundings possible.

Still today that spirit lives on because after dinner, of the finest smoked salmon and venison in the oak panelled room with the roaring fire and elegant drapes, when you retire to the lounge, you simply mingle with other guests as though in someone's front room. You just help yourself to drinks, and if someone is left out, there is the court jester (as I named him) who sported a Billy Connelly type goatee and wore a flamboyant red tartan suit. *He'd* make sure everyone knew each other. It went something like:

"Have you met Anita?" he said linking my arm. "She flew the contestants from the TV show the Apprentice up here today."

"Hey howya doin' Aneeda."

"This is John ... John owns ... is it err ... it's Kentucky that you own isn't it?"

It turned out that the glamorous New England golfing party whose wives all resembled Christie Brinkley had Massachusetts sewn up between them and the others had a firm grip on the Boston banking scene. I had a lovely chat with the couple who 'owned Kentucky' and they dazzled me with their itinerary which included South Africa, St Petersburg, and Paris. Meanwhile the rotund smiling, ever so slightly mad butler kept cruising around with his tray of fine brandies and whiskeys. It was like waltzing into the shimmering, taffeta world of an Agatha Christie mystery. Though in spite of these flamboyant personalities, I hoped there'd be no appearance of Hercule Poirot after a gunshot from the library that night!

"Have you seen the dining room?" asked the court jester as he held his arm out pointing the way. It was magnificent – a fairy tale. Dark wooden panelling gently toasted the room which was beautifully proportioned and furnished and had the sort of table from which you wouldn't want to excuse yourself early. What feastings and banter must have taken place there. It was fabulous.

We stayed up late, chatting on the huge squashy sofas in the drawing room, the fire crackling, the Lagavullen slipping down with ease. James and Sirah were on great form, brimming over with optimism. Antique oil paintings of the Scottish mountains and portraits of various important Lairds hung on the walls around the grand piano on which sat some fresh flowers filling the place with gorgeous scent.

Breakfast was in the great hall. Inside the huge ornate silver ice bucket were nestled the finest frozen vodkas and champagnes. Freshly squeezed juice accompanied them. On offer were scrambled eggs, caviar, smoked salmon, fresh fruit, and of course toast and marmite along with every tea known to man. Meanwhile, in the background the man 'with the owl' had arrived. In between bites of beluga caviar and shots of vodka you could wander over to the fireplace, don his thick leather glove and feed a beautiful little owl pieces of raw chicken, whilst the organist, aloft, hammered out a bit of Bach. Not exactly your standard 'brekkie'.

A piper clad in tartan kilt blew on his bagpipes outside the front door. This was heralding the start of the falconry display. A bonny lad (perhaps son of strapping chap on the porridge oats box) with a winning smile and a palpable love for his birds put on a terrific show. He had several birds, but his 'jewel' was the peregrine falcon which swooped down at breakneck speeds – these birds are *fast*. He swung his dead chick around on the end of his rope and the bird shot past low level, almost shaving hair from our heads then climbed up around the turrets, settled on the chimney pot and eyed us up for a minute then shot down again like a bullet locked onto his breakfast being lassoed around. He finally landed and won his prize and devoured the dead chick, accumulating a fur ball in his throat which he then bought up!

The falconer filled us in with fascinating facts and stories about his treasured birds, their feathers, their habitat, hunting techniques and marvellous eyesight – what? Spot a vole seven miles away! He finished by putting the little leather cap over the bird's head. It completely covered the little head so it was blinded, apparently they love this! It was very fetching with its little tassel and bell on the top. At this moment when the hooded bird was perched on his master's arm, an American voice whispered from behind me, was it the banker from Boston? I believe it was.

"Gad, that's kinda kinky … I like that, it's sorta like the one I got you for Christmas last year honey."

The day at Skibo just got better. I went from there to the archery – my respect for Robin Hood rose because it is *very* difficult. Then it was clay pigeon shooting, a bit of riding and some tearing around in the off road vehicles. There was a minor emergency when the two girls from the film crew came running into the foyer red faced, they had got their golf cart stuck in the mud and needed a tow! The grounds were exquisite and enchanting. There was a delightful pool and spa in a Victorian/Kew Gardens style building – all glass and wrought iron. Round every corner, views just stopped you in your tracks. Scenery which had you building palaces in your imagination.

A quick visit to the golf club was a 'must'. That boasted what *had to* be one of the top club houses anywhere. Big picture windows gave on to panoramic uninterrupted views of wild Scottish countryside. It was like the painting you see on a whisky bottle! All throughout the golden ripe landscape were large clusters of mauve heather. Nature was respected everywhere, fishing was done from a boat so as not to disturb the habitat of certain animals living on the bank.

I loved the fact that cell phones were banned and butlers were on hand round every corner serving drinks. Another appealing fact was that it didn't matter if you were God, the pope or first president of earth, you couldn't just rock up at this place with wodges of cash and ask for the imperial suite, no, you have to be invited and become a member and so on, protocol you know. Normally money can buy absolutely everything, so I found this just a splash refreshing. One of the tweed clad groundsmen told me that they'd had one of those "Do you *know* who I am"?!! sorts turn up once and it manifestly didn't matter **who** he was, he was *not* staying the night. He was rather drunk also which didn't help. He was politely rejected along with his ego and money. I entertained a rather tickling thought of self-appointed 'Lord Pooh Bah' being turned away, a gilley on each arm disappearing into the mist towards the Aston in a series of ever decreasing little explosions.

I returned my Barbour and wellies to the closet in the great hall and left to smiles and handshakes.

"Goodbye Anita, hope you've enjoyed your stay."

"Yea well, it's been so so I suppose," I joked with the manager.

It was the most personal and special hotel experience of my life.

Our little Cessna Citation was all alone on the ramp parked under a livid sky. Bluish black storm clouds rushed along and icy gusts signalled an approaching storm. Our two guests arrived in their Range Rover and jumped aboard all smiles, seemingly having had a ball. No matter what the outcome of 'The Apprentice', I'm sure they would both treasure the memory of having been inside the walls of such a magical place.

Funnily enough having done this exciting trip for Sir Alan's contestants, I ended up one year later flying the man himself. During 2005 I worked for a company who boasted amongst their clients the Sugar family, and the Pears family, we just needed 'Cream' family and we'd have had the sweet trolley! The Pears were a charming family of brothers who had *so much* property … everywhere. The Sugars – well I think most people know Sir Alan. He went often to his Malaga home with his lovely wife and son Daniel. Once having picked him up from there, we brought him back to Stansted, and while taxiing in, Sir Alan noticed that one of his *other* smaller jets was out on the ramp – not in the hangar.

"What the **** is my plane doing out there then?"

"Oh they've got a British Airways Embraer in the hangar, for its maintenance so they will have towed yours out to make room I suspect," I said.

"Well I'll be expecting a bloody refund on my hangarage fees then," he said quick sharp. You can see perhaps why people didn't get away with much with this man who didn't miss a thing, and drove a granite bargain!

There was obviously never a dull moment. A keen aviator himself he enjoyed sitting with us in the cockpit and joining in. He sat beside me one day as we flew the approach into Stansted.

"Stansted Tower Golf Sierra India Romeo Alpha, fully established ILS 23," I piped up.

"Romeo Alpha you might well be but this is Stapleford airfield, suggest you try Stansted tower 123.8."

Oops I'd dialled the wrong frequency; I expected that finger to come up in front of me with a "You're **Fired**"! He keeps one of his planes at Stapleford so knows them well and actually found it very amusing!

Me with Jo & Caroline, at the
World Cup in Athens.

Athens Airport: with
colleagues, World Cup

Jeddah, Saudi: with Julie, my friend
and hostie, in the Darth Veda kit,
mandatory before disembarking.

Derby Day, 1987: my mate Jenny with her
helicopter pilot, Adam & engineer, Mike

Derby Day, 1987: the helicopter crew's lunch.

North Weald, 1986: Carrie & me, Stomp biplane.

Kidlington, 1985: Marwan, Carrie and me. The first Beech Baron of 'Gama' – now a hugely successful company.

Uni mate Sonia on 'just graduated' hols to Kenya on Egypt Air. Cockpit visit.

Coventry Museum: larking about doing the 'dam busters' with mum.

Isle of Wight: Willz, fellow instructor & good friend, doing 'comms check'. "Read you fives"

Mike Woodley stands proudly on the wing of C119 In front of warbirds at his hanger in North Weald.

Spotted on a trip to Florida – Good advice!

The indomitable Brendan O Brian, having landed on the moving truck – his party piece!

Berlin – Tempelhof

I was as pleased as punch when operations informed me that I was off to Berlin for a couple of nights. Our airport would not be the usual Schoenfeld, it would be 'Berlin-Templehof' (just its name has a certain ring). Rumours were that it was about to close, so this made the chance to see it one last time even more attractive. It's a hugely important airport historically, the production place for the Stuka and the Fokewulfe aircraft, the embodiment of Hitler's quest for supremacy, and of course it was the airfield used during the tearfully impressive Berlin airlift when human dedication and courage kept an entire city alive.

We left Venice for Berlin. The contrast could not have been starker. Venice is so intoxicatingly ancient and artistic. The crumbling walls, creaky shutters and struggling foundations of the watery city with its romantic disappearing backstreets, and colonnaded piazzas full of music and masks, is so vastly different from the strong, Teutonic sturdy looking Berlin which lay in front of us as we approached on to the westerly runway. The most striking thing about landing there is that you are smack bang in the middle of the city. It's rather like landing in Green Park in London. Most airports are traditionally out of the city but this one is right in its beating heart. Berlin personifies the bohemian lifestyle of the thirties, the smoky jazz bars, the sleazy cabaret shows, the song and dance, experiment and expression. You instantly entertain images of Liza Minnelli in her fishnet stockings, bright red lips and high heels dancing raunchily on that chair.

I caught sight of a beautiful old DC4 parked on the far side of the airfield, a memory of the old 'Candy Bomber' days of the Berlin Airlift. Our passengers left, we were escorted to the handling agents' office. We engaged with a very helpful and likeable handling agent called Rick, who responded to my hopeful request re aircraft museums and told me that the old war birds including Wellingtons were over at Gattow, quite a drive. He suggested Check Point Charlie which we'd visit anyway, but what I *really* wanted was a tour of the unseen side of Tempelhof itself.

"This guy does guided tours sometimes, try him." He gave me a card.

Sadly my endeavours brought no joy, for when I did try I had a rather interesting conversation with a lady who spoke no English at all, and since I speak no German either we managed an impressively long exchange considering. We found some distant thread of common Anglo Saxon lingo – somehow! I got the gist of it, the tour was for groups only, and, had to be booked in advance. Very disappointing. But all was not lost for in the middle of our wanderings through the heroic, and sometimes tragic stories of escape exhibited in the Check Point Charlie museum downtown, my mobile rang, it was Rick who'd kindly set something up for us with the 'tour man' that afternoon. He'd mentioned our keenness and the man (Klaus) had obligingly agreed, on his day off.

It was a bitterly cold autumn afternoon, leaves spun and swirled through the air, people marched, heads down, hands thrust deeply into overcoat pockets, and even the dogs didn't look too keen. We met Klaus, our guide in the entrance hall of Tempelhof. The hall, which is 'Grand Central Station meets the Vatican', had an awesome grandeur. Lofty, solid and made of the most gorgeous marble, it's symbolic of that German aspiration (and building skill). Klaus, closely connected with this airport all his life, was a fount of knowledge. We stood under huge marble pillars, admiring the scale and dimension of the shining interior.

"But wait till you see zis," said Klaus as he gave a little toss to his enormous bunch of keys and turned on his heel so we should follow. Directly above the entrance hall where we had stood was another room, in other words a false ceiling had been put in which halved the height of the entrance hall, it *was* nineteen meters high. The Russians had taken off a load of marble for use elsewhere and the Germans had destroyed some of it too (a sort of 'if *we* can't hang on to it *you're* not going to enjoy it!' attitude). The Americans had patched it up as best they could but it was still a shocking assault on what was truly a foyer to rival any. At the end of this room was a spectacular photograph of the whole airport taken from outside showing the might and symmetry of the buildings and its futuristic architecture. Whatever your politics, you can't help being struck by the grandeur and sheer scale of the undertaking – so visionary and so ahead of its time. I could see the 'Fuerer' screaming out his 'uber alles' speeches and hear the clicking of jackboots.

Hitler had planned an enormous restaurant on top of the main building. The roof was designed to open up; it was never completed but would have been quite the place to dine. Klaus with a twinkle in his eye continued to toss the keys around like worry beads and pick out the right one and lead us up yet more hidden internal staircases through locked doors and into abandoned areas. We entered what would have been the magnificent restaurant and it had been turned into a basketball court, bowling alley and snack bar by the Americans during their long custody of the airport (the Marshall plan gave Templehof to the Americans after the war). Like all US bases round the world it had that 'just like home' feel to it, they like their creature comforts and familiar touches like pizza and the ball game. The Americans had the airport between 1948 and 1993. The day I saw it there was sadly yellow tape all around the basketball court because Health and Safety had deemed it unsafe, so you could no longer walk across the floor. I think Klaus found this ridiculous, because as he told us, he jumped up and down on the floor and punched the pillars and walls with his fist.

"You can see how weak and dangerous zis is, ya? All about to fall down around us," and laughed sarcastically with a shake of his head, implying of course that it was as solid as a rock which was probably true. It just added to the pathos.

It is the shape of Tempelhof which makes it so unique. It resembles a huge eagle with its wings outstretched and curving forward forming a crescent moon. The main building being the terminal and the two curved wings being a series of massive hangars. Everything is constructed of pale golden marble.

The enormous eagle, several meters across, wings at full stretch sat on top, right in the middle. Every detail is designed to be showy and full of statement. The Americans painted the head white to make it look like a bald eagle (very politically correct). Eventually in about 1962 it was removed altogether and now just the small head sits inconspicuously in a hedge outside the terminal, a decapitated fraction of its former self.

Because of the unique design they used to taxi the aircraft right up to the terminal building literally under the awning so they could avoid the rain! It was revolutionary, other major airfields, Heathrow included were still like huts in comparison. Considering it was built in the 1930s it's a work of art, it was the biggest structure of its day and the 7th biggest in the world during the years that followed.

Hitler had planned to have thousands of seats on top of the two wings; this would have effectively turned the place into a stadium to host big events and air shows. We climbed up more staircases, while Klaus buoyed by our enthusiasm and flow of questions continued to file through the jailer's bunch of keys and open more doors. We finally made it to the very top outside and just soaked up the glorious view of both the airfield and the city. He opened his file and showed us some *fascinating* old black and white photos of the building and emergence of the airport (one I remember was taken just after the First World War and was of a uniformed man in a small hut). This was the very beginning of Tempelhof. The photos of the 'grass strip' days, came out and he explained how, to indicate runway direction they'd have little pointers on the grass, which of course changed according to the wind.

We looked at the runway where we'd landed yesterday.

"Ze Americans put perforated steel planking down for ze runways after the Russians had gone."

Then two new runways went in for the Berlin airlift of 1948. He pointed far away to the stretch of water where the Sunderland Flying boats, laden with supplies, would have landed. I was just choked when I thought of the round the clock efforts of such brave pilots. Over 270,000 flights were made, many at three-minute intervals and 2 million West Berliners were saved. (In fact the Russians finally lifted the blockade when the Americans threatened them with atomic bombs, which arrived from Roswell into Mildenhall and were to be put on the B29s.)

There is the most captivating painting on an entire wall in the departure hall downstairs of all the different scenes, DC4s, flying boats, US Pilots in their flying jackets and a young girl with long blonde plaits giving a dashing young American pilot some flowers to say thank you. I was touched when Klaus explained that recently they had a commemoration of the Airlift and both *that* pilot in the painting (now in his 80s) and the girl (also now elderly) were reunited.

Perhaps the most interesting part was when he took us into the burnt out archive bunkers. The Germans had kept films and other top secret material in these rooms deep underground. The Russians who had possession of Tempelhof for two months between April and July 1945 could not open the huge steel doors, so they blew them up with dynamite – but unfortunately blew everything in there to smithereens. What was so special – it had been left *exactly* as they found it. The place still stank of old fires and burnt out remains, old doors with heavy locks, lay propped up against the walls much as they do outside people's houses when they are waiting for the skip to arrive. It was eerie and chilling, a bit like seeing a shipwreck on the ocean bed. In one room was a huge air conditioning machine comprised of bulky iron humidifiers and gigantic air filters – all very modern for its day. It reminded me very much of the underground hospital on the island of Jersey which is full of fine examples of German engineering. God only knows what was lost in that tragic and unnecessary inferno. I was glad they hadn't turned it into a museum and tidied it up; it was exactly as it had always been. But many secrets were lost forever in that explosion.

Outside, he showed us the production line for the Stuka which was made there during the war. It was a tidy set up. They enclosed the awning running along the main structure and erected big doors to make it secure. This made it into a vast corridor which was exactly the width of the wing span – a sort of a huge motorway tunnel – the bare frame started at the beginning then bits slowly got hammered on as it made its journey towards the 'light at the end of the tunnel'. Once the wings were bolted on it was wheeled out and off it flew. Shifts were from 6a.m. to 10 p.m. and there was no slacking.

"If you didn't like it you were transferred somewhere else usually much vorse!" said Klaus as he showed us some more fantastic old black and white shots of hundreds of Fockwulfe 190Ds and Stukas being churned out. There was a little railway track running the length of the tunnel bringing supplies to the production line. These Stukas had anti-tank missiles on them to attack the Russian tanks. The airfield was never used for sorties only for production, when they were finished they flew off elsewhere.

As the Allied advance closed in on the Germans the bombing intensified. Klaus showed us the last secret of Tempelhof, which was a series of underground bomb proof shelters where hundreds of people huddled for safety. My intuition told me that he had been a boy during this time because of the poignancy with which he described the scene. Maybe he had been interred in this bunker during the last days of the German defeat.

We descended down dimly lit concrete staircases right into the bowels of the place, preceded through the huge creaking doors and into two stark rooms – just four walls, a ceiling and a single bulb hanging. A small partition in the far corner provided scant privacy for a toilet. There were cartoons all over the walls of funny benign characters, these were painted to keep the children amused and offer a modicum of relief and humour in that terrifying situation.

"Sometimes there would be over seventy people in here, you could hear the planes flying overhead, some children would be crying … and *that* over there," he said gesturing towards the make shift toilet, "was just a sand pit … they were in here for many hours." I detected a lump in his throat, maybe he was reliving it somehow.

As we walked back down an avenue of autumn trees, leaves fluttering around us, Klaus told me about the last commercial flight of the war to fly *out* of Tempelhof. It was 1945 and it was a most unfortunate Fokewulfe 200

Condor enroute to Madrid. It was shot down by its own people – the Germans who had mistaken it for and Allied bomber. The Lancaster, Fortress and Sterling were all four engined bombers and this doomed passenger plane looked very similar to the B17 Fortress.

However, we spoke of the happier days and as I looked out over this poignantly historical airfield, I pictured a scene from the past. I saw the glamorous days of pencil skirted women in pill box hats, gentlemen in double breasted suits and brogues glancing sideways from under their trilbies, while tapping a cigarette against an engraved silver case. People alighting from the incomparably beautiful Lockheed Constellation right underneath the awning just feet from the terminal. Those heady days of scent, of hats and gloves, of boxy tan coloured leather suitcases, of reserved yet seductive chat and journeys on large propeller aeroplanes which took days, not hours. The distinctive sound of the roaring propellers on classic aircraft carrying sartorially perfect ladies and gents off on clandestine adventures. Flights filled with novelty and glamour during which you'd be served by a lovely Lauren Becall lookalike. Flights, when service was polished and manners impeccable, yes there would have been many such flights out of there, in that shadowy 'art deco' world, a world of 'The Third Man' and 'Casablanca'. I thanked Klaus and left the airfield with my mind full of imaginative wanderings.

I was grateful to have seen 'the other side' of Tempelhof in the magnificent city of Berlin.

Football & Fairy Tales

Not an obvious connection, but nonetheless an interesting one. A weekend featuring Billy Connelly's "Pint o' crème de menthe" Scottish fans in kilts, swilling 'White & Mackay' *and* ...'Thumberlina'! We flew the team and their immediate entourage out to face their Danish opponents. The pickup was from Edinburgh, always such a picturesque approach, sweeping in over the Firth of Forth turning west towards the city with its great bridge spanning the estuary, and Kirkcaldy off to the north.

The lads (Hibernium football team) emerged from the bus in matching tracksuits with spiky gelled hair, clutching their water bottles and bounced across the tarmac as young fit lads do! Out we went on the westerly runway at Edi, straight ahead, a nice departure which affords great views of Glasgow and Prestwick and their associated golf courses. We turned back east for St Abbs on the north-east coast caught sight of Berwick on Tweed out of the starboard window and then out over a rather grim looking North Sea.

The destination was Odense in Denmark, somewhere I'd never been so I didn't know what to expect. I had *just* read earlier that week in the paper that Denmark was the 'happiest place on earth' according to the world's first 'map of happiness' Britain came only 41st and I was pretty happy in Britain so I was all geared up for a positive cornucopia of conviviality.

It did not disappoint, it was a charming clean town. The buildings were sympathetic to the spirit of the place and much of the old traditional style had been preserved – no modern concrete monstrosities anywhere! There were 'gingerbread' shops and quaint cobbled streets. Cheery and manicured little parks with fountains and benches were dotted around. During my meanderings I came across a blues band playing in the main square outside the town hall, some people danced, some just sat with their beers or coffee taping their feet, then, a tango class in the park where anybody could join in. The town was pretty and well proportioned, a crystal clear river flowed through it, with little wooden bridges crossing here and there. Window boxes full of bright flowers splashed colour throughout and loads of people cruised around on their bicycles. The streets were brimming with cafes and restaurants, the people all seemed to be good looking and friendly.

Of course being the birth place of Hans Christian Anderson, the whole place is imbued with his spirit. Outside our hotel was an eye catching bronze statue of the man, seated on a bench, with his top hat on, his cloak outstretched inviting you to sit next to him. Adorning the entrance was a bronze fairy tale figure twisted and inverted as though diving through weeds in a pond. Along the corridors were excerpts from his work. Tender words described Thumberlina enclosed in a walnut shell floating down a river covered with violet petals. The words were lightsome and cheery transporting me with ease, back to my childhood.

I exited the sliding doors in the lobby adorned with the fabulous dancing, prancing fairytale bronze figurines and walked straight into a lively and colourful market, selling everything from cheese to Bizzie Lizzies. It was a colourful array of olives, salamis, fruit, veg and bright flowers – everybody was smiling, the sun was shining, it was great. I began to see why Denmark had won its position in the 'happiness table' it was most deserving of the mark of favour conferred upon it.

I clocked with interest the amusing names of shops and businesses, some familiar, some just gobbledegook (to me!): 'Blond bicycles' then 'Erjelejlighedbutikken' 'Happy Chicken' and the universally recognisable 'Hong Kong house' and 'Apotek'. There were little spots of Anglicism such as 'Beauty Zone' or 'Fast Food' next to raw Scandi speak such as Jan and Bo Lystfiskershop. There was 'Benies bagle'– fair enough but then there was the more intriguing and rather eyebrow lifting 'Slutspurt'. I spotted a shoe shop called 'Kazanova' and, expecting to see some seductive masculine leather boots, was surprised by a window full of bright plastic round toed sandals. Somehow, not what I imagined Cazanova to be wearing as he slid down sheets and leaped over a wall in his velvet coat escaping a jealous husband!

Into the Hans Christian Anderson museum I went. What a beautiful place. There was a comprehensive introduction to the era in which he lived. A time when life expectancy was low, (only 60% of children survived infancy), wars raged everywhere (uncovered by media), and poverty was crippling and widespread. I followed the chronology of his life. From such adversity, this man came up with real glory. In his family genes were insanity and alcoholism, he was raised in gruesome poverty. From an early age he loved to entertain people; there is a sweet and moving drawing of him dancing kicking up his skinny long legs for some seated washer women; they saw him as a bit of an eccentric. He would read out his little stories for whoever would listen. He did many tough, soul destroying jobs including working in a tobacco factory which he finally packed in before heading to Copenhagen, never relinquishing his dreams. He wanted to be an actor but the principal of the theatre, one Madame Schall, believed him to be mad and dismissed him from the theatre in 1822 blaming his "lack of cultivation". At school he was bullied by cruel teachers who were unreasonable and malicious, but in true 'Dickensian' fashion along came a kind benefactor who encouraged him. No wonder dark and light came to define his work.

"Den grimme Aeling er en afspeiling af mit eget liv," he said, which means 'the ugly duckling is a reflection of my own life'.

On display were beautiful and innocent 'paper cuts' which he had crafted. A real example of his creativity, while he spoke and entertained the children with a story he would be cutting and folding paper and at the end of the story, like a salute or finale he would unravel a little work of art of such intricacy and originality.

"I am like water," he said. "Everything is reflected in me."

There were phones on which you could listen to any fairytale. I chose 'Thumberlina'. The stuffy old mole who wanted to marry her, drag her off underground and keep her in his dark and friendless hole showed surprisingly how sympathetic he was to women's sentiments!

In spite of everything this man ended up travelling extensively and meeting other luminaries of the literary world all over Europe. "At rejse er at leve," he exclaimed, which means "To travel is to live". I empathised deeply with him as I stared down at his quotes, wondering where on earth I might be next week!

His photograph reminded me a bit of Disraeli. He had a big nose, deep set eyes and although not handsome, he had a face full of wit and life, 'his figure stately, his bearing elegant'.

His mother, the alcoholic washer woman was distraught when he left home but was comforted by a fortune teller who told her not to worry, for one day the town would honour her son. On Christmas 1867 they gave him the title 'Freedom of the City' and there was a torch procession in the streets for him. A creator of so many of the world's greatest fairytales, his own life in many ways became one!

From the shadowy, peaceful museum dedicated to this great spirit, I emerged into the bright sunshine, turned the corner and was met by three Scotsmen wearing horned metal helmets with gaudy ginger wigs, sporting 'White and Mackay' T-shirts, kilts, and Doc Martins. They were wailing out their football anthem, and clutching their tins of beer. Suddenly Hans Christian Anderson, the large caped visionary, the bearded poet, along with his ducklings and his fairies disappeared like a miniature vaporous cyclone 'Schluuump'. The genie spiralled back down into his lamp. I had to smile.

Kick-off was at 8pm. This freed the town of the riotous spectators and meant the restaurants were fairly peaceful. I'd never been to a restaurant with its own watchman. Whilst sitting in a rather special 17th century building (one of the oldest in Denmark) known as 'Den Gamie Kro' or 'The old Inn', surrounded by minstrels, galleries, beams, wrought iron torch holders, wooden balconies and vaulted cellars, in walks a character of most impressive countenance. He was like the old city guardian, he held a large pike with a spiked orb on top, had a long and splendid full length double breasted coat with gold buttons. He had high leather boots, a huge medallion and the biggest set of keys ever. He unfurled some document from which he read, it was compelling and I was sorry I couldn't understand, but after two hours with Hans Christian, my psychic antenna were up and I got the gist of it! He necked his glass of wine and went on his way to walk people around the town and entertain them with folklore and anecdotes. What a civilised tradition.

And so it was, we departed the next day. I saw all the footballers (in their matching tracksuits and gelled hair) at breakfast in the hotel, despite their loss they were in good spirits. Some recognised me as their pilot and we had a friendly 'och aye' chat over the croissants and coffee. I had enjoyed a little glimpse into the life of one of the greatest and most enigmatic creators of fairytales. It must have been his spirit because the trip had felt somewhat like a fairytale itself! All made possible by a football match!

The flight back to Scotland was quite beautiful. After crossing over a rugged cold North Sea we were cruising along at 10,000 feet – just above a thick layer of cloud a gorgeous late afternoon sun filled the skies with warm light. I knew at the next descent instruction we would lose our light and descend into the dull, dish water grey which lay below. I inwardly said goodbye to the sunlit evening and to the great poet and author. It had been a lovely introduction to Denmark and a snug and happy revisiting of childhood memories.

Jungles and Jet Planes

The clients were five senior executives from a Texas oil company. They were off to Malabo in Equatorial Guinea and then on to Yaounde in Cameroon. (Believe me the *only* reason any Texan would be going to Malabo is for oil revenue.) Having sagaciously decided *against* using the internal regional flights within EG (as they called it) they paid the hefty sum of over eighty thousand to hire our luxurious thirteen seat Embraer biz jet complete with bed to do the whole trip. Unfortunately we set off at 9.30 at night from Luton, landed in Palma for fuel at around midnight then had the long all night slog across the Sahara.

On the ground at Palma, 'José and Jose-b' struggled with their fuel tank which was 'muy problematico' so it delayed us quite badly. Just as your body clock is winding down you face the prospect of three hours of absolutely *nothing,* except a thirty second solitary twinkle as you pass Tamanrasset in the middle of the desert. However, it **is** rather nice the way we say hello to one another up there, as a plane passes directly overhead or underneath we turn on our landing lights for those few seconds. It's just a touch of camaraderie, creating that 'Jodie Foster' moment: "We are not alone!" It's the airborne nod and a wink as you fly across swathes of dark barren desert.

But the song 'You'll never walk alone' has a certain resonance because up there at thirty something thousand feet, we all talk indirectly to one another. Due to being out of VHF range for ground communication, every aircraft gives position reports on 129.6. So for example you will hear:

"All stations. this is Virgin Nigeria southbound London to Lagos on upper romeo 978 checked tango golf uniform at time five four, estimate bravo osca delta at 01.33 flight level three seven zero. Virgin Nigeria southbound London to Lagos."

Very tidy arrangement, because as each aircraft checks in on that frequency with their time over a waypoint and estimate for the next, you glance at the map and pinpoint them. The Lufthansa even announced on frequency when he was starting descent for Lagos. It had a sort of 'wish me luck guys' ring to it.

Pushing through the dark African skies, I remembered the last trip a few months earlier, when we flew from Geneva to Dar Es Salaam in Tanzania, to deliver a hunting party to Serengeti. In the middle of the night having made a few unsuccessful attempts on the HF radio we suddenly heard this African voice in our headphones (must be said in Strong African accent).

"Lima November x-ray four two five Romeo, can't you hear me callin' you, what is de matter wid you?"

Startled we looked at each other and transmitted back to him with an apology and to go ahead. His reply will go down in history, I had to make a logbook entry it was so funny.

"Lima November x-ray, is dis your fost time? You can't com heeyah, der is a war, you most go a-way."

We explained that *this* is how our flight plan was filed, we were sorry.

"You most go NOW to Djibouti, Eritrea and Ethiopia border is closed, say again, you most fly to Djibouti!"

We had already retarded the throttles back to a setting for maximum range. We were only doing .72 mach, so this news was not good since it would add another hundred miles at least and we didn't have lots of fuel to play with. But what a moment, it had my very humorous Captain, Peter, who is a 'half-moon specs' sixty-year-old grandee of aviation, (ex-British airways) lifting his shoulders with laughter and he said, "I am glad that my career lasted long enough to hear *that.*"

We made it ... and were treated to the sight of Kilimanjaro at dawn peaking up through a collar of soft pink clouds as the vast plains of the Serengeti continued to the horizon. I barely felt the fatigue burning my eyes as I caught my first glimpse of the tropical islands, Zanzibar and Pemba sitting like jewels set in the turquoise ocean.

Back in *West* Africa we had one hundred miles to destination, good, time for the descent. We were talking by now to Nigerian ATC. Windshield heat on, retard the throttles, set new altitude in the window and brief the descent and approach profile. There was no radar available (just the ticket when you're dog tired!) so we positioned ourselves for a VOR approach onto the westerly. Despite being exhausted after a sleepless night, your body scavenges every nook and cranny and obligingly pumps round that last bit of adrenalin needed for the approach and landing.

We descended into a hot, steamy rain forest-y landscape and crossed the water towards the island just off the coast of Cameroon where Malabo was situated. It was pouring with rain, big cumulo nimbus clouds towered around us, shadowy and ominous in the thin light of dawn. It was thirty degrees already. On our starboard side as we descended onto finals we saw the VAST industrial oil and gas plant with its towering chimneys and columns of smoke, on the port side … shanty town and bush.

The Americans had all slept (six people can lie horizontal in the interior), they were well pleased with the comfort and standard of the flight, they thanked us profusely as they disembarked pulling jackets on over crumpled shirts, into the damp humid morning and climbed into their waiting 4x4s.

We set about the post flight duties, the first thing was fuel which had been arranged on account by JetEx an international handling agent, but of course 'De paper no dey come' and the refueller kept repeating "Dollar dollar" and I kept saying "It's on account, it's on account!" and we went back and forth like a baseline rally for some time. Eventually I gave him a Shell credit card which seemed to placate him. Whenever we go to this type of place we carry about ten thousand dollars in cash but I certainly didn't want to start buying fuel with the money in case we needed it for more important things – like a quick exit!

The guys came to service the toilet – they certainly pumped it out but "no water for put in". So I settled for 50% job done, maybe no flushing on the way home – that could be interesting. I hoped Cameroon the next stop might do better. We would see.

Two guys in bright African print shirts with their fluorescent vests over the top cruised up in the potable water wagon to refill our water tanks. He had a hose but the nozzle was wrong so there followed a comedy sketch in which the three of us were fiddling with screwdrivers and jubilee clips laughing as we got soaked each time the hose flew off, all this while communicating in broken Spanish/French and pidgin English. When we finally located the hose securely I leant against the back of the truck and they rushed up saying "non non!" and pointed to the wet paint. I pulled away with a freshly painted white hand, which stayed on my skin for most of the trip. As for my handprint – well there is a part of me forever immortalised on a clapped out old water truck in Equatorial Guinea. Not *exactly* the stars handprints in the Hollywood pavement, but a small memento nonetheless!

Chris, a local, was the driver for Noble the oil company. He was, as the Africans would say 'a Propa *guy*' He had big snake skin shoes with square cornered toes, a tight trendy shirt with serious lapels and huge white wrap around shades – those which look like a close up of a fly's compound eye.

After washing the crystal glasses, putting all the bedding away and hiding the cash, we shut the aircraft down and climbed into Chris's truck.

"I am at your disposal so whenever you want me to show you around … I can do that," he said as his keys clinked against his gold rings.

He drove us to the hotel but stopped at the Noble offices and left us in the cabin of the pick-up with all our baggage and flight bags in the open part behind. I had just got to the bit in the 'How to survive Malabo' brief prepared by the Americans which said 'Never *ever* leave belongings unattended because of the street crime and robbery'! Some men were indulging in dogfights in the road just nearby. We were sitting ducks. If they approached I wasn't going to take on five barefooted, stoned members of the Mongomo Fang tribe from Bioko Island with flick knives and four snarling wounded pit bulls as back up. Nooo nooo they could have my flight bag with passport wallet licences and IDs. They could even take my nectar card and my favourite discontinued lip salve from the health food store in Guildford.

I took a moment to flick through the "Risk Summary" brief. It wasn't exactly Enid Blyton but it made interesting reading. There was enough going on here to keep you on your toes, let's see: human rights abuses, mercenaries, coups, political oppression, crime, torture, violent suppression of opposition, robbery, mugging, civil unrest, extortion, vote rigging, fraud, monstrous nepotism, poorly paid undisciplined military at check points demanding money from foreigners, decades of mismanagement, dreadful disease (including cholera which was hushed up), and the whole jolly place run by a repressive tyrant whose political elite and family enjoy *all* the wealth from the oil and....wait for this – my god would you believe it – he doesn't put *anything* back into poverty alleviation for his people. Another graduate of the Mugabe school of humanitarian studies.

Apparently some fire fighters had been arrested for impersonating policemen and exhorting money and documents from foreigners. Staying with the fire service, they were mobbed for not attending a fire even though their station was only 100 meters from the scene. Here was a good one: the shanty towns had no electricity and all the open cooking caused fires. Slum fires have increased – it is illegal to rebuild houses that have burnt down. It turns out that real estate companies have paid youths to start fires to forcibly evict residents. There is a real housing deficit and rents are going up because of the need for premises for oil sector companies. The police made some perfunctory measures against the youths **but** (and this may come as a surprise) it is unlikely that such clearances could have occurred without (quote) "some sanction from well-connected individuals".

Chris returned. I closed the booklet. We moved off. From the radio came mellifluous and haunting African/Creole music called 'zouk' sung in Spanish and French.

"What are they doing?" I asked pointing to a team of 'ghost buster' like men in white overalls, breathing apparatus and big canisters.

"They are spraying against the malaria and the mosquitoes."

Sisyphus and his pointless 'pushing the rock up the mountain' exercise came to mind. We crossed the river on a rickety looking bridge, below you could not see the river because it was full of garbage and mountains of rubbish were piled high on each side. It was an open sewer – the stench was ghastly. Yes I'm afraid despite the most valiant efforts by Geldof, Tutu, Kofi Annan, and Angelina Jolie, and other charitable 'lovvies' the place is buggered.

The rain had stopped and the broken roads were literally steaming, Hibiscus flowers the size of dinner plates opened in front of your eyes, you could almost see the plants extending. Wretched scabby dogs drank from puddles and scratched furiously. We drove down a road to the hotel and admired the imposing outline of the Basile Volcano which towers over the town. I saw a sign which said 'Acqui hay electricita'! Spanish for we have electricity here. It was written on a piece of torn cardboard box and had a sense of excitement and breakthrough about it.

Equatorial Guinea is the only Spanish colony in Africa, it was strange hearing pidgin Spanish.

"Vamos a tomer!" shouted friends of Chris when they caught sight of him in the car. "Ola!" he kept shouting from the window as he cruised through town, he obviously had an enviable job and he enjoyed the pose. He said to me, "You see we have inherited de Spanish way – wine and women and fiesta. This is why we are lazy and jost hang out drinking. You see in Nigeria dey had de British who taught dem that it's work before play. So dey are more advanced."

He went on to tell me that he had sent all three of his young children to be educated in Nigeria and live with his parents. His poor wife losing all her kids, especially since one of them was only six months younger than the other. He saw my puzzled look and said with pride, "Yes bot dis one is from anoda woman."

He drove us through an area called Los Angeles. More "Ola amigo". The similarities between it and say Santa Monica were not striking.

I remarked that considering the place was so poor the airport really was quite impressive.

"You know a few years ago the airport was jost a shit place like dis building here, a big storm came with big winds and it jost ... took de roof off. The roof was jost blown into de air, so after dis they decided to build the new airport." Sounded fair enough.

We turned into the drive of the hotel Tropicana. I saw fake black and white brick façade and steel rods protruding from the fibre reinforced concrete awning over the entrance. I glanced into the bar adjacent to the foyer. It was dark and the row of optics was adorned with flashing fairy lights. It was obviously a refuge for the many contract workers who were doing 'month on month off' for big money in the oil and gas business. It was smoky and cosy.

"Aye the bloody winters in Aberdeen ..." I heard in broad Scots from a table of guys, some of whom were Scottish, others English or Dutch. They were swapping stories and drinking vast quantities of local beer – a palliative to the grind and depravation of living in a disease-ridden cesspit.

Up in the room I sat on the brown velour sofa after pulling a cold beer from the fridge. There was no bottle opener. I walked down the corridor and saw the barefooted cleaning girl in a sarong. She had been granite faced when I passed her the first time, now she positively stuck her nose up and looked sideways. I guess they tire of the European guests.

"Excuse me, could you open this bottle for me?"

She took the bottle, put it between her back molars and before I could say 'no you mustn't ...'foam was oozing from the top.

"Ah sissie," I smiled, "I can't believe you did that, that's amazing ... you African chicks eh."

I laughed and gave her five and said thank you. With that she became an entirely different personality. She blew a laughter raspberry and went backwards like a released balloon, doubled up with laughter holding her tummy, then showed off the most dazzling set of white teeth, started clapping and literally danced back down the corridor to her bucket and mop. Isn't life amazing? All most people want is just to be acknowledged.

I cleaned my teeth in Evian and perched in the bath (which had no plug) and with the hand shower, washed away the grime of eight hours of engine bleed air. I turned up the rattling air conditioner and sat watching a crackly CNN fade in and out in time with the ceiling light as the voltage fluctuated. Outside the rain fell unrelentingly, car horns were bibbing everywhere and cockerels crowed. I swigged my beer then swatted the biggest cockroach I had ever seen, it was like a baby terrapin (the telegraph just wasn't man enough, I actually had to throw my suitcase down on it). I stood on the case and jumped about to make sure. Being chicken I couldn't bring myself to lift it up and see. The next day when I packed and left, I was anticipating the large flattened corpse as I moved my case. It had gone – no sign of the squashed cockroach. It did occur to me that the case had moved a little across the floor – it was definitely nearer the window when the murder happened. I bet the thing came round, pumped itself up, rebooted its shell back then stood up like mighty mouse threw the case off and scuttled away.

I finally flopped onto the king size, rock hard, cream and black lacquered bed with inset art deco mirrors. The furniture was the same as my friend's apartment in Sharjah. It all comes from China. I went for the bedside light switch but it was on the far side of the lounge. Oh well it is Africa. I fell into a coma.

Chris came by at four o clock to drive us round town. We meandered round the streets and neighbourhoods of Malabo – a town which made Lagos (my birth place) look like Nice. This was **poverty**, my heart went out to these people who are victims of greed and tyranny. You could witness little desperate attempts at survival, but the stench of hopelessness was everywhere. A Bushman with matted hair and caked in filth wearing nothing but torn trousers sauntered into the road in front of us, he was barefooted and had two small plastic bags stuffed into each ear and was having a very animated conversation with himself.

"Loco," smiled Chris and touched his temple.

He drove us through the bustling, crowded, rubbish strewn streets up to the Palacio del Pueblo. This looked more the ticket, ah ha, it was the president's house, well anyone with a name like president Teodoro Obiang Nguema Mbasogo needs a pad I guess. There were a couple of decent looking restaurants and hotels around with views of the port which, explained Chris had sprung up recently to service the 4,000 foreigners who now work there. He said there was nothing here a few years ago you wouldn't see a car in the silent streets.

Everything was owned either by the president, his wife or a member of his family. Not surprisingly his son is tipped to succeed him. We drove past another of his residences; it looked like the Ewing's house from Dallas. His wife's was of similar proportion on the other side of the road. No wonder there is widespread discontent amongst the 500,000 people who live on less than $1 per day.

"It is so unfair isn't it Chris, does it make you angry to live under such inequality?"

"Yes but dis is **Africaa**."

"It must be soul destroying for the people, seeing all their country's wealth creamed off by one family."

It is what he said next which made me realise the place will *never* change:

"But if I was in his place I would do exactly de same, I would look after myself and not care about the others."

Amen.

We drove to Punta Europa; this is where the American compound is. Our passengers were staying here. There were manicured lawns, big houses with Toyota Land Cruisers parked in carports. The club house had tennis courts, a nice bar/restaurant, a games room, big screen TVs and a beautiful swimming pool. When I saw the size of the mosquito corpse floating in the pool I reached for my malaria tablets.

Funny that the Americans do not require a visa to visit this country. The catchy little calypso song kept skipping through my mind as I looked around "Workin' for the yankee doll-arrr".

On the way home we passed an extraordinary line of luminous plastic palm trees on the side of the road; they were radioactive orange and lime. A sizable building was undergoing construction behind them.

"This is going to be a huge shopping mall built by the Lebanese," explained Chris.

Far more beautiful were the absolutely gargantuan Ceiba trees which proliferate all over. Their roots like the great fins at the base of a rocket were above ground, they towered majestically high into the sky.

We thanked Chris when he dropped us off and headed for the bar in the Tropicana. It was still full of tired ex-pats drinking beer. Two beautiful long limbed local girls sauntered in with the elegant gait of female giraffes. They had 'plenty bling', hair extensions and necks like gazelles, and were – I was told – trawling for business. Very tempting I'm sure at times if you're stuck out here but I *did* really hope the lads would give just a cursory thought to their subsequent swollen black gonads the size of netballs before they committed to the horizontal lambada.

We had been told it was the best restaurant in town (The Parisien) so we looked forward to some fresh fish. He didn't have any of our choices so I went down the menu item by item.

"This one?"

"No sorry."

"How about … this white fish?"

"No sorry." He did say it with a big apologetic smile though.

It turned out they had a few frozen prawns which had come over by boat from Douala Cameroon earlier that week, but the good old standby pasta was there. The place did have a painted Eiffel Tower on the wall though!

We left for Yaounde Cameroon the next day. Chris picked us up, his mood had completely changed: he was morose, preoccupied and texting continuously on his mobile.

"What's up Chris, you ok?"

Then he told me that his friend (a girl) from Cameroon had been tortured by the police and she was in hospital, he'd had a call late last night – if he hadn't intervened she might have died. I asked why.

He said something about her not having the right papers, she was an illegal. It's no picnic by a stream living out here.

"Very cruel de police here … ayee, I'm telling you," he shook his head. I didn't want to imagine what they'd done to her. Just part of the tragic brutality of life there.

God there is nothing like seeing a gleaming chunk of $25 million private jet sitting there when you are in blackest Africa and the keys are swirling round your index finger. It looked almost as good as that helicopter must have looked to the stranded Andes crash survivors who were wondering which dead limb to chomp on next. I know it's awfully childish but I do like to indulge in the attribution of animal characteristics to my aircraft. I imagined her to be a golden lab who sees her owners coming back after a long night in the yard all alone, the tail wags furiously and the legs (undercarriage) start to bounce up and down. "Let's get outta here!" she barked. Oh well, a bit of imagination never went amiss.

I turned the key, raised the big red handle and pulled the door down. It lowered slowly, the six steps falling neatly into place as it reached the end of its travel. I went straight in to check the bag of money, still there, phew. I turned the batteries on and put one avionic switch on to check the voltage.

"Aural unit … OK," came the familiar voice chime.

I performed the fire check, then started up the APU. Always a relief to get those electrics on line and watch all the screens come to life. Then the air gets introduced so we can have full air conditioning (we must wait three minutes for the pneumatics so as not to overload the APU). Air con packs go on and voila, beautiful cool air.

I sat in my seat loading the flight management computer with the flight plan for this next short leg (only thirty minutes). Thank god for satellites and databases, this computer knows every single little insignificant waypoint in the whole world. I wished that Orville and Wilbur could come back for a day and see what they started.

Just then, a monstrous bolt of fork lightening zigzaged to the ground, it was followed by a clap of thunder so loud it made me jump. This was serious weather, but we were, after all cycling distance from the equator. Then something extraordinary happened – it was as though we went from day to night, someone just turned the sun off. The world turned charcoal grey, a great cloak of darkness enveloped us, and boy did the rain come down. Raindrops the size of eggs fell in curtains and it just got heavier and heavier, I glanced out, I had lost contact with the other side of the airfield, then the runway disappeared. The thunder roared and the clouds got blacker. This was certainly the weather which got Noah reaching for his toolkit. The apron flooded, there was so much water it was flowing in rivulets, tiny waves were breaking. Frogs, if they had been so inclined could have surfed on them using lollipop sticks. I reached for the 'Wet V1'card. A wet runway reduces your decision speed because you need more runway to stop in the event of an aborted take-off.

"Think we'll wait for this lot to go through," grinned my colleague raising his eyebrows and cocking his head towards the storm.

I checked the airways map and located our destination, about due east inland into Cameroon, it was only a thirty minute flight. There was just a VOR on the field and again no radar. Our weather radar would definitely come in useful – so with a bit of storm dodging we should be ok.

We did a thorough walk round checking the wheel wells and inlet ducts. It's always wise to be extra cautious in these type of places you never know who might want to 'take out' some Americans. In our security lectures which are a mandatory part of training now, we are told if you are flying high profile people who might have enemies, *or* you are in slightly dodgy countries, be extra vigilant on the walk rounds. Private planes are the perfect targets for sabotage.

The Americans arrived, with that 'glad to be leaving look' they climbed the steps with strained but smiling faces:

"How ya doing? nice to see you."

They fell appreciatively into the capacious leather armchairs and dipped into the nuts. The storm had gone, brilliant rainbows had replaced it.

Our hostess Caroline pressed the 'door close' button and the hydraulics went to work lifting the door which she then pulled into place and locked. The African colleagues lined up to see the plane off.

"Cabin … secure, beacon … on, fuel pumps … on, hydraulic pumps …off, park brake … set."

"Okay starting engine one."

It turned and accelerated, oil pressure, ignition, fuel flow, turbine temperatures … it was all there, that familiar cycle.

We taxied out and turned slowly onto the runway which stretched out shiny and wet after the storm, the clouds were dissipating leaving great holes through which the blue sky shone. The black ground steamed in front of us.

We didn't have to worry about noise abatement take-off here. The power levers came forward, I released the toe brakes and enjoyed that meaty power and wonderful acceleration. It's a rush every time no matter how many times you have done it. Faster and faster we moved forward then I lifted the nose and punched through the vaporous clouds which bumped us around a bit. We retracted the gear and accelerated away towards the next adventure.

"One zero one three … set."

That completed the after takeoff checks as we set the standard altimeter setting of 1013 millibars and headed east.

We flew across dense jungly landscape, the sort where the gorilla programmes are filmed. A long twelve mile arrival procedure during which we slowed to one hundred and eighty knots afforded us views across the dense green bush through which snaked a muddy terracotta river. We turned onto final approach.

"Lima November X-ray 469 Bravo, you are cleared to land, wind is one nine zero six knots," came the African voice from the tower. I flew her down the final approach savouring the unique moment.

We landed at Yaounde in Cameroon. Our passengers were met by smiling African colleagues, there was much hand shaking and greeting, then they were gone.

A surprisingly comfortable hotel minibus came for us. What followed was undoubtedly one of the most interesting taxi rides from airport to hotel I'd ever had. The first roundabout featured a beautiful golden lion in its centre.

"Is that the Cameroon national symbol?" I asked.

"No it's for our football team!" said the driver which had me rolling my eyes thinking 'can't get away from it'!

The long congested road into town was basically a drive through department store – one big market. There were huge three piece suites everywhere (the old familiar brown along with the lacquer from China were there again). God only knows what they did when the rain started, but the people were undeterred, dining room furniture and huge bed frames, sofas and armchairs filled the sides of the road.

One stall just sold 'junk' or what looked like the entire contents of the cupboard under the stairs – pieces of wire, old lengths of cable, rope, balls of string, old screws, hose attachments, torches, you name it. There were stalls piled high with mangoes, papaya, and plantain and different fruits and veg. African 'high life' music played and everyone bustled about. I saw a fat woman in what must have been a size 44 FFF bra with a sarong round her waist, her head covered with bright plastic curlers. She was running her salon under the concrete arch of a bridge and was busy doing hair extensions for a woman who sat on an upside down milk crate in front of her feeding her baby. She waved her comb at me and smiled as we went past. Refreshing to see people so unaffected, uninhibited and resourceful.

Little picins (their name for children) with bulbous belly buttons wearing underpants ran alongside the bus waving and giggling. Loads of little children in matching blue school uniforms, and satchels on their backs pranced and played on their walks home. Babies slept on their mothers backs, wrapped in yards of cloth, their little heads flopping backwards.

Ah, more home furnishings on sale … a life size gaudy orange, red and blue lacquered crucifix complete with Jesus nailed up full of arrow wounds (extra blobs of red lacquer!). Mary and another woman stood on each side weeping tears of blood. Oo you could have matching sofa with red and orange lacquered trim. Right next door to this gruesome ensemble was a guy selling hundreds of old tyres and bags of granulated potash and … stink fish.

Guys played serious games of backgammon while friends looked on spinning on the spot and jamming when a good move was made. Motorbikes were being repaired under tin roofs while chickens pecked at the garbage. Little kids who were just starting out on their trading careers had just an empty 'Bells' bottle full of groundnuts or a few packets of cigarettes and matches. I noted with interest the contents of a barbecue which was smoking away on the side of the road. Beside the corn cobs, there were water rats roasting nicely, crickets and what looked like squirrels and the head of some strange creature. (I thought of my colleague Astrid who told me that when she flew the president of Rwanda his catering order was 'fish heads and porcupine', which he enjoyed immensely as did his wife who was head to toe in mink, with dark shades!)

Right in front of our vehicle stepped a well-dressed man with a shoe on his head, a nice brogue actually, perfectly balanced. He had four right shoes in each hand and a backpack obviously holding the left. He didn't have premises so he was his own walking shoe shop. He couldn't manage the last one so he put it on his head – good arrangement, and seemingly very good for his deportment.

There were many hair salons. One, just a piece of asbestos roof with plastic curtains around. Signs simple and unsophisticated had 'coiffure' in bright uneven letters next to a painting of two black women, one with an afro, the other with long straight hair. The next sign raised a giggle in the crew bus: there was no subtlety in it. "Tit Bar" it read with an out of proportion picture of a girl in shorts hanging on to a pole! Trouble was she had a cardi on; it looked like Joan Armatrading in an M&S twin set. I thought it was rather nice actually. All the signs looked like they had been painted by kids, a bit crude and simple, but it made them somehow more interesting and likeable.

The hotel was comfortable – you could detect the French influence – nice croissants on the breakfast tables! There was a kerfuffle going on in the bar. A mountain of a man adorned in sweeping embroidered robes, obviously indicative of his rank, was standing with cross, staff, ceremonial cloth, pointy hat, and other pontiff regalia. He was the ecclesiastical equivalent of David Beckham I suppose. Little men whom he dwarfed jostled around with microphones interviewing him. He spoke quietly in deep enigmatic rumblings. When they had all finally cleared off, he slumped, expanded into an armchair and had a cold beer right next to me. He then lit a cigarette, I topped my beer at him in a 'Cheers' gesture. I should think all those blessings and liturgical posturing not to mention the accountability of those Vatican funds must take it out of a man.

We finally took off from Cameroon for the long flight back to Paris the next noon. Our passengers were going from Charles De Gaulle to Houston via New York – a long old slog! The flight home was infinitely more enjoyable, being a day flight, we could appreciate the landscape of Nigeria as we overflew the River Benue then the cities of Jos and Kano then into Niger. The desert is somewhere you don't want an engine failure. Looking down at that terrain made me marvel at the caravans of travellers who trek with camels for thousands of miles. It was at times spectacular, with its perfectly round dunes like Chinese hats then at other times just hostile flat and featureless. We saw beautiful wavy dunes shaped by the wind. And spectacular rock formations, one looked just like the back of a crocodile half-hidden in the sand and about twenty miles long. Using the 'seriously handy' satellite phone in the cockpit, we called our operations in Essex, so they could call ahead to Paris on our behalf, plus to describe exactly what we were seeing out of the window. Sharing the moment. They appreciated that.

We couldn't quite make Paris on the fuel we carried so we came down to top up. A huge full moon hung over the bay of Palma when we turned onto final approach. The lights twinkled all around the coast and the lit cathedral was towering above the buildings. Boats bobbed in the harbour – it was serene. The next stop was Paris where we landed on the easterly runway getting an unobstructed view of the city. The Eiffel Tower (last seen on restaurant wall!) was prominent and all the buildings were crystal clear. The whole city was encircled by the snaking lights of the 'Peripherique'. We said our goodbyes and pushed on to London. Quite a day.

I located some 'zouk' music on my return. These haunting, mellifluous songs, sung in French, had played all the time we were in Chris's car as he showed us round Malabo. It will always transport me back to those steaming humid streets, the smoky bars full of contract workers, the warm rain and the smiles and the waves of the kids as they ran alongside, through rubbish strewn streets. Best that they don't dwell on the iniquity and corruption, better they smile and dance. They all have to be tough and resilient down there, even the cockroaches. I have to admit I was glad the cockroach made it!

Exporting Thierry

Not being much of a football fanatic, I had serious egg on my face when I said, "Who's he?"

Then my hostess who is a very 'up to the minute' devourer of Heat magazine and all things 'media' said, "Oh for God's sake Anita it's Thierry HON-REE – he's only like THEE most famous footballer around."

"Oh sorry," I said not meaning it at all.

He climbed up the front steps, he was well-dressed and he very politely came into the cockpit, shook my hand and said hello pleased to meet you. He sat down with his two colleagues, there were only three of them in a huge thirteen seat private jet. They could have chartered a much smaller plane – oh well money isn't exactly an issue, when you earn more in a day than most people do in a year.

On the taxi out I had an unexpected call.

"Lonex six five five romeo from ground."

"Go ahead."

"Could you tell your passenger from me … thanks very much!"

"Okay I'll pass that on, no problem."

When our cabin attendant came up to give us the 'cabin secure' I told her to relay the message. I wondered what that was about and asked my colleague if they knew each other perhaps.

"No no I doubt it, he's probably an Arsenal supporter and is saying thanks for all the contribution to the team."

They seemed to enjoy their flight and were deep in conversation. We landed in a sun drenched Barcelona, approaching from the east which afforded magnificent views all along the coast and the entire city. From the starboard window the bizarre towers of the famous Gaudi Cathedral gestured skyward above the mass of buildings. The monument perched right on top of the mountain was clearly visible, and all the beautiful buildings of old town and the port shone in the sun. I could just make out the glorious statue of Columbus and Las Ramblas. It is hard to beat Barcelona, it's got to be one of the greatest and most vibrant cities in the world. Lucky Thierry I thought if you're going to be 'bought'– may as well be by Barcelona!

"Ola, welcome," said the bronzed Hispanic beauty who came on board clutching her clipboard once we had parked.

"Do you need any fuel, any service?"

I was actually returning on an Easy Jet flight back to Luton because I was needed for another flight the next day, so I asked if she could send the handling agent to pick me up.

"Err we are very busy now, so better if you come together with passengers to terminal, ees okay?"

"Yes no problem," I said and wished my colleagues a pleasant night in Barcelona and I walked down the stairs and into the waiting bus where Thierry and his two friends were in the back. I sat up front with the driver.

"Okay," he started in a strong and utterly charming Spanish accent. "We go to another place for the immigration to make the pass through, because otherwise there will be ..." he rotated his hands in that very Mediterranean gesture which normally means 'palaver' of some sort and cocked his head and raised his eyebrows.

"Muchas gente?" I suggested pleased that I could remember a few words.

"Exactamente," he nodded, "muchas gente aqui for ... to see us, so we go for a different way to avoid the cameras and all this things because they know we are coming."

I made a joke about the paparazzi.

Well that didn't raise a dickey bird of a smile anywhere. I was only trying to be light-hearted but it was a nonstarter. Oh well just because you can go right foot, left foot, chest ... right knee, left knee, back of neck then seamlessly back to the right foot, left foot, chest, a thousand times with a ball and never miss a stroke, it doesn't mean you have to have a sense of humour does it. I guess tensions were high.

"Okay we get out here," said the driver a bit conspiratorially rather enjoying the cunning plan to avoid the crowds of fans and cameras all waiting in the arrivals hall. We were going to dupe them – I was just hoping we would have a more cheery ending than Diana and Dodi. When we finally dismounted in a remote low key place, it looked like the sort of entrance where the baggage handlers would come in for their lunchtime coffee and hang their fluorescent jackets up. There was one guy who had been placed there to check the passports and that was it. But we had not been out of the van ten seconds and the ground staff on the airport were following him in.

"Perdon! Perdon!" they were saying as they proffered their folded footie magazines and pens hoping for an autograph. He obliged very politely.

"Gracias, gracias … buena suerte!"

Even in this remote place which looked like an underground bunker, girls had still managed to sneak in and were waiting with their cameras at the ready. The four of us filed through together showing passports, meanwhile the girls and a couple of photographers almost shooed me out of the way, heads like metronomes trying to eliminate me from the picture. You know it's heartbreaking being a nobody! (Tongue in cheek).

"Thank you very much," said Thierry to me in that distinctive French accent and held out his hand.

"Oh you're welcome," I said sincerely, "hope it all works out for you."

I'm sure he wasn't at all, but, he suddenly looked a bit vulnerable. I thought of those kind words of encouragement that my mum used to give me if I was nervous or if I was going off somewhere.

"And if you don't like it Thierry, you give us a shout and we'll come and pick you up."

What a silly thing to say, thank God I didn't ask him if he had a clean hanky.

The kind Spanish handling agent whose radio was blaring overtime with colleagues wanting to know how it was going, pointed me towards the Easy Jet terminal.

"Gracias."

"De nada, hasta la proxima." (You do become acquainted with the handling agents at airports you frequent a lot such as Malaga, Barcelona and Nice.) I strode up the stairs feeling grateful I had a book with me, I would probably manage a hundred pages as I queued up to get through security.

There it was – the ghastly depressing line of slow moving demoralised dispirited humans filing unsmilingly towards the 'ping' machine. Shoes, belts, jackets, hope, it was all being removed. After the *third* showing of the passport and the boarding pass we were finally on the Boeing 737 bound for LA which is our affectionate term for Luton Airport in the trade!

I managed to get the front row aisle seat. On my right was a very gritty middle-aged German woman of the 'Mother Nature' variety – big sensible sandals and backpack. She was on the final leg of a tour which had featured sleeping with tigers and monks at a tiger sanctuary somewhere in the east. On the other side of the aisle was an Irishman who had had just completed a large part of the pilgrimage to Santiago de Compostella. I got chatting to him because we both ended up laughing at the presentation of a Gin and tonic. It came in something neither of us had ever seen before, wait for it – yes a little plastic sachet like those containing ketchup or mustard. He tried in vain to tear the corner off, then tried the other corner, rotated it, inverted it, still he could not rip the plastic. Suddenly, having made a tiny hole somewhere, a big squirt of gin shot straight out at him – all down his shirt. Ah the joys of budget airlines.

"Malt whisky in a cut glass tumbler with chilled spring water, *this is not*," I joked from over the aisle.

"You can say that again," he came back.

That little comment didn't fall on deaf ears. He went on to tell me that he ran the Glenmorangie distillery in Northern Scotland!

The cabin attendant in her orange and grey work outfit noticed my ID pass and asked me if I worked at Luton, she was very friendly and I told her we had just dropped off Thierry Henri for his new contract. She went into convulsions, hand coming up over the mouth.

"Who else have you flown ... who else?"she asked eagerly.

Without a word of a lie I reeled off all the celebrities our company had flown recently.

She rushed to get her card.

"Will you call me and send me your company email so I can write in."

"The grass isn't always greener," I told her, "sometimes you just trade one set of chores and problems for another."

"But at least yous serve yer gin from a damn bottle," chirped up the Irishman who was still wiping his shirt.

"Yes but *you* get to fly the player, we just get the drunk fans."

"Oh I have been there ... trust me," I told her remembering the chaotic football charter flights I did on the airline out of Stansted and Gatwick.

When it comes to the 'footie' spectrum I had certainly been at both ends! Quite by surprise I ended up at an England match during the summer of 2006 – the World Cup! I was flying the Embraer 135. We night stopped at Stansted ready for the morning departure to Cologne in Germany. My dear friend the beautiful Emma-Jane, (EJ) cabin attendant on this flight was sitting with me in the bar at the Stansted Hilton, two guys entered, sat on the adjacent corner and we started chatting. A good half-hour passed then:

"Where are you girls off to tomorrow?"

"Oh we are taking a bunch of 'corporates' over to Germany."

"Oh right you are crew then?"

"Yes."

"Oh great where are you going?"

"Cologne."

"Oh so are we ... what time?"

"Eleven."

"Oh same here ... you're not ... the Citylynx flight."

"Yes ... oh you must be our passengers!"

It turned out they were top performers from a big computer company and they were throwing a large hospitality day for their loyal clients and indeed for their own top sales guys.

On arrival in Cologne, EJ (as she was fondly known) slid her head round the cockpit door with a big grin and said, "Neets, they've had two 'no shows' and have invited you and me to the match!"

I knew this was not an opportunity to be missed. A very comical scene followed of the two of us in the back hold amongst all the oily rags, the tow bar, boxes of drink miniatures and peanuts, hopping around, heads bent trying to pull on jeans. We grabbed our bags, jumped down and went off with them in their coach, leaving the male members of the crew (we were two planes that day) rather riled. Yes I know you might be a devotee of the game and know the offside rule, but, EJ **is** stunningly beautiful and we are mates … ciao. (There are *very* few advantages to being a girl in this world so on the odd occasion when it works in your favour … take that ball and run with it!)

The day was a straight 'TEN'– amazing lunch in lofty chandeliered room in beautiful five star hotel/mansion which looked like Versailles. Then the build-up outside the stadium of people drinking beer, socialising, soaking up the electric atmosphere, then the seats themselves …in the middle down near the pitch. Superb! For someone who had never been to a football match in her life I guess this was a good way to start. I got to see Beckham and Rooney and all the other heroes of our team and I must say seeing all the action close up like that made me realise what a fast and skilful game it is.

It was England vs Sweden. We sat with the two guys we had met in the bar at Stansted and they were perfect hosts, very polite, charming and funny! On our right – the Swedish fans were in fine voice wearing brass horns and blonde plaits singing under metres of flowing blue and yellow. It was an exciting match although it resulted in a draw.

For Emma-Jane and me, it was definitely a 'Score'!

I read in the papers a few weeks later that although Thierry had split from his girlfriend he was doing well at Barcelona.

The Pop Stars and Musicians

It's rather a breath of fresh air when a bunch of musicians climb on board simply because, compared with 'the suits' who are often anxious and unsettled about their next deal; musicians are usually fun and splashy, dressed in crazy bright clothes and whistling a tune. Plus they stick their heads in the cockpit and say catchy little things like, "Yo sister howzit goin?" and smile and shake your hand. Most of them are expressive, and refreshingly 'whacky'.

Over the years there has been Rod Stewart, Mark Knopfler, Roger Waters of Pink Floyd, Velvet Revolver, Beyonce, Jayzee, Barbara Streisand, and Craig David amongst others. The Brazilian made Embraer (which is widely flown as a 37 seat passenger regional jet) has its executive version – the Legacy – luxurious and spacious inside, and unlike its airline sibling, the Legacy has winglets, (very stylish) long range tanks and bigger engines – two Rolls Royce Allisons, *and* … thrust reversers (very handy for those short strips like Cannes!). Being a roomy thirteen seater it lends itself well to bands. This was the aircraft in which we flew the talented Mark Knopfler (of Dire Straits fame) and his band to Rome for a very memorable concert.

He was surrounded by the very best musicians, both American and English – they had played with the greatest, and made up a treasure chest of talent. His 'wing man' as I called him was a fellow master of the guitar, on stage, he often stood side by side with Mark and was clearly 'his man'. He was a small bearded American – an outstanding, consummate guitarist, who was friendly well-mannered and without ego. He shared some of his special memories with us, especially the Neil Diamond tour!

We got to know them, after every show they'd bounce back on board, each one had their own unique style and greeting. The keyboard player (whose tipple was gin and tonic) had a birthday during the tour, so our crazy Scouser hostess Suzie had a brilliant blue cake made for him in the shape of a Bombay Sapphire Gin bottle. We carried it *to* and *from* the aircraft in its box, through terminals on trolleys, successfully keeping it hidden from him until disaster struck in Cardiff where we checked into a nice hotel on the water front. Just before departing for the concert, Suzie lifted the designer cake off the front desk to ask them to store it in their fridge and it slipped from her arms and landed upside down squashed on the floor. The whole foyer rushed over to help put 'humpty together again'. Laughing, we reassembled it, while Susie treated us to a few Scouser expletives! It didn't spoil the celebrations one bit.

"What would you guys like to eat on the onward flight?" we'd always ask. They changed from their usual sushi that night to curry. So we found an Indian restaurant in Cardiff, where the manager must have thought it was Christmas, we bought about four hundred quids worth of curry! We laid it all out for them on the polished credenza, they loved it. One thing about *this* band is they got stuck into the bar – polished all the gin off on one sector! – *and* they loved to eat. The next stop was Rome.

A gorgeous balmy evening settled over Rome. We jumped out of the taxi at the arena just outside town. It was 'bellissima'– there were crumbling, honey coloured ruins and old pillars around which snaked ivy and wild flowers. The air was filled with "Ciao Fabrizio…eh Ciao Maddi…" as young people, in brightly coloured jeans swung their heads to kiss their friends. Shiny Vespa scooters were pulling up, I saw tight brilliant turquoise Armani jeans, helmets being removed to reveal tumbling dark curly locks – and that was just the guys!

We had a real problem persuading the Italian security that we were with the band and our complementary passes would be waiting inside the building. He was only doing his job – our air side crew IDs meant nothing to him. Having said that, he was a bit of a brooding, high collared, *very* tight jeans type who enjoyed saying 'No' and shaking his head with a 'tch tch'.

Suzi sounding like Lilly Savage got her mobile to her ear and shouted, "Could one of you tell these bloody gits out here that we need to get in!"

She was a 'no nonsense' sort!

The phone was passed – a piccolo chat followed with Mr Love Myself Italian security man and…

'Che Forte!'We were in! We went backstage and had a drink with the band and entourage. It is invariably the same sort of scene at these shows. Great cold draughty corridors filled with black boxes and sound equipment, platoons of long haired roadies and 'sparkies' dressed in black busying themselves with duties and having a smoke. Thousands of metres of chunky cable are strewn all over the floors and high-pitched squeals come from the concert hall as they 'sound test'. There's always a special canteen with travelling chefs who churn out very good food. I had a fruitful chat with the tour promoter who had booked the plane. He loved the Legacy and we discussed the opportunities for future bookings – he organised many tours for bands. A bit of PR is always constructive!

We slid in at the front just next to the stage. The place was echoing and booming with that classic 'Dire Straits' sound, "We are the Sultans ... we are the Suuultans of Swing!" duh duh duh ... Magenta and turquoise lights swirled around in the roof and there was a faint trace of spliff in the air. What a consummate musician he is, one minute he is sitting down strumming his guitar solo singing folksy ballads wearing a cardi with a cup of tea next to him reminiscing about Lonnie Donegan, and then the next minute he stands up and under an explosion of crazy rotating lights brings all the band together and pounds out the grittiest and most incendiary rock. He has a knack of standing, relaxed just oozing cool as he journeys up and down the length of his guitar with precision and brilliance sounding sensational, and looking like the quintessential rock star even though he is dressed like a dad.

We stayed in the beautiful Hotel da Russie in Rome, which had a delightful courtyard with trickling alabaster fountains. Some of the boys partied till the wee small hours of the morning. Suzie our flight attendant joined them sometimes and had many a laugh – you only live once!

Mark sat up in the cockpit with us on the next leg into Naples, we cruised past Vesuvius and landed towards the sea. He took an interest in what was happening and chatted about various instruments, and gauges. This was their last Italian gig and I must say Naples and the warm glowing Amalfi coast was enchanting that evening as I flew us down towards the runway, the sea glinting beyond.

I have never had a crush on anyone (well maybe David Cassidy and Donny at school!) and don't get in the least bit star struck but I must confess to being a total Mark Knopfler fan simply because his music just 'gets you'. It has depth and soul, it is ...'meaty' the kind you want to crank up if you're driving, roof down through spectacular landscape doing a 'Thelma and Louise'! So ... it was nice to have him there next to me. I don't normally ask artists about their work – I don't like to pry, but I did on *that* occasion. Just before saying Goodbye:

"May I ask you Mark," I said, "the lyrics to 'Follow me home' on Communique – I love that song and I'd like to know, is it about some sort of pagan gathering...I mean 'Celebrations in the town tonight' and 'slaughtering upon the stone' and the priest and all that or ... what ...?"

"Oh it's funny you should mention that one," he said, "because they have just asked me to make it into a trance track."

I was none the wiser. He obviously didn't want to say what it was about. That's okay, I had an unforgettable moment in the Yorkshire Dales when I first heard that song in a storm and it will always conjure up certain images to me and as the saying goes, "You create your own reality!" Rather than be disappointed I have chosen to enjoy the multiple interpretations which are my own ... but thanks to him for really brilliant song.

The up side of flying bands around is there are no early starts and many parties, or so I thought until I then flew Rod Stewart who wanted to be home every night because Penny was pregnant, so we rushed back to Stansted each time with him.

We were flying his Scandinavia tour and after a successful concert in Karlstaad one night he came to join us the cockpit for the take-off at half past eleven at night – the sun was shining brightly.

"Blimey should have bought my suntan lotion!" he said slapping his cheeks and putting his shades on. We stayed with the lingering sun as we gained altitude; it was wonderful having so much light at nearly midnight. I suggested a song title 'Chasing the Light'. Years ago, he used to live near me in Sunningdale, I reminded him of his zippy yellow sports car I used to see screeching up the local pub – the Crispin. What a nice bloke Rod was. I remember dancing around with all my mates at school to Maggie May and 'You wear it well' in my denim skirt, so it was *great* to meet him, he was easy to please – he didn't mind if it was pizza and Chardonnay. Wears great jackets too!

Doncaster was the venue for one of his concerts and we landed at the newly converted RAF Finningly airport, now known as Robin Hood. We wished him good luck and asked what he'd like for the way home – he said lamb stew. We shut the aircraft down. First off; the APU which gave its familiar whirring down sound, then, clicked off both battery switches which leaves everything dark and silent. We climbed off and shut the air stair which lifts hydraulically using a switch on the outside panel – then off we went. We climbed in a taxi and went downtown Doncaster looking for Rod's lamb stew.

In a row of shabby terraced houses in a rundown part of town, we found a gem of a restaurant. The taxi driver had recommended it – it was owned by his buddy! Some shops and houses were boarded up, I saw broken panes and graffiti, you'd never think there could be a decent restaurant there. But here was Omid Jalili's double, a rotund Iranian living with his mum who only made a handful of dishes, and my word, this was gourmet Eastern 'family' food. He explained with passionate hand gestures.

"Lots of turmeric, salt, and long slow cooking until the lamb falls off the bone." We ate at one of his three little tables with plastic table clothes, it was manna from heaven. Mum came out and said hello though she spoke very little English. We loaded up with Rod's takeaway, gave him a big tip and returned to the airport.

Often one of the tasks assigned to us during these tours if there is no catering facility at the airport is to go downtown and buy food for the return journey. In Aalborg, Denmark we found a great little place and asked for their help.

"Okay, so you want grilled fish and steaks and mixed salad and vegetables for Rod Stewart's band?" they said with a grin.

"Yes that's right, and can you put it in …*these* foils which fit in *our* oven?"

217

We strike up a certain camaraderie sipping juice in kitchens round the world, chatting with chefs in white aprons and tall hats as they 'knock something up' for a famous singer.

While watching them prepare our food I remembered a very funny 'catering' moment with Diana Ross back in the late eighties on a Citation when I flew her from Heathrow to Dublin for a show which was sensational (she kindly left two good tickets for us). The funny thing was I had ordered first class canapés from the Meridian and rather nice nibbles, thinking with her incredible figure she'd be a 'stick of celery' girl and *wouldn't* be a big eater. When she got off she said, "D'you have anything different for the way back, I don't really like this very much."

"Yes of course, what sort of thing would you like?"

"Oh I don't know something good … err fish and chips? … tomato soup?"

Wow I thought, good old Diana. So I busied myself buying a thermos and some Heinz tomato soup and bought a fish supper from the chippie! She loved it. Who would have 'thunkit' as they say.

Rod would usually turn up after the show in a good mood, singing, and smiling in his flamboyant stripy blazer. I always thought it very endearing the way he could just snooze off on the seat, with a blanket over him. We all love a snooze – he looked so peaceful. But then in true Rock Star style he'd pull his bright red Ferrari up to the plane at Stansted and throw his stuff in, and whiz off.

We have a little pull-out bed in the more private, *back* section of our aircraft it has been popular. We've had businessmen crashing out through exhaustion, two gay guys disappearing behind the door for a long while! (Strange little white crumbs found on bathroom marble after *those* two! One of our politically correct Captains – insisted it was mints.) Various famous couples have had a little kiss and cuddle in there en route to Paris or somewhere romantic. Then Mr Mittal (the poorer of the Indian duo, he of only hundreds of millions not billions like big brother) would be a frequent snoozer since he regularly took off at midnight. But the band members loved to have a stretch out. The drummer for the heavy metal band who we flew around Scandinavia was partial to the couch. It's been a life saver for many an exhausted passenger including Mrs Beckham.

As in any walk of life there are those who are miserable and those who are amiable. I must say though, no matter *what* job you do, a simple please/thank you or a smile go a long way. At times it seems as though the accretion of wealth and status is directly proportional to the decline in manners or what Chaucer so aptly called 'gentillesse'. Not always – but sometimes.

We flew a famous R&B singer who found fame at a young age. I respectfully appreciate you don't want an exchange of life stories, but *one* greeting or a 'thank you' to the people in whose hands your life rests during that week would be – well call me old-fashioned but, courteous! He did perform with a certain narcissistic finesse and clearly knew about the bull**** which goes with 'pop stardom'. In one of his songs, he sang about how (and I may be quite wrong) when you suddenly 'make it' your friends change and your life changes – he seemed to be the living example of the lyric, in which there was, a hankering after the simple pleasures with real mates in the 'poor years'. It wasn't *exactly:*

"... then you become so arro-gant yeah ... and everyone becomes a syco-phant..." but it was a smidge along those lines.

It's true though, when you have nothing you get offered nothing ... you make it big and suddenly you can get a table anywhere and everyone *wants* you on their boat!

Wow what musicians he had though, they were from West Africa and boy what talent. I told them I was born in Nigeria and we spoke pidgin together!

"Ahh sissie I see you sabi de language oh!"

One of them was the son of the drummer from a West African band called Osibisa whom I had listened to as a teenager in Lagos. I remember well the honeyed black voice at the beginning of the album, we recited it together with laughter and nostalgia. He was astounded that 'female English Pilot' would know the album – what were the chances? I received all sorts of complicated 'bro' handshakes and knuckle presses for that one!

"Osibisa ... criss-cross sounds dat explode with happinessss ... we start ... early one morning in de heart of **Africaar**!" There followed drumming, thunder and the sound of rain and birds.

They invited us to the gig in San Gregorio next to the San Salute *right* on Venice's Grand Canal. The venue was stunning – a private square villa with open courtyard in the middle – typically Renaissance in style. The large rooms on the upper floors had huge windows which opened onto the canal. It was the last word in elegance and luxury. Someone told me it had been the residence of an ambassador – I believe the Hungarian. Anyway it was an exquisite, gorgeous spot. There were two balconied floors above, people leant over to watch the show. It was sponsored by MTV and was quite small and exclusive. The ceiling opened onto the night sky and you could see the twinkling stars and the lit dome of the gleaming white church next door. I had a little boogie with the musicians at the party after the show. I felt all their African sunshiney warmth and I instinctively turned to it like a smiley yellow sunflower turns to the sun.

There was one prize winning musician – he was small and wiry but an endlessly firing synapse. A human firework. He played the keyboards but frequently picked up various guitars which he played with equal confidence. He jumped up and down feeling the rhythm with every cell in his body. I inwardly nicknamed him 'perma grin' because he never stopped smiling, sweat was pouring off him as he leapt about in transcendental ecstasy. They can feel the ancient drumbeat of generations, it's engrained in their bones. They've got that 'let it all go' hip swinging abandon. That rhythm. Every time he boarded the plane he literally leapt up like a young hare and put his perma grin face in the cockpit.

"Hey sista," he would beam and then give me the 3 stage handshake which I learnt quickly, the normal shake then the thumbs up, then the finger curl one. He was a happy soul.

When we left Monte Carlo where they had played at the wonderful Princess Grace stadium, we noticed on the headcount that we were two short.

The 'main man' our star and bodyguard had decided to stay behind! I wondered if it had anything to do with the bevy of naked Uzbek beauties frolicking in the sea.

Who else … oh yes Beyonce. I had no idea (being an Earth Wind and Fire girl) that her boyfriend is one of the biggest superstars in the universe.

"Omygod Jayzee," my friend said astounded. "What d'you mean *'who is heee'*... you don't **know** him? He's huge! – God what are you *like*?"

I was just aware of a bunch of very casual looking guys and girls in 'trakkies' with barrow loads of 'bling' and little kids who were identical miniatures and everyone's name seemed to start with a 'J'. They asked for banana nut bread or fried chicken. Sadly we didn't have either. If only they'd let me know beforehand because my mum's banana nut bread is scrumptious, I could have brought some along for them and I'm sure they would have loved it. Having turned down our normal catering they did get stuck into the red wine (quite right too). I liked the way Beyonce had a good drink after her show. There is nothing more uninspiring than the skinny stars of lotus blossom tea fame. It was just a shame that an entire glass was spilt that night all over the owner's favourite white cashmere blanket.

On completion of her concert in Dublin where we picked her up and flew her to Nice at one o'clock in the morning, she was out of her angel and sequin outfit and into her velvet tracksuit by the time she got to us. I was struck by the long amber coloured hair, serious nails, and never ending eyelashes; she's very sexy. She lay face up, stretched out on top of her boyfriend, they watched a Spiderman Three DVD. Well I don't suppose you want anything too deep when you're unwinding! They looked dead comfy and that's what we aim for!

In all my years of flying I have never seen baggage like theirs. When it was offloaded from the truck outside our cargo hold, my knuckles were in my mouth. Considering there were only a few passengers, here were bags for twenty and each one was huge and heavy, it took two guys to lift each one up and we had a hell of a time fitting them in to our hold which is *big!* No they certainly hadn't mastered travelling light. We flew them down – arriving in Nice at sunup and sparing a thought for the skipper of the boat who would take charge of them for the next week as they embarked on their luxury sailing holiday. Hope he had lots of room!

Fun in Finland

This had to be one of the stranger moments of the career. Mid June, standing in the middle of a field at Finland's version of Glastonbury in blazing evening sunshine, dressed in my uniform (sensible navy M&S trousers and white pilot's shirt) surrounded by thousands of *SERIOUSLY* drunk and stoned people – all head banging. I saw the entire 'brochure' of piercings – there were pointy cones – three in a row protruding from lower lips, there were swords through brows, studs through chins, multiple earrings and nose rings. One girl had about twenty rings in her lip it looked like a miniature slinky – and these were just the *visible ones!* And dreadlocks ... blonde ones! Enough dreadlocks to tether an airship. They must have looked at me and wandered what on **earth** someone *that* un-hip could be doing there!

The band – a very well-known heavy metal group were pretty wild to say the least. Some of them used to play with Guns and Roses and I could be wrong but perhaps dear little Axel Rose poppet that he is, became impossible to work with. I guess there are only so many drugs and so many 'no shows' you can get through. They were a very cool bunch. "Hey you guys wanna come to the show?" the manager chirped up in Vaasa in Finland.

It always beats sitting in the aircraft for six hours so we accepted. The manager said he'd have tickets and VIP area passes for us at the entrance, so having learnt the price of a taxi we decided to hire a car from the very dour Hertz man who tried to charge us 180 Euros. (The place is famous for good herring but not bargains.)

"We only want it for four or five hours," we protested and unsmilingly he agreed on one hundred. He had a vibe best described as Jack the Ripper-esque. Off we sped down the country roads of central Finland, it reminded us of the mid-west USA with the flat fields, red wooden homesteads, barns and grain silos, a scene made so much more lovely by the thousands of wild purple lupins.

My friend and colleague Caroline, who was the flight attendant on this trip and a lot younger than me, was able to fill me in on the music scene being a Radio One listener. (I having defected quite some time ago to Radio 2.) Allegedly the guitarist (half black, top hat, long dark frizzy hair, black leather, and massive tattooed biceps) could claim something not *many* people could claim in this life – to have died *twice* . He had been revived so rumour has it, I found this rather impressive. That is a mortal coil that does not want to be shuffled off! No wonder he wears black and never takes his shades off – probably staying *away* from the light!

The drummer wore a hat with 'In Funk we Trust' written on it, he was always bleary eyed and crashing out on the bed in the back. The other two were also true 'Rock Stars' – open shirts, covered with tattoos, chain-smoked and were recovering alcoholics. All of them – dead friendly.

Even with the help of two 'chicks' from California to assist them, not once did they get off the plane, go to a gig and actually remember to take everything with them. *Every* time someone would call and come back to collect a top hat or a garment or just 'something'. They had numerous big round hat boxes with toppers in and a very fetching cane – they always seemed to forget *one.* I thought of my friend Jo who had flown Guns n Roses; she too said that *every time* they would send someone back because they had forgotten something.

So, in I walk – the frumpy traffic warden, sober, and straight. There were over five stages in this vast park and it was just choc a block with young head bangers: Goths, piercers, hippies 'born agains' you name it. I stood on my own (having declined Caroline's offer to get near the front – I saw too many plastic cups full of beer being thrown around up there!). The band came on to screaming applause and rotating lights.

"How are all you Mother F****** do-iiin?" was the opening line screamed out by the guy who'd sat in the front seat of the aircraft snoozing like a little church mouse or reading quietly.

"Let's rock this mother f****** place up!!"

Rapturous applause followed and much jumping up and down on the spot, head banging and fist punching in the air. Then the whole band burst into, well, what would you call it … noise.

The guitarist of black top hat fame played his guitar upright sort of north/south, rather that east/west as most people do. He was undeniably striking. The lead singer was a bit Mick Jagger-ish mincing and strutting, he was never without his ciggie. The tall blonde who looked like a Californian surfer took his shirt off to the screams and whistles from various 'Scandi' babes (amongst those who could stand up and focus) and he too played a mean guitar and leapt frenziedly from dais to dais like a nimble insect.

Patty Smith had been on before them so a huge crowd had already assembled, I was leaning against the end of some sort of barrier and actually had a great vantage point. This was definitely a "Drop some pills and get some thrills" type of venue! These are just a few the things I saw.

A girl in a tiny white crop top and cut off shorts was perched on the shoulders of her boyfriend; her bare feet grapevined round his back – for balance. He brilliantly managed to keep her up there and turn round through 180 degrees so his face was now right in her crotch. His friends applauded him heartily; quite rightly so it was an impressive manoeuvre, she certainly didn't seem to object. Then a girl floated past in a little 'hippie chick' dress, she was being dragged by her boyfriend through the crowd right in front of me. She had two high pigtails, a round freckly face, and her eyes were like saucers in her Cheshire cat face. She was as high as a kite. He was pulling her too fast because she wanted to take things in, like me for example, she looked with this huge grin and wide eyes, staring me up and down – how could *anyone* be at a concert like this looking as pitifully un cool as me! I swear she thought I was an alien. She giggled with her hand over her mouth and smiled almost sympathetically!

There were three very drunk bare torso guys dancing and drinking on my right passing a joint around. They were all out doing each other on the air guitar. Suddenly one of them just went *straight* down, he was out cold. His mates laughed at first and tried to roll him over with a flip flopped foot. But when he didn't move they tried to bring him round by slapping his face – but he was gone. I was on the verge of intervening with my 'ABC' of first aid training, but fortunately he came round five minutes later and staggered off in a daze – maybe to find the saline drip tent.

A thought flashed through my mind of the previous summer, when almost to the *day* I found myself in Kiruna in Lapland on June 25th. A mining town famed for Reindeer and big drinkers where the architectural highlights were called the 'Snuffbox' and the 'Spittoon'. Long haired guys wore 70s style Hells Angels leather jackets with Eagles on the back. That night we were marooned in the only 'happening' bar in town (it was like the bar from Star Wars – full of strangeness) with live music and a bunch of crazy 'Scandis.' It's no wonder you never get that 'One for the road feeling' when the sun is pouring through the windows at one o'clock in the morning. We left when the inevitable fight broke out!

Back on the stage our band were giving it some black blooded, nasty, savage 'welly' insulting everyone and smoking like chimneys. I did notice among these 'Scandi hoolies' there were some 'not so stupid' ones who had bought earplugs, – I thought at first they were little Martian aerials but then I realised they were just little earplugs and boy would I have paid any money for some!

I thought back to my university days schlepping around in mud at Glastonbury, eating lentils from a tent which had a sign: 'GOOD F***** FOOD' with my fellow graduates. I recalled the kegs of cider going overhead at Castle Donnington when Van Halen and AC DC played. I remembered the girl who walked stark naked, but for a daisy chain, right through the crowd to the bar for more drinks, she got rapturous applause. So I reminded myself that I *had done* all this stuff once, but boy was I **over** it! The fact that I found it unnecessary and downright rude to call everyone mother f****** was the final nail in the coffin and convinced me beyond all further doubt that I had finally become my mother! The fact that I could not evince the slightest trace of melody out of this music made me face the fact – I was condemned to the world of smooth jazz and radio 2 along with all the others who can't find their glasses!

"I liked the Mark Knopfler concert," I argued with myself internally I can't be *that* square.

"Yes but he *did* wear a cardi," went on my internal adversary.

Oh to hell with it I concluded; I'm happy to like Abba!

I stayed until almost the end and then thought I'd better find my colleagues and get back to the jet to fly this gaggle out to Rotterdam. We panicked when unable to find the airport on the way back, (different exit) I managed to flag down the only two Scandinavians in the world who didn't speak any English at all. We then stopped for gas and the pump didn't work. Panic stations – we didn't want to arrive after the band. But all was well because they were *very* late, no surprise!

I looked out across the deserted airport of Vaasa on the west coast of Finland (there was just one controller in the tower and a fireman who had stayed on duty for our departure). Though nearly midnight the sun was still up, it was molten and syrupy – quite beautiful. The band arrived all bouncing about like Zeberdees. Of course they had forgotten something but decided to say to hell with it.

They took loads of pictures outside the plane with their mascot, which was a cute stuffed toy – a little black bear. They held it out of the cockpit window.

"Hang on," I said and put the headsets over the toy's ears as if he were the pilot. They loved that!

"Oh cool, hold it there," they laughed and clicked away. Then I straddled it over the pitot tube for them … more laughter.

I noticed that I didn't see the Californian chick on stage who had sat up in the cockpit with us for my landing in Vaasa. She gave me the impression she was a singer … I didn't see her.

Later on the aircraft when they all piled on, I said, "Hey I didn't see you on stage, I thought you'd be coming on with your black leather pants and peaked cap. What happened?"

"Oh well I only kinda go on if they **really** need me, otherwise I just kind of help out."

The two or three remaining Fins on the airfield really wanted to see the back of us so they could knock off.

We fired up engines one and two.

"After start checks please."

"Electrical … checked."

"Hydraulic pumps … Auto."

"FADECS … Reset/alt."

"Ice protection … as required."

"Air conditioning … set, APU off,"

"Rudder … checked."

"Flaps … set 9"

I was anxious to go, it was midnight, we had over two hours to Rotterdam and I was catching a 7.15 flight in the morning back to London, it was my day off and I was attending the Falkland celebrations. I would have only two hours sleep in the hotel. We were *just* about to taxi out and in burst one of the band from the back.

"Hey guys, can we all just take couple more pictures, we didn't get one with *everybody* in it. Can we just jump out for a second?"

"We'll have to shut down an engine," I explained with undisguised lack lustre but it didn't matter, they wanted some more pictures. They have *just* spent fifteen minutes taking pictures I said banging the heel of my hand on my forehead. Oh well it all went hand in hand with the 'forgetting things' theme.

There are two answers to questions like these. The one you **want** to give and the one you **actually** give.

The first one has to be said in a 'sarci' John Cleese/Basil Fawlty voice, "Yes okay we'll just shut down this multi-million dollar engine which loves accelerating up to 800 degrees Celsius and revving up all its systems, its pneumatic starter valves, its ignitions, its digital electronic control, its fuel lines, and then being stopped dead and turned off, and cooled down only to rev up again three minutes later. No problem, what's another cycle for heaven's sake I'll pick up a couple of titanium turbine blades from Halfords when I'm next there you inconsiderate MORON..

Then the second one. "Yes okay no problem."

We had a no smoking policy on our jets. It was easy for the girl who manages cabin services from the office in Essex to say resolutely "They cannot smoke". I'll challenge *anyone* to tell this lot they can't smoke. A recovering heroin addict whose mood swings are anyone's guess, whose life is madness and methadone, asks with a predatory rumble for an ashtray, isn't going to take kindly to hearing "Er sorry but you can't smoke". Nah. Best not to go there.

Something quite revealing about the characters who surround these people happened on the final leg to Rotterdam. The manager, I think with the advice of the personal trainer (now *there's* a job) told Caroline to take the booze off the plane. The lead singer gets on board after the exhausting gig and asks for a scotch.

"Um we don't have alcohol," said Caroline in an innocent Saint Trinians sort of way.

"What d'you mean, you had scotch yesterday! ... so **where** has it gone?"

He leant over her rather menacingly with eyes that bored into hers like drill bits. I was actually quite scared Caroline admitted later, 'cause he was **not** happy'. Don't you think **that** would have been the moment for the manager to pipe up:

"Er ... actually it was **my** idea to remove the alcohol, so don't take it out on her!"

But not a dickey bird. This, the very manager who'd earlier criticised *other* band managers for telling the lead singers what they **want** to hear. It looked very like a repeat performance to me. The female assistant (of no-show on stage fame) chirped up with:

"Oh we meant everything off *but* beer and wine."

It was a meek offering. In fact Caroline had been told to remove all alcohol.

"Where's it gone!" he growled mutinously.

"Oh we ... er... had a clear out," came back Caroline valiantly.

"**You had a CLEAR OUT?**" came back the scream which had Caroline's head tilting away and her ponytail practically lifting horizontally.

Then the manager and trainer knew they might have a problem on their hands so abandoned their sensible ideas of sobriety and concluded: "We need to find him a scotch ...**now!**"

With that Caroline disappears into the hold to rummage through mountains of bags to find the scotch before the plane got torn apart.

I do sympathise with the hassle some of these tour managers have to go through – it can be like looking after a bunch of kids. On this occasion I asked the manager if he'd enjoyed the show.

"God no, I've been on the goddam phone to New York and Paris, calling Fed Ex."

"Oh dear what's the problem?"

"One of the band just informed me that he's about to run out of *medication*."

"What do you *mean*?" I said genuinely concerned. "What *type* of medication?" (Crew **do** have to be informed of medication.)

"Oh dernt matter ya know ... medication."

"Oh ... right," I said.

"Yea he's got enough to get him through tonight but that's it, so I've been trying to get some couriered over and it's a hell of a job."

I was suddenly rather relieved I was getting off in Rotterdam and another crew member was taking my place. I had images of Jekyll and Hyde – black shirts being ripped open, incoherent ranting, bubbling spittle, perhaps the crash axe being pulled from its harness. Yep these were *proper* rock stars – no orphan hugging UN peace ambassadors amongst this lot.

As we lifted off into the night sky to fly south-west, we crossed the coast which was just breathtaking. Hundreds of little fingers of land and small islands gestured into the sea which had the texture of mercury in the dwindling rays of light. It was like a lovely painting. Despite being gone midnight the sunset was still going on! The thousands of little islands were of the deepest black colour – like the paper used for silhouette cut-outs. They somehow looked content to be remote and unvisited. They lay silently and serenely as though they were sleeping. It was the landscape of ancient myth and legend, of wolves and eagles, of Viking boats with woollen sails and a high prow, giant men in bearskin capes called Laaksonen or Arvid. I kept glancing back at them until they were out of sight.

Just hours later, the following day I was sitting in Horse Guards Parade in London in my dress and hat, with HRH Prince Charles, Baroness Thatcher, Tony Blair and other important figures nearby, listening to the military orchestras, while memories of the Falklands were recited. It was formal and grand. The RAF were there – 'Per Adua ad Astra' as were the Fleet Air Arm, navy, army and many Veterans adorned with their medals, marching alongside the bearskin hats and royal marines and I thought to myself 'talk about from one extreme to the other'! What a world away from those Nordic nutters and wild Finnish Rockers! Well ... they do say variety is the spice of life!

A Few Others

During the next few months our company flew Aerosmith, Red Hot Chilli Peppers, The Eagles *and* The Who. It was quite a summer for bands. I was touched to hear of Roger Daltry drinking camomile tea. I wonder if he listens to classic FM as well. I know Alice Cooper is partial to a relaxing round of golf these days. In that one summer, the company I worked for flew Daniel Craig, Joan Collins, Hugh Grant, Brad and Angelina, Posh and Becks, Beyonce, Barbara Streisand, George Michael, Tony Blair, Westlife and a host of others. I flew Cameron Diaz, (boy has she got the 'ditzy' giggle down) Jude Law and Kate Winslet to Madrid on the promotional tour for their film, 'The Holiday'.

Timbaland was an interesting one, not being into rap music, I thought we had the manufacturers of the outdoor shoes coming on board. I was momentarily hopeful for a new pair until my much younger and more 'with it' flight attendant told me not to be such a plonker and 'how could I not know who *Timbaland* was for Chrissake'! I did a bit better the following week when I took Jensen Button down to Hyeres in the south of France. "He played Joseph in the technicoloured dream coat musical didn't he?" I joked just living up to my reputation as an uninformed 'duh'.

The one for whom I suspect the company would *not* take a rebooking, was the 'Oh so haunted' and severely etiolated 'Mr P' shall we call him – well famed for his supermodel girlfriend. I personally wasn't on his flight but my colleague told me he trashed everything, from the lounge at the airport to the inside of our aircraft. A few broken glasses is okay but when there is blood ... perlease. Could someone, *anyone* tell me what the attraction is? I trawl my mind and engage my deepest reserves of charity and still all I see is a screwed up vacant junkie who can't sing or string two words together, who has lost all elasticity of mind and body, a blithering freak, in desperate need of a good soapy wash, a square meal and perhaps some music lessons.

Ireland was the venue for George Michael. We asked the manager for three tickets and attended his show in Dublin. It was absolutely sensational. What a funky performance and quite the most fabulous original stage I'd ever seen. It was like a moving escalator, (all multicoloured) which ran along the floor and then up vertically behind him – all very high tech. His was a fun filled show full of spirit, dancing and plenty of audience interaction. The three of us – Caroline, Ian and I had great seats and danced the night away. He was a fabulous performer and the Irish – hardly a 'reined in' lot, absolutely brought the house down with their dancing and singing.

He came on board with a big (and I mean big) lady who was, chatty and friendly. I understand it was his sister. I've always tried to find the good in everyone but his boyfriend was ...not the friendliest... Wouldn't you think that flying around with a superstar in a private jet having whatever you want might raise a smile? Nah, not for this sour-faced grumpy. Maybe he didn't like flying you never know. Not once during the trips did we get a smile, a hello a goodbye or any eye contact. Just shows, you never know people's inner turmoil. Despite all the froth and frill of jet setting, despite enjoying every material endearment life can offer if you're not a happy soul ... that's that. George, however, was a pleasure to meet and what a great concert.

Posh and Becks, or Pecks and Splosh as my friend Mike calls them (he can never get it quite right) were our passengers to Cannes on the south coast of France. I'm no football fan but David you can tell is just 'good guy' warm friendly and had a great smile! He said to his kids as they disembarked in Cannes.

"What do you say to the nice lady and man?"

"Thank- yoou," they chirped. How refreshing that was. They sat right at the back on the sofa bed for some peace and quiet and left their kids to play in the main cabin with a girl who was perhaps the nanny? They were normal little boisterous kids exploring all the drawers in the plane and having fun.

My colleague from Signiture – the handling agent at Luton told me that Victoria had wanted to get out of her dress which was a bit tight to fly in, but her zip had got stuck, she asked for her help and they spent fifteen minutes in the ladies trying to tug at the zip. But my friend couldn't budge it either. They were having a good laugh. It's not everyone who gets to help posh out of her dress!

You never see too much of Victoria with her peaked hats and dark shades, but she was very polite, she told us she was *really* "Ti-yerd" and in need of a break, so went straight to the back to lie down on the sofa. She really did look exhausted. They were going on an anniversary break in the south of France just prior to the move to California. We gave them the bottle of champers and a card and wished them well. Of course with that figure she doesn't eat much. (I suspect she's *not* a member of the Sunday night Chicken Tikka Masala and a pint of Cobra club.)There was one of the best seafood platters I'd ever seen on board for them. I must say it would be nice to see her 'chill out'. it must get exhausting having to 'hold that pose' every day of your life. Maybe in America or one day she'll be able to run carefree down a beach trailing a kite with the wind in her hair, laughing. I must confess I loved the Spice girls when they came on the scene, they always cheered me up enormously! We wished them a fabulous weekend in the south of France and good luck the USA. I'm sure she'll 'fit *right* in' in Beverly Hills and that Tom and Kate will loan them the Gulfstream if she misses Sawbridgeworth!

Rocking and Rolling with the Stones

This wasn't a post gig party with the Rolling Stones, (sadly!) it was a bit of severe, unexpected turbulence which suddenly rolled the jet through ninety degrees and had Ronnie Wood's drink flying up the wall of the aircraft. We flew to Berlin Tempelhof (ah wonderful) to pick up the band after the film festival at which the Martin Scorsese feature about them had been promoted. Everything went swimmingly with the movie so I heard, and we flew some of them back to Farnborough.

Charlie Watts looked like a proper 'city gent' with his dark conservative overcoat, scarf and clean cut look – a real contrast to Ronnie Wood who was delightfully 'nutty'– a little Jack in the Box. Charlie told him off for smoking on board! Ronnie was hilarious, just bouncing around like a 'free radical'. I've never seen thighs so thin on a man. What struck me is even after all these years of being a global mega star and jumping from private jet to limo endlessly – he *still* seemed so enthusiastic about it all and came out with the odd "wow check this out!" like a child finding the electric window knob for the first time. He was giggly and smiley – *and* he gave me a big kiss when he said goodbye! Plus any OAP who still wears coloured plimsolls and kaleidoscopic scarves at a granddad's age gets my vote!

It was during this flight that I experienced a real moment of terror for the first time! We were cruising at thirty-six thousand feet on a perfectly still night somewhere over Holland and suddenly the plane just went out of control. The autopilot snapped out, we lost 300 feet and we were vibrating and shaking violently. We were *almost* going inverted at one point and it lasted about twenty seconds. As part of our training we are forever watching videos of crashes – I know … nice touch isn't it? I thought instantly of the DC10 which lost its controls because something severed the hydraulic lines. They had no ailerons or elevator, just differential thrust on the engines in order to turn. Could this be **it**? I thought to myself, I'm going to end it all splattered across some 'corner of a foreign field' in the Netherlands! Fortunately we came out of it. We discovered that we had strayed too near the aircraft in front which was a huge Airbus; that night there was absolutely nil wind and without a breath of wind to disperse the vortices we had flown straight into his wake. That was scary..

Poor Caroline, our flight attendant who is tiny, had been knocked off her feet and there was broken glass everywhere and food all over the floor! I went back to explain to the passengers what had occurred.

"You could have waited till I was out of the loo!" Charlie said taking it all in his stride. I could imagine him bouncing off the walls of the back loo like a squash ball being knocked around the court! Red wine and bloody Mary had gone all over the beautiful suede upholstery on the walls and over the carpet. That would please the owner!

Ronnie Wood seemed unphased – well it was 'only Rock n Roll' I guess.

"Was that *you* driving darlin'?" said the hefty geezer (one of the entourage) as he disembarked.

"Blumin' women drivers ya see!" he joked as he squeezed my arm and gave me a cheeky wink.

The fleets of gleaming limos purred up to the aircraft, gloved drivers opened doors and 'Jumpin' Jack Flash was gone. It had certainly been a 'gas'!

The Unknowns

Although not famous, there are musicians out there whom I've encountered because of this job, who, I feel really deserve a mention. I flew some businessmen once to Albania. In the capital Tirana, I heard THE most expressive, soul stirring violin music I've ever heard and it came from a gypsy man – about a 100 years old who had gold teeth! I will never forget him. He journeyed zealously up his strings, lower fingers vibrating madly, as the bow danced vigorously left and right over the beautiful worn battered instrument. His eyes were closed; he was with God. He held such an impossibly high note at the end, it was as though miniscule winged fairies were tiptoeing in teeny satin ballet shoes up the tightrope of his string as he beckoned them ever further towards that high point. Then suddenly as the refrain achieved orgasmic resolution, they all scampered down the instrument like a nimble gymnast flik-flaking down the beam for the big dismount. Then came the four big closing notes: 'te da da **DER'**. Everyone in the restaurant had lowered their knives and forks and was utterly absorbed in this old man's genius. Here was a real life Orpheus playing for his Eurydice. One clap started a torrent of applause as the old unknown gypsy with the crumpled bronzed face looked up to his God to thank him for his company! Another was in Cuba. It must be something about communist countries – maybe the lack of distraction and opportunity which hones such masterful talent. We were having dinner in a 'parti'cular' in Cuba – that is someone's house – it's how they make a bit of extra money. In walked a beautiful old lady in black. "Tengo noventados anos" (I am 92) she announced proudly and started to strum her guitar and sing old Cuban songs with the sweet tunefulness of a little nightingale. It was as though angels were kissing your ears. I'll never forget her either. Both she and the

Albanian gypsy – very elderly – never left their countries, and both, produced 'blink back the tears' music from deep within their souls!

All Above Board Hoskins Old Chap

The flight on the Embraer Legacy started at RAF Conningsby in Lincolnshire and went down to RAF Northolt near Heathrow. Military airfields offer a different experience, as civilians we don't frequent them much, therefore it's a nice change. With these high ranking men came plenty of braid and 'scrambled egg'. We had Major Generals, Lieutenant Generals, his Excellency this and his Imperial Excellency that. Those were the Saudis; batting on *our* team we had Air Vice Marshall 'X' and squadron Leader 'Y' amongst other luminaries of the military world. There were many 'bins' on their team and many DFCs DSOs on ours. There would be forelock tugging today.

A huge black storm cloud edged nearer Conningsby as we approached low level from the south. There is always a lot of 'chat' when you visit the military, they tend to say more on their radio than civilian ATC they make damn sure there is no margin for error.

"Contact in your one o'clock no height information – read back QNH – report checks complete – report wheels down." Often for training purposes they will give you a PAR (precision approach radar) when they 'talk' you down with radar steers. It's exciting, and very accurate (and makes you concentrate!). It is busy with the 'crabs' as our airforce boys are affectionately known.

Having landed, we taxied in and parked near the beautiful Lancaster bomber. A few minutes later a quite breathtaking display took place featuring the spitfire alongside the typhoon Euro fighter, the old and the new! It was beautiful … and very moving. Great clouds of vapour formed on the topside of the fighter's swept wings and the air condensed out in the great pocket of low pressure. There was a distant slice of lemony light under the purplish storm cloud and this made it even more dramatic. The easy climbing rolls of the spitfire and its familiar growl were just fantastic as it spiralled and looped around the stormy clouds.

"That was jolly nice of them to do a show for us!" we joked with the squadron leader, who was a Harrier pilot, and had come on board to greet us.

"Yes well we aim to please," he retorted. He came on board first to introduce himself and do a quick inspection of the aircraft. He was a chirpy sort, and was very pleased with our aeroplane.

The Saudi dignitaries were lined up outside a nearby building clearly having enjoyed the show.

They walked past a line of 'chests out' upright saluting airforce juniors in their distinctive blue uniforms, then climbed on board. The spaciousness of the Legacy is what catches everyone's eye when they first embark. It is roomy and luxurious. All the formalities were strictly observed as they embarked. Having copied the latest weather we called for start and taxi. The sky was still thundery and moody, walls of slate coloured rain fell from distant cumulo nimbus clouds. Thunder rumbled like a retreating beast.

We enjoyed the short low level flight across the green fields of Lincolnshire, Leicestershire and Bedfordshire and down to RAF Northholt our prestigious military field (which seems to have become the 'plane park' for Net Jets). More red carpet and saluting military personnel awaited.

After night stopping at a local hotel, we returned to Northolt the following morning and went through the rigorous security at the gatehouse. There was a small queue so I had time to glance about the place. There were formal photographs of men of great rank and power. I saw braid, medals and immaculate uniforms; serious expressions on faces which meant business. The whole alphabet seemed to be displayed under some of them – KCB, CBE, ADC, DFC, FRAeS, BAR. This was the 'puissance' of the Royal Airforce.

Northholt is a strange place, just in case the Royal family land there it has to be nice and quiet (I know – it's too insane!) so … you have to shut down your APU; this is the little jet engine that powers all your services on the ground. One poor American Captain in a Boeing Business Jet (BBJ) had just loaded his entire flight plan for Chicago only to be told by ground crew to shut down – thereby losing everything he had loaded into his Flight management system.

All this so that the Royals don't have to put up with that annoying thing called noise – it's an airfield for God's sake.

"You know what? I bet there isn't a single member of the Royal family who condones this or even wishes it – I mean most of them fly themselves anyway," I suggested.

"Just protocol and tradition," came the answer from the man in blue.

"Maybe, just maybe it's time to review rules made in 1935 which applied in the days of Handley Page Heracles."

Funnily enough nothing changed.

The flight that day was up to RAF Warton near Blackpool in Lancashire. It is a BAE Systems airfield where the Typhoon is assembled. Again we enjoyed the contrasts between the military and civilian procedures. We waited in a little pilots' lounge with baggy sofas at the end of the operation room and watched television and made endless cups of tea. BAE run some of their own aircraft for business and we had interesting chats about their routes with the operations personnel. They showed us the extensive area full of hangars where people beavered round the clock building the prestigious jet fighter.

The meetings came to a close, we received a heads up and walked out to get things started. I noticed some poor lady in her fluorescent jacket had to stand next to our aircraft in the rain until the passengers actually arrived. I asked her why, and whether she'd like to wait on board.

"I can't love thanks anyway, it's just the rules, I have to stand guard while we have visiting aircraft on the ramp."

Yet another one of the mysterious erratic notions of the new and totally unfathomable health and safety that we all have to endure these days.

The flight went swimmingly (literally, with the torrential rain and crosswind at Luton, so much for the merry month of May). After a marathon innings of handshaking, smiles, nodding and hand to shoulder contact – they were gone. I jumped in my car and turned on the radio to hear a lively debate on the unprecedented amount of corruption recently revealed within our military. It had a bearing on the trip I'd just done.

"The MOD are fully incriminated," said the guest speaker, who was explaining the scandal to the DJ and taking calls from the public.

"The fact that this money was supposed to be for the payment of fighter jets but went to Prince Bandar as shall be revealed in 'Princes, Planes and Payoffs' on Panorama is really something of great concern."

I hit the usual three lanes of stationery traffic with five thousand cameras and two million cones, commonly known as the M1 so with resignation and I can't deny a fair bit of interest I cranked the volume button.

"Yes but we have signed an agreement to stamp out bribery, how can we therefore show bare faced indifference to such appalling double standards," said one caller who obviously still thought there were morals in the world.

"Well yes I fully acknowledge your point," replied the DJ sympathetically, "but isn't this just a part of big business these days?"

"I think Bob Dylan had it right you know when he said 'steal a bit and they put you in jail but steal a lot and they make you King." She left the airways in a palpable aura of disgust.

"So what is the significance of having such a high profile Saudi involved in this way?" asked the DJ.

"Well," continued the pundit. "The fact that the SFO shut down the enquiry is really quite significant, I mean we are talking one hundred and twenty million a year to one person who is the ambassador to Washington and this money probably went through BAE Systems with the full knowledge of our Ministry of Defence."

"Let's just bleedin' face it," chirped in a caller from Chigwell, "this is how business is conducted nowadays, I spent years in Saudi and all round the Middle East and I can tell ya if it weren't for bribery and corruption there wouldn't be no business, know what I mean?"

"Okay," continued the DJ with a neutral kind of 'keep the calls coming', tone.

"But how can our own Prime Minister condone this by saying it's good for British business?" came the retaliatory shot back over the net from another idealist.

"Well John from Chigwell what do you say to that?"

"What I say is this ... that he's right *it is* good for Bri-ish business and it's the way of the bleedin' world now mate, and another thing ..."

And so this lively debate continued which I thoroughly enjoyed – it helped relieve the boredom and drudgery of the motorways. As I stirred my pasta sauce that night I thought about that debate and the type of punishment a crime like that would exact, and concluded absolutely *none*. With that I enjoyed my pasta and felt rather chuffed that I had played a miniscule part in a rather huge scandal and confirmed inwardly that the last laugh went to him on the receiving end of one hundred and twenty million. It was a tad more than my pay checks anyway. No one **ever** said life was fair! – But it's still good!

Three Men from North Africa

Tangier

Property developers! We would be idle and quiet without them. We flew a group of about twelve to Tangier and on to Marrakech. They were looking to put some 'high end' hotels such as Kempinsky's into the place and were excited about the potential growth in Marrakech.

Normally when down *that* way, we are landing in Malaga. But because we were over flying that day we enjoyed the magnificent view at thirty-nine thousand feet, off the straits of Gibraltar. You could see in one gigantic scene as though viewed from space, the outline of the Spanish/Portuguese coast, the impressive 'Rock', North Africa, the blue Mediterranean and the Atlantic beyond. It was a quality shot!

A savage wind was blowing in Tangier when we landed. We had all day there so jumped in a taxi to have a tour of the town. We had a right character in the shape of our taxi driver, he had a huge hooked nose like Fagin and beady little eyes which narrowed further through his thick specs. But he was a one man show. Being a French speaker I sat up front with him and he called me madam after every sentence. There is a real charm the way the North African speaks French, it is almost 'pidgin' like but very pronounced. I commented on the wind and I got North Africa's King Lear.

"Oui madam, nous avons L'Atlantique, **et** Le Mediterranée, (he lifted his index finger and thumb) ils se marrient et … ahhh plein du vent." (He waved his hands in the air in crazy circles.)

"On dit le **Rrroi** du vent. Nous avons plein d'oxygène ici a Tangier madame (he thumped his chest heartily). La mer est très agitée et nous avons toujours du vent madame. Nous dormons bien ici madame."

He whizzed around town pointing out things of interest such as Malcolm Forbes's house.

"Ici la maison de **Forr-bez** madame – il etait très rich et il aimait beaucoup Tangier. Maintenant le Rrroi a acheté pour ses in-vités quand ils viennent ici pourrr dorr-mir madame."

It became hot in the car, we asked him for some air conditioning. He turned to me and opened the window and said proudly, "Voila air condi-shon madame!"

Since he only had the two top canines and the bottom two incisors it made for an interesting smile, his mouth looked like a staple remover. I couldn't help thinking that perhaps this was the real living example of the man who talked the hind leg off a donkey hence the ruined teeth. He showed us the market places the hotels and the restaurants perched high up on the hill overlooking the whole bay and then went into an animated explanation of 'les bateaux', which steam back and forth between Gibraltar et Malaga.

Naturally he tried to pull a fast one when it came to pay time. Having said initially that it would be "Cent diram madame" it suddenly became "cent cinquante diram madame."

"Mon dieu," I joked with him and remarked in French that inflation was "très rapide" in these parts. After fobbing me off with the hundred dirams being just "allez" rather than "allez-retour" he shrugged his shoulders and drew all his fingers into a point in front of his mouth and moved them back and forth; this is a sort of international language for 'I have to eat'. After many mercis, shukrans, and a load more "bonne journée madame", and "bon voyage" to all of us we went our own ways after a very entertaining and informative afternoon in windy Tangier.

Marrakech

Our well-dressed, well-heeled passengers grabbed their brief cases turned on their mobiles, said thank you very much and alighted on to a baking hot apron at Marrakech airport. I passed their bags from the rear hold down to the handlers who loaded them in the boots of the Mercedes and off they went to try and find extensive chunks of arid desert to turn into lucrative five star hotels. Soon, where there had been nothing more than a few goats milling round some rocks, there would be a shiny magnificent structure complete with swimming pools, fountains, lofty mosaic foyers and willowy palm trees around whose trunks thousands of fairy lights would be wrapped.

We headed for the famous square in the middle of the city. Wow if you have never been, this is truly a place worth seeing. The square is jam packed with musicians, jugglers, tumblers, and dancers. The centre is lit up with sports stadium strength lights. In the centre are a hundred different outdoor eateries, food is being chopped and tossed into giant sizzling woks and smoke fills the air. Tables with benches surround the whole area and people of all nationalities are eating. The souk is open, selling everything imaginable. Boys in fez hats with tassels move their heads round so the tassels are constantly rotating like helicopter blades, then they cartwheel and flic flac in their bright silk costumes across the square – a real spectacle! An old man with hands like knuckles of ginger was pressing olives in an antique wooden press, the contents being poured into old Evian bottles – fresh cloudy olive oil, I bought a bottle for pennies it was the best I'd ever tasted. Traders were selling cloth, shoes, jewellery you name it and all around are dozens of freshly squeezed orange kiosks. Then a very lively character came skipping up trying to coax us into his al fresco restaurant. His patter was superb.

"Where you from?" He obviously has a well-rehearsed 'spiel' for *any* nationality.

"England."

"Oh lovely jubbly, come eat … we have lamb, fish everything." Learning one of us was vegetarian he was off again, undeterred.

"Look lovely jubbly vegetables, salad, couscous."

And when you say you're going for a wander and might be back he said, "See you later alligator … in a while crocodile."

Before you could retort he's spun on his heel and was accosting the next passer-by.

The next hustler we encountered was even funnier, he had pictures of Rick Stein *at* his restaurant, he threw his arm round my shoulder, tapped his picture of him and Rick which he'd laminated and shouted, "Look look! Rick Stein was here, very good! Very good! He like very much. He friend. You want fish kebabs? We have, you want lamb? We have eeeevery thing we have the best the best, come look."

Then he continued "Gordon Ramsay, Nigella Lawson but…" and then turned and patted his bottom and winked, "Asda Price!" When we turned him down (our flight attendant didn't want to risk 'Delhi Belly') he raised his finger to his mouth, cocked his head and said, "Am I bovvered?"

They were all impressively up to the minute with English characters from television!

Moroccan families were all out together, girls in frilly dresses, boys in their best attire eating ice cream as they strolled. Old story tellers sat cross-legged round fires recounting ancient tales and myths. It was quite enchanting.

I wanted to do a tour of the city, the rest of the crew chose to stay at the hotel and relax, so I wandered outside the hotel and did a deal with a taxi driver for the whole day – it amounted to twenty-five euros. I didn't know him from Adam and maybe it was a bit risky but being the wrong side of twenty-one for an abduction, I went for it.

He said he would take me to all the important historical and cultural spots and wait for me while I looked around. And sure enough every time I exited from a palace or a museum, there he was drinking coffee and chatting to his mates, but he was always looking for me and when he saw me he sprung up and waved like a parent meeting a child at Arrivals in the airport. It was all very 'Ali Barbar', I was half expecting a low flying carpet overhead!

He dropped me at the fourteenth century palace of the sultan which is a dazzling museum, at the Koutoubya mosque, and the ornate building where the harem was kept. As he drove me between sites he filled me in with entertaining detail (in that lovely French /Arabic accent) about the founder of the city Yusuf ibn Tashfin and the French conquest of 1912. We became quite friendly and it was good for me to practice my French. I winced at the poor wretched horses who slaved away under that merciless heat. Some had arthritic hips, their backs bowed with toil. All round the streets, you hear the clip-clop of horses' hooves, beaten on into unwilling and exhausted trotting. He told me that I was as bad as Brigitte Bardot with my overboard concerns about them. Oh well, I knew nothing would get done to ease the animals' burden, and I also knew that would be the first and last time I was likened to Brigit Bardot!

He could see I was wilting in the heat – though the windows were down, the blowing air was hot! But before he took me back to the hotel he insisted on introducing me to his family. We parked up on the outskirts of town and walked down a rather shabby alley. His mother and grandmother were sitting outside making cheese, he had an uncle there also and he introduced me.

"Voila mon amie d'Angleterre, tu sais ce'qu'elle fait? tu sais?… Elle est **pilote** eh, c'est bien eh?"

They were all so friendly and mama wiped off the upside down bucket so I could sit on it.

"Asseyez –vous," she said and then some youngsters crept out from behind a beaded curtain. I was introduced to everyone even the family goat which I had to hold.

"Mangez, mangez!" insisted grandma and she handed me some delicious homemade cheese. They asked me what I was doing in Marrakech, I explained about the passengers being property developers looking to build hotels. It seemed a world away from them somehow, and although they would benefit in no way, they nodded, smiled and repeated "Ah les nouveaux hotels, ah c'est bien" and seemed to think that was wonderful. I thought it was pretty wonderful sitting in that yard stroking the goat, eating homemade cheese with a Moroccan family, it was a lovely little bubble of experience. The taxi driver dropped me back, we shook hands and I tipped him for having been such a good and reliable companion and showing me what is really an exciting and vibrant city. He smiled and gave me his card with an "À la prochaine"!

Libya

On board our jet that day we had some American oil hunters and one very influential Libyan businessman. The idea was to explore the possibilities of drilling and exploration and he was like 'their man in Havana' only on this occasion 'their man in Tripoli'. One hundred miles out is when we usually start our descent, we were left high by Air Traffic, they gave us descent clearance at about sixty miles so we did a very memorable 'dirty dive' approach over the sea and landed on a coastal airport. I soon got the gist of how important our passenger was because the red carpet was spread at the bottom of our air stair and men in uniform stood saluting whist others shook his hand. I was almost expecting the fanfare from the bugle players. The large black Mercedes limo purred up alongside.

Goodbyes and thank yous, said, I went over to the building to pay the handling fees. I said to the man in the uniform and dark shades behind the counter, "Wow what a reception, our passenger must be a real VIP here in Libya."

"No no," he insisted shaking his head and tutting, "he not VIP, only Gadaffi is VIP in Libya, this one not VIP."

"Oh, well who **is** he then if not a VIP?"

"Ah," he said thoughtfully, "he is … yes … he is a very important person, but **not** VIP this man, only Gadaffi is VIP for Libya."

We went to a beautiful hotel right on the coast in Tripoli. We had an evening stroll round the souk. Our very generous and very important passenger (but not a 'VIP') had kindly arranged for us to visit Leptis Magna the next day. There are several important heritage sites in North Africa – such as Trasamine and Carthage, but they don't come much bigger than Leptis Magna. It was founded in 600BC by Phoenicians and annexed to the Roman Empire in 46BC. One of the emperors (Severus) was actually born there. It is home to some of the most fascinating archaeological treasures in North Africa. As we wandered around we saw, ancient walls, baths, forums, columns, temples, and much more. This is one of the most important ancient Roman cities in the world. It was fantastic.

On the way back our driver (who was clearly enjoying the protection of the diplomatic plates) was tearing along the roads at breakneck speed with loud Arabic music playing. If he'd gone any faster we might have actually gone back in time and seen the Romans in their skirts marching along the roadside. He pulled into a cliff top restaurant, we looked puzzled and he said it was the pleasure of our host and passenger Mr 'A' and we should enjoy lunch. We sat at a long table overlooking the ocean chatting with some locals. What a wonderful treat, and how generous of our 'Very Important Person'. He wanted to make sure that we enjoyed the treasures and hospitality of his country.

I had a feeling that although Gadaffi might have been the figurehead, it was certainly *our* guy who actually got things done in that country.

From the Jet to the Super Yacht

One day, I had an irresistible opportunity to see aboard one of those mega yachts – the type Bond would crawl aboard with a knife between his teeth, unbeknownst to the baddies who lounged around on deck 2, while armed guards patrolled the helicopter pad on the aft deck. It was in a covered dock in Kiel in north Germany. The family *owned* the jet and I flew them to a military base called Hahn and they very kindly invited me along, I accepted gratefully. It was the day on which every single craftsman who had played a role, in this three year project would be acknowledged and treated to a slap-up lunch on the owner. It was a day of speeches, thanks, breaking the champagne bottle and the unveiling of the name (and much celebration!). I was captivated by the workmanship on board this floating palace.

Naturally it was the last word in opulence and luxury. It had a huge Jacuzzi on the top deck – ideal for those starry nights, bars, lounges, dining areas and many luxurious en suite bedrooms. A concealed spiral staircase disappeared down from one of the rooms into a little secret area – all very intriguing. The décor throughout was just exquisite. The chief designer walked with me for a few moments and was telling me it had the most sophisticated fire detection and extinguishing system in the world today. The environmental and air conditioning systems were also very advanced but it was little touches which really fascinated me, namely the carpet in the bar. It was just like sand, it was made into wavy ridges. I had to ask. The carpet maker had used a sheep sheerer on a deep pile white carpet and after hours of assiduous work had literally carved out the form of sand ripples. It was impressive. A jagged crystal ceiling (like Swarovski crystal) created beautiful patterns of blue light overhead.

Then there were the toys – the smaller boats and jet skis to go ashore on, they were tucked down below the party/sunbathing area from which it was only a short stroll to the extensive bar! It was incredible. The head honcho of the boat building company gave a rousing speech thanking the owner and his wife for their kind patronage over the last three years and he acknowledged *every single* person who had worked on it. Food and drink followed and I had the opportunity to chat to the boss's wife who was clearly delighted with the result. She personally had done so much of the shopping – she told me of all the goods she had bought from the White Company and other shops in London describing the effort and energy she had put into all the choices. I must say all the cushions and furnishings as well as all the lamps and ornaments were all her choice and they were lovely.

"I bet you can't wait now to have her in the water down in Cannes and actually have a drink on the back deck, watch the sun go down and celebrate," I said with sincerity.

Her answer really startled me.

"Oh I'll never have a drink on it … we've sold it already."

"No ...? why?" I said genuinely surprised as to why you'd take the money when you are already billionaires. I couldn't understand it. She probably thought how naive I was.

"We're having a bigger one built, they have started it already."

The German designer on my right could see my surprise. I said to him, "I have a boat you know."

"Ya?"

"Yes it's an inflatable kayak, cost a hundred and ninety quid from the chandlers in Chertsey. I keep it in the back of my car, I inflate it with a pump that plugs into the lighter, it's got telescopic plastic oars and a little skeg and two inflatable seats – I take it to the river, I have SO much fun on it – don't think I'll ever sell it!"

"Ya but I don't think anyone would offer *You* a few million profit for it."

"This is true – my running costs are probably lower though – don't need any crew for a start."

We chuckled.

I learnt from that experience. Rather than get attached to the boat for them it was more of a project. It was certainly an extraordinary opportunity being shown this massive undertaking known as boat building from the great engine room, the fridges in the kitchens, the tiniest wiring harness, to the bridge and all its state of the art 'satnav' and radar, oh and not forgetting the enormous lazy susan in the middle of the vast dining table! I wondered if they would sell the next one on. Probably. But I hoped they would get the chance to enjoy it. Oh well I felt sure I'd get to the water first with my foldaway kayak and have fun paddling to the Montague Arms on the Beaulieu river in the sunshine.

Whatever the outcome I was grateful for their invite and felt fortunate to have had a rare glimpse. We all left in two taxis and drove back to the airport where their gleaming jet was waiting – the only civilian plane amongst all those German fighter jets. The stairs were down, ready to welcome them back on board – the *other* toy!

And now, Please Meet...the Passengers!

*There are certain 'types' who seem to crop up on private jets. We've all been told **not** to make generalisations, but what the hell, let's make some. It's all very light-hearted. You do get certain types who frequent this exclusive world of 'leather and pace'!*

The Designer Wife

The designer wife is usually groomed like a Crufts winner, she can be fairly stressed and a tad unfriendly. She is dressed in tight designer jeans and has an expensive long suede coat of incomparable softness, the seams of which are trimmed with luscious fur (the hide originating from rare newborn yak dwelling on unpronounceable plain in somewhereystan). She wears long pointy boots, and tosses the tumbling shiny hair from side to side, and is constantly inspecting the acrylics (nails) using one as a tool to clean the others. You would think that folks who spend their lives hurling around the place in a beautiful private jet avoiding that agonisingly depressing thing known as 'check in', would be, well, on the whole quite cheery wouldn't you? Well, not so, because for this 'type'(the spoilt wife) it seems sometimes that no garnish on her cream cake of a life is ever good enough.

The average stay for the kid on the sideways thrust bony hip is about two minutes before it is plonked in the arms of the patient and smiling Slovakian nanny who is rotund and a bit plain so as not to attract corporate raiding hubby. (She must make sure that it is *only* company assets he'll be stripping!) Mummy releases the child with undisguised relief and moans something along the lines of "For God's sake Tabitha you're driving me insane." Then she catches sight of the other little monster who's found the toy truck in one of the shopping bags and is steering it along the floor making 'broom broom' sounds.

"Tarquin please don't get your clothes all dirty *dah-ling.*"

At this point it's all too much and with a huge sigh she starts rummaging in the cauldron sized Louis Vuitton bag for the much needed headache pills. Then when she 'pings' at the security machine and gets frisked, we get a "For God's sake" and a murmur about anyone thinking they were common criminals and weren't they supposed to be exempt all this nonsense. She glances at hubby, her enhanced lips pinched into a tight grimace, her raised eyebrows and tilted head saying to him – 'I thought all *this* nonsense was just for plebs, can't you sort it out sweetie?'

All this strain and hassle of actually *getting* the kids, the nanny, the hubby, the luggage (*AND,* most importantly the twenty-six shiny boutique shopping bags, each decorated with seductively attractive lettering and filled with pretty tissue paper) *from* the hotel into the limo and *onto* the waiting private jet, is indeed tiresome; but it's nothing that the good old stalwart friend "Hello" magazine can't sort out and once she has picked that up and started flicking through, she's happy – well as she'll ever be.

But the one thing we must remember about *wives* is that they are terribly useful as recipients of the assets which are deftly shifted by a rich husband. Get her a non-domiciled status and …another chunk of tax saved. But keep her sweet! Otherwise they move on to become the 'decked out doyenne of the divorce' and *that,* gets painfully pricey – we've had plenty of those.

When together with fellow designer wives their conversation tends to revolve round fashion, spas, restaurants, shops and recent **'fab'** holidays. There are many who have been my passengers but one in particular came out with what I think must be one of the iciest and most snide comments I ever heard.

I was chatting once to a gentleman about his friend's aircraft – a Gulfstream 550, *very* nice too. The conversation got on to various people, Paul Green the well-known British business maestro and funnily enough a girl named Robin whom we both knew. Through my brother I met this young lady whose banking and investment brilliance was earning her a fine reputation in the city. I knew she was a friend of Mr Green. She made tons of money, was very aggressive in her pursuit of business. I attended her 40th birthday party in Florence, Italy. It took place over a whole weekend and was truly the most spectacular and glorious party I had ever been to.

So I would say Robin was not only a high achiever, a wealthy forty year old, but a great party girl, with an eye for the aesthetic.

Her name cropped up in conversation.

"Did you go to her party in Florence by any chance?"

"No sadly I couldn't but I heard it was marvellous," he replied.

Then from around his back emerged the wife wondering what on earth we could be discussing.

"What's that darling, who are you talking about?" she said making sure she didn't lower herself to anything as unsavoury as eye contact.

"Oh we were just mentioning Robin."

Then, pushing the Dolce and Gabanna shades up onto her head, she looked up at him with a frown so deep – and came out with the corker:

"Oh God, *she's* rather yesterdays news isn't she?"

Another unforgettable line came from the American wife of a billionaire who enjoyed every possible endearment that could make life comfortable. Although not feted for her deep love of culture, she was very good at interior design – *that* by the way means you spend all day in Harrods! I flew her to Scotland where she'd never been, so I took great pleasure in giving her a quick overview: granite mountains, lochs, beautiful scenery, salmon fishing, roaming deer, bagpipes, tartan, haggis, fine malt whisky and so on. After her brief stay she arrived back at the jet to go to a high dollar resort in the Mediterranean (much more her scene) and I asked with enthusiastic anticipation, "Well did you enjoy yourself, did you like Scotland?"

"Mmm. Well not really," she said screwing up her nose and shaking her head. "It was kinda cold and kinda old … there's not much there for me really, I don't think I'll be back."

I instantly thought of the American tourist, checked pants, camera round neck, emerging from the Prada museum in Madrid, saying to his wife, "Nah I don't think there's anything in there for us honey, howbout a carfee?"

And so … I thought, that's *it* for you Scotland, you are *off* the Christmas card list. You can keep your mystical lochs, your Robbie Burns poetry, your majestic mountains, your enchanting castles, and sound of distant pipers, you can take your malt whiskies and fresh salmon and glorious islands and stuff them up your jumper, because Miss West Palm Beach doesn't rate you!

Another was quite a different creature, she was the wife of the super brute, the modern day Herod. After several trips collecting and dropping off various mistresses all round Europe for him, we finally got round to collecting her. He wagged his finger and drew it across his neck and said "This is my *wife now"* which roughly translated means 'so keep shtoom about all the girlfriends and illegitimate children otherwise it's going to get expensive!'(Crikey if I had a grand for every secret I'd kept for men and their peccadilloes, I'd be flopping about on a blow up pink caddi in my *own* kidney shaped pool in Juan Les Pins.)

I waited dutifully and correctly at the top of the air stair just outside the cockpit ready to greet her, with, I must confess a tiny trace of sympathy and affection for this woman, who I suspected may have suffered with his vile temper and sexual peregrinations, so I was ready with a big smile and a warm handshake. She alighted from the shiny Mercedes, in an elegant well-fitting suit and high heels, she was sartorially perfect, slim, beautiful, manicured nails, hair in a bouncy ponytail and big dark shades. She looked like the sort you would see in a Parisien 'Salon de thé' sipping floral tea with her favourite designer while stroking a freshly groomed lapdog. I held out my hand as she climbed the stairs and ten seconds later I was feigning an inspection of my own nails because no hand was forth coming, in fact no eye contact and no smile. She walked straight passed me and turned into the cabin just stopping with a critical 'tut' to straighten a mat on the floor which was a smidge crooked.

It made me want to pick up the crew phone on the front bulkhead and say: "Er hello … is **anybody** out there actually happy? … do we have *aaaaneee* happy campers at all in the audience? … lady in the lovely suit, front row with all these millions, private jets and diamonds? No? … C'mon any takers for just a smile …"

But I didn't.

Ah yes … it was another marriage made in Reno!

The Hunting, Shooting, Fishing Chaps

These guys are Fun with a capital 'F', gorgeously debauched and boozy. They invariably turn up late, a bit drunk, due to extended lunch, they are covered in mud, wearing plus fours, green chequered caps and red socks. They have many fine guns in leather gun cases which gives the security staff at places like Humberside airport (affectionately known as The people's Republic of Humberside) a field day because they can go into a 'jobsworth' overdrive.

I picked up three chaps there who'd been shooting birds on the Yorkshire moors and were about to fly to Germany to shoot wild boar in the Black Forest. One of them was a Count or Baron, his splendid Teutonic name sounded as though he should be ensconced in the lofty heights of Neuschwanstein. I remember he just stood in the middle of Humberside airport and changed his clothes, no fuss. It *was* very quiet – with no one around, but still, he went from mud splattered tweeds and deerstalker down to socks and boxer shorts in seconds, completely unabashed. Next minute hey presto he's standing in his mustard corduroys and blazer before you could say 'hand me my Rigby'.

The other chap was an exemplary HSF. His frame was a testament to the copious amounts of foie gras, game pies and oozing cheese boards which had been helped down with the lubricious assistance of Volnay, and Beaune. He was jowly like Willie Whitelaw and he was … great!

When the security manager who was queen of all Snagglepusses saw his gun cases, she moved in brimming with self-importance determined to bring these 'toffs' down a peg or two. (I'd already ascertained her paranoia when she wouldn't let me step back through the sliding door I'd just walked through to retrieve my mobile from the aircraft. Despite being the only plane on the ramp and it was *'just there'*. I had to go through the 'ping' machines *all the way* through security, wear a yellow jacket, be accompanied by one of their staff, go through three doors with secret codes and produce my licence.)

We were very late already and keen to go, but she set fire to every hoop imaginable and made us jump through the lot. She wanted, licences, documents, papers, the whole nine yards. She looked down the barrel – I guess for some sort of registration number. He was losing his cool especially when something she insisted on seeing was in the bag, which he had innocently tossed on the luggage belt and was already on its way to the aircraft. When she instructed him to keep the bullets separate from the gun he exploded like a gouty brigadier.

"Yes I suppose I am *very* likely to shoot myself with my own bloody shotgun on the plane!"

Not the teeniest trace of a smile softened the gimlet eyed, pursed lipped, granite faced woman who had just beaten Sinead O'Conner in the 'shortest hair in the world' competition.

"If there's to be any f***ing shooting it will be *you my dear!"* I heard him mutter under his breath as he struggled red faced with all his clobber to the security machines. I laughed inwardly.

The HSF's (huntn' shootn' fishn') love a good time, they all drink to excess and travel with 'the chums'. In this environment they can indulge their passions for boyish pursuits and associated toys. They love their guns, game, red wine and black Labradors. Politics, port and the Sunday papers are also favourites. It is heartbreaking (happened to me in Hamburg) to have to tell them when you are in a foreign country, departing early Sunday back to the UK that you *have not* managed to get the Sunday papers (the delivery is just not early enough).

On the whole the HSFs are good-natured despite the odd arrogant one. Their irreverence for inane rules and their 'two fingers' to all this ridiculous health and safety nonsense and for spineless political correctness are bracingly refreshing. Compared to some of the fat free, bean sprouting, colonic irrigating, no meat no fish, no diary, 'all ribs and self-denial' types, they are, a breath of fresh air!

One chap I flew was such an eccentric, when he alighted from his Range Rover on the ramp I gasped, he was a giant; he must have weighed twenty-two stone, a veritable blunderbuss, how *on earth* would he fit in a Citation? He somehow managed to occupy both seats at once (one on either side of the aisle), his head strangely cockeyed and brushing the roof, he just wedged himself in. He actually brought his dog along. It was a huge lumbering old golden Labrador, which had been sedated for the journey. We all helped it up the steps of the Citation and once on board he just plonked himself down in the narrow aisle between the seats. He closed his red droopy eyes and didn't move one inch after that, just grunted and snorted and became a source of bad smells. It shed so much hair we had to get an industrial cleaner to vac the carpets after the flight.

But the chap was most convivial and with the practiced skill of a veteran boozer polished off a bottle of brandy and demolished every scrap of catering, with the help of the dog who he would stir occasionally when his master boomed out his name: 'Hine' (obviously his favourite brandy) then toss him a huge slice of rare roast beef which the hound would gulp down in one and then drop his head heavily back on to his paws with a small grunt and another smelly emission.

Both he and Hine alighted with awkward difficulty at the destination. They made quite a pair, he stood there tucking metres of stripy shirt into red cords while the dog, still dopey, stood devotedly next to him with his front legs not directly under the shoulders but splayed out like a set of compasses. They looked as if they would collapse beneath him any minute, but his tail wagged benignly. Off this most unathletic duo went, to shoot something or other, frankly I gave whatever bird or beast it was, a damn good chance of seeing another day!

The Aristocrats

The next hunting trip I flew was down to Seville on an Embraer Legacy, thirteen seats (and bed!). When you think it normally seats forty passengers when in airline configuration it gives you an idea of the space. I carried ten of England's finest 'Aristos'. They were all Dukes, Lords and Earls and there was one Lady in the shooting party. There were long established names including Percy, Peel, Grosvenor, Douglas Home, not forgetting the delightful Lady Leonora Litchfield. Yes the hydraulic fluid may have been purple but the blood was blue. I have never been among such polite and charming people. They were so well mannered, whenever they asked for something it went, "Would it be too much trouble to have a drop more scotch?"

This was such a breath of fresh air after the uncouth boorishness of the foul mouthed wide boys who love to show off.

"This champagne is sh** luv 'ave you got anyfing else?" (It was Dom Perignon!)

"I told you we should have put the Cava on," we joked afterwards!

It was *really* pleasant after the finger snapping arrogance and acerbity of various Sheiks, or Nawabs from the Sultanate of 'Mhine al Mhine'.

I personally loaded up the rear hold with the help of my baggage handler friend at Luton. The luggage was marvellously expressive. As I handled a few hundred grand's worth of Purdies and other fine guns, I admired the craftsmanship of the worn hide gun cases with gold initials embedded deep in the leather. Then came the standard navy globetrotter suitcase, beaten and weathered with large square locks, and covered with old sticky labels. The Hercule Poirot style thirties suitcase was there, the sort you would see nestled in the net baggage rack on the Orient Express. The sides of the lid were so worn they could no longer hold the contents properly and a small piece of a pink striped shirt popped out.

The lovely thing about the Aristos is their casual and effortless eccentricity. They are just ever so slightly frayed at the edges and are not quite sure of the *exact* programme. We saw a couple of them waiting in the car at Luton.

"You can come and sit in the lounge at Signature and be comfortable if you like, you don't have to wait our here."

"Oh may we, okay super, thank you vair much."

Four of them were on board having a drink and a Marlboro, reading about themselves and their vast lands in The Field magazine, the slot was approaching so I went back into the cabin to ask them how many more were coming, to get an idea of time. I cannot recall the *actual* names but it went something like:

"Is James coming?"

"Well as far as I know, isn't he with Christopher?"

"Not sure … I *think* so."

"What about Andrew?"

The suggestion of a phone call to their friends' mobiles to check progress, would be a bit crass. Better that we just 'jolly along' in this slightly hazy yet rather comfy bubble because "Everything will be alright, I'm sure."

There was no urgency, it was delightfully haphazard and all sartorially perfect of course. There were maroon cords and mustard coloured trousers, red socks, tweed shooting jackets, with patched elbows, silk ties and smart handmade brogues. This was the world of hunting pinks and cavalry twill and a splash of pink gin. One, sported long hair, which just added a bit of 'mad Count' to the party.

After their three day bird shoot just north of Seville, (who knows maybe with the King) they returned with many large wooden boxes, nicely crafted – and plenty of them, they were filled with special bottles of quality olive oil. I asked about their shoot, they told me they had got plenty of birds and it had been terrific. We parked up on a cool rather blowy dark evening at Luton. They thanked us profusely and loaded up the vast spoils of an Iberian 'castillo' weekend and slid into their waiting cars to head off to widespread country seats throughout the land. They were courteous and civil and so profuse in their thanks. I enjoyed meeting them. Once home they could, if so inclined, scale the turrets of their country piles and take in three or four counties through the zeiss 'binocs' no doubt!

The Geezers

"If you get up early, work late and pay your taxes, you will get ahead – if you strike oil."

245

Just as hyenas or wolves hunt in packs, well so *this* type – the 'Geezers' travel together, in a pack and have nasty 'boys weekends' away. Neither grammar nor the Queen's English are big features with these guys but they are masters of cockney rhyming "me old china plate" and have bucket loads of charm and cheek. 'Geezer speak' is pithy fast and occasionally filthy, it features words such as 'wonger' or 'readies', 'the folding stuff' and they all seem to have the knack of making plenty of it! There is also, it comes as no surprise, the odd lewd reference to female anatomy. Some geezers don't like the 'bird' around when they are getting stuck into the nitty gritty of whoring, gambling and drinking or talking about boxing, punch ups, sport and fast cars. They always call girls 'sweedart' or darlin' and on some occasions they just want a 'dirty bird' for a bit of fun and games.

These are the confident, risk taking, balls out 'largin' it', shirts outside, LADS. "And another bottle of the pink please darlin'!" Some are clever and crafty and get rich selling repackaged debts which most of us don't have a hope in hell of ever understanding!

They have been known to dismiss a needy girlfriend with a fistful of readies and a sneaky wink, saying, "Look Sweedart I'm talking to Meat hook Mike 'ere, so why don't ya go and buy yourself a nice dress babe and get summing nice for underneath! Know what I mean darlin'."

Geezers have rollicking personalities and like to talk in "Millw-yons" and get 'wodged up' and "pull a cork" on a nice 1994 chateau something or other and light a big fat cigar. These guys are terminal womanisers and flirt suggestively with the flight attendants all the time, trying their luck. These geezers indulge in noisy, slack jawed boasting. Some, (not all) love a bit of bling or an outsized jewel encrusted medallion (best one I saw was a curvy elongated teardrop, just covered in diamonds).

But the prize for bling on a geezer has to go to one I met in Jersey which along with Guernsey is a popular destination for private jets. He was a diamond dealer and had made millions fixing dog races. He actually explained to me *how* they would pull dogs up and fix the outcome of the race – he made a mint! He looked like a cross between Arthur Mullard and Vinnie Jones. He was huge and on his wrist was a watch with three concentric rings of sapphires, rubies and diamonds, which when rotated and lined up spelt 'I Love You'. Round his neck he had gone to quite another level of 'medallionary'. Not content with one jewel there were loads of them – every three inches round the chunky gold chain. We had rocks, ores, ingots, precious stones some intriguingly wrapped in swirling meshes of gold (like a model of the Jupiter with orbiting satellites), diamonds, rubies – in fact half of Namibia was there. He had a big ring on every finger and bracelets galore! He bought more pink Laurent Perrier champagne than I thought was available on the island. He was a generous, likeable man, I guess the prototype 'diamond geezer'.

Some of these 'polished' geezers are just successful hard working city boys – bright, sharp, risk takers. These guys do 'cheeky deals' over a 'cheeky' lunch. They talk:

"Discount market, forward transactions, Libor, letters of Credit, liquidity, and hard arbitrage." Where else would I have learnt that CDFs (credit default swaps) is a 45 trillion pound business? It's all banking jargon and over my head but they certainly seem to have a tight grip on the whole caboodle, but don't forget 'OPM' darlin' is *always* the best way (other people's money).

"Don't worry mate I can get that sorted for half a percent over base!"

Stags in Rutting Season

Stag parties are common features of private jet flying, and 'whooah'... have I witnessed some boys weekends! Sometimes it is *one* guy with the money and the rest of the pack are his mates, *he* can afford the £3,000 per hour flying costs but he doesn't want to be 'Billy No Mates' so along come his pals to accompany him to some Mediterranean island to see how much beer can be drunk, and 'totty' can be chased.

A jollier crowd of Staggers there could not have been, the day I flew to Ibiza. They were irrepressibly ebullient. It was a category 'A' weekend, the head of the party was a very successful South African who, was in the restaurant business. I first caught sight of them on the ramp at Luton as they zigzagged over the tarmac – shirts out, jackets slung over shoulders and shades on. A true 'laddish' advance. It was mid-afternoon, they had enjoyed a very liquid lunch during which the blow up doll, the rubber gag and fur lined handcuffs and edible thongs had been unwrapped and thrown about with much hilarity. I remember these because they left them on the plane and I looked at them as I tidied up – I was astonished at the *price* of these objects! (Good business to be in.) No wonder the owner of the famous sex shop flies around in a Lear Jet!

They drank every drop of alcohol on board and got louder and louder. One (a South African) was passionate about flying and spent the flight with his head in the cockpit telling us over and over again about his trip on Concorde which had recently finished its service so we indulged in some Concorde nostalgia. His bloodshot eyes were almost tear filled as he gushed with brandy scented breath.

"God it was just *ep-solutely* f****** awesome I swear ... aahh lecker hey it was lecker."

I was super impressed by these chaps because being in the catering business they had a feel for running a tidy ship and one of them asked for the bin liners and he proceeded to put every empty tin and bottle away and secured the plates in drawers for landing, now *that* was a first. We like tidy staggers. They actually did their own 'cabin secure' check.

Next sighting of them was in San Antonio in one of the many heaving bars. I nodded hello to the 'Concorde' chap but he didn't notice, due to his fevered interest in the well-oiled girl thrashing about in a cage wearing no more than a broad belt doubling up as a miniskirt and two Dairylea triangles threaded onto some string over her boobs. He lifted his beer bottle to his mouth but missed a couple of times, then finding his lips tilted it back and emptied it in one, then returned open-mouthed to the swaying hips of the caged girl. He looked like a character out of Close Encounters who'd just seen 'the light'. I am grateful to those 'Staggers' because unfamiliar with the Ibiza scene, I was unaware that 'clubbing' was an activity for which courses should be run. People take this *very very* seriously. I was queuing for the ladies on the fourth floor of a bar, next to me were three girls in white PVC nurses' outfits complete with white fishnet stockings, little hats and thermometers.

"Wow," I said, "you look terrific, you must have been to the fancy dress shop here."

"Oh noo," they replied in broad Geordie. "We brought these over with us in our luggage like."

"What just for this nightclub?"

"Oh yea, we've got a different outfit for each night, this is the tame one we've got schoolgirls and devil woman and Betty Boop dominatrix."

"Gosh that's not exactly travelling light, I guess the flip flops bikini and couple of T-shirts is not de rigueur on Ibiza."

"Well you know people take it really seriously here so you've got to come prepared."

"So where's the dance floor?" I enquired .

"Oh *this* is not the nightclub, this is just the bar people meet in beforehand like."

I was amazed because it *was* a sizeable place and the music was booming. But around midnight people went on to a club which was twenty times as big and could accommodate thousands of revellers. There was a massive traffic jam, just miles of headlights as cars piled in to this nightclub. Girls in fetish gear, and rubber, all flocked like pilgrims to the club the size of Heathrow airport. There, on numerous different dance floors and chill out rooms people would rave away until noon the next day when they would collapse at three o'clock on the beach and try to rehydrate. (By the way I'm not knocking it!)

The journey back from Ibiza was somewhat more subdued, the sleep deficit situation was fairly apparent and the guys slipped easily into REM. Not one beverage was consumed. They'd had a great time, but their livers were having a well-earned day off. They donned the shades, thanked us very much and moved off towards their limo. My colleague and I had a chuckle over the sex toys which they had left behind.

All told, the rather endearing thing about the Staggers is that they give you a glimpse into what true and unconditional love really is. The team spirit and bonding engendered during the skirt chasing ribaldry often creates real blokey emotion. Elegiac and wistful memories of their friendships give rise to poetic outpourings of love for one another:

"No but I fuuuuckin love you Gary," said one as he hung round his mate's neck and pushed his fist gently against his jaw, just before falling into the back of his taxi.

At least we had the full complement of lads going home, on a previous occasion when I took seven lads to Dublin for a stag night only six came back. They didn't seem to care or have any cohesive explanation either. Poor bloke was probably handcuffed, half-naked to a rubbish bin in Malahide.

The "Too Important to Speak" Types

The "too important to speak", or should I clarify and say "too important to speak *to you directly*" types have definitely become victims rather than masters of their money. Nobody can respectfully appreciate more than we the crew, that sometimes you want peace and quiet, privacy, no interruptions and the general exclusivity that private jet travel offers. That is absolutely understood and we bend over backwards to make life comfortable and exclusive for these people who are, after all paying huge sums of money, I feel strongly about offering them the exceptional and privileged environment that they want.

Am I strange or is it normal for someone to arrive on an aeroplane, fly with you, then get off without ever uttering a word.

"Gosh he didn't say anything," I told one of my colleagues after flying a very high profile Italian who owned a racing car team.

Oh that's fine if he doesn't say anything at all he's *really* happy, and that's cool. Okay I thought. But *he* had the engagement and the empathies of an agony aunt compared to the chaps I know who wouldn't actually speak to you directly, if they spoke it was to their managers or PAs who were standing right there, who *then* passed the question on (which of course you had already heard, but pretended you hadn't). All very bizarre – made me glad to have studied the 'theatre of the absurd' at uni as well as Stalin and Caligula, it gave me an insight and an edge into weirdness.

I know it is hard to believe but when discussing this phenomena with a colleague one day he told me of a Russian (obscenely rich category) who actually phoned his contact in Russia who would then call the crew and pass on his wishes. I know, I know, I am flummoxed also! As they say in Yorkshire: "Ee there's nowt so queer as folk!" I've certainly come across some with the warmth and tenderness of old Robert Maudsley himself, aka Hannibal Lecter.

Funnily enough, when I had the good fortune to stay in an exceptionally exclusive hotel in the UK, I met someone up there who said that a very famous guest who had exhibited the same trait. She had asked about seating arrangements by addressing her questions to her *own* member of staff. I can only imagine it must have gone something like:

"Ask him how many people can fit round the table?" Then he would dutifully turn to the banqueting manager:

"How many does the dining table seat?"

The answer would come, *but* she could now receive the information because it had come out of the apparently uncontaminated mouth of *her* member of staff.

An Indian gentleman with his own jet exhibited this same unfortunate encephalitis type of condition. He was showing the signs of strange sickness. My colleague who flew him said he would place the cup of tea in front of him, then as soon as he was back in the galley he would hear frantic ringing of the call bell and the boss would summon him back:

"Stir it some more!"

The same man would stab at the call button again and again and demand that the volume be turned down or the channel changed on the TV or DVD player, yet the control was *right* beside him. He would make the flight attendant lean over, he almost had to remove *his* resting hand from the control panel to reach the press buttons himself. I've heard them encouraging their kids to "leave it on the floor- the steward can pick it up!" Another super rich Indian with an inordinate amount of power in the world, actually used to twist the plastic cap just a tad on every little bottle of Evian and then see if they had been replaced on the next flight, by sealed ones. Oh it's a funny old game sometimes!

He seemed to enjoy seeing their submissiveness, (which he demanded) maybe it gave him the same prurient thrill. Maybe he was bitter and vengeful or just deeply unpleasant. I thought once again of the Middle Eastern man I flew for once who would stand like a statue in the bedroom, arms out like the hilltop Christ of Rio, and make the two flight attendants undress him from his suit then redress him in his robes. Is there a word for the latter stages of egomania? They don't walk through a door so much as ooze their way under it.

We have had, over the years, some big stars and celebrity 'A listers' and their demands and their 'diva-ness' is absolutely beyond the bounds of credulity! When it comes to the American ones I think – how different they are from their pioneering ancestors who fought and struggled and endured every hardship to establish a life in America. They would be grateful to find an overhanging rock to shelter under during the ox and wagon trek out West. Now some of them are reduced to stroppy adolescent fits of rage if the flowers aren't quite right or the drapes are the wrong colour. "Get me my complaints secretary!"

The 'Never on Time / Change my Mind' Types

I flew for a devastatingly rich Asian who, just *could not* and indeed *would not* ever EVER stick to his original time of departure. In eight flights he never showed up on time and to compound the problem changed the estimated time of departure *five times* without the tiniest crumb of concern.

Can you explain to me how you end up owning half the world's mineral wealth and you can't stick to a departure time? Oh well I guess we will never know. What he clearly *never* considered was the fact that a crew would arrive two hours before departure only to wait around, all day and then he would expect to fly a seven hour sector having turned up six hours late. Such arrogance and lack of consideration is *very* irritating. Types like this have an absolute unshakable belief in their superiority. He just messed everybody around – people were moons, **he** was Jupiter – end of story! There was only one schedule and that was *his*. Isn't it unnerving how sometimes as power increases, the responsibility for its application diminishes.

Yes millionaires and billionaires have worked very hard, taken risks and should enjoy the luxury of flexibility. Nobody minds if someone has hit a bit of traffic and is delayed on the M25, but this guy, he was something else.

When a flight is *private* rather than *public*, that is … for the owner, the rules on duty periods change – there aren't any basically. This means the crew can keep going like 'Eutelsat' circling the planet. (Rules have since changed.)

Here is *one* example that I lived through. We went to Tbilisi in Georgia. The departure time was changed four times – believe me our operations department used to dread calling us with yet another schedule change, they would get an earful from us and then have to moan.

"It's not my bloody fault, *he's* phoned and changed it again."

When you were rostered to fly him you never knew whether to go to bed early and get up early as per the *latest* departure time, or to catch a few Zs *anytime* you could, not knowing which airport or country you would be hanging around in all day.

Off we went, from Luton at quarter to eight in the evening – hurrah that *was* actually within six hours of schedule take-off time. Because there was a bed in the back of this jet, he understandably spent most of his flights sleeping which is why he did so much night flying. We landed at twenty minutes past midnight. We always go through those very comical and meaningless motions just before the passenger disembarks.

"What time would you like to depart on Thursday, sir?"

"I will probably depart around three o'clock in the afternoon," he said with a very convincing wobble of the head. "But I will let you know." (And the cheque's in the post.)

So it stayed at three o'clock for the record linear time stretch of one whole solar day. That meant that the flight attendant and I decided to meet at seven for a drink and a mosey around the town to experience some Georgian cuisine and culture.

She was funny … she'd sat round the pool that day while I read a book and chirped up after a half-hour fidget and said in a strong Morecambe Bay accent, "Oh how can you read books Anita, I can't stand them, they're mingin', I get so flaming bored, I can do me magazines and I like me soaps but Oo … I just can't do books!"

This compounded with the news of her strict vegetarianism had me wondering what we would have in common – as it turned out we had a really funny time. However, we did find a place perched atop a steep dark river canyon with a view of impressive medieval spires. We were just missing the swooping bats. It was very 'Transylvania'.

That afternoon my phone rang – our operations in Oxford:

"Mr X's assistant has called and he *now* wants to leave at seven in the morning." Okay, I calculated quickly, with the time difference that means a four a.m., (English time) rise, so, better get a very early night. Consequently we binned the evening out in town and planned an early night. Just as I was settling down for another exciting evening of BBC World and a cuppa, the phone rang, it was operations.

"Don't tell me," I chirped, "but there's a change of plan."

"Yes I'm afraid so," said long suffering Tim.

"It's now been put back to fifteen hundred local."

So, we rang each other and the hostie and I went off to eat. Tbilisi was certainly different. Gypsy women with missing teeth and mangy cats for company were sitting in asbestos shacks selling extremely good quality vodka in bottles adorned with ornate Slavic labels for a staggering £3. That certainly reawakened our interest in the place. Amongst the rubble and the broken pavements and dug up roads, there was the odd little bar adorned with an umbrella. It was a bit like a hopeful clump of wild flowers growing on a landfill site. It reminded me a bit of Albania.

There were the impressive statues of great military men on horseback – so typical of *that* part of the world, and just feet away, ram shackled old huts selling everything from soap to salami. I noticed how beautiful the writing was – pretty and swirly not unlike Thai. Just as we were strolling along the banks of a river admiring dark pointed castles which were quite Dracula-esque, my mobile rang, it was ops. Here we go.

"Hello."

"Anita, I'm really sorry but he's just called again and wants to leave at seven in the morning."

Dinner then became a hurried affair, after which we walked back up the steep hill to the hotel picking a few more local goodies on the way.

The night was short. The hotel phone rang at four in the morning English time. We went through the usual rigmarole of catering. On early starts, we'd ask the hotel to prepare all the food and juices, especially if the airport is not equipped to provide first class catering. It was wheeled out on a baggage trolley, piles of flimsy cake boxes, sandwiches wrapped in Clingfilm, juices, canapés and trays of patisseries, way too much stuff and all difficult to carry!

Into the sparse and basic airport of Tbilisi we went. Just as I was looking about for our handling agent, my mobile rang, it was the assistant to the 'big man', with his obsequiousness now at an all-time high, he informed me:

"Allo Miss Mays yes, it is (unpronounceable Indian name). Yes I am wery sorry but Mr XX vill not be leaving today until fifteen hundred, this afternoon, I am wery sorry but his meeting with the minister got put back …"

(And if you believe *that* I've got some nice beachfront property in Birmingham you need to look at!)

"Oh Yes and orlso, Mister X would like to go hom wia Geneva."

This went down very well with the black hating, Indian hating, women hating, Jew hating, in fact everything and everybody in the whole world hating, Nazi Captain from Austria with whom I was crewing this flight!

So we *could* have had another five hours in the hotel, but now we have to hang around at an airport with one tiny bar full of smokers where the only thing to eat was pink flabby frankfurters served up with a piece of bread which could have passed for a lunar specimen. This windowless room was smoky and dirty, it had a tiny television showing a football match with loud distorted foreign commentary, and two severely pissed off waitresses who chained-smoked, had cherry coloured hair and couldn't raise a smile between them.

It was raining that day and I had to stand outside while we refuelled with no umbrella. Zoe, our flight attendant (Miss GHD) who is never more than a flex length away from a hair straightener would simply NOT and I repeat not go within fifty yards of a molecule of H2O, even in suspension, for fear of her hair going frizzy. If she had to step out of she'd armed herself with hood *and* a brolley. She looked at me in absolute horror, I thought she would burst into tears – it was as though she was looking at a car crash victim. I looked like the albino love child of Don King and Joan Armatrading. Her hand actually came up over her mouth. She rushed to get the straighteners to try and save me. I told her it was no good. She tried half-heartedly to offer encouraging words.

"You must have been 'well in' during the seventies."

I think she'd only seen people with hair like mine who were of mixed race on old record covers wearing *really* flared jeans and platform boots.

The passenger was told in no uncertain terms by the Austrian Captain that we would *no*t be going Geneva due to duty hour restrictions (mentioning duty hours to someone like this passenger is like telling a joke in colloquial Inuit).

When the passengers finally did arrive at the airport, the handling agents were busy. My mobile rang five times in the space of twenty minutes and I had a frantic Indian voice which got higher and higher.

"Ve have been vaiting now for five minutes and still nobody coming here isn't it."

We were preparing for the departure, loading up the GPS, running check lists and acquiring departure clearances and so on, all I could do was reassure him that the handling agent knew of their whereabouts and would be with them soon.

'So *you* are getting well-hacked off after a ten minute wait, try waiting six hours pal,' I thought to myself.

We took off for London, I flew the same guy four or five times again and every time he changed the departure at least three times. I will be forever grateful to one Captain called Tony who finally said the magic words "NO" and he abandoned the trip unwilling to tolerate the flagrant and outrageous disregard for our fatigue levels. He was going to Nairobi (via Tripoli for fuel). It went from mid-after*noon* to mid*night* out of Stansted via Luton to pick him up and then into the thousands of miles of African desert. All three of us (the crew) had been called incessantly whilst trying to sleep during the day and being constantly woken with changing updates, is, believe me, distressing.

Another Captain through exasperation had the good judgment to say: "I know you change your departure time so people can't track you (there is a website where you can see every take-off and landing – anywhere) *but* even though you want to remain elusive, (sort of guy who *could* have lots of enemies!) you have to keep **us** in the loop."

What was so amazing about this guy who incidentally awarded himself a *yearly* pay rise of over fifty million, he never once tossed a twenty pound note in your hands and said thanks have a drink on me. Not even when you had spent all your days off, your bank holiday weekend (and beyond) flogging around the world changing time zones being ceaselessly messed around suffering fatigue and disruption. God I would be tipping like a dumper truck if I had that kind of money. You have to laugh in this job otherwise you go mad.

One of my fellow pilots, well famed for mimicry and imitation used to get the hump with this tardy passenger and his entourage of deferential 'orbiters'.

"I bet he's even got someone to wipe his arse," he sneered one day, I burst out laughing especially when he then grabbed a loo roll got down on all fours outside the luxury toilet on board, knocked softly on the door and said with a strong accent.

"Hello Mister XXXX I have extra soft Andrex for you – perfumed one, are you ready for me …?"

It *was* actually extremely comical. You had to be there!

Oh well, this is life. He and others like him are machines of acquisition. How does that quote go?

"The meek may inherit the earth but *not* the mineral rights."

A quote which he had definitely *not* learnt in school was: "Punctuality is the politeness of kings."

Another Similar.

Rakes, libertines, womanisers and corporate raiding shysters – we couldn't do without them! As mentioned previously, men who make a habit of annexing great swathes of a country or a couple of its major industries into their personal portfolio are constantly jumping on and off our private jets. We meet some who are positively Emissaries of Beelzebub.

I met an absolute gargantuan personality one day. This guy won the joint prize of womaniser and bastard in walkover style. He could literally eat people for breakfast. Every time I saw him I tried in vain **not** to think of paintings by Francisco Goya during his 'dark period' of terrifying, *very* bad tempered giants plucking men from the ground and biting their heads off. He was from Europe and without *any* doubt was the mould for the ninth century marauders with bronze horns and wheeling swords. He would have had the biggest horns, the deadliest sword *and* the fastest boat so as to be first in the queue for rape and pillage. He had done some deals with the Russians (aforementioned carver uppers of state mineral wealth). He was 'well in' and he was well minted. He *also* changed his mind re-destination, intention and timing on **every** occasion, but he had the clout of a pile driver and thought this was part of the package. We landed in Germany to just pick up a passenger and he said, "Actually I think I will go to the farm and see my race horses, I'll be back sometime this afternoon."

Of course this should be a right they can exercise **but** unfortunately in this job we must be furnished with departure times for slots and Air Traffic control. *"Sometime this afternoon"* just doesn't cut the mustard with 'The System' headed up by the mighty Brussels flow control who must know **when** exactly we are going, these choices are not ours.

Flying into Russia and former Eastern Bloc countries can be dogged with dreadful bureaucracy. The place might be open for trade but it is held back by these apparatchiks. You can't just jump in and go … "Oh nyet, nyet", they need paperwork which renders Dostoyevsky a short read.

Myself and my colleague were briefed to go to Moscow, St Petersburg and somewhere, more remote, in Russia (you never want to see that on a flight brief, anything east of Moscow is going to get rough). So being December we packed thermals, fleeces, hats and gloves. We ended up in Dubai! Not a T-shirt between us.

Our operations had not managed to get the necessary over fly and landing permits for the Russian destination – result one very **very** angry passenger, who was already a big devotee of the 'F' word. He went into overdrive.

He stormed off the plane in Scandinavia effing and blinding saying that he was going to charter '*that* Challenger parked over there'. It was a local company so they would know how to operate properly unlike us who were a bunch of idiots. Just as we were shutting the aircraft up and going to the hotel, awaiting further instructions, he came marching back across the ramp. Oh no, more hell and damnation!

"The f****** Russians have gone home for New year. I am too late for my meeting because we waste so much time with your f****** operations trying to get the permits!"

"Go to the hotel, sleep and await further instruction." This was the instruction from our ops department. The next morning at five a.m. my Blackberry rang and woke me.

"Hello?"

"So I am standing at my f****** plane there is no one f****** here!" Without having to ask … I knew who it was. He was touchingly disinterested in time wasting formalities like 'Good morning this is …'

"Oh and a very good morning to you … so sorry Sir but our last instruction was to go to the hotel and wait further instruction after they have secured the permits for Russia."

"Your f****** people can't give instruction they can't organise anything" The one thing with this chap was that you never had to turn on your insult detectors, it was a both barrels, close range, sort of experience!

He was a lion with toothache. I hammered on my colleague's door and said we had to scram – **NOW!** He (the Viper, or The Priapus) as I affectionately named him was still working on the *original* departure time which indeed *had* been six a.m., but without the permits we could go nowhere. Maybe he thought these offices (**and** our ops) stay open all night to obtain them. Sadly it was not the case, but all was not lost – we were privy to a fairly realistic example of what will happen when Yellow Stone Park finally blows.

So we abandoned the mission and set off for Eastern Europe. This was to pick up a girl.

"By the way this is NOT my wife, this is *just* a girl who has given me a son," he said flatly.

I know – it's one of those statements which has you clasping your heart and scrunching your nose going "Aaaw" as you reach for your hanky – the tenderness of it all is just too much. Just for a bit of leg pulling which he was not adverse to I said, "Ah the affection and compassion you show Mr X … it's moving."

"Ah f****** affection, romance I don't bother with all this crap anymore," waved his hand in a circular motion, lit another Marlboro red and downed a Red Bull, squashed the tin then started yelling at some poor bastard in Estonian down the mobile!

A famous anchor woman was on board also with another man, they were all off to Dubai for New Year's Eve to meet racing drivers and models. (He actually changed his mind due horror of inactivity and wanted to return home to Farnborough on the *31st* itself.) It would have been closed by the time we arrived – this forced him to stay in Dubai. Why anyone would want to leave on New Year's Eve and get caught *between* celebrations is beyond me. He was easily a match for the Asian man of 'change my mind' fame. He never once stuck to his original plan and added on or removed sectors and legs constantly. The moral of the story with him was ... pack for all weathers and for many days away.

A girl with an extremely long blonde hair got on in Kiev. I instantly named her Rapunzel. She had all the right attributes for a mistress. She wore designer jeans and had diamonds the size of Rice Crispies on her watch, and was jumping about the place excited at the thought of another 'celeb' studded, champagne party followed by *not* having to see *him* very much. *This* one had had a child though so she had secured the money.

I engaged in yet another minor argument with the clearance frequency who told me we had 'no authority' to be there and we were not allowed to leave until further paperwork arrived. God, it has you cradling your forehead in your palm – once again. It's never straight forward! Sometimes I feel like standing in the middle of the ramp in Russia with a megaphone and shouting, "You know what? ... we don't even WANT to be in your poxy country."

Via the Blackberry I called ops, they thankfully sorted it through a company who specialise in permits for *that* part of the world. The very fact that such a company is *necessary* shows how difficult it can be. God only knows why it's so tricky, it's no doubt all about *money* and demanding lots of it from those who wish to conduct their business there. We left – 'Spasebo Bashoye'! The corruption in Russia gnaws into the bones of the country. It leaves you weary.

I did the landing into Dubai on a perfectly calm night, we landed to the north so flew over the coast admiring the futuristic spectacle of lights and buildings. The place is forever multiplying. We stayed at the **airport** Marriot which, despite its proximity took us forty minutes to reach in the taxi. Traffic is a problem there!

A week later I flew to Cannes to drop off an Arab passenger and his seven pieces of luggage, and was told to go straight to Prague to pick up the 'viper man'. He'd just called. We did so, then continued to another city to pick up the ... **wife!** I got the old 'shhhh' sign again with index finger in front of mouth and line across the throat!

"Of course sir."

The Suits (aka Dodgy Dealers)

As Balzac said in his wisdom: *"Behind every great fortune there is a crime".*

"Choose a scandal – *any* scandal ... don't show me ... I bet there's a private aeroplane involved. It will be warming up in the corner of some remote airfield *somewhere*."

Yes ... a lot of these masters of cunning and opportunism need to make a quick dash from time to time! People grabbing their passports, briefcases and flying out the door stuffing handfuls of cash into the inside pockets, whilst doing a runner for the private jet, are jolly good for business quite honestly. Remember Mr Nadir of Polypeck who legged it to northern Cyprus? Remember the chap from Investors International who scarpered with everyone's money? What about the insurance tycoon who disappeared in an HS125?

Enron, Guinness, Ronson all names which spell 'Let's get out of here!'One minute you're tearing around in your Lamborghini with the world at your feet, next minute you're shielding your eyes from flashbulbs, pushing, head down, through a crowd of obnoxious reporters.

All these backhanders, insider tradings, and disappearing millions, they all generate business and have us filing flight plans at ungodly hours. Even though some of these people can't even lie in bed straight, you have to grin at their ingenuity. One chap on the wanted list put on a false beard, disguised himself and announced he was going on a day trip to France, jumped in a Piper Seneca and fled – *for good!*

Another who went to jail was released early on the grounds of mental illness – good one! (A sharp lawyer is useful.)

These guys come in different shapes and sizes: they are invariably men of brisk wit and whiplash one liners. I flew a chap around the UK back in the eighties, he was of the 'mansion in Hampstead' gang, always wore immaculate suits with a bow tie, he was a snappy dresser and oozed confidence. The huge Filofax and first edition mobile phone (size of a brick – remember) were common accessories. He had narrow gimlet eyes and a hooked nose and moved fast like a weasel. He looked like the sort who could survive below ground as well as above it. I read about him shortly after in the paper, being detained at her majesty's pleasure. Despite being personable and charming somehow you just knew he had the trustworthiness of a Medici court usurer, but these are the pinstripe villains – we read about them every day.

When you think of all the scandals and illegal activities which get covered in our press everyday you realise that corruption is throughout every strata of society. In some ways we are no different from the Nigerians, just a little bit more subtle perhaps. (A rather amusing little detail here – I once worked for a jet charter company in whose operations manual it was actually stated that when flying Nigerians the money had to be paid *in full AND up front* ... no credit for Nigerians!)

Things started to get worryingly slow in the early nineties but phew, along came Yeltsin the vodka swilling buffoon who was controlled by all the oligarchs who meant business and demanded remuneration after securing his re-election. Yes the Russians have had us pilots marching down to Transair pilot shops throughout the land to purchase new log books because the flying hours are rolling in.

The Nick Leesons of this world are men in Yogi bear suits at the entrance to Disney Land compared to the new villain which had come amongst us. These are men who bribe, murder manipulate and control. Men who get rid of their enemies with icy ruthlessness. Men for whom contract killings carry the same gravitas as a parking ticket.

I have met some who make Cesare Borgia look like Noddy. (Our friend Cesare by the way acquired renaissance notoriety for hideous extravagance, vice, poison, incest and murder.) These are the predatory players in the game. Greed, venality and self-aggrandisement certainly keep the old fan blades turning.

As the film Layer Cake tells us, one minute you are doing a bit of small time money laundering skipping across London in your pointy Italian shoes with a briefcase full of 'dosh' on behalf of the big boss, next minute you are *with* the big boys (well, the good ones are) in the back of the private jet; your hard-earned wealth and power buying you immunity from what you don't want! Yes many of our passengers are breathing that 'rarefied air' at last.

Rich people are moving money around and often need a fast machine to help them slide round the planet. Let's be honest, no matter which party is in power, the super-rich are just too good for party coffers.

All this is rudely good for business, offshore companies must be visited and days must be spent abroad, the jets must be filled with fuel, and fly them around we do! As one of England's erudite satirists said: "Laws are like cobwebs which may catch small flies but let wasps and hornets break through."

Having super yachts built (of the Jet Ranger on the aft deck variety) seems to be a good old favourite and crops up with a reassuring regularity. Groups of very creative and *very* well paid accountants help with these endeavours.

With all this money floating around at the moment, buying a private jet can be very tax efficient – all the running cost can be offset. Of course most of these shining sexy jets are owned by companies not individuals, and provided that the company is making a good profit, all running costs are offset. **If** they sell the jet on for a loss after a few years, there will be no balancing charge. (It must be said though that most of them hold their value.) If they sell it for a profit they can roll it over into another aircraft (every four years) rather than pay the tax.

I have known of some, who in their need to 'get rid' of a bunch of cash will, say buy a second-hand jet in the Cayman Islands, keep it on their register. It comes as no surprise that the jets with long range capability like Challengers and Global Expresses are flying off the shelves, they can get to those handy places like Bahamas – and the occupants aren't just going just for the lobsters and cocktails! Another interesting little point is that there is no VAT on planes over 8,800 kilos. It is in the back of *such* jets where this 'happy breed of men' are clinking their schooners of Grey Goose.

Many passengers are just hard working success stories from the city. Let's face it with such punitive tax laws and chancellors trying to homogenise the human race and starting to tax *retroactively* offshore trusts and disallowing *any* decent system of inheritance, it is no wonder some of our smarter citizens have to get a bit creative; good luck to them. I flew one of the biggest mortgage brokers in England into City airport. Like so many of these wealthy businessmen – great when happy, but woe betide when their tempers fray. Well stress does make one ratty doesn't it? He used to slice through his opponents with spiky little phrases like:

"Don't talk to me about second best. *SECOND* is just first loser," or:

"I don't want to hear about the **problems,** Mark. Tell me about the bloody solution alright?"

Then with a smile and a patronising pinch on the cheek of his long suffering manager, he'd slide his 'Jermyn street' cashmere overcoat down his upheld arm and stride across the apron at City airport jabbing numbers into his mobile. A dark blend of wit and menace.

One fund manager came aboard bound for Zurich to go skiing. A small truck pulled up at the steps of the jet and boxes of computers were unloaded. These were indispensable for the week. He sat in the front seat of the cabin pulled out the shiny table and placed his array of mobile phones upon it – a Blackberry, an Apple (we could have a pie here), a Nokia and an Ericsson. He looked like a drummer in front of his drum kit, I wanted to bring the telescopic tripod to his side so he could mount the Ericsson like a symbol in his two o'clock high so he could just press loud speaker should it ring and still have the Nokia to his ear. Yes it looked like another relaxing week in Verbier. Still he would probably make a couple of mill by the time we crossed Dover at 29,000 feet.

I was informed of a particularly interesting villain by my fellow pilot one wintry night in Ayr, Scotland. He told me of a Gulfstream jet which would fly regularly to Russia, it was often seen in St Petersburg, but it would also frequent 'less well known' airfields.

"What, sort of remote strips, where the lights would go on for the landing, then off again after departure?" I suggested a bit sardonically.

"You're not too far off I can tell you!" Someone would emerge from the shadows jump on board – a deal would be done right there and then in the back of the plane with the engines still turning and burning. Then they'd disappear off into the night again. He was always being chased by Customs, and *was* eventually done for VAT fraud and did 'time' but his wealth had gone up so much by then *and* he accumulated more whilst in prison. (Can't keep an old dog down).

Apparently if you put old thru'penny bits into gold it adulterates it, so, if it is stolen gold it can't be tested or traced. I am no mineralogist but apparently if you add another metal into the smelter it alters the footprint – useful if you're in a hurry to legitimise a bit of gold you've just nicked. Come in man with smelter and a handy 'skill', a man obviously in great demand amongst those in balaclavas, keen to legitimise a few barrow loads of gold bullion. In Hogarthian speak they'd have been the roisters, the cardsharps, the jacknapes!

They *do* have a knack of rising from the faecal matter and smelling of roses. It was decided that since he'd been found guilty by the press already no jury would be unbiased, and *that* (push out bottom lip here) just wouldn't have been fair to the poor man. So … Gran Canaria or Caribbean here we come! *That* was a very busy business jet! Well done him for making it into the Sunday Times rich list I believe at a not altogether unimpressive 700 million. Also it has to be said these types are very good to their mates, he bought one of them a helicopter. He bought properties and cars to launder the money and gave them as very generous gifts to friends who 'protected' him. So … a good mate to have. One does have to give a cursory nod to their ingenuity sometimes, one of them started off putting sawdust in the gearboxes of Morris Oxford cars to stop them rattling, obviously from the seeds of this nascent small time 'crookery', grow large trees, nay forests of swindling and vice!

I feel a cocktail should be named in their honour. For one in particular whom I met I have rustled up a little 'drinkette' and named it:

"Slow comfortable screw against the Odds"
1 part hoodlum chopped
Two heaped spoons bribery and corruption
One adversary (crushed)
Dash of tourettes
Shaving of murder (optional)
A twist of tax avoidance (careful to remove pips)
Large slice of immunity (available from specialist metropolitan outlets)
Put in blender with sharp blades until unrecognisable.

Serve with dash of bitters, and drink while strolling through Cap D'Antibes in £1,000 shirt with large lapels and medallion preferably with three 'poitrine' enhanced models who think you're great and will never know any better.
CHEERS!

I had a 'call out' one evening for Moscow– this is an unscheduled flight for someone who has decided they want to go somewhere – *now.* It was a cold wintry night, the thirteen seat Embraer Legacy was despatched to pick up *one* guy (obviously money no object). This was at a time of the evening (roughly eight p.m.) when there were many commercial flights – British Airways and other major carriers. So it is not as though he were stranded. This would be about a £25,000 flight. We picked him up at Vnokovo in Moscow. There were bags and bags of 'gifts' being marched on board by his assistants. Thousands of pounds worth of caviar – serious caviar. He looked very dodgy. It was my sector to fly, I pushed up the throttles and hurtled off down the rather bumpy runway, pleased to be leaving. We climbed away and headed back for London. Halfway through the cruise, my flight attendant and friend came into the cockpit giggling.

"What's up?"

"Look at this!" she said as she flashed her hand which was adorned with the most exquisite emerald and ruby ring and matching bracelet. I turned round to have a chat and she pulled her hair back and said, "And that's not all, clock these!" There were matching earrings and necklace.

"What's going on, he hasn't given them to you has he?"

"No," she said giggling and holding her fingers out in front of her to admire the stones."He's asked me to wear them and then at Luton I should walk across the ramp and go round the back and see him in the car park and hand them back, Isn't that hilarious!"

"Jan," I said, "take them off, you aren't getting paid *nearly* enough to do *that!*"

Forgotten How to Have Fun Types

"The world is not enough." This was the catchy title of a James Bond movie not so long ago. It would also be an apt caption on certain passengers' business cards. They are just compulsively acquisitive. Even when they have more than they could ever spend, they cannot stop. Whereas *we* would think 'yipee' I can buy that boat, take a few years off, travel the world, learn to windsurf, take music lessons, buy a house in Gascony, fill my garage with the best wine, ski all winter in Switzerland. (God, worrying how I could go on unimpeded here for quite some time.) They don't have any of these frilly capricious desires. No flirtations with nonsense like this, noooo noooo noooo.

These men's idea of hell is sitting on a beach relaxing or having to endure that ghastly, empty thing called 'leisure'. One Arabic guy who owned his own jet and who was very personable despite his wild temper, took his whole family and the crew for a holiday to Phuket to say thank you. We were supposed to be there 4 days but on the second day he decided he could stand it no more and everyone had to pack up and go, he was itching to do another deal. When you are the size of a walrus, with the drive of Gordon Gecko (of red braces in Wall St. fame) sitting under a palm frond watching a sunset in an area with no mobile signal, clutching a cocktail with an umbrella in it, just does not **do it**. They don't have the appetite for it – it simply does NOT have the same allure as sitting in an air conditioned office in London or Kuwait engaging in cut throat negotiations for the next skip full of commission. These people have formidable appetites for things like … er …*countries!*

Yes I have learnt through exposure to the sort of people who can affect the economy, that it is no longer about earning enough to afford things which bring them pleasure. Some don't actually *understand* pleasure and leisure anymore, it is not on the agenda. The only turn on, is the next deal.

Along with the faculty for moral discernment, the desire for a giggle or a simple pleasure has vanished.

Some of them sit there with penetrating moroseness. You will occasionally hear a self-congratulatory 'humph' and almost detect a smile as he reads about a share price plummeting which will adversely affect his enemy.

I used to fly such a chap out of Farnborough, he sometimes went to his house in France with his wife and kids but they never stopped arguing. Instead of laughing and cherishing their good fortune it was nonstop bickering from wheels up to wheels down.

I know kids can be difficult but honestly isn't making money all about having fun and enjoying your life? It seems with so many of them, their exalted status does little to remove the grim-visaged scowling. I don't know much but what I *have* learnt is that boats, planes and exotic locations can never underwrite our happiness, just as bills, the weather and the M25 cannot sentence us to misery. Ultimately it is what's going on in the mind that counts. I think we have to address *somewhere* along the way our psychological needs, friendship, respect, decency and meaningfulness perhaps a scruple or two. If you are anxious, selfish, fearful or miserable you simply *transport* those problems to a 'holiday brochure' location, a palm fringed beach won't expel them. "Anyway," I can hear my passenger sneering, "enough of that New Age crap".

"Why are we bloody waiting so long to take-off?" he barked once when at the hold of the runway in Madrid. (In Spain you can forget an expeditious departure – they will let every single Iberia flight take-off in front of you no matter how long you've been waiting.) Lo Siento! We try our best to go next but, we must do as we are instructed by the tower.

Once lined up we would do the last few checks, with the added seasoning of his commentary.

"Strobe lights ... on."

"God don't tell me we are actually bloody going".

"Transponder ... on."

"Bout time."

"Ignition ... on."

"Landing lights ... on."

"Halle, bloody lujah."

Isn't it funny how you tend to enjoy your first car so much more than your last somewhat flashier one. Vanessa Feltz once said on her radio programme, when they were all impecunious students living on 'spag bol' they had no money so had to stay in every night having sex because they couldn't afford anything. They longed for the future as well-paid journalists living in fine houses. When they got there, they experienced great nostalgia for the old days admitting the 'spag bol' and sex was rather a good era after all. I have seen couples between whom the tension is palpable and around whom there is a septic and unhealthy atmosphere. Do they sometimes look back on when the boat or the house in Sardinia was a dream and they were happily and positively striving for it? Perhaps? I have dropped off families where *he,* po-faced with the pressure of work has been on the laptop all journey, *she,* bristling with resentment has struggled with the kids. You can only imagine the rows that will erupt when they get to the villa, which has been empty for a while if the electricity doesn't work or all the beds need making up because the maid has scarpered with the 'dosh'!

They say money doesn't buy you happiness, but one thing's for sure with these types, it is at least buying them a more comfortable state of melancholy, *and* they can be pissed off in more exotic places and have their arguments over fine wine!

With some passengers – like the fabulously rich property developers I flew on numerous occasions it's not so much they have *forgotten* how to have fun, it's more that they have tempers that can curdle steel. They hate inconvenience of any kind and are seen frequently shouting and moaning. Once, because of the foreign passport of the Philippine nanny, they had to go to immigration rather than just jump out into the waiting Bentley. This delayed them and he was absolutely livid.

Similarly we had a guy, en route to the Rugby world cup final in Paris between South Africa and England, he was positively apoplectic. There are SO MANY slots and restrictions on such a day and there is no getting away from it! Can you imagine how many people are trying to get to Paris? Again it is totally out of our hands. We are all flying into the regional airports like Toussus and Pontoise, and it is strictly controlled.

"I could have got better service on f****** Easy Jet, this is bloody ridiculous!" he snarled. He was almost rabid, and nearly took a swing at the Captain. He was incandescent with rage. We had to ask him to control himself in the end. You can totally understand the grief and disappointment (just as I did those guys at the Milan Grand Prix – we were three hours late) but unfortunately these things are just impossible to control. But passengers can be 'off puttingly' volatile. On that occasion I had to explain that the Italians are actually not able to run a bath let alone an airport on a huge event. Anyone out there thinking of using Milan Linate on a big event day I urge you to stay home and watch it on television.

The Obsessively Fussy

I worked for an Indian man who was, no argument, *brilliant*. He was chairman of one of the world's biggest corporations and multilingual. And I don't mean Urdu, Punjabi or surrounding dialects I mean Russian and Japanese amongst others. He was the only foreigner invited to speak at Putin's important televised conference on the Black Sea, to which I flew him. He was no doubt extremely erudite and percipient. His opinion was highly respected and he was good! *BUT...* fussy or WHAT!! You wonder how such pettiness can come from such a mind. He didn't eat any meat or fish and woe betide if any came near his private jet, even if guests would have enjoyed some – it was forbidden. It simply didn't matter what we ordered it was never right. If you can imagine the cat in Tom and Jerry when he's putting the brakes on before crashing into the sleeping dog's kennel – hair on end, claws out, wide-eyed horror – that's the expression if he so much as spied a slither of a prawn's tail.

We'd have to be fumigated as though we were returning from Barundi. One night having picked up catering from Delhi and it was again, unsatisfactory, I had the temerity to suggest that since it was the best efforts of *his* people in *his* country along with the best 5 star hotel in the city, perhaps it would be better if a) he suggested what we should get, **or,** b) bring his own.

At least my previous boss – the 'Fat Man' as he was affectionately known (after his gambling scandals in London) brought his own grub. He was a haven of practicality – he'd just call the Fakreldine, on Piccadilly order ten grands worth of food, have it loaded into a limo which would follow his up to Luton – job done. That's when he was alone, if he had guests it would be more like twenty grands worth. I'm not saying lambs tethered to spits would be marched aboard but it wasn't far off! Everyone was happy.

But this Indian, well it just didn't matter what you did it was NEVER right. There's only so much you can do with executive canapés armed only with yoghurt, a chickpea and an egg. Oh yes lentils and tangerines were allowable items too. He made micro biotic Madonna look like a beer swilling omnivore dragging her hand across her chops after a full Sunday roast and cheese board. When his parents were on board he was ten times worse, complained about absolutely everything, even the chocolates which came in their own handmade wooden box with individual drawers – they made Godiva's look – well council estate. Yup even those weren't right. Funny thing though when he was on his own he insisted on a paper napkin and nothing fancy, didn't want to waste the money. I'm sure he'd have been happy with a paper plate – so it was all for effect. A stunning young blonde Ukrainian employee who'd just joined the company came on board one day, he obviously had the hots for her she was allowed to sleep on HIS bed – nobody EVER had HIS bed – he went into the cordoned off sleeping area as well with her (there were two big reclining seats in there also). Promotion would, undoubtedly be swift.

Because of his obsessive tantrums we had two hosties walk off. I'll never forget my friend and colleague from Manchester kneeling between us in the cockpit, flinging her tea towel over her shoulder.

"Eh guys I'm really really sorr-eh, but I just can't stand this bA-stad anymore, I'm gerrin' off as soon as we get to Luton – I don't care what happens to me, all right? Sorry! I don't care about being paid, I'm leaving!"

Yes the day he's happy will be the day Jeremy Clarkson turns vegetarian and rocks up in a pair of sandals driving a hybrid Hyundai SUV to a conference on global warming with his good mate Peter Mandelson.

God, he and fellow super 'fussys' made me long for that happy go lucky 'Oirish' charm. Benny Dunne and other Irish millionaires just never 'gave a monkeys' if you were delayed.

"Och that's okay Aneeda," he said to me once at Dublin airport when we had ATC delays going to Malaga.

"Could yous just order us op another five bottles of the fizz and have it sent to the lounge and give os a buzz when yers ready."

I'll never forget him swaying on the tarmac at Malaga trying to persuade me to stay and have a short holiday with them as he told me the joke about the

Indiana 500 for the fourth time and peeled of many fifties and pushed them into my hand with a wink. What a fabulous guy. Which brings me on to that rare and special creature – the happy man!

Not everyone is an angst ridden, snarling egomaniac. Some are brilliant, hardworking, undoubtedly very clever people and cheerful! Some have fantastic relationships with their families – let's raise our glasses to the 'Happees', they are out there and boy they are a breath of fresh air. A few come to mind...

The Happy Ones

I flew for two Welsh brothers who sold their food company for millions and bought themselves a Swan yacht and a private jet, and moved to Partyshire. Now these boys knew how to enjoy their cash. They remembered their friends (many were Welsh rugby players) and were constantly engaging in those typically boyish activities of drinking, eating, golfing, flirting, larking, frolicking and merry making. They partied with a capital 'P'. I remember actually having to take one of those three foot high metal swing lid ashtrays of one guest's shoulder as he trotted out of the airport with it at Le Castellet in France, after a full day of golf and drinking.

"Just the ticket this I can put it in the garden ... lovely see," he sang in broad welsh as he zigzagged his way to the aircraft.

"Monsieur monsieur, you cannot tek ze cendrier eh," said the little French man who came running out of the terminal chasing him.

This 'A' team of mischief makers loved to laugh – the music was always 'full blast' and being Welsh of course every flight was a 'singspiel'. Roxette's 'It must have been love' was a party favourite and once, while turning onto final approach at Prestwick, a champagne cork flew straight into the cockpit bounced off my instruments and landed in my lap. This sent them into convulsions of laughter. They would often give me a kiss goodbye on the cheek at the end of the trip when we returned to Cardiff after a 'boysfest'. One of them got a bit carried away once and muttered "You're lovely" and locked his mouth firmly on mine in a tight embrace only to be pulled off by one of his mates who slapped him about the head cursing him:

"Get off the pilot you filthy old ... .sorry Anita ..." then almost picked him up by the collar of his overcoat and threw him to one side. He apologised like an errant schoolboy and went staggering off in completely the wrong direction before being rounded up by his mates again. It was hilarious.

They all went to play golf at a very exclusive course and as was our habit we went to collect their clubs an hour before they came to the plane, that way we could have them all loaded and put away.

"I'm afraid madam you can't come in here," said a very polite Scottish voice, "no ladies allowed."

"Oh!" I said rather taken aback but not in the least bit angered. "It's just that we have come to collect the boss's clubs and take them to his jet so he doesn't have to bother with them later."

265

"Well your colleague will have to do it," he smiled politely but blocked the way in no uncertain terms with his outstretched arms, one of which pointed to the door like a great weather vane. I had just enough time to pad across the monogrammed carpets and see the wood panelled walls, the rich heavy curtains, chandeliers and ornate fireplaces. In the drawing room was the odd flicking up of a broad sheet after it had fallen on the nose of the dozing reader in the high backed leather chair, no doubt snoozing off the excesses of the cheese board while elsewhere in the room the ships decanter slid across polished mahogany tables. Very nice.

In the winter we flew to Chambery most weekends and all went skiing in Courcheval. The trips were a little different depending on whether it was 'the wife and kids' or just the boys. I don't think that needs any elaboration. They all enjoyed the mountains and skied hard and it comes as no surprise that they were masters of 'après'. They indulged in the good food and wine and often included us in the party which was kind. Such great people.

They did huge amounts to develop the docklands area of Cardiff and enjoyed aligning themselves with good causes.

Another luminary of fun and master of his success is one Sir Tom Hunter. He owns a jet which I had the pleasure of flying. He threw a party in his house in Cap D'Antibes in the summer and we shuttled back and forth bringing various people down and back (Jamie Cullum and Sophie Dahl on one occasion). His kids and their friends were on board and everyone was happy. He had everything transported by road down from Kent in England – the tables, chairs, drinks, absolutely everything because apparently it can be a little unreliable in the south of France. The Christmas before we had flown guests up to his place in Ayr where he threw a party at which Lionel Richie was the entertainment. This man has it down.

Here is a man who has staggering wealth and whose fun metre is in the red. He is always smiling and upbeat. The fact that he looks like the baddie from a Bob Hoskins movie makes it all the more fun. The incredible thing about him is he gives most of his money to charitable causes. Greed is just not part of his make-up. He works closely with Bill Clinton in his Tom Hunter Foundation and he is the driving force behind ethical and compassionate causes all over the world. He is a deeply likable man brimming over with courage vision and belief. I flew him home to Prestwick where he lives and his brand new Rolls Royce convertible was parked waiting. I went to have a look and wished him well.

"I'll be going back to Chambery next weekend, so I'll see you then," he said through the open window.

"Right you are sir" I replied feeling decidedly like the girl chauffeur from 'Foyle's War'.

I gasped when I saw how many peoples in the world he helps. He has embraced altruism and humanitarianism with a commitment, which is truly inspirational. Here is a man who loves to party and who has adorned the very highest flights of philanthropy. Beat that.

Having mentioned Tom, I couldn't leave out Don. Sir Donald Gosling, another quite excellent human being. As much as I have railed against the price of NCP car parks where he made his fortune, I have to say meeting him made up for all those ruinously high charges. I flew him to Klagenfurt so he could buy boxes of fine wine – how's that for a bulls eye. He was unfailingly courteous and polite, but best of all, which is where so many passengers fail – he was on time! When you say to him "Farnborough closes at nine o'clock so if we're a minute late, we **will** be diverting", he actually *understands* this, so, he gets to the airport in really good time AND calls en route to let you know he is coming. He was charming and well dressed and always wore that one thing which makes everybody look fabulous – a big smile (doesn't cost anything either!). One thing which really impressed me was that he brought his own bacon sandwiches that morning.

"Here," he said as he put his face into the cockpit as we were starting the engines.

"My housekeeper made them for me just the way I like them, I brought two extra along for you guys."

Wow, I could have somersaulted with joy. How utterly fabulous was that. He handed them over in tin foil.

"Fat is cut off, and a bit of brown sauce."

That did it – he got my vote for first president of earth.

Another very chirpy party animal was the owner not only of a premier league football team but of his own jet. Sometimes he used to have very late nights partying then get on board and crash out. Once I flew him to the Caribbean where he was going off with the likes of Bruce Willis and a few Hollywood 'celebs' to a private island off Turks and Caicos to do a yoga retreat.

"Wow I didn't have you down as a yoga man."

"Nah, yer right I think I'll just find the local talent and have a bit of a party," he joked with characteristic mischief. We didn't see him emerge from the bedroom until we landed in St Johns Nova Scotia for fuel. The wind gusts of forty-two knots and freezing cloud woke him and true to form he sat in the cockpit and watched me battle down through hideous conditions to the aural accompaniment of "Wind shear! Wind shear". The next approach across the turquoise lagoon to the sandy island was somewhat more gentle.

Anyway this very generous man once gave the flight attendant and I one thousand euros because we had no overnight gear with us in Seville where he was meeting some famous 'footie' manager. He had announced last minute that he would have to stay the night. We were both on 'day off' the next day, therefore unprepared, so jokingly said, "Oh but we've got absolutely no overnight kit, no clean undies for tomorrow."

With that he peeled off a wodge of Euros and with a wink said, "You look like La Perla girls. 'ere you are, go and buy yourself something nice!"

We promptly bought a 2 euro pair of 'nicks' from El Corte Ingles and indulged in a slap-up dinner of Lobster, prawns and chilled white Rioja! He was always jumping on yachts and enjoying fantastic holidays with his family or his mates. He loved using the sat phone in the cockpit to call anyone who'd listen. He was indeed a happy camper!

The Freebies

They say that the stolen apple is always the sweetest. Another bunch of people who REALLY enjoy themselves are those on a freebie. These guys drink every drop of booze, slide the window blinds up and down, eat every morsel of catering, laugh out loud, sing and shout, move about the cabin, put the music on loud, flirt with the flight attendant and have a thoroughly good time. There's always one who wants to sit in the cockpit with us for take-off and landing which is great, we explain everything, run through the avionics and point out places on the ground.

"That's the Isle of Wight coming up, there's Hayling Island straight ahead and Bournemouth on the left."

"Wow superb, and what's that instrument telling us?, what speed are we doing?" and so it goes on. They have a refreshingly unalloyed excitement about life! This is because it's a treat and a rarity to be on a private jet and boy they are going to get every drop of pleasure out of it.

I flew a group of young people who were the top sales and marketing performers in their company and this trip to Marrakech was their reward. To hell with 'moderation'. We didn't have a scrap of food or a drop of drink left! Well played.

A group of top 'household appliance' salesmen and women were our passengers on a Champagne tour of Reims in France. They returned after much merriment and were definitely 'Appellation *un*-controlee'.

Some 'Royal Bank of Scotland-ers' were off to the Grand Prix in Milan. I couldn't resist a little dig at the 'team leader' sitting in the cockpit with me. "Oh so *this* is why you guys can charge us like an injured bull with all those crippling, punitive bank charges; *this* is where our money goes, on fancy outings eh?"

"'Fraid so," he returned with a laugh. We did have an interesting exchange about things I'd never heard of like fiduciary issues and medium term notes.

"A banker is a fellow who lends you his umbrella when the sun is shining and wants it back the minute it begins to rain," I joked, remembering the quote. He laughed but tried earnestly to convince me that they *too* have problems when the credit crunch comes, the loss of confidence means *they* have difficulties borrowing from other banks. We managed to hold back the tears!

The Heart Attack Candidate

We flew a rather large man from Farnborough to Venice. He owned his own jet which I believe he kept in Van Nuys California, it was in routine maintenance, so he chartered our Legacy. He arrived two hours late in a helicopter and climbed on board. The plane keeled slightly when he put his foot on the airstair. We are talking 'Big Man'. He insisted on smoking. We had a quandary because it is a no smoking aircraft and obviously the brokers had not told him – no they kindly leave those 'minor details' to us.

He looked days away from death this guy, completely obese, short of breath and very stiff – he did not move well, the chair could hardly support him. At one point he had a ventolin inhaler in one hand and a cigarette in the other. We were put in a very difficult position by refusing him the cigarettes. The actual owner of that particular jet was a smoker so I voted to let him smoke. These people have paid an awful lot of money – they should have what they want. Sometimes the temper tantrum they get into is more dangerous than having a lit cigarette on board – I learnt that on the heavy metal tours. Rather have a three inch skinny stick of tobacco burning than a human bomb going off – that could be quite incendiary!

He was going down to his villa on the Grand Canal in Venice. He mentioned being very friendly with the lady who organises the famous Masked Ball in February (Balle de Doge). For this party he had packed up huge parcels which we had to dexterously load into our cargo hold. There was a huge solid silver ship with sails – this was the centre piece for the table. There were ornaments of all description, incredible lights and a warehouse of valuable luxuries all to decorate tables.

We (my colleague and I) painstakingly unloaded this 'Handle with care' heavy cargo from the back hold – it was a tricky, drawn-out job. He didn't thank or acknowledge us – and my fellow pilot who had just truly exhausted his reserves of solicitude for the arrogance and rudeness of these people – went into one of his thigh slappingly funny routines during which he did accents, little sketches and all sorts to make us laugh. He stood correctly on the ramp seeing the limo off and said under his breath in an Italian accent:

"I hoppa your boat sinks on the Grand Canal eh!"

Oh well, as the saying goes, "you gorra have a laff".

The Uber Rich Families

I used to say "**I'm dying to fly**" but with these types, it's more a case of "**I'm flying to dine**".

"The catering bill was about six grand, I kid you not!"

"What!" I squawked, "I mean I know catering at airports is **thee** most overpriced commodity in the world, but six blumin' grand!"

My colleague Bill was telling me of his flight earlier that week of one of England's richest 'old money' families. The trip was a short hop from Croatia to Luton. They requested that rose petals be strewn down the center aisle of the jet and crystal glasses full of the finest wine and champagne be waiting for them as they climbed aboard.

"What on earth did they have, kilos of truffles in saffron and fois gras?"

"Well there was an abundance of fois gras, lobsters, sea food and pepper steaks. They had different delicacies, salads, huge cheese boards and exotic dishes with all the trimmings."

Excellent and why not. I named them henceforth the Dukes of 'Gormandy'.

Names crop up such as Hermione, Amarinta, Peregrine, Sophia (pronounced So- **Fire**) not humdrum pedestrian 'Sofie'– that's too like a settee or the capital of Bulgaria rather than this haunted pre-raphaelite beauty before us. Sat in the cockpit perusing the passenger manifest, I see names like Helena, Persephone, names which make me want to ask jokingly as they climb on board.

"Will Lysander and Demetrius not be joining us?"

Some of the names of the nouveau riche kids – the 'jeunesse doree', are interesting – Jewel, Saxon, Gulliver, Atlanta, Phoebe, Thalassa and Ciel. (Sea and Sky in Greek, those last two – rather lovely!)

Most of these families are pleasant enough – polite and gregarious. Some of the children, particularly teenagers can be tousled haired fops who are pretty feckless and vain. Some are just out and out Hogarthian rakes and braggarts. I suppose it does shave the edge of your hunger and the desire to catch the 06.42 every morning if you are going to inherit, say, a twenty bed roomed country pile and half the county it stands in, *or* a network of private banks.

The children (and their mates)can often be a handful. The kids of an Asian money maker were fainéants, naughty and untidy. One teenage boy whom we nicknamed 'blubberotis' was horribly overweight and just watched porn DVDs which he hid from mum and dad which was quite amusing. Food was always left all over the cabin and floor.

On another occasion we had *just* the kids of one of our wealthy clients. Neither Mister nor Missus Millionaire could accompany them to the chalet in the Alps poor things so they had to go on their own. It is generally a noisy, crisp chomping 'trasherama'. One of them managed to step on a pat of butter and tread it into every inch of carpet, along with some squashed raspberries. And how *do* you manage to get *that* many crisps into that very tight bit between the seat and the arm of the leather chairs?

Staying with the 'ubers', I flew a small party of Rothschild's back from a hunting trip in Africa. On the outbound journey **to** Africa it was just the Baroness on her own, Peter my Captain, went back to the cabin before take-off to see if she wanted anything. She replied she wouldn't require any food or service because she intended to sleep all the way (seven hours).

"Yes, good thought, that's probably what I'll do," replied Peter wryly, tongue very much in cheek and in best British accent. She thought this was most amusing and laughed out loud.

The return journey from Dar Es Salaam to Switzerland had the men on board, a very nice crowd (her husband and some mates). I still have to this day as a souvenir a lovely half-full bottle of Absinthe and another of Cane Spirit, which they kindly left on board. No wonder they disembarked in somewhat of a haze back in Switzerland. After I tasted some I had a better grip on why

Vincent lopped his ear off after guzzling the stuff! Yes it was a proper spirit fuelled odyssey that night as we moved silently across the darkness of Sudan towards Cairo. We came down at night into the city of the pyramids, their guardian sphinx and the snaking Nile. Lovely.

These were serious partiers. On the bottle of Cane spirit was a label – it read produced and bottled in St Kitts distilled by Baron De Rothschild CSR Ltd – CSR being of course Cane Spirit Rothschild. I knew they did the finest wines but *this* was most impressive. But it was the bottle of Absinthe which held my fascination. I have kept it. On it there stands a tall skinny magician dressed in black with a demonic grin and his foot on a naked woman in stockings and heels who is lying dead on the ground, with a cross plunged through her heart. He points with gloved hand to an owl holding a clock and calendar which reads Octobre 7 1910. I could only assume this was the date the wicked liquor was legalised, because across the top are the words 'Messieurs c'est l'heure'. Large black pterodactyls fly across moonlit mountains and across the bottom are the words La Fin de la "Fee Verte" (suppression de l'Absinthe en Suisse). I found it all very intriguing and I hazard a guess that an evening spent at one of *their* parties would be an extremely lively evening indeed! They certainly had their own version of the great Cartesian premise, '*I drink therefore I am.*'

A wall mounted photo of old Templehof.

Just landed, Dar-es-Salaam,
with Peter Britten.
Note: Party in background.

Me with Ronnie Wood – Berlin

Early days of Templehof.

Templehof: 'Deco' elegance of restaurant

Waiting for passengers in Luton.

Driving the water truck,
Yaounde Airport, Cameroon.

CHAPTER FIVE: Random Rolls and Turns

Introduction

Just like a wing, life is not always smooth and laminar flow! There can be a bit of turbulence, some interrupted airflow! You meet one person somewhere and whoosh it takes you down a different road. Along the way, outside the stretches of employment different opportunities have cropped up – working for a film facility company, learning to fly a sea plane, taking part in the odd Air Show. Being between jobs or 'working your way up' can often be a chance to discover something else. As they say: 'when nothing is sure everything is possible!' These are some of the 'rolls and turns' along my flight path. It is not chronological – just a glimpse at some other activities over the years, within the aviation world.

After that fortunate opportunity to ferry a B-25 over the Atlantic I was asked to stay on for a bit and fly on the television series for which it would be the camera plane.

FLIGHTS, CAMERA, ACTION!

It was May 1988 and unusually warm, what a glorious and memorable summer, the rape was so vivid that month, fields of brilliant yellow patterned the English countryside. I took part in an LWT (London Weekend Television) production of "Piece of Cake" a series about the early years of the Second World War. My role was as co-pilot on the B-25 bomber which was the camera platform from which all the aerial filming was done. Most days I flew with five Spitfires and three Messerschmitt 109s. On location we also had a Junkers JU52, a De Havilland Dragon Rapide, a Hawker Hurricane and a Tiger Moth, so plenty to keep the enthusiast happy. There was a finely restored German Heinkel 111 also which was used in some static scenes.

We'd basically fly a racetrack pattern and I'd endeavour to keep us **all** out of controlled airspace (sometimes tricky with eight high speed fighters considering the distances they needed for the 'run in' into shot and for their own separation!). I had my work cut out being unfamiliar with the area and armed only with my aeronautical 1:5000,000 scale map. Duxford in Cambridgeshire and South Cerney in Gloucestershire were the locations. We had one cameraman (Simon Werrey who I've since seen on so many credit lists) hanging out the back of the aeroplane and another amidships, both with lenses protruding from the aircraft. The director had his head in the bubble right at the top of the aircraft where he benefited from a 360 degrees view. He spun around like an owl shouting orders – my God when you think of the money spent per minute with such a fleet of aircraft airborne, you really *have* to avoid error as much as possible. The hourly price of these flying war birds is prodigious.

The aerial unit also used Friston on the Sussex coast which was particularly poignant since it had been the site of a wartime airfield used by the RAF, and of course the White Cliffs of Dover are quintessential when it comes to conveying any wartime fervour.

We would brief the sequence of the action and then **we** would get airborne first and wait until all the fighters gathered in two groups on each wing. Then on the directors command… 'whoosh'… they would all break and dart around for the fight sequences, always returning to us – the steady mothership as we described our race track pattern over the ground. From the cockpit of the B-25 I was treated to **the** most wonderful sights as Spitfires and ME109s came hurtling towards me breaking off at the last second, planes were disappearing underneath us and rolling over the top of us and heading full speed towards us! It was certainly a little more invigorating than flying two hundred passengers straight and level down to Alicante.

The first afternoon, we, the aerial unit met at South Cerney. Vernon the American Captain (a feisty and highly experienced septuagenarian) gave me the leg from North Weald. He talked me through the descent profile, power settings, speeds and flaps, and I landed on the grass strip at South Cerney, quite a challenge! I was captivated by the place – it was as though time had stood still, it held all the inherent charm of a World War Two aerodrome, all grass, large 'period' hangars, a thirties flat roofed control tower and a 'peri' track circling the field. The much loved and well known father and son team of Ray and Mark Hanna were the leading two Spitfires, and some others were there including Stephen Grey, Peter Jarvis, and Hoof Proudfoot. The Messerschmitt pilots – Nick Grace, Reg Hallam and Walther Eichorn introduced themselves.

What followed was simply glorious. Some of the Spitfires took to the sky one by one and performed a little show – a sort of warm up before tomorrow's filming. One of them I learnt later was a cannon armed aircraft built at Vickers Armstrong in the Midlands. G-ASJV was its registration and it had been based at Hornchurch in Essex and had done bomber escort missions in 1943, flown by a flight lieutenant from Natal. It had two Focke Wulf's and a Messerschmitt to its credit. It was magnificent, roaring around like an unchained beast relishing its freedom.

Then another went for its take-off roll across the grass, lifting its tail and slowly and effortlessly ascending into the air, the pilot dextrous in his control of the swing caused by the torque. G-AIST was its registration, a Mark 1A built by Westland at Yeovil in 1941. It had been operational at Hawarden near Chester and lived now at Old Warden, as part of the Shuttleworth collection. She had starred in the film the Battle of Britain I believe and was then sold to The Honourable Patrick Lindsay, whom I saw one day at Wycombe Air park flying his beautiful toy.

Another, G-BJSG, I was told had been saved from a storage unit in India, transported to the USA and then bought by a British collector and shipped back to England. It had flown with 443 squadron out of Ford Airfield in

Sussex. One of the others G-PRXI, was, I learnt the most expensive spitfire of all, the owner had paid around £300,000 for it. A nice little touch was the fact that a girl – Lettice Curtis of the Air Transport Auxiliary service had set a speed record (over 300 mph) while racing in *that* particular Spitfire.

I felt so lucky – it was simply beautiful, a very special sight. It was a 'first' for me, and I was choked with emotion. Then I heard some male voices chatting behind me. I naturally assumed they would be sharing in the incomparable joy of this moment, but instead I heard words which really surprised and unsettled me. Looking skyward with hands shielding the sun from their eyes …

"He just never seems to get that roll off the top quite right."

"Yea that was a bit loose."

They were actually criticising each other! I was astonished. Being so new to it, it all looked marvellous to me; my eye was untrained and uncynical. That was my very first encounter with 'The … Ego'. I have had untold meetings with it ever since.

The summer was just beginning and haze filled the air around the beautiful landscapes of Gloucestershire, Oxfordshire and Cambridgeshire. It was magical but at times difficult to navigate with the reduced visibility. I felt the pressure having to keep such a formidable fleet of aircraft out of harm's way, most of the fighters were without comms and it was my responsibility to talk to air traffic. Luton, Lyneham, Brize Norton and Cambridge were all very accommodating and requested the odd fly past. On one occasion we were flying back from Little Rissington to Duxford and the Spitfires –five of them were on my wing, they formated on us and the cameras were rolling. It was grand. *But* they could not hear my conversation with Luton air traffic who actually vectored me through their zone for a closer look. The spits thought I was lost so Ray Hanna, in the lead plane performed the silent message 'follow me'. This involved a very close flypast across my window, inches away from my windscreen. He frightened me half to death as he shot across my bow from right to left – (certainly a fantastic photo opportunity!). He then disappeared off to the north.

Once on the ground we all exchanged a few heated words but it was no disaster, the most upset party was Luton who missed out on their spectacular flypast. The film crew were a bit miffed as well having lost some shooting opportunity. As well as excitement there is a lot of confusion and frustration involved in the execution of these scenes, and we were for ever having problems with the radios.

The day for the main action arrived. We were all getting airborne for a long dogfight sequence which had been briefed. Vernon and I would launch first, circle the airfield and wait for the Spitfires and Me109s to take-off and come and formate, after which we would go off to the local area, fly the racetrack around which the dogfight would take place over the sleepy fields of Gloucestershire and Wiltshire (not your average hum drum sight for the residents for whom noise was usually the traffic on the 419 from Swindon!). We took off, I raised the gear and flaps for Vernon who swung her wide downwind and we watched eagerly as the former adversaries took to the skies together.

There followed a remarkable incident, which none of us really understood until we landed back minutes later having aborted the mission. The ME109s and some Spitfires were all bobbing up and down around me like race horses tossing and pawing getting ready for the 'off'. Then we heard Mark's voice in the headsets talking to his father in one of the other spitfires. "Okay that's a hundred and twenty knots … one hundred and ten knots … okay that's fine."

Ray must have lost his pitot static instruments I thought to myself and therefore have no indication of airspeed. So Mark is acting as his wing man feeding him speed information and talking him down the approach; very tidy and well managed. The director wondered what the hell was going on, nobody really knew but we all realised it was aborted – there was no shoot without the two lead spitfires so we headed back.

After only one circuit and feeling robbed of a much anticipated sortie, we lowered the gear after only just having retracted it and hauled her round onto final approach to land on the grass. The noise from the engines increased then decreased as Vernon made small power excursions up and back on the throttles to get this heavy chunk of metal over the bumpy uneven surface. Once parked, I saw the two Spitfire pilots had alighted from their respective planes and were standing over the wing of the lead Spitfire in their green overalls staring down at something obviously quite distressing.

"Well let's go and see what the hell's goin' on here," said Vernon in his Texan drawl. Our engineer snapped open the lower hatch and we climbed down the ladder.

Everyone had gathered around and now the horror was revealed. The tip of Ray's wingtip was missing, the unmistakable elliptical tip, so classically

'Spitfire' was nothing but a rough jagged edge, torn and shredded. There was disbelief from the film crew and the other pilots were deeply shocked though very sympathetic. We all knew this was going to be *expensive*.

"No filming, ok, and no bloody reporters in here to cover this!" Ray said, angry at his mistake.

He had performed his hallmark take-off which involved keeping it very low, skimming the ground and banking round as the wheels came up. Normally very impressive, only *that day* he wasn't reckoning on the huge great lorry driving along the road just outside the perimeter fence. Yes, it seemed that the normally so accurate flying ace had put his wingtip into the roof of a passing lorry. Well we are all human after all. Mmmm I could imagine the comments from the drivers' mates when he got to the depot in Bristol or wherever:

"Got a good tip today then Reggie!" as they all stared in disbelief at Spitfire wingtip lodged in his roof.

Vernon, who had by now suffered days of 'scorn and contumely' from the British pilots who never *really* trusted the Americans – (certainly not aging Southern rednecks) seized his moment for a bit of banter and a touch of payback.

He ambled on his bow legs over to the plane, removed his baseball cap and scratched his head then readjusted it on his grizzly head.

"Hell Ray I gotta hand it to ya, you could make a mess out of a steel ball with a rubber hammer."

Well that seemed to go down like a sideways bone, so I sloped off and let the big egos deal with it.

We successfully finished the shooting there over the next couple of days.

We spent a few glorious summery days at Charlton Park near Malmesbury in Gloucestershire. It was supposed to be the majestic French chateau 'St Pierre' and actually looked quite the part. It had been turned into apartments, the residents were delighted at the prospect of Spitfires landing on the front lawn every day. I don't think they were quite so taken when the special effects team had to blow the place up!

To see RAF pilots sitting on their wicker chairs, with a cigarette and the newspaper wearing battered old flying jackets, with the old tea urns standing on the trestle table on a glorious summer's afternoon was *so* nostalgic and really transported you back to war days. We just needed a bit of Tommy Dorsey playing and it would have been perfect.

The film crews had had to widen the grass runway at the country house to accommodate three spitfires taking off together. Another unfailingly evocative sight! The ground had been worryingly boggy during February when Ray Hanna landed there for the press day. (In fact several burley men had had to remove the plane from its huge rut!) Winds and rain had been against the Spitfire pilots and a few of them diverted to Lyneham, and doubt remained as to whether it would be suitable for so much aircraft movement.

However, good fortune came our way and by May when we filmed the sun shone and the grass grew over the widened strip, which was ready for the onslaught of aircraft repeatedly landing. Imprinted on my memory is the unmistakable De Havilland Rapide trundling benignly around in the butterscotch sunlight of early evening with the golden Cotswold stone of the mansion gleaming behind. This aircraft has the charming appearance of a baby dragon. It is a big biplane, the covered struts of the undercarriage make it look as though it has furry forelegs – not unlike a cocker spaniel and its shaggy little feet. They were built as little passenger airliners (only six or seven passengers) and after war broke out they served in the RAF as courier aircraft or as training aircraft for communications and navigation. They seem to encapsulate the spirit of that age.

I gained a unique insight into the filming techniques. It was delightful sitting around on folding chairs watching scenes of replica Spitfires being blown to pieces, or taxiing into the side of a dispersal hut. Special effects teams attached tanks of petrol to the nose of the replica and set off explosions by radio control. Some replicas, which had to move under their own steam had little motorcycle engines to drive the propeller and another small motor to turn the wheels. There were gripping moments – like the one when the Spitfire came hurtling towards the camera and then nose-dived into the grass and bent the propeller, and another in which it left the runway and ended up in a ploughed field. It was an education seeing how these scenes are constructed and shot.

The very last sortie for me was from Little Rissington in Oxfordshire. Having just completed many months at the flying training school at Kidlington nearby, I couldn't resist a little 'hello' to my friends in the control tower there.

"Oxford, good afternoon this is N1042B."

"N1042B, Oxford tower pass your message."

"N1042B is a B-25 from Rissington to Duxford, two thousand feet on 1023, just approaching Woodstock."

"Roger N1042B, the QNH is 1023 maintain 2,000 feet, no known conflicting … is that you Anita?"

"Affirm."

"Any chance of a flyby?"

I asked Vernon who never passed up a chance for a bit of hell raising.

"Yes we can do that."

"Okay runway in use 20, you can join right base for a flypast, as low as you like."

I explained quickly to Vernon that *this* is where I had done all my flying training recently, it had become a home away from home, I knew all the guys and girls here.

"Well hell you take it Aneeda and have yourself some fun."

I knew this was my last flight in the B-25, the aerial shots were complete now the rest of the shooting (the famous Spitfire under the bridge – Ray's moment) was to be in Durham and the rest would be shot from the ground at Friston on the south coast.

I took a firm grip of the yoke, put the nose down and came down to about seven hundred feet, spotted the familiar white chimney – Smokey Joe as we called it – a godsend for finding the airfield. There would be no flap or gear on this one I'd just make it low and fast.

"N4102B right base for a flyby."

"Roger, one in the circuit downwind clear for flyby."

I pushed her down, opened the throttles, "here goes."

I lowered the nose, the speed and noise increased rapidly and we went down to about seventy feet. Wow, what a feeling and what a great tank of an aeroplane. I flew her right down the middle of the runway flat out and pulled her up steeply at the far end for a sharp right break back towards the north. It was a 'good rush'.

"Thanks very much guys that was fantastic, you're clear depart to the north, contact Brize on 134 decimal 3, goodbye."

"You're welcome! Changing now Brize on 134.3, so long."

It was the cherry on my 'Piece of Cake' and a great way to end.

(I was fortunate enough to be asked to fly it again for the filming of Memphis Belle, but I was employed full-time by then so could not, but the B-25 was the camera ship in that movie also.)

Air Shows

The Nazi JU 52 Junkers – Brize Norton

What luck – it was the summer of 1988 and I was invited to have a go in the German Second World War Junkers JU 52 and attend the Brize Norton air show. I'd recently acquired my Commercial Pilot Licence and therefore legal to fly right hand seat. This war bird is a three engined tail dragger made of corrugated aluminium. Somewhat prehistoric in appearance, it lumbers around slowly at 70 to 80 knots. It was particularly significant for me because on the day of my *first* ever solo at Fairoaks airfield in Surrey, they were filming the Dirty Dozen with Lee Marvin using that same Junkers; apparently I came in to land in the middle of their shot forcing a retake. It was not every day that a load of Nazi generals in jackboots and 'Seig Heil' jodhpurs queue up for a mug of tea and a bacon sandwich at the airfield café. Poor old, war veteran Ted who cut the grass and had advancing dementia was reduced to lip trembling murmurs, as he stared, pointing his shaky finger in confusion thinking he was back at Arnhem.

After climbing up the steep incline of the main body to get to the cockpit, the Captain Peter Hoar, (British Airways) familiarised me with some of the controls, we settled in our seats – big old iron bucket types with lots of old padded, faded quilt everywhere. Although enthralled, I was grateful for the progress we have made! The propeller blades have to be pulled through by hand to clear the cylinders of any oil; a long pole with a loop to hook round the prop, was provided. We put the fuel selector switch to start, then used the manual wobble pump. There's no primer so we pushed the throttle back and forth few times to squirt fuel into the cylinders. Then on go the four position magneto switches, the generator and battery switch. The fuel/oil selectors (can't miss them!) had large yellow and brown balls on the end. In fact miniature billiard balls dominate the central quadrant – black ones on the end of the mixture levers and white ones on the throttles.

Everything is full on, big and bold in these planes, there are knobs, levers, handles and huge great taps everywhere, the dials are enormous; all very mechanical! The engine was a huge nine cylinder air cooled radial – from that bygone era.

Even when the engine fires you still keep wobbling the pump, we put the fuel/oil selector to fully open and the engine driven pump kicks in. At about 600 rpm it stabilised and we stopped pumping. Then we repeated the same procedure for the other two engines.

It was all a bit cumbersome, but so clever too. I cannot pretend casual indifference because it was absolutely brilliant to handle an aircraft like this, even its smell – it is *so* unique and distinctive and it never seems to fade. I was imagining both the Germans and the Spaniards (who operated them during the civil war), how modern and high tech they must have been then. As for the designers and inventors – you have to admire their resourcefulness and intellect; such seminal minds.

There are certainly some quirky pieces of engineering, for example the propellers cannot be feathered, they just windmill if the engine fails, not only that but it was designed for the oil to run out, the shaft to seize and the engine to fall off! No weight penalty from a dead engine after that. I was tickled when Peter the Captain stood up to taxi it out. You really can't help feeling a bit Nazi-ish in that position. He stood upright in the middle of the cockpit with both hands on the throttles as though he were driving a tram, it's the only way to see out. The rudder pedals are huge metal plates, they had no control as such, they just angled back and forth, and they were connected only to the rudder so provided no assistance for steering at low speed.

The fact that this was obviously not a 'speed' machine was evident from the props, which are fixed pitch; they can only be adjusted on the ground by an engineer. But they built it like this for a reason – higher revs normally mean shorter life span, so they were keeping them low. Also the landing gear is fixed, this means loads of drag! Unlike the little elevator trim wheel of modern light aircraft which sits neatly between the two seats, this one was like an old nineteenth century spinning wheel – a huge round wooden affair which moved the whole of the tail plane rather than a trim tab. But what was remarkable was the fact that when you pulled a lever next to the trim wheel it became the flap selector!

I was amazed to discover later that these planes flew with airlines in Bolivia, China, Belgium, Ecuador, Denmark, France, Hungary, Italy, Poland, Czechoslovakia and many more so we are talking about a huge success story.

You know those big red taps you might find in the loft to turn off the water supply? Well here they were! These were oil temperature controls; similar large blue taps were for the brake accumulator. And Oh! pneumatic braking, this was a 'goodun' – new territory for me. There would be a hiss of pressurised air whenever we applied the brakes, and lots of smoke, because when you brake, effectively you're torching the centre engine, starving it of fuel so the *excess* fuel burns off out of that exhaust.

A fascinating fact – the brakes were not operated as they are traditionally by the feet, but by the throttles. You'd pull the centre throttle back to idle, *then* ... bringing it *further* back turned it into a brake lever. The sharp injection of air from the brake cylinders to the wheels made the loud hiss. The 2000lb bottle of nitrogen was good for two hundred braking actions. You couldn't help feeling part pilot, part steam train operator, and part boiler room engineer!

The instruments were archaic but had that exquisite 'made by hand' craftsmanship about them. There was no missing the three red fire extinguishers, nor the bulky carburettor heat levers – you didn't have to look hard for stuff in *this* cockpit, it was pretty much jumping out at you.

The radios were surprisingly clear when I contacted Stansted (our controlling authority) to tell them of our impending take-off from nearby North Weald. As we lined up I felt we had the aerodynamic profile of a London bus and as we trundled slowly down the runway, it did seem to take a while to accelerate. Peter pulled her gently off the ground and banked right towards the west. No undercarriage to raise, it was fixed – the Germans certainly weren't looking for 'velocity' here. I was impressed by lift generated by those bulky great wings, and by the ease and grace of her movement in the air. I held the topographical map and started to navigate towards Brize Norton in Oxfordshire.

Is there any greater felicity than a slow low-level flight over England in the summer? It is unfailingly beautiful. Green fields stretching away to the horizon, soft hills, and meandering rivers catching the sunlight occasionally. I looked down affectionately at our country houses with the occasional 'folly', the cricket greens, snaking hedgerows and pretty villages. It is a friendly patchwork dotted with church spires, small towns, disused airfields and miles of railway. Cross countries are marvellous. One of the glories of seeing it from the air is the sense of connection. I love to imagine our ancestors, the ancient Britons, building their burial mounds and stone circles, leaving their great chalk drawings for us – did they laugh when they thought of future generations enjoying the inordinately well-endowed giant of Cerne Abbas in Dorset? How nice it would be to go back in time just for a day. They trod that same turf. They no doubt played and hunted in that ancient woodland and fished in that river. Did people hide or lovers meet in those dense copses on top of that hill? I'm sure they did.

Something which brought a smile to my face, was the oil contents gauge – it was *outside* on the centre engine nacelle and was totally inaccurate, as were the fuel content gauges, (der kraftstoffanzeiger!) which were the 'float' type and were situated on each wing, so you couldn't actually see them. You were obliged to use the old-fashioned method of time and fuel burn to work out how much you had left! Mmm, glad we weren't on a long journey.

I took hold of the big wooden yoke, worn by decades of hands. It felt solid and strong and despite her bulk she really handled beautifully. As we neared Brize, we saw the long impressive runways and resident VC10s, along with the huge gathering of planes for the air show including World War One vintage, Spitfires and F16s. Our first stage of flap came down at ninety knots followed by full flap at seventy-five knots. The approach speeds were similar to those of the little Piper Cherokee that I'd learnt on – remarkable. I could see eager crowds lifting cameras and binoculars as we turned gracefully onto downwind. Peter put her on the ground very deftly and we taxied to our stand, hissing and lurching with Peter stood up in the cockpit being the tram driver again, moving levers up and down and back and forth – excellent! Our display was one of the very last, so we had plenty of time to wander around the whole place.

I managed to talk my way into the cockpit of an A10 Warthog from Lakenheath. The pilot was from Arizona, we were laughing at the difference between the old Nazi garden shed which couldn't outrun a greyhound, and his titanium plated, missile loaded, high tech, 'faster than hell' killing machine!

It was like the 'Battle of Midway' as we watched the high performance piston fighters take to the skies – the P51 Mustang, a Thunderbolt with a Hellcat, a Bearcat and a Corsair, and of course the beautiful navy Sea Fury. All those gravelly rumblings resonate through your chest. They roar like unchained beasts as their huge propeller blades split the air and the pistons – hot and furious work at unbelievable RPMs to give out those distinctive and triumphant growls.

The air is bursting with noise at air shows especially when the Vulcan is at full chat, swooping around like a sinister caped devil. A most loved veteran

Dizzy Addicot and Bob Thompson flew the Vampire and Venom, then up went the red Spitfire – well what can you say.

When the military jets start, conversation stops. Against a backdrop of perfect blue the jets went through their motions, slicing through the air low level charging along the runway then snapping up into a vertical climb, displaying their incredible power. They'd almost disappear into the neighbouring village – their turning radius was so large. Someone told me that the Blackbird SR71 was so ridiculously fast, it would have to start its descent at Shannon in Ireland to make the correct profile for an airfield in Eastern England! After the military jets – F111s, Phantoms, Tornadoes and the great Harrier (which of course ended its display with its customary bow to the audience) I carried on meeting some more pilots.

A robust little English chap (Linton Moss) was standing by a three quarter size scaled down replica of a Fockewulfe – he had built it himself, just as well, he too, was very small. Moustached and feisty he was springing about like a 'jack in the box'.

He told me some of the leg pulling pranks they played on new recruits in the RAF in Oman where he'd been stationed. During their first sortie, someone would pipe up on the radio.

"Watch out lads, I think Jones is about to pile in; silly bugger took that one a bit late."

Then... someone on the ground would set fire to a pile of tyres sending up a cloud of black smoke. The leader would call an early landing, they'd all gather round for a debrief in front of the new guy who was now sweating for Britain.

"Darn shame eh, but these things happen, he was new, didn't really know the routine, don't let it get you down young man!"

And they slapped him on the back ... Sods!

He very kindly invited me to Booker airfield in High Wycombe to fly with him in his beautiful, high performance Cap 21 aerobatic aeroplane. The following week I did just that and was treated to a roller coaster, white-knuckle ride over the countryside of Buckinghamshire and Oxfordshire, swooping, spiralling and pulling bags of 'G'. It was made extra memorable because he had an old, Alvis car, which he had lovingly restored, we had a little jaunt down to the pub, after the flight. It was dark blue with polished brass trims, big old steering wheel, tidgey little windscreen wipers, cracked leather seats and a chirpy 'noddy type' horn complete with squeezable black sack. It was like jogging along in a little biscuit tin, absolutely spellbinding and quite the jolliest car I'd ever been driven in. So glad to have met him that day at the air show, someone told me a few years later he had died. I was so sorry.

Back at the air show ... the Lancaster bomber flew past flanked by the smaller more nimble fighters, a sort of mother duck with her chicks; this one always has people humming the Dambusters tune. Then we were treated to the B17, followed by dog fights, aerobatics, tumbling biplanes, coloured smoke trails, soaring motor gliders cruising around to Pink Floyd, and, of course the dazzling and unfailingly accurate, Red Arrows.

On the ground the army did a wonderful job of entertaining kids on mini assault courses, the RAC looked for new members, and as always, people propped up bars in Guinness tents. Glamorous 'Promotions' girls in 'zip down' matching boiler suits were selling tickets around a flashy sports car on a rotating platform.

The smell of frying onions and hot dogs wafted around the temporary gazebos. All around brightly coloured bunting fluttered in the breeze. So much was on sale: second hand military gear, old stamp collections; prints and postcards of wartime aeroplanes, Battle of Britain memorial tea towels, nostalgic books, uniforms and medals, even old war time 78 records. It is a typically English summer event – a great day out and very educational. No event seems to combine the charms of history and future, of preservation and invention so successfully. As much reverence is heaped on the 1915 canvas biplane as on the futuristic fighter jet. It is every man from Orville and Wilbur to Neil Armstrong.

Unfortunately we didn't do our display – we had a technical hitch (so common with these old planes.) Ray the engineer discovered a throttle linkage problem – die anschlüsse ist kaput! (my entirely made up version of events.) Nonetheless, the journey home was beautiful, the early evening sky, was full of planes returning to their various bases. With our sauntering pace of eighty knots, we were easy to catch, so many of them slid over for a spot of formation flying with the old but 'herrlich' German flugzeug – the Junkers trimotor.

Danke schön.

The Spitfire and Messerschmitt Together as Friends

On May 15th 1988 right in the middle of filming ITVs 'Piece of Cake', we had the North Weald air show. By this time the good old Mitchell B-25 was a familiar friend. It was a sunny May day and the aerodrome (such a great word) was alive with activity, aircraft were arriving from all over, buzzing round the circuit waiting their landing clearance. Awnings and flags flapped in the breeze. The polished and precise English voice of the commentator boomed out from every speaker, telling us *what* was tearing through the sky above us and *who* exactly was flying it. Thank God we put together such days, not only for pure enjoyment but for the preservation and celebration of history.

Our detail was at two fifteen in the afternoon, we'd do our usual fly pasts then we'd be joined by Walter Eichorn in the ME 109 and by Mark Hanna in the Spitfire – how different would be their meeting now from the white knuckle ones they'd over the channel nearly fifty years earlier. Both aircraft would be sure of returning unharmed back to base.

I pushed the bottom hatch open, slid it back and climbed up the metal ladder into the cockpit with Vernon the American Captain and Ray the engineer. The start sequence is *not* from the 'press to start' school. Ray pulled the propellers through by hand to clear the cylinders. I opened up the throttle levers half an inch, the *left* engine boost pump went on 'emergency' until we read ten PSI then we selected 'normal'.

We checked the 'all clear' with the ground crew. Ray turned the props through nine or ten blades. We engaged the starter and put the magneto master switch to 'on' and the left mag to 'both'. On went the priming switch. Sometimes the blades would turn and then judder back into position – a non start. You try again, then that wonderful sound of the starter, a seconds hesitation then she bursts into life. Flames roar from the exhaust and white smoke engulfs the cowling of the chunky Wright Cyclone engine. As soon as she fires up we prime, then mixture lever – RICH. We ran her at about 1000 rpm until warmed up and went through the same process for the *other* engine. We checked all the instruments and ambled slowly out to the hold.

We heard the loud and unmistakable commentary, he introduced the B-25 giving a brief history and said it was currently being used as the camera ship in a television series. Then he introduced us and away we went belting down the runway! It's always a joy to break free from those terrestrial tethers and get into that sky once more. The gear came up with a muscular 'clunk' and we fine-tuned the throttles and props to eliminate any asymmetric whirring.

We cruised north away from the London zone and after a minute or two, turned back for the airfield and prepared for our low fly pasts. The first was slow, flap down, so people could have a good look. Then we dropped it lower and performed the exhilarating 'full speed ahead down the runway' manoeuvre. With the extra power we pulled up into a steep climbing turn and 'winged over' into downwind.

Then came that magical moment when a much quicker, niftier aircraft comes alongside. It was the greatest and most beautiful of them all – the Spitfire on our left wing and its erstwhile adversary the mighty Messerschmitt 109 with its German cross, on our right. To fly beside the Spitfire and behold this thoroughbred at such close quarters, was … well … overwhelming really!

I could clearly see Walter the German wearing a mask, he just popped up alongside appearing out of nowhere and waved, and for that one, brief, brilliant moment we were together, floating along sharing a wink and a smile in the 'footless halls of air'. It's such a buzz when you see a plane *that* close, because it's only *then* that you feel their buoyancy, that slight keel and bob, the minute sliding movements which suggest they are on that cushion of air. We did a formation fly past together down the runway which had the fun meter hard into the red!

The two fighters peeled off, their grace and beauty bought a lump to my throat. But it is the *power*, of those machines considering their age, which is nothing short of amazing. Before the jet age, here is an aircraft doing nearly 400 miles per hour and climbing at more than 4,500 feet per minute. Well done Reginald Mitchell the inventor of this supreme fighter, the paragon of aeroplanes! They flew all around us sliding underneath then slipping over our heads, putting on quite a show.

I thought of Churchill's 'We will fight them …'speech, of grass airfields where pilots would run, parachutes slung over shoulders to their waiting Spits, not knowing if they'd come back. I thought of the mess room after a sortie;

kettles steaming, camaraderie and courage and the ghastly unbearable tragedy of lost friends. How can I ever grasp the terror of spiralling down to the ground having been shot? I shudder. Thank God I am enjoying these wonderful war birds in *this* environment. I did feel a soaring gratitude and my thoughts were, for a brief but very profound moment, with those young lads whose bravery was consummate. When the ME109 was leaving he came close to my right wing once more, then the pilot just lifted his hand to his brow in a jovial salute then showed me the underbelly of his plane as he peeled steeply off to starboard and went on his way … superb! We landed back and taxied in to the ramp. The rest of the afternoon was spent chatting to visitors, journalists and crews – and enjoying the displays.

Jobs loomed and I had to get serious, (oh well!) but I got *one* more show in luckily – the West Malling air show the following year; we did a formation fly past with the B17 'Sally B' and the DC3. Now *that* was a terrific day. The film 'Empire of the Sun' was being shot at around the same time so we met some of the cast and crew.

Sadly there is a gloomier side of air shows and that is when someone crashes and dies. Having done this spectacular display with Mark Hanna, I was horrified to learn he tragically died in his ME109 at an air show in Spain. Such a great loss to British aviation. I saw with my very eyes the tragic loss of the Hurricane pilot who was displaying ay Shoreham in the summer of 2007. There were many aircraft including Spitfires, ME109 and 108s taking place in this dogfight, I happened to be focussed right on him as he made the fatal error. It was just so tragic to see that Hurricane pile straight into the ground just outside Lancing College in Sussex and then the fire go up. It made my blood run cold. His buddies went into the 'Friend missing in action' formation which was very poignant. Silence fell over the airfield but his friends insisted the show should go on to the end since that is what he would have wanted.

Just a piercing reminder of what a dangerous game it can be.

Two Girls, One P51 Mustang

The other air show in which, with the greatest of fortune I became a participant, was held down in Tamiami Florida. I was doing my FAA Airline Transport Pilot's Licence at the American Flyers School in Fort Lauderdale, which took several weeks and was, I have to say, pretty tough. During my Aces High days I made two great contacts: Kermit Weeks – pilot and collector, and his girlfriend Lynda Myers. They lived in Florida and were organising an air show. I called them just at the right time:

"You must be burnt out on all that studying and flight training, how d'you fancy coming down and joining in the air show?"

I was ecstatic.

I hired a car, bought some soft drinks and a bag of Lays sour cream and onion crisps – a new and exciting discovery, cranked the radio and I was off down the Florida Turnpike singing along to the Eagles. I arrived in good time at their home, and went along with them to the airfield. Linda, was a champion aerobatic pilot and was very deft at flying pretty much everything in Kermit's collection. I wandered around the displays admiring the impressive collection. A Curtiss P40 and P47 Thunderbolt caught my eye, the latter being the largest single seat fighter of the Second World War. There was much to marvel at from little biplanes and Hell Cats to the majestic B17. The Corsair was parked there – very arresting with its characteristic folding wings. God it's a rugged looking thing, not the sort of aircraft you would want to see coming straight at you in the binoculars as you're stood on the deck your ship. It first flew in 1940 and with that huge great 2000hp engine I am told it was a supreme naval fighter as well as an outstanding ground support plane.

Kermit had a special penchant for his flying boat the Grumman Duck. He invited me to accompany him on the flying display which chuffed me to bits naturally. The amphibian is such a strange looking aircraft, rather cute actually. It is like a stubby fat biplane mounted on enormous protruding hull which looks like a banana! Under the hull protrude the two wheels and one tiny wheel caster at the very back. Under the lower wings hang two large floats. Aptly named, 'duck' seemed far more fitting than 'heron' or 'egret'; there was nothing lithe or predatory in her lines, she was just a fat little waddler. It first flew way back in 1933 for the US Navy and it became an air sea rescue plane in the late forties. As I approached to climb aboard I realised how big it was. I was surprisingly 'high up' as I lowered myself in behind Kermit. He fired up the big radial piston engine and the sound was just perfect.

Off we went to the delight of the crowds because she was obviously quite rare and special. Kermit flew her around with manifest delight, he was very proud of this machine I could tell. We circled around the local area and flew up and down the runway. The high profile drag precluded any great speed but it was nonetheless a delight. Such a visionary, Kermit. On his business card are the words, 'FLIGHT... more than anything on this planet symbolises man's desire to go beyond himself.'

I couldn't believe my luck when towards the end of the day Linda, who was going to display the P51 Mustang, said to Kermit.

"Why not take Anita up with me, she's never flown one before, two girls, that will be a crowd pleaser," and in typically laid back style he agreed that was a great idea. Don't know about *crowd* pleaser but it was certainly going to please the living daylights out of *me*!

The P51 is seriously top notch. Fast and strong with aesthetic lines and undeniable beauty, it was an army pursuit aircraft though there was a photo reconnaissance version. It looks more British in its design than its contemporary American fighters and I believe this is because the RAF had far reaching influence in its design specification. The wings are laminar flow and the airframe low drag. When the Allison engine was replaced by the Rolls Royce Merlin it transformed a good aircraft into an outstanding one. Its performance and manoeuvrability were astonishing. Little touches gave it an edgy and winning profile; for example, the inline engine, the 'set back' radiator which improved the streamlining and also the teardrop cockpit for enhanced pilot visibility. It had great endurance, a powerful engine which gave it speeds of nearly 500 mph and rendered it the best dive bomber of its day.

Lo and behold here I was climbing into one just before sunset behind a pilot with long blonde hair!

Linda talked me through what she was going to do and said once we got out into the Everglade area I could have a play on the controls. OHMYGOD prepare for fun meter to twitch on full red! Off we roared, I felt the raw and surging power as she pushed the throttles. Everything was there, strength, agility and grace, this was an aircraft which would never know 'struggle'. She did a few manoeuvres for the spectators, low fly past down the runway with a dramatic and steep pull up at the other end and a wing over, then after a few barrel rolls she flew off into the local area really for my benefit – I was blown away. The swamps stretched out before us like a vast soup. They looked beautiful and in the setting sun, though I didn't for one second underestimate the deadly contents of their still and inhospitable waters. I knew all sorts of wild and slithery creatures must be lurking in the deadly depths waiting to snap off a limb should one be forthcoming!

The sky was a symphony of citrus, fish bones of wispy cirrus were edged with orange and peach. The colours reflected in the flat waters which were broken by the odd protruding dead tree or by the late air boat whizzing around leaving swirling wakes on the glassy surface. I took the controls and banked left and right doing a few steep turns, it felt … just so right. I tried to imagine what a dogfight must have felt like in one of these – so liberating yet so terrifying. We had a black tie ball throwing it around, diving and climbing then swooping low skimming the surface of the dark mean swamp scaring the gators into a bit of tail flicking retreat.

Linda took us back to the air show to finish off the day in perfect style with a final crowd pleasing fly past at full speed followed by a gear down, flap down, slow one. We landed beautifully just as the red sun sank below the palm treed horizon. I had certainly 'slipped the surly bonds of earth and touched the face of God' on *that* little sortie. Unforgettable moment.

It's just those crazy women in the P51 again

That night we all shared a big tub of Florida stone crab claws, a new experience for me. You crack them and dip them in melted butter, they are seasonal and now was the time. They were absolutely delicious and I was so happy to hear that the claw grows back after it is removed – isn't life magical sometimes. Kermit told me of his plans to move his collection to Polk City in central Florida, he would have one of the biggest collections in the United States. Many years later whilst doing a sea plane rating in Lakeland I flew right overhead and sure as shot, there it was, he'd pulled it off.

Good man.

Aces High

During those uncertain years after you have acquired a private license, but before you adorn the lofty heights of a commercial pilot and then encounter that wonderful stuff called money … life can be a tad shaky.

There are all sorts of companies who have their offices on airfields, and Aces High with whom I became friendly, was a particularly interesting one, run by a husband and wife team, their activities were widespread. They sourced planes for films and TV, they were involved in warbirds, vintage planes, air shows, buying and selling just about anything, and renting out hangar space for aircraft parking *and* film shoots. Their hangars were at North Weald in Essex (more recently at Dunsfold in Surrey). The Chairman Mike Woodley (ex-DC3 pilot) and aviation advisor on the last six James Bond films, along with his wife Caroline are life-long friends.

In fact Aces High had just acquired the first Russian Mig-15 in the UK. (Ex-Polish Airforce and now in Royal Navy museum at Yeovilton.) They also claimed amongst other war birds a DC3, DC4, a Lockheed Constellation (now in Wroughton museum) C119, a Miles Jet and a Lincoln which had come from Bitterswell, one of only three in existence, the others are in Cosford, England and Buenos Aires.

The next few stories are all about the 'missions' I was involved in around 1985–1988. I was building hours, so to make myself a bit more marketable I did a twin-rating over a weekend on a Grumman Cougar in Southampton and also acquired an IMC rating, i.e. basic instrument rating. Those, combined with my enthusiasm, enabled me to take part in some of the projects and adventures. I had been cleaning planes and amending paperwork (airfield plates) to earn hours so this was a notch up the ladder. Some of these aircraft can be flown on a Private License with a twin rating, and furthermore I didn't want *paying*; I was just happy to fly anything, gain experience and *learn* about the industry, so, it worked well.

At the time there were a few 'deals' going on in the States; one was the purchase of a PBY Catalina flying boat in Hawaii, another was selling some Venom jets to private owners in Vermont; and another was selling a Lancaster bomber (in bits) to a Florida museum, then there was a P51 Mustang sale to an ex-hippie who had just inherited a chunk of Florida's citrus farms. Last but not least was the purchase of the B-25 Mitchell bomber, on which I flew as co-pilot on the ferry back to England.

During all of this I was lucky enough to indulge my passion and be the guest of some pilots who took me on some memorable 'jollies'.

Catalina Flying Boat – Hawaii

The Catalina flying boat 'deal' was full of promise and excitement and Woodley (owner of Aces High) fully intended to buy it for resale purposes, and I was hoping secretly for a ride in the beautiful thing. It turned out to be quite farcical. Woodley had said he'd go along with the deal if they flew the plane as far as California and that it proved airworthy. Using the pool of accumulated 'airmiles' we eventually flew to Maui. The white flying boat was visible on the other side as we landed. It was on the Canadian register – C-FSAT. We walked up to the plane, the tropical sun shone down, the palm trees were swaying, the ocean glinting in the background – it had all the feel-good charm of a nice corny 1950s musical, I was ready for Jimmy Stewart or Richard Widmark to alight from a military jeep with a "Howdy".

Woodley was clicking away with the camera and the engineer (a walrus of a man) was ready to do a full inspection; he was a big florid and sweaty and did look a bit comical with the lei of purple flowers round his neck. (We had all received one at the airport with an "Aloha"! from a petite Hawaiian beauty.)

We started our walk round, took pictures, and the engineer looked closely at the wheels and fuselage. I was just like a dog with five tails letting my imagination drift freely into those magnificent journeys of nostalgia, picturing vigilant World War Two pilots in oily flying suits over the Atlantic. Then I entertained the very stimulating thought of flying in it – maybe on some film shoot or air show. (What's that song...? *"Just my imagination; runnin' away with me"*).

We were just in the middle of all this when suddenly the side window in the fuselage opened and out popped the very sleepy, bleary eyed face of a hippy. He had long matted hair and bloodshot eyes and scratched all corners of his skinny frame.

"Oh hey, you guys. Made it huh?"

We were a bit startled to say the least. This guy was a sort of caretaker, looking after the plane on behalf of the owner who was in Canada. I imagine the boss would have given some instructions along the lines of:

"Take care of my flying boat, keep it clean make sure nobody tampers with it. If it needs to be towed, supervise that, and show any prospective buyers around," and so on.

Naturally, as is the case with most, teenagers and hippies, interpretation is an inexact science!

"Surely that means I can live in the plane, burn josticks, smoke grass and sleep with my girlfriend all day and night, maybe even light the odd camp fire? I mean, hey dudes what's the panic?"

We climbed in. I found the cockpit quite different from anything I'd ever seen – how wonderful to have the throttles in the roof. The two pilots' seats were side by side in the bow cockpit (a turret) with big windows all the way round. In the bow was a sighting window protected from the salt water by a blind. The wingtip floats could actually be retracted electrically, so that in flight they formed the wingtips; very clever. It was designed in 1935 and transformed the patrolling capabilities of the US Navy. There were many flying at the outbreak of the Second World War, and even though the next generation of flying boats had been ordered, the 'Cat' had a long and mighty life. It was one of the slowest war planes but its power lay in its range and endurance. It was reliable and rugged and of course brought many crews safely back to base on both land and water. I thought of the story of the RAF pilot in 1941 who whilst far out in the Atlantic, spotted the Bismark, which had eluded its pursuers for over thirty hours! He was able to radio the position to the British fleet.

To cut a long story short, Aces High agreed the deal **if** it was flown to California and was confirmed airworthy. Well, after some maintenance (I suspect that even Heath Robinson would have been proud of) it did indeed take-off from Hawaii but the wheel apparently fell off on the take off run and it went rolling unceremoniously into the water – well maybe not a problem for a flying boat, but the plugs were not in so it filled with water and sank; hard to believe but true. They tried to lift it with a crane and this actually broke the plane! – conclusion: this deal was not meant to be. As the saying goes – 'you can't win 'em all!'

Ironically enough, the Insurance Company pointed out that on such an exceptionally long leg as Hawaii to USA, it would have to carry so much fuel, that this would preclude it from staying up on one engine in the event of a failure. But if you dumped fuel or came down in the water, you would never get it airborne again, because it certainly couldn't take-off on one engine.

It's a slow old plane, only goes along at about 120 knots, so it would be a very long journey, and maybe as much as nine hours from land. In the war, although they stayed up a long time, they were, I believe always nearer the coasts.

A Catalina did make some appearances in England at various air shows. It was owned by a company called Plane Sailing and was flown by a John Watts who sadly died in his Tornado.

Aces High did eventually acquire one too – a serviceable one, *not* the ill-fated one from Hawaii … Aloha!

Fast Jets 'n Fast Cars

We happened across a rather interesting character from Florida, about whom we read in an advert in an aviation magazine (they are a buoyant and reliable source for all types of deals). He had recently inherited about half of Florida's citrus farms and like so many of those people for whom the biggest problem in life now is how to spend it all, he slipped with consummate ease into the 'new toys' department. What's the saying? "A fool and his money are soon partying!"

What he wanted was a P51 Mustang (fast furious high performance piston – sort of American version of our Spitfire) and he was offering good money for this. Then as a little side deal, he was contemplating buying a Venom (small, early jet) and for that he was offering a brand new Mercedes Sports and a red Ferrari. I offered to drive one of them up to New England (well that's just the kind of self-sacrificing gal I am!) where a colleague of Aces High had a shipping company.

We had a rendezvous with our buyer in a hotel in Fort Lauderdale.

"Any distinguishing features so I may recognise you?" I asked him on the phone.

"Not really," he said, so I gave a brief description of myself and said we'd meet in the foyer.

When a six-foot-six man with a beard and a ponytail, fringed jacket and size 15 snakeskin cowboy boots strolled through the foyer I thought 'Oh, ZZ Top must be playing tonight'. I also thought that can't be him because he said he has no distinguishing features. Eventually I realised by the way he was looking around that it had to be him. I approached. I was right; it was the man – Steve.

Feeling very diminutive and quite school ma'am-ish, I challenged him on the 'no distinguishing features' bit.

"Way-el, ah rully didn't theenk ah gard eeny."

"What about the beard, the ponytail and the height?"

"Alright yeah, ah didn't theenk o thay-at." – God, were these the fruits and nuts of the granola joke fame?

Off we went to get into his waiting car. I forget the make but what I do remember was that I'd never seen anything like it outside cartoon movies involving villains in mythical cities and steaming manhole covers. It was a black two door super charged beast. I climbed into the rear, he was so tall that his seat back was also in the back, and the ceiling was low and sloping. I was squashed up with neck bent, like some puparial insect in a Dali painting, trying to hatch from of my black pod.

I thought he had bought a cooler of drinks to share with us but then realised, when he sucked on the straw coming out of the top of it, that this was simply a '*large*' in the new and fascinating world of American iced drinks "to go". I had never seen a vessel that large without a matching spade.

VVROOOOM!! We were off! This was the scariest, fastest drive I had ever had.

"I thought the speed limit over here was 55!" I challenged feebly with a nervous laugh from my larval pod at the rear.

"Yeah I know but that sucks!" he moaned as he changed down and did some spectacular weaving across four lanes.

I was terrified. He took this apt moment to explain to us why he'd been late getting to the hotel – the cops had been chasing him and he'd had to 'shake em off', but he actually got a ticket.

"So what have you guys got goin'? Ya know I'm real inerested in buyin' some planes off y'all, I mean the Pee fifty wuun is great and I wanna git me one, but I'm real innerested in sum fast shit aswell."

"Yes you might be interested in a Lightening or something like that. It climbs at forty thousand feet a minute," chuckled Woodley, who stared straight ahead, hand, permanently pressed against the glove compartment.

"Okay, okay," he nodded with a smile, not getting the irony.

"I think Steve might like the Venom, the black one with the skull and crossbones on, or maybe the Saab Drakken, *that* does Mach two doesn't it?" I chirped-up from the back again. We finally made it, never have I been more jubilant to alight from a vehicle.

We met his partner and their wives that night to try to conclude some sort of deal in a nice restaurant. I became acquainted with the 'southern belle'. With maybe just a smidge of exaggeration, but not much, the intro went something like;

"Now Melba, Lee, Rosie, Sue honey, I'd like ya da meet Aneeeda and Maaak."

"Well howdy – pleased ta meetcha," returned the perfect porcelain doll.

Out came a tiny hand with flawless nail extensions and about a hundred grand's worth of diamonds. His partner introduced *his* wife – something like Stephie sugar pie. The meal was good fun. The wives were very young, both had a bunch of kids and had achieved the triumphant 'meringue' march down the aisle, good and early. One of them mentioned 'the Lord', a lot. She beamed as she described Li'l Carlton Junior and Bobby going off to school in their matching dungarees. "God I swear they looked as cute as buttons."

293

They were very congratulatory on my being able to fly but thought I was crazy wanting to mess around with all that "dirt and oil n' stuff" when I could be "takin' care of a good mayn and a whole bunch o' beautiful bay-bees".

She explained: "Yeah, mah husband's learnt to flaa, and I'm real proud a hiy-m, he's always traa-n to git me to go up with hiy-m but I just cayn't stay-nd it, I'm so frightened see I'm real chicken. So we don't flaa tageether." As she spoke, she held her fork as though it were a dagger, pinning the meat to the plate then cut it up with the steak knife; that was a new one on me.

In the middle of dinner, one of the guys received a loud buzzing sound from one of his impressive array of electronic gadgets.

"Excuse me," he drawled and picked it off his belt. "Go ahayed." A crackly voice came from the hand held gadget, I could vaguely make out the message.

"A'm at five thou buddy in the Lear, everthing's faaan, I'm gonna bring her into Kissimmi, so talk to ya'll later."

"Okay buddy that's copied, call me when ya'll land." He switched it off and held it at arm's length.

"Hell I gotta tell ya I lurve this shit – we can connect, he can drop in from faave thousand feet to say howdy and I'm sat here having wild turkey and coke!" (It *was* 1986 so that was impressive technology then – such things are incorporated in your wristwatch now!)

His wife fluttered her eyes upward at her hubby and looked over to me with a scrunched nose as if to say 'Isn't he just daaarlin'?

She had asked me so many questions about my boyfriend, who I described and talked briefly about. "Well when d'yall think you'll git married?" When I said I had no immediate plans, she couldn't believe it, her face crumpled. It was as though I had told her I only had days to live. We changed the subject but at the end of the meal she leant over, touched my arm and whispered in my ear. "Ya know Aneeda, if the shoe fits… *Wear it.*"

The company did indeed sell Steve a P51 Mustang, which had been acquired at Paul Raymond's Auction in London (Paul Raymond of Revue bar fame). He declined the Venom so I didn't deliver the car, but I certainly enjoyed a spin in the Mercedes Sports round the block, my first experience of a sports car and of turning right on red light. We found a great place which sold fried alligator and sat and watched the float planes coming and going. Little did I know *then* that fifteen years later I would be back in Florida actually learning to fly sea planes – Anyway *that's* another story.

In America there seems to be a sense of abundance. I was amazed at how many light aircraft there were in the sky. That abundance spills over into *everything*… I had never been exposed to so many salad dressings. I was swept up in the torrent of choice from the waitress, fascinated by her delivery during which she didn't stop for breath – blue cheese, honey mustard, ranch, strawberry vinaigrette, Italian, French, house, thousand island, creamy this, low fat that, and so it went on. The breads were the same: poppyseed, pumpernickel, rye, sourdough and whole-wheat.

I noticed *how* many exercise machine adverts there were on TV. Tanned men with bodies like a Giambologna statue in a Florentine piazza were striding out on the latest impact-free fat burning apparatus. His legs were going flat out on two swinging under-slung pedals and he smiled with dazzling white teeth at his female partner who was doing the same and smiling back, in a matching outfit, in the comfort of their own living room. Other adverts were so short and garbled – just fifteen seconds of someone talking flat out about Toyotas and listing the showrooms, you couldn't possibly follow, then he was cut off crudely midstream due to total lack of editing. Other ads had someone at the end gabbling at six words per second about terms and conditions or side effects –all legal jargon, waste of time really since there was no hope whatsoever of keeping up.

The other thing which fascinated me was the religion on sale. I lay on my hotel bed one night absolutely entranced as a short, smiling, blow-dried creep with a sunbed tan, and gold jewellery sold hope and salvation in the Church of 'Jesus' children'. At the end of his terribly cheesy and unconvincing talk about selflessness and good deeds there was a picture of all the credit cards they accepted including Diners, American Express and Visa. I had seen more crafted subtlety in a Nigerian ad which simply had a man leaning into a car saying: "My friend, use Mobil anti-wear oil for your enjin because it's de best!!"

"Who the hell subscribes to that kind of garbage?" I asked the concierge.

"Oh you'd be surprised, obese women in tent dresses living in trailers from Tallahassee."

I noticed also dry cleaners where you could drop off ten shirts in the morning and pick them up after lunch all for a few bucks. I marvelled as I thought of the dry cleaners in my village where it's about £35 for a suit, and 'express service' means they'll have it back to you at the breakneck speed of next Wednesday.

But one of the *greatest* things I saw in the hotels was the 'All you can eat Sunday brunch with unlimited champagne'. It was incredible! Can you imagine if they did that in England? There would be a sing-song, some bottom baring, a fight or two, girls falling over on the pavement showing their knickers, loads of photos of drunks hugging the waiters and perhaps even a saline drip at the end of the day with some paramedics saying "Move away folks" as they removed a flaccid body in an Umbro football shirt.

It was all very enlightening and educational being in America again after the Cessna Skyhawk ferry trip. Florida had been wonderful but now it was time to carry on up to Vermont where Aces High's associate at the time, a guy infelicitously named Dean Martin had found some customers for the Venoms.

The Venom of Vermont

It was the time around 1985 that the vogue for owning your own fighter jet was growing. The company had recently acquired some ex-Swiss airforce Venoms. For those not familiar, a Venom FB5 is a single seat, jet fighter bomber with twin booms, the elevator stretches across from the left to right boom at the back–very similar to a Vampire. I used to help out in the office, and saw one being fired up one day at North Weald. They were started with cartridges which would fit into a kind of breach on top of the engine. The exploding gases went down a pipe and engaged the starter, then fuel would then be put in from a control in the cockpit and away you go. The start I witnessed was a bit different. It had me running for cover behind the hangar door! It looked more like an unplanned explosion – it happens apparently (so I was told by Ray the Venom aficionado) during a wet start and there's not enough RPM, so, the fuel goes in but a subsequent fire breaks out all over the tail plane. Aah the good old days of hand swinging props and explosions on start up. It's all so easy now just pressing a button, no risk of severing a limb or being burnt to a crisp!

His associate in this little venture (or *Test-Fest* as I called it,) was one Dean Martin. When I heard this name, I entertained images of a smooth, swarthy, twinkly-eyed ace with immaculate dress sense. He would have the manners of Don Juan and the heroic conviction of Errol Flynn. But I was … well … a few degrees off track.

Here was a man who looked like he could single handily put Dunkin Doughnuts into the FTSE 100. He had a piggy face, wore specs, had savagely high blood pressure, a sweat problem and wore jeans (which showed off both the crack and the beer gut), and, of course, a flannel shirt. He swore like a tourettes victim, went bright pink at the merest peep from the sun and consumed the same amount of beer as, say … Zambia.

He poured vodka straight down his neck from a bottle with a handle in it and never left home without his gun. His favourite saying was four expletives put together; he obviously couldn't bear to leave one out. It went; "*aah, shit-piss-whore-dog-&-suck*". A sweet man!

I witnessed him go to the salad bar. He was cursing his doctor who'd told him to cut back on the fat, to eat more salad and veg instead of ribs. He just emptied the whole potato salad container onto his plate then added about five spoons of cheddar and smothered the whole lot with the blue cheese dressing. "F******rabbit food," he said, as he tipped the basin of banana chips into a bowl for dessert.

Notwithstanding this, he was an excellent source of contacts for brave young guns who wanted their own fighter jet. We met one such quintessence of manliness with a dangerously tumescent ego who bought a jet, painted it black with skull and crossbones and was oft' seen whizzing over Lake Champlain in Vermont. It was educational for me learning about the sale, the handing over of manuals, the spare parts and the associated paperwork, accompanying the trade in these 'special category' planes.

We were invited to a dinner party one evening. It was late summer, the house was enchanting – log cabin style with spacious sprawling decks overlooking acres of hazy mountains, pretty woods and a sizable garden. The man (a PHD in showoff-ology) who had bought a Venom was there, bursting with confidence and self-aggrandisement. These aircraft were slick, fast and dangerous and selling like hot cakes amongst the thrill seeking young daredevils with an adrenalin addiction. Egomania is rudely good for business. We were hoping to sell another couple or at least arrange a test flight.

Amongst the party was a smart, well-groomed woman, exuding sexual energy, clearly bored to tears with her boring, aging millionaire husband who was a public figure (I nicknamed him the Senator). A few more people arrived – a stud and another couple. It was all happening. The meat sizzled on the BBQ and the huge American cocktails were in good supply. A serene lake graced the middle of the garden, ducks quacked around on it and a huge boulder stood on the far side. Chatter and conversation filled the air and there was a palpable feeling of opulence and comfort. The hostess glided around filling glasses. Shouts of, "Anyone want it rare, it's ready!" came from the squinty-eyed chef armed with tongs at the BBQ.

The sun was paying his complements, the last rays, like a long invisible paintbrush, playfully dabbed new colours here and there, dusting the faces of the guests with flattering hues of amber and rose. Molten light flooded the deck, breathing warmth into the brick and wood. It turned the Chablis into buttery gold as it sloshed around in the crystal glasses, which were held unsteadily now by laughing guests. Fire flies were beginning their mysterious gavottes in the woods, the golden retriever was managing record 'wags per minute' from his thumping tail and never took his eyes off the chef. It had not escaped my notice that the well groomed 'bored wife' had disappeared, as indeed had the hunky young stud.

A short while later "Owch! Sonofa-bitch" came sharply from behind the boulder at the end of the garden. "Jesus Christ" the voice of the victim continued.

I happened to be down some steps so I heard it quite clearly. I had a pretty good idea of what was occurring and thought to myself 'Wow there is no end to the bravado – not content with a fast jet, we have to take the Senator's wife right under his nose – mmm, nice one'.

They eventually emerged from behind the boulder and as they passed me looking a bit flushed I asked if everything was ok.

"Yeah just got stung by a hornet, jeez those sunsa bitches sting." I noticed he was rubbing his backside – I didn't ask. The party continued, her eyes never left him. Her husband, no fool, probably knew but chose to ignore.

The stud made his excuses fairly early and disappeared. In my mind's eye, as he left I had him turning round, topping his hat and saying, "Hey, I've got a lotta ladies out there, only fair to … share myself out." He didn't actually say that, but what he *did* do was buy an aeroplane and master it very well apparently, and I feel sure he took many a girl for a spin over the hills and valleys of Vermont, and undoubtedly enjoyed experimenting with his 'lift' and his 'thrust'.

Aerobatics in Burlington, Vermont
Christen Eagle Aerobat

Whilst waiting for the final remedial touches to the B-25 bomber which I (and three others) would be ferrying back to the UK, I became acquainted with some rum characters on the airfield of Burlington, Vermont. I was rather glad there were a few last minute glitches, it afforded me time to get to know them a little. Our daily trips to the airfield daily to check on progress meant a sort of fraternity built up.

"Hey Aneeda how's the 25 looking, you guys leavin' yet?"

There are more privately owned aircraft in the USA, it seems more common for people to own their own planes. Of course there is always the 'ego' factor with which I became quite familiar. When expensive or rare toys are involved men *can* indulge in a bit of chest thumping. One guy had an old vintage biplane and a Staggerwing, the next had a fast fighter jet like a Saab Drakken or a Vampire. I'd wander up for a chat while they were pottering in their small hangars. They were good company but they couldn't resist the odd dig at one another especially if someone else was in the limelight. A guy called Hoover had recently earned himself quite a valiant reputation with a video of his hallmark 'one wheel landing' in a Rockwell Commander turbo prop; these grizzly old guys with baseball caps on couldn't wait to tell you what he was doing *wrong*.

If someone in a neighbouring hangar had done some heroic stunt, I'd hear, "If bullshit was music Aneeda I sware to Gad that sonnufabitch would be a brass band".

One particular man who looked just like the baddy out of James Bond asked if I would care to go for a flight in his Christen Eagle aerobat. This is like a Pitts Special, tandem cockpit and very high performance aerobatic biplane used for displays. Not wishing to pass up an opportunity like that, I just overlooked the fact that I don't have the inner ear for these antics and I have lost touch with my 'bat' side therefore feel quite out of sorts when hanging upside down. It was a beautiful plane, jovially painted with bright stripes down the fuselage. I buckled up into a robust assembly of straps. There would be no slipping out of this harness. I sat in the front, which gave me that feeling of raw exposure – like being in the first car on the roller coaster. I started to feel a slight quickening of the old heartbeat as we taxied out because he was coming out with those pithy macho comments like, "Alrighty Aneeda you ready for the bone shakin' rahd of your life? Hang on girl 'cos we gonna do some rockin' and rollin'!"

I could feel the icy hand of panic starting a little squeeze of the chest, 'deep breaths, deep breaths' I would mantra to myself. Of course he was going to turn it up a notch because the 'show off' factor was now in the equation. I was battling to expel images of display pilots crashing into the ground and being mangled in hot burning metal. Dougie Bader and his tin legs were haunting me. We got our take-off clearance from the tower,

"Wind three three zero seven knots, clear take-off, you all be careful."

I didn't like that sound of that 'be careful' bit at all, did they know something I didn't? Maybe I was strapped in just inches away from a nutter. Oh well. We went straight into a vertical climb; the power of this machine was overwhelmingly evident. Straight up into the blue we soared, he was the token homesick angel. The speed gradually decayed. Oh god, what's going to happen when we run out of puff, it's not going to be gentle that's for sure I muttered to myself. At the stall we started to tail slide then suddenly he put in an unholy boot full of rudder and 'whoosh' we flipped into a violent spin corkscrewing around towards the earth, the wind whistled around the frame, fields rotating manically as if they were going down some great plughole. I saw the stick go full forward between my legs, thank God, the recovery. Back into straight and level flight then before I could say phew, I was snapped abruptly into a four point hesitation roll, so now we were flying with port wing up and starboard wing down, straps digging in, right cheek sagging. I had just enough time to confirm that I didn't like that position when 'whack' we were upside down – hey that previous position wasn't too bad after all. I saw my bulging red inverted face in the glass of the altimeter, now both straps were sawing into my shoulders, I was looking forward to the last cardinal point of the roll when I'd be back on my side. Snap, snap we were upright again, but I knew it wouldn't be for long.

"You doing ok?" he shouted from the back.

"Yee ha, absolutely loving it!" I lied.

"Ok we gonna turn up the heat a bit, I'm gonna go through my routine for the airshow, need to practice!" he shouted.

"Yeah, go for it," I said bracing myself knowing my cheeks would soon be on my shoulders and I would be that person on the roller coaster, when being filmed from *very* close up.

Well, we went zooming and darting through the sky like an overfilled balloon when it is suddenly released. At times we were swinging rhythmically then tumbling down untidily. He did rolls, loops, hammer head stalls, back flips, front flips, barrel rolls, lazy eights you name it. I was aware of coming out of my seat, being unweighted and momentarily floating then being jammed down with a devilish gravity so hard I couldn't lift my hands off my legs. The little plane, was in full flow now roaring and fighting, revelling in its own excellence. The load he was placing on those wings with some manoeuvres was staggering. With the wings and the props acting like samurai swords, we were slicing and splitting through clouds. The 'G'meter was smoking! But those muscular little wings were tough, this aircraft was like a fine athlete capable of exceptional performance. Armed with such a gutsy engine, every manoeuvre was smooth and penetrating, he carved the rolls with absolute precision, no jerking, no loss of altitude, the propeller pulling us effortlessly up, and still up into the never ending blue. It was aerodynamic and graceful and it cut through the air like a little rocket just overflowing with stamina. The pistons were thrashing, sunrays bounced off the wings, as we went screaming around our nebulous playground.

"Here, I'll show ya where I live."

"OK great," I said, expecting a low flypast of his house.

He turned, fighter pilot style and swooped down into a valley. We came down to about five hundred feet and slowed down.

"Ok watch this," he said and he pressed a diode in his instrument panel and we did a straight in approach to a private strip. We landed on the left wheel with a little screech and he held it there until the end of the strip when he allowed the right wheel to fall. Then with another touch of a button a large door opened and in we went into a hangar with a red carpet. My first carpeted hangar! Unbelievable, it was covered from floor to ceiling with pictures of naked girls. He cut the mixture and the plane was silent and stationary once again. He jumped down and helped me out.

"Well how d'you like that? Ain't that just such a rush?"

"Thank you so much, that was certainly ... a bone shaker – great fun," I said trying be cool, in fact trying just to stand up straight like a spirit level and allow the scattered fluids of my inner ear to drain back down to their sumps. I felt as though I'd journeyed through a wormhole.

In the corner there was a fridge which was the size of a garden shed. He strolled over and shouted back over his shoulder, "You wanna beer, they're real cold!"

He opened the door and grabbed a beer from the well-stocked shelves, then in one fluid movement, he pulled the ring, emptied it down his open throat and crushed the can all at the same time. He then threw me one. "Miller Genuine Draught, hope that's ok."

"Cheers!" I smiled as I opened mine and sipped it a bit more slowly, but it still ended up in both nostrils.

I was checking out the wall decoration, there were big breasted, tiny waisted girls draped over Hellcats, and Tigercats. Naughty spanner wielding 'engineers' in stilettos going to work on a B17, nut brown babes with perfect bikini lines leaning into the cowlings of P51 Mustangs and grinning girlies in stockings and suspenders straddling T33s. Blondes with nothing more than protective goggles and pouting lips held welding torches. He saw my 'I-don't-bloody-believe-this' expression and drawled, "Yeah pretty hot chicks huh? Ya know Aneeda they probably don't know the front of an engine from the back but they sure look better than the oily, bearded, crotch grabbin' sweat hogs who normally work on ma planes. You know what aam sayin'?" He let out a good belly laugh and strolled back to the fridge.

"Well yes, now you put it like that, I must say I do agree," I said as I turned just in time to catch the second beer as it came spinning across the hangar at me. Only in America.

In Search of War Planes and a Visit to Star City – Russia

When you think of how cheaply Second World War aircraft were sold off immediately after the war, and what their subsequent worth became, it makes you want to get out there and look for a few! I heard about Spitfires being found in places like Israel and Burma. I spoke to a man once who found one in the playground of a Kibbutz – it had been put there for the kids to play on! I know of another collector who found many in India and had the lot – for very modest sums; they soon became worth hundreds of thousands of dollars. So such a bounty is worth a bit of a hunt.

One of the less successful missions with Aces High (in terms of a result) but still funny and hugely educational was to Moscow in search of a B-25 and beyond. News had recently gone round the industry of a Focke-Wulf 190 in excellent condition, found in perma frost. It was a coup. When this single seat fighter-bomber (Germany's answer to the Hawker Typhoon) appeared in September 1941, it was a force to be reckoned with, although not as sleek or as beautiful as the Spitfire it dominated the skies for almost a year and remained one of the best fighters in Europe until the end of the war. It was bought by an

English owner and was probably worth around two million dollars. Buoyed up by these possibilities, Aces High felt a trip to Russia was worth it.

This was 1991, well before the tide of modernisation and change. The hotel was a bit 'tired' but had an old-fashioned elegance reminiscent of wartime. The dining room was huge and lofty, massive chandeliers hung from heavily decorated ceilings. Local families were filing in for an 'evening do'. For the young girls it was a big night out, they had kilos of make-up on and pouted indifferently, hopeful for some romance. Little boys dressed as Cossacks and played hide and seek under the table. The Russian folk songs would have the wide girthed women with towering hairdos tapping their feet. Mothers and sons, sisters and grandparents all dressed in their Sunday best whirled each other round the dance floor. When they had exerted themselves royally they retired to a table to nurse a bottle of vodka. It was all very 'Fiddler on the Roof'.

We met our contact that night at the Aerostar Hotel, and he escorted us round Red Square. It was my first time, therefore utterly thrilling especially after a childhood of knowing communist Russia as 'the enemy' suddenly it became stripped of its secrecy this made it all the more enchanting. We were finally getting to look inside a hidden treasure chest, to taste a forbidden fruit. The onion domes of St Basils church glowed against the starry sky. I was spellbound by their wonderfully exotic shape and colour – such a departure from any architecture I'd ever seen.

I would return to Moscow repeatedly ten years later on the private jets when trade and business had opened up, but sadly when, septic corruption had started to poison the place. I would stay in luxurious '$390 a night' hotels, where shady villains lurked in the foyers and people disappeared. So ... the first trip to hunt for war birds had a hint of that 'old communist' nostalgia about it.

Our colleagues were serious, correct and greeted us most formally. Full of expectation we entered an office eager to see pictures of the B-25 in the frost and to our horror they showed us some footage of an old wreck at the bottom of a lake. To make matters worse it was salt water so the condition would have been very poor.

We tried as best as we could to explain that it wasn't quite what we were looking for. Reluctant to give up they showed us all sorts of other 'bounty' but nothing was very valuable.

However the upside was that they insisted on taking us around Star City or the Cosmodrome their astronaut training center, a few hours' drive away. Apparently we were amongst the first twenty or so Europeans to go there. It was shortly after Helen Sharman made her mark in space and she featured widely at this institution – good for her, what an achievement. We were shown around the mock-up of the Mir space station which had cost them hundreds of millions and had sunk into a low orbit. There was no space shuttle or similar, back then to despatch and lift its orbit. They offered it to us for a mere (no pun intended) sixteen million dollars! No wonder they were trying to sell it off cheaply. If I recall correctly it finally burnt out and fell on Australia – just as well it's a damned big place. (I loved to indulge my imagination on such occasions and hoped that a couple of flip flopped hippies were on a 'find myself' journey in the desert, asking for a sign from above, then ....voila! One Mir space station.)

I saw my first centrifuge – built by the Swedish; then their fascinating underwater training facility. The Americans apparently trained by flying a parabolic curve but the Russians achieved weightlessness by being submerged.

The museum, featuring Yuri Gregarin and his colleagues was superb, everything from the history of the spacesuit to the building of a rocket was explained. Medals for excellence and achievement were on display and breathtaking photos of orbiting capsules and planet earth. Shots of men drifting around on ropes against the blackness of a never-ending universe, what a magnificent endeavour.

The next museum they took us to, was like the props department of a Flash Gordon sci-fi set – an entirely different world. It was a sprawling gigantic yard full of old Soviet planes. Professor Boviosky showed us the secret experimental plane the Stomovik two, their equivalent of the A10 thunderbolt they wanted to put it into the next James Bond movie. It was a large square tank buster.

Then we saw the B29 and of course that always reawakens the horrors of atomic warfare. I saw crude angular and clumsy shapes in these aeroplanes which stopped me dead in my tracks. Some of them seemed to have the aerodynamism of two mobile homes mounted on a semi articulated lorry. One flying machine had me in state of silenced bewilderment, I had to get the camera, no-one would believe it. It was a monster with a set of rotating blades on the top of each wing. A strange and ungainly marriage of fixed wing and helicopter. The blades drooped despondently, the whole thing looked like a huge sigh. The Russian equivalent of Concorde was parked there, its huge pointed nose dropping down, a wonderfully thought provoking plane but it fell well short of the grace and beauty of Concorde (not that I am biased of course).

I saw so much which was new to me and our hosts were informative and justly proud. Being a little unpractised in the art of doing deals with Westerners, they had, I thought a modesty and a slight awkwardness which somehow embodied those 'old style' manners. There was no pompous arrogance. Negotiations have become a lot more cut-throat and edgy now. They took us to a street in Moscow which had hundreds of medals for sale, I believe they had been taken mainly from the uniforms of dead Germans.

Although we found neither another Focke-Wulf, nor a World War Two bomber, we had a lively look round some new and interesting terrain. They assured us that they would be unrelenting in their search for any war birds crashed in lakes or forests, and be in touch if they had any luck. It is always worth upturning a few stones in that part of the world because there are treasures to be scooped and coups to be had in the pursuit of war birds.

Lancaster Bomber Deal Ends with Surprise Trip to Belize

This was another interesting assignment from the company Aces High whose forte was buying and selling old war birds. The mission: to sell a Biggin Hill based Lancaster bomber to a south Florida flying museum. Happily, the deal went ahead and they achieved their objectives. Despite being a seriously affluent inheritor, the American pilot and collector, booked, for the meeting what must have been the grottiest airport motel in Miami, the sort where the odd gang shooting might take place. All decent hotels were full due to a huge conference.

It added a certain 'je ne sais quoi' talking Lancaster bombers and shipment details and rather hefty sums of money in a pokey little reception area next to a dying cheese plant sitting on old rickety velour chairs next to two pots of stewed coffee and a bowl of half and half creamers, under an ancient air conditioner which made about as much noise as the departing aircraft.

The deal became quite interesting, because not only was the Lanc being sold to the American but *he* then sold his Heinkle 111 bomber (which was built by General Franco's airforce in Spain) to Aces High. I had the opportunity while in Florida to see an impressive collection which included a Hell Cat, a P51 Mustang a Sunderland Flying Boat, a Grumman Duck, a Corsair, a P40 a B17 and many other Navy planes.

The mobile rang a couple of days later. It was, a long standing friend and associate of Aces High (a Californian) who had dropped in occasionally at North Weald, and who had, at one point asked Mike to find an aircraft for him. He happened be in Miami.

"Hey why don't you guys come to Belize for a few days fishing before you head back to the UK?" Having no permanent flying job to go back to I was keen. I had never fished for tarpon or bone fish or been to Central America.

Miami airport is Spanish. End of story. If you don't 'hablar' you don't get far. It made me determined to buy some tapes for the car so I could 'escuchar' and 'repetir'. A little Hispanic boy saw me looking for a trolley (you have to insert a dollar bill to release one).

"Hey Meeees you have dis trolley for fifty cents," and pushed a trolley towards me.

"Who are you then?" I asked with a grin.

"Who care? You win I win, here take it."

I couldn't argue with that, I tossed him two quarters and admired his entrepreneurial spirit – collecting trolleys from outside and flogging them for half price. I would probably read about him in ten year's time in Forbes magazine.

Within two hours a small group of us were south-west bound on an American Airlines DC9 flying over Havana, Cuba admiring the Caymans off to the port side and heading south towards Belize.

The aisles were full of suntanned Americans in shorts and straw hats. There were a handful of businessmen, some military boys but mostly scuba divers and fishing enthusiasts. I sat next to a college student from Miami, she wore faded dungarees with a sleeveless vest and 'sneakers'. We had a beer together and she told me her story. She had to find her buddies who had a sailboat down there, she hadn't communicated with them because they were on the boat but they knew she was coming *sometime that* week. But it would be ok because they would 'hang out' at the harbour. I was used to the strict ETA and ETD culture (estimated time of arrival/departure)endemic in aviation, so this loose knit arrangement seemed like a nightmare to me but it was a jolly good story and I was enjoying it. They certainly hadn't put this together with any precision whatsoever and *she* had taken eight weeks off school.

"I figured f*** it ya know I can study anytime this is a great opportunity to take a long sail round the Caribbean, ya only live once," and with that she raised her tin of Coors and beamed from ear to ear.

"Actually he was the *most awesome* lay I've ever had and I just gotta find this guy!"

"God it sounds brilliant," I said, "hope you find them!"

"Oh it's cool, it'll work out, besides I got my guardian angel with me," she pulled a strap down to reveal a little winged angel tattooed on her shoulder. "He's got one of the devil on his butt so I know we're made for each other, we gotta be soul mates right?"

Belize airport was typically tropical, hot and chaotic, locals in flip-flops hustled everywhere selling jewellery and carvings, and shouting out prices for moped hire. Flies hovered around the overworked ceiling fans. The bar was lively, but since we had a couple of hours before our connection to the island called Lighthouse Reef, we headed downtown.

The streets were buzzing. Noisy music blared out from speakers which shook under the strain, tinny and distorted reggae filled the air. Plump women with big white smiles were selling delicious fresh fruit on the side of the road. The ubiquitous Bata shoe shop was there and of course the chemist where no prescriptions were necessary. A river reminiscent of Bangkok's floating market was host to several fishing canoes in which men repaired nets and gutted fish – fish packing is the main industry. This river in fact flows west and is navigable almost to Guatemala. Timber and wood are important there also but sadly like so many places in that part of the world, Belize was devastated by a hurricane in 1961. Rickety makeshift asbestos shacks housed old cars, the sort that can be fixed with a hammer rather than a computer. Local guys milled around panel beating and leaning into engines.

Being the capital of British Honduras, you could see the vestiges of the old colonial style, elegant houses with attractive colonnaded balconies lined some streets and vibrant puce and tangerine coloured bougainvillea grew rampantly among the railings and palm trees. Bright garish adverts sang out on billboards, classic examples of retro chic "Smoke Business cigarettes and be Cool!" Others had the perfect family with brilliant white smiles, she, elegantly coiffed and he in a smart suit looking at their perfect child; and all that promise just in a bar of soap!

After a mooch around and some local beer we headed back to the airport to catch the regional flight to the island. A huge glass of apricot punch with umbrella and chinking ice cubes was waiting, it certainly got everyone in the mood and subdued any fears of light aircraft. The De Havilland Twin Otter taxied in – looking like the reliable old 'tail wagging' dog. Its thin fuselage houses just single seats down each side. It was starting to feel more like a 'Hercule Poirot' island adventure now.

I was getting to know some of the 'fishing' guys, particularly one humdinger of a man I immediately named 'Uncle Buck' because of his similarity to John Candy the likeable, overweight actor who is invariably the luckless buffoon. He had a big belly, booming voice, a baseball cap on back to front and Marlboro's stuffed in top pocket of Hawaiian shirt. I thought the 'fat yank on holiday' was a thing of the movies but I was wrong. He was hilarious and boy he had packed more fishing tackle than I had ever seen.

The party bound for Lighthouse Reef was split into two, the divers and the fishermen. The former were nature loving eco-freaks, the latter spent most of their time shooting or catching anything that moved. One in our party had just hunted deer in Argentina, salmon in the Soviet Union, buffalo in Zimbabwe and was now after tarpon in Belize. I sat opposite Uncle Buck and commended him on his impressive array of fishing paraphernalia. He took me through the different hooks, one looked particularly sharp and I said just for a bit of a joke, "You wouldn't want to be casting *that* one and catch someone in the eye with it."

That unfortunately was the prompt for one of his stories.

"Gad I was down in Cabo and I sweardagod I caught my buddy right in the back with that goddam hook."

The look on my face said 'no please *don't continue*' but once he was off there was no stopping him, he really was the mould for the 'bull in a china shop'. The sort of guy who, even when his listener had turned green and looked away, would just steam right ahead with the story while yelling to the waitress, "Can we get a couple more beers here please!"

"That poor sucker, my buddy Dave," he chuckled with a shake of his head, "he had chunks of flesh poppin' out of his back, every time I tried to free the hook that sunofabitch just ripped more skin up." This really pleased the Birkenstock wearing, anti-hunting, vegetarian newlyweds from Taos New Mexico in front of us.

The propellers whirred up into high RPM – fine pitch and we descended steeply. The island, part of an archipelago lying in a sea of heavenly blues and pea greens you find in only the most translucent waters. We all helped unload the bags onto jeeps and then just walked down the sandy path lined with gigantic red hibiscus flowers, to the little reception hut where another tropical drink was waiting.

The island I found out was owned by an American who had worked for (I *think)* AT&T. He headed up the operation to install the telecommunication systems in Belize after independence. He apparently became friendly with the governor and expressed his desire to have a piece of paradise one day, so when the island came up one day he was notified and bought it. Not sure how accurate the story was but it sounded to me delightfully like Jimmy Buffet's 'Margueritaville'. It had been kept as natural as possible. There was a small runway, a large generator, twenty or so small bungalows and a central bar/restaurant which was no more than a beach hut. The staff consisted of a manager, an assistant, two dive instructors and three fishing guides, a frisky mongrel dog and a bright green parrot who never left the managers shoulder, oh and of course the iridescent iguana. A handful of locals helped in the kitchen and bungalows.

The entourage was indeed mixed, I think I was the only aspiring pilot there though there were a couple who had their own plane. A guy you could have taken for a surf bum with a long ponytail and flip-flops was a top lawyer from New York. There were doctors, dentists, electricians, artists, musicians and businessmen. 'Corporate raiders' alongside the tofu types but all shared a love of the ocean even though some were diving and some fishing.

We *had* to get to know each other because there were only a few tables for breakfast and dinner. And there were some lively debates.

"You torture those poor fish with your hooks," complained the two feminists from Wisconsin – both dentists. "And as for hunting game where do you get off on *that!*"

"Well you eat meat, don't you … have you ever seen an abattoir, oh that's *real* nice?"

And so it went on.

The beach was paradise, swaying palms, hammocks, and sand like milled white flour. The sea, was a pale aquamarine near the beach, then deepened into rich emerald then brilliant azure and deep navy near the horizon. The colours were fresh and 'zingy' like sherbet. Halfway out, little reefs and sandbanks broke through the clear minty water and formed small mini beaches and lines of rippling surf. The only sound apart from the breeze in the trees and the lapping waves was that of the Red Footed Boobie birds who lived in the swamps behind – how funny and quirky they were.

The peace was broken one morning though as I woke to the distant shouts from Uncle Buck.

"Try over here Gavin I saw those sunsabitches jumpin' right there."

What a sight, he was wading into the shallows with his baggy shorts, T-shirt and beach shoes. His hat was on backwards and his cigarette pinched between his teeth. He had a large sling around his neck holding up this huge tray (à la ice cream lady in cinema), which rested on his belly. It was a divided up into compartments and little drawers each jammed with squashy creatures, rubber fish, jellies, lures, feathers, hooks, fake fish of all different materials from steel to lime green rubber. Fascinating. He was a constant source of entertainment and he was amazed and I'm sure, a tad annoyed the day I caught a jack fish, a grouper and a barracuda. Funnily enough I had a fish on my line which I was reeling in when suddenly all went slack and when I plopped the catch up on the boat it was just the rather sorry looking head, the rest Uncle Buck, reckoned had been eaten by a barracuda.

"Well I'll be goddammned," he said and launched himself into a committed and unrelenting search for the beast, casting his line over and over, alas but he never pulled the monster from the deep.

A tropical storm approached one night, rumblings of very distant thunder could be heard miles away and the wind in little flurries then sharp bursts ripped and curled through the palm fronds. The sea changed colour and went quite mat and the little boats tied up to buoys near the beach were rocking and bouncing ominously. The maids were scurrying around bringing washing off the lines and stacking deckchairs. The fishermen pulled their boats ashore and the mongrel dogs sniffed the air with more purpose than usual, then scuttled off round the back of the huts. In the small reception come lounge area, a video played (*that*, and some cards and backgammon were the only entertainment). Playing, at that moment was the first James Bond film 'Dr. No'– Perfect! Ursula Andress emerging from the blue Caribbean waters with her conch shells. The wind really started to blow, an umbrella tumbled and spun down the beach, the little wooden windows propped open with sticks began to rattle. Then I saw something amazing, a Harrier jump jet just screamed past at breakneck speed inches above the water. It was absolutely deafening and made me jump. It was like something out of a science fiction film, it was there, then it was gone, but it was a Harrier alright. A split second later a fierce bolt of fork lightening came down on the horizon and the sky was charcoal grey. I can honestly say *that* was a photo opportunity!

White caps tripped and tumbled over the agitated water and then the rain (and my God do I mean *rain*) came down. It was ferocious, the sea now dark and cloudy was dimpled by the huge drops; the lightning struck everywhere and the thunder cracked so loudly it had me grabbing on to the side of the wicker chair. Heavens, no wonder this sort of thing would have our ancient and unknowing ancestors rushing out to kill a goat or a virgin or something, *anything* to placate the wrathful Gods. It was a real howler, and before the mysteries of meteorology were known to man, it was not surprising that the ancients attributed it to God's tantrum! Crikey I had a CPL in meteorology and it was frightening the living daylights out of me.

"Wow what was that Harrier doing out there?" I asked a guy in a shirt with big hibiscus flowers on it nursing a beer at the bar with a sort of 'seen it all before' kind of look.

"Trying to get his ass back to base ahead of the storm most probably."

"But what are they doing here?" I asked with a 'Mary Poppins' innocence.

"Well," he said unexcitedly. "You want the real reason or the pretend reason?" and he necked the dregs of his beer.

"Oh, um … let's have the pretend reason?"

"Okay … well they are supposably (it's an American thing, a 'b' instead of a 'd' in that word) here to fight the Guatemalans and stop them invading, see they want a channel to the sea. So as a concession the Americans with all their Hum Vs and stuff are helping them have a route to the sea. But they are tryin' to kid everyone that all these military helicopters and Harriers that *y'all* have got down here are to fight the Guatemalans, kinda keep 'em at bay."

"Is that not true then?" I offered moving on to the next bit which I could feel he was ready for.

"Well it's probably a smidge of an overkill to have supersonic vertical take-off fighters, Gazelles, Pumas, Rapier missiles and the whole enchilada against a bunch of beaners."

"I see, so what's the real reason then?"

"Well I figure the CIA are paying for this whole show to try and stop the drugs trade, they need to have a presence down here so it's easier for them to hide behind you guys and your jolly governor and British flag and all that but really they're shootin' the asses off the drug barons with all this equipment."

You live and learn stuff everyday don't you, I enjoyed watching Dr. No with him as the storm raged then eventually passed. Maybe he was ex-CIA and really in the know – maybe he was a mumbling idiot, it didn't matter, I found it all very gripping. Huge great anvils on top of dissipating storm clouds now towered against a new and quite baby blue sky at the horizon. The wind had done its worst, the lashing had stopped and the palms just waved gently in the breeze. It was getting dark and the first star appeared.

George was our Belize fishing guide; he was famed for his beer consumption, his right hand which had only two digits and his yellow oily anorak with matching hat (endearingly catalogue-ish). Having only two digits didn't make him any less adept at cracking and opening hermit crabs or removing hooks from fish. He sang rather than spoke, in a Creole patois and called me Miss Aneeda and the others Mista Boyd and Mista Stan. One scorching hot day he took us all round the other side of the island to catch snapper in the mangrove swamps. The art is to cast the bait *just* in front of the roots where the fish rest on the bottom. Too far and the hook snags on the mass of tree roots, and not far enough and the fish won't bother to come out of their shelter. I managed to catch two and was once again royally entertained by Uncle Buck who journeyed over to the trees to untangle his hooks from the branches muttering 'sunofabitch' as the sweat poured and then nearly capsised the boat as he clambered up the back step.

We were on the silent pea green water when once again out of nowhere the penetrating shriek of jet engines exploded in the air. He was pushing it to the limit, seriously low, almost leaving ripples in the water. It was as though we had been in a tranquil glass bauble which just exploded into a trillion shards, flying outwards.

God he must be having fun, I thought with a little teeny bit of jealousy, then I realised he was because he pulled up in a sharp climbing turn and promptly came back over us again. We were ready this time and blocked our ears. We all waved and he disappeared.

"Well that's *your* tax for the year gone in one flypast!" piped up one voice.

Just then I saw a huge grey shadow in the water, it swam towards us, I took it for a shark then suddenly George yelled, "It's de dolphin it's de dolphin!" I had heard about this resident dolphin from the man with the parrot. I had the mask and fins on in record time and in I went.

What a frolic! I touched him and swam alongside him, he wouldn't let me hold his dorsal fin but I got close, very close. It was his eye, which moved me.

He really looked *at* me. This wasn't a flat empty fishy eye, it was an eye full of intelligence and expression. Although small it was somehow deep and mesmerising! He knew I was having fun from my squeals and when I couldn't keep up with him he came back and nudged me. What a treat! A meaningful and profound engagement with one of earth's most beautiful creatures. An encounter without fear or dominance just mutual admiration and curiosity (and lots of playfulness). He had probably surfed the 'tube', porpoised along the bow waves of ships and done somersaults at Neptune's wedding! He came alongside for one last orbit, then he was gone – leaving riddles in his wake.

That's why they're called jump jets

The last night was the beach party, lots of rum, reggae music and fresh grouper and snapper on the fire. Andy the young English wind surfing instructor in the uniform of the beach, shark's tooth necklace, bleached curly hair and colourful 'jams' circulated among the guests. Uncle Buck called him over for a drink with us.

"Let me ask ya some'n Andy, how the hell do you ever get laid out here, I mean you can't screw the guests huh? ... too bad."

He lit a cigarette and leant back in his chair which was bowing dangerously. Andy blushed and admitted in his correct Hampshire accent that it *could* be quite difficult at times.

"Jeez," continued Buck, "life's a bitch isn't it, when you're a young good lookin' jock like this guy and got everything goin' for you, you got no goddam money, then by the time you get old enough you've got all the dough but you're just a fat old ugly drunk like me ... son of a bitch."

The next day the staff headed by long John Silver and his parrot walked us to the runway. There were lots of handshakes photographs and exchanging of cards. After what had been a brilliant few days, we all headed back to an American collector's fixed base operation in Florida to see if there were any more sales deals to be had. I learnt quickly that there's always *someone, somewhere* who wants something. Having contacts to source them, was, I soon realised the name of *this* game. Sure enough some enquiries had come in about the purchase of some DC 4s for the film Candy Bomber. Aces High did end up acquiring them and they are at North Weald to this day.

The Name's Bond

The movie with a new James Bond (Daniel Craig) was in the pipeline. My old friend Mike from Aces High days (who has worked on the last six Bond movies coordinating some of the aviation shots) asked if I would like to go along, help out and team up with some old friends from across the pond. Normally the 'full-time employee' status puts the mockers on such an opportunity, however my last company had just got rid of all their Legacy jets (my type) so we were laid off. I was between jobs and therefore able to accept. It was February and the drizzle was falling in England ... no hesitation!

The scenes with the helicopter and the sea plane were to be shot in the Bahamas. It was a great opportunity to observe different aspects of movie making. I know little about it, at this top level, so it was *very* educational.

Much filming had been going on in Prague so our journey (on a chartered Monarch Airlines Airbus) started there. Bond was on board along with Judi Dench and the top executives – Barbara Broccoli and the team. It was a 'cakes and ale' type of flight, everyone had plenty of room – a row to themselves and the drinks and catering just kept coming. Although there was no first class section all the top brass sat up front and the rest of the plane was filled with cameramen, grips, sound technicians assistant producers, caterers, make-up and special effect artists – the whole shebang. It was like being at a party with everyone milling around, leaning over seat backs chatting.

Azores in the middle of the Atlantic was our fuel stop, an unusual place – Portuguese, and allegedly the last remnants of Atlantis. You certainly wouldn't want to overshoot that runway – there would be a rather large splashing sound! I saw the first officer supervising the refuelling outside so I sneaked into the cockpit to have a chat with the Captain. A few seconds later Dame Judi walked in entertaining the same idea. We chatted about the routes and the Captain showed us the flight log with all the great circle routes, magnetic tracks, distances and PNRs (points of no return). Looking at the North Atlantic maps prompted her to talk about her very special time filming Shipping News in Nova Scotia. She shared a few poignant memories about the terrain, the people and the bleakness of the place. It was a good moment.

Loads of people had gathered on the air stair platform enjoying the sunshine, getting some fresh air, a few having a smoke. The impossibly good looking young flight attendant with the perfectly waxed eyebrows and sunbed tan was mincing beautifully up and down, tea towel over arm, with his bottle of champers filling everyone's glasses.

We landed at Nassau that night and all dispersed to our various hotels. The logistics of moving a huge group like this in a controlled fashion is considerable and I must say the organisation was excellent.

Shooting started the next morning very early at a beautiful location called Albany Bay. (This is where the gorgeous bikini clad Italian rides her horse along the beach.) It was colonial elegance at its apogee – a long hibiscus-lined drive, lush gardens, baby pink walls, huge rooms with ten man sofas, ethnic wooden furniture, ceiling fans and big hardback books on coffee tables. Balconies overlooked the turquoise ocean, and hammocks swung lazily between bent palms as the mini waves lapped onto the white sand. There was a pool, and a helipad, no detail had been overlooked even down to the exotic fish in the pond. I do believe Tiger Woods had his eye on it.

Certainly the first impression I came away with was *how long* it takes to do just one shot. Hours and hours can trudge slowly passed filming the same thing over and over. I remember Bond standing in a little gazebo putting his hand through a metal loop (some form of identification) and they did it **SO** many times people were finishing their long novels!

I decided to stroll down the beach, passing many beautiful homes, and ran into a skinny overly tanned woman from New York walking her dog. She'd obviously heard about the film.

"Oh yea," she kept saying. "I wanna see the blaandie Baandie." I took that to mean the blonde Bond. Anyway she was pleasant enough in a potty sort of way. She was parting the palm fronds trying to peer in.

"Where's the blaandie Baandie is he there?"

"No he's round the front putting his arm repeatedly through a ring … it's actually a bit slow right now."

"Oh okay … well do you wanna come and have a beer with me and the General?" she chirped suddenly with a huge smile and raised eyebrows.

I think years of eating disorders, LSD, Vietnam and 1960s New York had just ever so slightly interfered with the neural firing. I rather enjoy her random, unedited thought flow, it makes a nice change from lengthy introductions.

So off I walked in a 'Wizard of Oz' sort of way with this eccentric woman who squawked and flapped like a little bird and her wiry hound.

The General, an old friend of hers and her host, was a striking and congenial man (sadly very deaf) who had enjoyed a long career in the airforce, fought in Korea and flown many types. Certificates of achievement, plaques, honours and medals were strewn around the walls. He had hundreds of photographs, some signed in that flowing penmanship so typical of Americans. His life was there: planes, aircraft carriers, military dignitaries shaking his hand in full uniform at black tie dinners in the Coronado Hotel, etc. We had beers, we chatted, I met the hippy artist with a bandana who was painting on the far end of the deck. His passion was collecting 'stuff' off the beach, painting it different colours and sticking to a black canvas. I met all the parrots, helped feed the neon iguana with diamante collar, and said my goodbyes and thank yous.

I walked back along the beach occasionally having to climb over great pieces of driftwood (the sort that would go for thousands in Harrods). When I strolled back onto the lawn, they were *still* filming Bond putting his hand through the loop.

The same happened with the helicopter which we filmed the next day. Over twenty shots of Daniel Craig alighting from the cabin closing the door behind him and walking across the grass. I thought he looked cool and suave every time and to my untrained eye each take looked identical but they did it over and over. They are obviously seeing *something* which the rest us miss!

The interesting slant on the helicopter shot was that the *owner* was actually flying it, he was not a stunt pilot, he had never flown in a movie before, he actually flew his own *very expensive* Hughes 500 Notar ('No tail Rotor') down from Baton Rouge Louisiana. (The original Jet Ranger that had been booked had a last minute problem and couldn't make it.) Therefore when the director asked him to come down on the lawn with a bit more aggression and speed in fact to whack it on the grass à la Magnum PI, the poor guy was in a bit of a quandary because that's a lot of money to be throwing around. His name was Tony and he was a very successful Businessman with a soft southern drawl and this was a corporate tool. He was there with his mate who had shared the flying with him. The gritty 'slam it on the deck' style approach of cops and robbers movies was a bit alien to him. He managed a good job though!

The seaplane arrived at the magnificent Atlantis Resort situated just off New Providence. The hotel (where Disney, Gothic and Narnia all come together!) is a colossus, a spectacular, turreted, creation in terracotta surrounded by pools of manta rays and sharks and other exotic aquatic creatures. It has featured in other films. It was built by the guru of leisure, the South African Sol Koezner of Sun City fame. It was a fitting backdrop for the scenes in the film.

The De Havilland Twin Otter on floats was painted in a refreshing minty green colour – most unusual. It belonged to the Miami Dolphins and had their famous helmet on the tail. I stood on the seaplane base to see her arrive, hanging on to my hat which nearly flew off in the wind from the jet Ranger which was just lifting into the hover to do a sightseeing tour. The skies are busy in this part of the world!

The little wheels protruded from under the floats as she taxied up the ramp from the water to the parking bay. The turbo prop engines made a hell of a racket as the pilot gave it a handful of throttle to climb up the slope. We were invited aboard and climbed up on to the float and up the steps into the cabin. What a terrific amphibian! We all introduced ourselves. Terry Sherman our contact from West Palm Beach had hitched a ride over with the crew. He was the American partner of Aces High who had sourced the helicopter and the seaplane for this movie. The Captain entertained me with stories of trips to the Virgin Islands and Florida keys where they would hook up with Jimmy Buffet's crew and fish off the back, dive for lobsters, drink margaritas and generally do what the Americans do so well ... have "Way too much fun".

"Here ya go Aneeda," he said and tossed me a couple of bright baseball caps in the same colour scheme as the plane.

We discussed the shots which would take place. Meanwhile the co-pilot who had disappeared fifteen minutes earlier suddenly emerged from the water scrambling up the mole of rocks, clutching his spear gun, fins, a handful of conch. Apparently this is standard practice as soon as they land, the co-pilot dives in and catches lunch and they crack it open and eat it or build a little fire and cook the lobsters. I imagined their shutdown check list … emergency lights … off, batteries off … mask and fins … on, Dive in! Can you picture us indulging in such practices after a landing at City Airport and sliding into the Thames to emerge with a haul of fresh whelks! I think not.

The shoot took place the following day at Atlantis seaplane and helicopter base. The ramp was swarming with film crews, extras, staff, microphones, clapper boards, Bond himself and the Director. And guess what? The whole afternoon was spent filming Bond walking down the steps of the plane with a bunch of extras. I think it lasted all of five seconds in the movie. The charming Peter Lamont (who won an Oscar for Titanic) was there and he explained to me the amount of preproduction that goes on and the hours and hours of creating sets and filming over and over for sometimes seconds of action. What a very polite, likeable, and talented man he is.

I had witnessed the *arrival* of the seaplane now I waited to clock its *departure*. I waited patiently to get a picture of it lifting off the water and nothing happened. I was poised with camera at the ready, but all I heard was a rather loud bang followed by no take-off. They'd had a problem with the wheels, (don't know but sounded to me like they had left them down for the take off!) anyway something had blown perhaps the engine and it had to taxi back in for maintenance – lucky it happened *after* the shoot!

The end of the shoot was a very happy day for me. Because we'd talked a lot of 'shop' the two helicopter pilots and I had become friends. One morning they called me up and said, "Hey we were thinking of flying over some of the nearby islands to check out some real estate, wondered if you wanted to tag along?"

I was out of the door like road runner, leaving small eddies of dust. I drove like a mad woman through the streets of Nassau to get to the airport. They let me sit up front to enjoy the magnificent views. He fired her up and we did the 'dragon fly bit' lifted a few feet off the ramp and cruised slowly across the airport close to the ground, then, when clear, he increased the power, then came that *sweet* moment in a helicopter when the nose goes down and you accelerate along the ground then lift up and away. We got a glorious view of the entire Atlantis resort with all its pools and towers. We flew out to a long thin island just to the North. Plots were being sold for development. It was like a long sausage which would be chopped up therefore you would get beach both sides of your plot – one side was rocky, the other flat and sandy. It was beautiful … one of those 'can't get any better' moments. Apparently Ritz Carlton were putting a big hotel on the end plot so that assured all the ancillary services would be brought in – making this a good investment.

We went flat out along the beach just feet above the turquoise water then turned sharply at the end of the island and came back down the other side for a landing. Tony the pilot put it dexterously down on a heli pad of an existing house there. We hovered down on to this postage stamp of a landing pad. Left skid, right skid, we were down. We waited for the cool down period, I hung the headset on the hook in the ceiling, opened the door and stepped out on to the skid. We walked down to the beach of the private house. It was all there – a big barbecue pit, a hammock, a gazebo for outside eating, and of course a gorgeous private beach where teeny little waves just nibbled at the shore. Does it get *any* better than that? I saw a pool, Jacuzzi and a big round lounge in the house affording panoramic views.

"Another lousy day in paradise" the owner must have grumbled each morning. I picked up a 'memento' shell and we climbed aboard, lifted off again like a giant bee rising vertically. He turned through 180 degrees and we bombed off down the beach back towards New Providence Island. I believe Bond himself was desirous of a flight in that helicopter (God knows he had alighted from it on the ground enough times) ... so I was exceedingly grateful to have such an invitation extended to me.

I came back shaken *and* stirred!

The Bond Plane Adventures to South America

It was time for the *next* Bond of 2008: Quantum of Solace. Aces High and partner in Florida sourced a DC3 which had to fly to Antafogasta in Chile. I took a week off work jumped on Virgin Atlantic and flew down. I saw the DC3 parked at a regional airport north of West Palm Beach. Filming had been going on in Mexico and *this* DC3 had to be made to match the other. Consequently it had been stripped to bare metal and was gleaming like a mirror in the hot sun. Boy there were logistics problems on this mission.

The sectors were exhaustingly long, some places would not have fuel so long range fuel tanks had to be fitted. As per 'sods law' a nice little dispute broke out right on cue. Venezuela, Equador and Columbia all decided to declare war just as our DC3 was cruising along through South America, without markings – which made matters worse because it looked exactly like an unmarked drugs plane. Most CIA aircraft operated like this too. (We don't realise when we are munching our popcorn in the Odeon Leicester Square just what has gone into this). To get round this, they heavy crewed the plane – four pilots, a hammock *and* a spare engine which was cleverly harnessed to the floor in the cabin. Simon, a friend (and owner of Me108) was on board, I said goodbye to him in Florida's Arcadia airport. He had never met his fellow American pilots with whom he would do this mission. He stayed the first night at their place in Florida before taking-off for Panama. He text me that evening – I had to laugh. "Capt F has **never** owned a TV and his son catches rats on the compound and mounts their heads on boards!" Christ these were his companions on a six day dangerous mission to Chile!

The Bond crew were already filming in Panama. (Meanwhile the star, his girlfriend and the two most important 'Bondarians' were en route to Galapagos on a private jet for a break!) I text Simon all the way down with progress through Ecuador, Peru then Chile.

The filming took place up in the mountains where the famous observatory is. There were many 'moments' such as the one where the mayor came screeching up and tried, for a publicity stunt, to stop the filming. This apparently was because they were portraying Chile as Bolivia in the movie – a country which had been their enemy. He was actually arrested by the police and removed. No doubt about it a James Bond movie shoot is a good place to get publicity.

All I can say is there are some extraordinarily clever people involved in these movies because over the course of three Bond films I have seen the pieces of battered looking junk in the hanger turn into something positively spanking in the finished film. The brilliantly engineered night shots of Miami airport in Casino Royale were all shot at Dunsfold in Surrey – where Top Gear is filmed. I noticed as I stood there one afternoon how ingeniously they created the effect of a city skyline at night. It was miles of lights pinned to the fence; they went up and down in a crenellated fashion to different heights. The result: Miami skyline at night.

Still ... only the best for our James!

The Glorious DC3

Sounds strange? Well it is ... One was an aeroplane, one was a car, and one was a wreck in the sea!

Who doesn't love a DC3? It's the lovely, friendly, wet nosed Labrador of aviation. I got the chance and seized it with both hands to fly G-DAKS a DC3 which had featured in the TV series Airline in the eighties and which was still painted with allied roundels and invasion day stripes. We took her for a jolly around the countryside of Essex and Cambridgeshire. It was the start of a loving relationship with this really extraordinary aeroplane.

During 'hour building' days, I was asked if I'd like to go and pick up another DC3 from Exeter. So, one fine June afternoon a highly experienced British Airways Captain called Peter, and I were dispatched down to Exeter in Devon. We did a thorough walk round draining the fuel drains under the belly, turning the blades round (this stops the hydraulicing.) In the cockpit, there's the familiar smell of old oil – everything looks old and solid. The brakes were on, and the gear and flaps levers split – they have to be split on the ground because if they are left in neutral they can, in the heat, build up pressure and burst the hydraulic valves. It's a term known by the pilots as 'split the lady's legs'.

We got comfortable, Peter showed me the start sequence (a tad more detailed than my little Piper Cherokee. So ... master switch on, the fuel selector to left or left Aux, throttles about half an inch open, left boost pump on and check the pressure.

Next ... we pressed the left engine energiser switch for twelve to fourteen seconds, followed by the 'mesh' switch adjacent to it. This meshes the drive and winds it up, the starter engages the engine after a few seconds, I watched as the blades rotated about nine or ten times, on went the Magneto master switch and immediately after – the left mag goes to 'both'.

Then, on to the cylinder prime switch to squirt fuel directly into the cylinders (you need four hands to start one of these things!). Next, the mixture lever to 'Auto Rich' and stop priming. If it splutters a bit, you have to re-prime, but our left engine burst into life. It's rather like a build up to a sneeze which won't come, – lots of jerky breaths and spluttering, holding off... and then suddenly 'ACHOOO' you're there. A relief of fire and revs! Not all Daks are like this but *this* one had Inertia starters. Quite a procedure.

Cowl flaps to open (in winter they remain closed until the Cylinder head temperature is in the green band). I put the battered old headset on and spoke to the tower who cleared us to taxi out.

Lovely old instruments surrounded me, the large but simple artificial horizon with its big white horizontal bar, and then the charming old compass complete with mirror! There are six levers in the central quadrant. Peter's deft handling of the throttles and brakes had us riding smoothly, noses in the air, out towards the westerly runway. The black coloured throttles sit in the middle between the red mixtures on the right and the white pitch (or constant speed) levers on the left.

"Golf Papa cleared take-off, wind two three zero degrees niner knots."

Peter advanced the throttles, she started to move slowly down the runway, as the speed picked up the rear wheel lifted off as the tail began to fly. We kept straight, I called eighty knots and rotate and we lifted into the fair and bonny skies of Devon on a bright summer's day. The wide horizons were as spacious and freeing as ever, and the sky – a duck egg blue.

The raising of the gear was curious, there is a little spring latch on the Captain's side which you pull first, *then* you raise the big lever out of its gate on the co-pilot's side. The gear retracts then you must set neutral because it has no 'up locks' to hold it up, so it's just trapped pressure in the hydraulic rams that keeps it up. During the cruise our cowl flaps go to 'trail'– the most aerodynamic we can be!

We flew east watching for gliders at Dunkerswell, then crossed over the pretty landscape of Dorset near Sherborne. We spoke to Yeovilton, flew over Compton Abbas and Salisbury then spoke to Boscome Down. Peter let me fly, and told me a few interesting 'DC3isms' especially about the landing characteristics of a tail dragger as opposed to a tricycle undercarriage. I just held a nice steady 'straight and level', helped by the perfectly defined horizon which was a pencil line that day. We flew round the top of the Heathrow zone talking to RAF Benson, and passed Leavesdon and Hatfield (sadly both closed now) then we spotted the distinctive lakes near Cheshunt and Waltham Abbey, then descended for our circuit into North Weald.

I selected the large red gear lever on my side to down, watched the gauge, it read about 750 psi hydraulic pressure, that means it's down, and again the handle must go back to neutral in order to get the three green lights indicating down and locked. It gear dropped firmly into place, The mixtures went to rich the props to fully fine. I followed Peter through on the controls putting the flaps down feeling the pitch change, controlling the speed and landing on the two front wheels, which let out a little screech as the rubber touched the grounds. The speed decayed, the little tail wheel fell naturally and easily finding *its* place on the ground behind its two big brothers up front.

I unhooked the bulky five way harness and climbed down the back. You have to lean back a touch and use your thigh muscles when you walk through the back cabin, it really sits at quite an angle. We hooked the portable stairs on and disembarked. It had been a cracking flight.

There are some books which never go out of print: The Canterbury Tales, Shakespeare's plays, Hucklebury Finn. There are some movies, which are always there at Christmas: 'It's a Wonderful Life' and there is one aircraft which goes on and on, that is the splendid and quite extraordinary DC3. One of the reasons it is so enduring is because it has no spar (the large steel section running through the fuselage to which the wings are attached). Other aircraft of its vintage; the Dart Herald, the Fokker 27, the Hawker Siddley 748, were all limited by their spar life (around 3,000 hours). Someone very savvy at Douglas made a good design decision many years ago, out went the conventional steel spar, and the magic wand was waved granting it an almost never ending service life.

As long as there was no corrosion it could soldier on. Because the spa didn't run right through the wing as in other aircraft, it was not subject to the same stresses. So this was as revolutionary as, say, Howard Hughes inventing flush riveting. Furthermore the wings were *bolted* on. The huge number of bolts meant it had to undergo frequent and thorough inspection *but* it was breaking new ground.

The DC3 or Douglas Dakota is the 'most versatile workhorse ever known in aviation' as I once heard it aptly described. This charismatic, muscular twin engine tail dragger can, it seems do just about anything! It is without doubt one of the greatest, ubiquitous and delightful aircraft of all time and one which is *always* present at airshows.

The spectrum if its duties is utterly staggering. It could truly multitask – it carried troops, pulled gliders, served as airliner, an air ambulance, it was used for training, it has made up squadrons of communication units and geophysical survey units and has been embraced and incorporated by many air forces and navies in multiple roles throughout the world. Derivatives of the Douglas DC3 are as far flung as Burma, Ecuador, Norway Yemen, Belgium, China, Thailand, Nigeria, Pakistan, Oman, Syria, Czechoslovakia and many more. There was even one on floats and many have been used as VIP toys! No wonder Eisenhower said that the C47 (as it is known in the military) was one of the four principal instruments of Allied victory in the war.

Hit the Road

Feet up on the table, nursing a cup of coffee in Fairoaks Flight Center waiting for the weather to clear one drizzly morning, I picked up a pilot magazine and read a fascinating article about this eccentric guy in California who had got hold of a DC3, chopped the wings off, modified it and somehow mounted the body onto a chassis and was driving it around as a vehicle on the road! What a lunatic, I loved him already.

I, like so many aviation aspirants chose to build up my hours in the States because it is considerably cheaper. Off I trotted with hopes of gaining one hundred and fifty hours for my log book and subsequently an instructors rating.

So, cruising down the 'freeway' one morning in an utterly clapped out old Datsun sunny called 'honey bee' humming along to KI Fm Smooth Jazz, I saw the DC3 on wheels.

"Oh my God!" I shouted out loud to myself, "that was the DC3." I was in fits, wriggling around and adjusting my rear view mirror to get a better look. *That* was the plane I read about in the magazine. I came off at the next exit and flipped a U-turn to see if I could catch up. Alas it had disappeared. Damn what a coincidence seeing that. I regretted that having come so near I didn't actually get close enough to touch it! Thank God for nut cases who do things like drive around the country in DC3s. So glad for a dash of insanity every now and again, really keeps the old world turning.

All was not lost, a few nights later was Halloween and you know how the Americans celebrate *that!* My sister had various friends over to her apartment and I had two English friends over (both friends from Fairoaks); Mike from Aces High was looking at aircraft parked up in the desert of Arizona and Mike Davis was my flying instructor who had come out to ferry the Cessna 172 back to the East Coast with me. We kitted ourselves up in fancy dress and went off to a party.

"Are you sure it's okay if we all go?" my sister asked her friend as she topped everyone up with wine.

"Hell yea," said the guy whose friend was hosting the party. "These people are really cool and crazy they won't mind if a whole bunch of weirdo Brits show up, especially since you're all into airplanes, he's gonna love ya!"

A whole crowd of us piled into one of those huge American cars, which had a bench seat up front. One chap pulled out what looked like a school chemistry set. It had tubes and pipes, little spherical chambers for heating the Potassium permanganate. He was packing down the weed or the 'giggly twig' as he called it and after attaching a suitable system of linkages and covering up the appropriate hole with his finger he lit up and inhaled heavily to the sound of a babbling brook. About ten seconds later he became an exploding beetroot, convulsing and coughing. I casually took a sip from my tin of beer (in 'Maui' cooling sleeve) because I hadn't finished it so I had brought it with me. Mike lit a Marlboro cigarette and opened the window. Next thing I know Beetroot head who was still wheezing like a harmonium, turned to me in horror and said. "Gad you can't drink from any open container in a car in the United States." and promptly grabbed my beer, emptied the contents out the window, crushed the can and hid it under the seat.

"And yuk, could you not smoke cigarettes in here, the smell grosses me *OUT!*"

And with that he went back to sorting out his Quaaludes and his stash of weed.

We cruised along, a right assembly, in our yank tank and then … my 'Eureka' moment. I couldn't believe my eyes. We pulled into the drive and there was – the DC3 in the garden. We had come to a Halloween party hosted by the mad eccentric –oh thank you angels of fortuitous coincidence! We piled out and I asked to be introduced. The friend led me into the house which was straight out of the Adams family. There were bicycles mounted on the walls, pictures of aliens, space ships, strange statues, models of atomic structures in colourful plastic, bizarre art and very psychedelic lighting. I met the main man who *did not* disappoint! He lived right up to his reputation as an oddball. He struck me as one of those guys who would happily be fired out of a cannon and sweep across the sky like a burning trajectory. He *had* actually been a NASA technician and was obviously a soaring intellect, very inventive and was a smidge bonkers too!

I eulogised about the DC3 and congratulated him on his efforts and vision.

"Oh yeah that was a lotta fun," he said modestly as though it was just one item from his menu of 'crazy creations'. He introduced me to a lady – a little, bald, plump alien in a blue leopard print toga. The cloth was wrapped around her 'cave woman' style and on her bald head were tattooed planets and stars. She was great, of German origin I believe, a perfect match for the firing synapse of a man. Both were barking mad.

The garden was beautifully lit with flame and torch. Everybody was dressed in weird and wacky costumes. The inside of the DC3 was quite bizarre. There were sumptuous purple cushions and velvet walls, richly coloured fabrics covered the two long bench seats which ran the length of the cabin. The windows were tinted and everything was dark, soft and velvety. It was like an exotic Turkish den full of fragrance and lustrous colours. This could have been 'flower power' tour bus for a 1960s hippie band. People were lounging about chatting and laughing. I recall Mike getting a small cigar out which he had saved from the Onslow Arms (his local pub in Clandon Surrey). He lit it and some creature dressed as Queen of the Lizards extended two fingers with long red nails and took it from him.

"May I?" she said raising one eyebrow seductively, thinking it was a joint. Poor old Mike was presented ten minutes later with a rather soggy cigar after it had done the rounds of the 'love bus'.

I went up front to see how he had modified it. It was cleverly done, he'd installed the dials and gauges he needed for the road – speedometers and so on and fitted the accelerator, clutch and brake on to the driver's side, (left). But he had left many original aircraft instruments in the panel as well, and on the right side were the rudder pedals. The throttle and mixture levers were still there protruding from the centre console. There was a compass and direction indicator and the good old artificial horizon. I sat in the driver's seat – a beautifully worn original aircraft seat, full of character and from which many a mission had no doubt been flown. The seat belt was the original harness. What a strange and marvellous oddity!

On each side were huge wing mirrors like those attached to a caravan. I looked through the original DV windows on the side and saw the Queen of the Lizards disappearing with Darth Vader from Star Wars behind a tree, while Sylvester and Tweetie supped frozen margaritas under a frangipani. The beach was nearby. I saw from my cockpit a luminous giant foam skeleton walking off with a witch – whose black cardboard cat was perched on her shoulder, to take a stroll on the sand. Behind them a man in a huge pumpkin mask laughed along with Judy Garland from 'Over the Rainbow' accompanied by Herman Munster. Well never a dull moment while partying inside a road worthy Douglas DC3 on Halloween in Southern California!

Splash

The location was the Bahamas, I'd heard about all the crashed drug planes which lay at the bottom of the sea – a Neptune's junk yard. The plane ride over was one of those which had you looking around rather a lot, pulling that seat belt nice and tight, and giving the old safety card a cursory glance and then perhaps another one. It was an old Embraer Banderante, and my God it had done some sectors, if the wretched donkeys in the streets of Tripoli had an aviation equivalent – this was it! It had been flogged to within an inch of death – daily. I took my seat and saw an intriguing notice pinned on the bulkhead in front of me it read:

CAT ISLAND

LORD HELP ME TO
REMEMBER THAT
NOTHING IS GOING
TO HAPPEN TO ME
TODAY THAT
TOGETHER YOU AND
I CANNOT HANDLE

It gave you that sort of 'mixed emotions' feeling. Much as I love a good 'sing song' to the Lord at Christmas, I'm just a tad uncomfortable when maintenance engineers or worse still, *pilots* invoke his help!

Terry a friend who sourced the aircraft and helicopter for the Bond movie, had a residence on Great Harbour Cay. Accepting an invite with alacrity I asked if it might be possible to see one of the wrecked DC3 drug planes.

"Sure no problem." (standard American response to just about everything in the world).

This particular island has an eerie and strange history. It was *going* to be an island paradise filled with the rich elite, the seventh best rated golf course in the world would number amongst its many charms. An exclusive country club was built along with many outstanding homes. The glitterati of America were heading there. You can just hear the 'but unfortunately' coming up can't you? Yes unfortunately like Esperanto it didn't happen, it very sadly got destroyed. Apparently the whole project collapsed, the investors lost all their money and hey presto the drug people moved in thank you very much. It was an unbeatable location for the booming trade. A notorious guy named 'The Rock' hung out there and of course with such villains, it always means bodyguards and bent lawyers are not far behind!

In the 1970s a DC3 was flying from Columbia to the islands. $10,000 was the rough amount the owner of this strip would charge per landing. Sounds a lot but it is 'tuppence ha'penny' in the scheme of things. The smugglers wouldn't pay, they thought they were being ripped off. Fair do's thought the owner, my strip is henceforth *not* available. To make sure he wouldn't get the Mickey taken out of him he parked a stonking great bulldozer across his runway and informed them the strip was closed. Undeterred they came, at night, as they had always done. The story goes that they saw the bulldozer only at the very last minute and performed an overshoot, they clipped it with the wheels and stalled during the overshoot. They caught fire and in they went to their watery graves. The crew were killed. The cargo burnt for over a day and the whole island was getting high on the fumes!

We approached in Terry's speed boat. I saw the top of the engine cowling protruding from the water, God it was creepy, I had never seen a submerged aircraft for real. I guess the 'boatie' fraternity of the keys and Bahamas don't bat an eye anymore, they are so used to them. I put the snorkel and mask on and jumped in.

Fish were darting in and out of holes in the fuselage, starfish were on the roof, fat sea cucumbers lay peacefully on the wing, all types of aquatic life were living in this small cosy city. One day just sand and rocks, next day – a readymade housing estate for these small creatures. The throttles and all the levers were still in the fully forward position, the seat frames were there and the undercarriage was down. God I shivered as I thought of the terror in the hearts of those guys as they went in. The fuselage was broken but the tail plane was all intact as was one of the wings. This was certainly *not* the unceremonious end they were expecting.

Tiny little shrimp were clinging on to cowl flaps and every tiny inlet door or scoop was the comfy home for something. Pretty little reef fish hovered vertically pecking at the algae growing on the damaged steel, it was quite a sight. The ghostly seats were still there with frayed straps.

I thought of the poem about the Titanic in which Hardy describes the sea slugs crawling all over the fancy mirrors – showing the emptiness and futility of the opulence now. This crew certainly never got their dream home with balcony and hot tub. As for the poor DC3 how all her charms had flown. The once proud and rugged torso beaten, broken, and rusting away. However, there was a certain peacefulness about it and just as no ounce of carcass goes uneaten on the Serengeti, so the fish were making full use of their new home.

The Hidden Messerschmitt

It was the sort of day that winter itself aspires to – frosty, bracing and clear as a bell. I had become aware, through a mate of a place down in Sussex where this ME109, which had been recovered from a lake in Russia was for sale. Never missing an opportunity to see a genuine World War Two aircraft I was pulling a sweater over my head before you could say 'clear prop'. The recovery specialist, was a likeable man called Jim, a very modest 'get on with it' sort of guy – dedicated to his craft. And without doubt very skilful.

I took my mum and we drove to a small village in Sussex where we had agreed to meet him in a pub. He came in wearing his woolly hat, thick sweater and old boots and looked like a local farmhand. We got into his little car, jam packed with tools and bits of junk. *"JUNK?"* he would no doubt demur in horror, should I have called it that. Those were his priceless tools I was referring to! So he drove us off to what seemed like a secret location. Mmmm…this is a bit curious I thought. We left the road and trundled over some rough ground and climbed up a steep, gravelly hill, which was full of potholes and deep ruts. There seemed to be nothing else around. Then as we rounded a corner the ground dipped and there, completely isolated, and off *any imaginable* track not just the 'beaten' one, was a grass strip, a windsock and two small hangars. Nice …*very* nice.

There was another chap in the hangar all rugged up against the cold, he was working industriously on some priceless piece of wreckage. There was a narrow upstairs balcony with a ladder, it was packed with more files and paperwork than an insurance office in the pre computer age. A workbench ran along the bottom wall and there were rudders, tail sections, pieces of fuselage, propellers, lathes, tools, wooden boxes and 'stuff' everywhere with hundreds of manuals and 'how to' books, drawings and schematics of every aircraft system imaginable, thumbed discoloured pages of complicated explanations for those with the patience of Job. What an extraordinary place. These two were *real* enthusiasts.

All along the walls were wings, wheels and ailerons. Wooden crates stood full of bearings and bits of engines. Undercarriages and tyres were propped in any available space. On the right hand side there was the precious item itself, the German Messerschmitt 109E. What was so incredible was how intact it was. The windows were still in place on the original runners. The body showed traces of the original markings, the German swastika. This extraordinary aircraft built in 1939 was in the Battles of France and Britain before being shot down by a Russian in the frozen North. There were bullet holes in the fuselage, these bullets injured the pilot, one Lt Widowitz and Jim showed me the big hole in the tail where he was struck. The strike which brought him down. He had done the most flawless landing choosing (wisely) the frozen lake rather than the wooded terrain. He managed to walk away. It was Lake Shonglgul-javr on the Murmansk front (brrr sounds pretty cold). The fuselage plate showing the manufacture and the year was there intact. The fresh icy water had been an effective preserving chamber. It sunk to the bottom of the lake where it remained for 60 years. Some important things (compass, radio, machine gun and instruments) had been removed by the Germans who went back shortly after the crash.

I asked Jim about the rescue operation, he told me that once it had been located, they sent out a team of English engineers to dismantle it (the Russians tend to go at it with a hammer). To illustrate their diligence he pointed to all the bearings and parts which were sitting in glass jars full of oil so they would not spoil during the journey. They forbade *anybody* local from working on it so it would not be torn apart haphazardly. I asked him about the logistics of working over there in Russia on such a project. He said quite nonchalantly that ex-KGB men are involved as are the mafia who protect him while he's there. It was dismantled with the utmost precision, care and expertise.

He told me the most extraordinary story about the aircraft itself and the man who used to fly it. His name was Widowitz – a German ace who was known as the man who always returned (usually in a Feisler Storch) to find his colleagues who had been shot down. He had a glowing reputation, obviously loved for his compassion and valour. The plane was built in 1939, and had done 1,500 hours of flying. When it was delivered up to the icy Arctic Circle for action on the Eastern front he claimed it, recognising its worthy modifications (an armoured windscreen) and the fact that it had been overhauled.

In August 1940 a German squadron of Messerschmitts110s was attacking in England. Treble one squadron (Hawker Hurricanes) based at Biggin Hill were returning from Middle Wallop that day, saw them and engaged in combat. One ME110 went down and crashed near the very hangar where I was standing in Sussex. It is still buried there. The sister plane to that downed ME110 was struck but managed to stagger back to Calais. The British pilot claimed one down and one 'probable' but in fact the German made it back. *That* ME 110 (M8ZE) was then sent to the Eastern front (to JG13) and was flown by two men called Grobe and Mendle, they were shot down and it was Widowitz who went to rescue them. How ironical that *his very* ME109 should be in *this* hangar in Sussex and the sister ship to the ME110 (whose stricken crew he went to save) is buried right outside the hangar doors!

Jim pointed to another beautiful picture of an ME109 which was flown by Ehrler, a true German ace. He had 199 strikes to his name. Apparently in November of 1944 he shot down a Russian Stormovik after a hell of a fight. Very sadly he was stripped of his rank, Iron Cross, Knight's Cross and Court

Marshalled. *WHY?* I asked amazed. Jim explained that on *that* very day we bombed the Turpitz. It seems the Germans needed a scapegoat and blamed him for not being there to help defend it. He was accused almost of fighting his own war, of upping his strikes. It was bitterly unfair since he obviously knew nothing about it. (Isn't war a strange and nefarious affair). Fool is he who thinks governments will be there for you when you need them! He became very disillusioned by all accounts and on his last sortie after running out of fuel he ended his life by flying into the tail of a B17 and slicing it clean off.

Behind the ME109 was a P39 Cobra, also fantastically rare. In October 1944 the Russians were pushing hard against the Germans in Norway, where the fighting had been intense. The story goes that the leader of a small squadron of these P39s broke right and lost his wing man who disappeared without trace. Many years later when the salvage team were pulling a Hurricane out of the lake, a fisherman approached them and said that there was another one 'over there' pointing to the other side of the lake, he said he'd seen it through the water. Lo and behold there was a Bellair Cobra. That's what you call a productive day out!

"What's that pile of twisted metal junk?" I asked pointing to an enormous heap of broken aeroplane. "That pile of junk," he said smiling, "is the remains of two Junker JU 88s and I just sold it for a lot of money!" Very tidy. Of course there are wealthy collectors who will buy this sort of thing. Microsoft's Paul Allen for example is a well-respected collector of war birds, and such people are vital for keeping these planes alive.

I asked Jim if he'd be restoring these fine old war birds and he said not until he had finished his *main* project, his first passion which was the Fockewulfe 189, a two engined reconnaissance plane. There it was in the middle of the hangar just the centre section, bare metal and hollow. The wings and engines were not attached yet. Jim had very cleverly *made* the frame for the cockpit into which the glass would fit. He showed me how he would copy surviving bits of framework and fuselage and recreate identical pieces and hammer them out on his work bench – he'd been at this project for years and years! If he didn't have the piece to copy he looked at pictures and reconstructed it that way. He said it would be worth four million when it was finished because it would be the only one in the world!

"Blimey you'll be a rich man Jim," I said with gusto.

"I'm not going to sell it, good heavens no, after all this I'm going to fly the bloody thing!"

I drove away over the South Downs with the fat red wintry sun sinking behind the hills. I felt very happy that I'd come across such an extraordinary and informative man in such an enchanting place. I'd discovered not the secret garden but the 'secret hangar'.

Learning to Fly a Seaplane

"Glassy water landings – you gotta nail them or else you won't pass the flight test!"

Those were the words on day three from the instructor, when I was struggling to get the hang of it. He was your typical Florida guy (shorts, deck shoes, Raybans and polo shirt). He was super 'laid back' even when I came a tad too near the shore line!

"That's okay, no problem everyone has a hard time with this at first."

I was in Winterhaven near Lakeland, Florida and the scene was idyllic I was transported into one of those 'Southern' movies where a swing settee rocks idly on a deck overlooking the water, gators slide around silently and the mosquitoes bite while the spongy red sun slips behind the bayou and smoke from barbeques unfurls in lazy silver spirals filling the air with good smells. How very different from the Oxford Air Training school.

The plane was as cute as a puppy, a little yellow Piper Cub on floats, boasting a massive one hundred horse power. It was your basic, stick and rudder plane but this one had a skeg too, under each float, she also had little water rudders on the back of the floats which you raised or lowered depending on the manoeuvre. What looked like no more than a non-stick patch was stuck on top of the float, it boasted the title 'Deck' and that's where you stood. The window opened for that 'elbow out' cruising along sort of look. That was a bit scary first time up, he opened both windows turning it into a semi convertible and I found myself on the vertiginous edge looking at a long drop down to the lake – it felt very exposed – not unlike a micro light!

The drag is very noticeable when you first open the throttle but you soon learn to find the 'sweet spot', which is the minimum drag point in the middle of the float that contacts the water when you accelerate, and the back and the tip of the float are out of the water. What a thrill to lift off from a lake for the first time. My instructor buzzed around showing me the local area. I clocked all the homely wooden cabins, each with its own jetty – so perfect for float planes and boats. Jet skis darted about and kids were fishing.

The first landing was a big Eureka moment. I flew her down the approach quite steeply, (the speed was only about sixty knots) then levelled off just above the water making allowances for the additional height of the floats then simply started to pull back on the stick raising the nose … waiting … it's there somewhere … and splash. What a great sensation to decelerate just like a boat, when the bow lowers into the water and you get that slight surge followed by the sound of the water sloshing up against the sides.

It is actually much easier to land on water when there is a little surface chop because it gives you depth and distance and all those parameters necessary for accurate judgment. One of the many exercises you have to perform is landing on water which is absolutely glassy and above which it is very tricky to judge your height. It's pretty tough, so the method is that you pick a point on the bank known as the Last Visual Reference or LVR which sounded a bit ominous to me! Last before *what* I wondered … a watery grave rolling around gently with the sea cucumbers on the muddy bottom? The patter they give you is as follows:

"Choose your LVR, approach the LVR at lowest safe altitude, establish correct glassy water landing attitude, get about 1700 RPM, do *not* flare visually, when you touch down, stick back." Roughly translated this means: dive nose down towards a bush on the bank, clock it properly because it's the last thing you're going to see before entering empty field myopia, pitch up when you're above it, hope it's about ten feet high, raise the nose just a tad, hold it for what seems like an eternity, whatever happens don't for god's sake lower the nose or look at the surface and try to flare 'cause your eyes will play tricks on you. Then pray that you haven't misjudged it 'cause if you have you'll either nose in and turn over or end up way too high, stall and fall onto the water!

"Always look for the band of calm water round the edge, that's the *upwind* side, and look for the smiles on the surface, read the ripples, the wind is blowing *into* the smile."

These and other fascinating little snippets of information from the instructor, helped increase my understanding of the wind and how to 'find' it. Smoke is a beauty because it is a sure fire signal. It is as good as having one of those gigantic foam hands on the ground pointing. If there is **one** imperative, it is that you land *into* the wind. But if the clues are scant you have to read the water, for example the streaks on the surface which are always parallel with the wind.

I learnt all sorts of 'neat stuff' as they say. I learnt about 'Power off sailing' in high winds, severe porpoising (not a good thing!) and rough water operations. The explanation of the stall characteristics was an interesting one:

"Yea ... it gets kinda mushy, the nose will drop and the door floats up!" *That* one rather tickled me.

"One of the 'must do' items is called Docking. You must show yourself capable of manoeuvring the aircraft on the water and parking it into wind next to a jetty.

"You don't wanna crash into your buddy' deck when you all arrive for the party," explained the instructor with a grin. So off we went taxiing around on the lake, sometimes we kept it slow (idle taxi) and the whole float was in the water, sometimes we opened the throttle for the 'step taxi'– full power, stick back which left a small wake. "You use *this* technique when your buddy's run outa beer and you have to go to the store on the other side of the lake and pick some up!" he said.

Because the dock which he *normally* used to demonstrate the exercise was occupied by a boat, he turned to plan 'B':

"Hell just use that big ole 'gator over there Anita, just pretend that's the dock and try and come up alongside it alright?"

"What that great big alligator in the water over there?"

"Yea ... see the twenny footer over there, just make out like that's the dock, I just need to see you control your speed and pull up alongside him."

Suddenly the flimsy, 'Fisher Price' toy plane in which I sat seemed thinner and flimsier than ever.

"But er … are you sure that's okay," I demurred. "I mean aren't they protected, we don't want to upset them in any way do we?"

"Hell no he's okay, he won't care he'll just move on if we piss him off."

Why at that moment did all the clips from 'Planet Earth' of Crocodiles eating fully grown wildebeest come nose-diving into my mind. There was Attenborough's soft voice again:

"Yes, they are the masters of the unexpected attack, supreme killers … once the prey is in the jaws, of this master predator it's all over, he spins it round and round shredding it then takes it to the bottom to rot."

"Right okaaay, so what do you suggest, sort of come in and face the same way as him or spin it around … probably best to just keep it simple." My attempts at the self-assured 'all in a day's work' lilt were quite pathetic, still I forgave myself because, after all, I *was* terrified! He did oblige me when I asked him to close the window. He made me do all the checks though: mag off, carb heat on, the 3 'H's – harness, hatch and headset, but he did exempt me from the final one which was 'jump out'.

We approached the gator, the little float which held us out of the water seemed awfully fragile. The animal didn't seem to mind that much, his jagged snout was motionless on the water's surface, but his eyeball was shifting about a bit. I turned the float to parallel the length of the beast, and became aware of my knees which had moved instinctively over to the far side of the tiny cockpit!

The alligator flicked his tail abruptly, showed a few teeth and sloped off under water. It did make me jump. I squealed something like "OHMYGOD" and patted my chest.

"Okay that's fine, I'm happy with that, just remember nice and slow and try to read any current and allow for that as you drift in.

"Absolutely … yep I've got that," I lied, "shall I put the power on and take-off again now?"

"Okay cool, you can always have another shot when we go back to base, you can park her up."

"Brilliant," I said, "let's get airborne shall we?"

I saw his shoulders go up and down with a small chuckle, he knew I was scared.

"Let's have a bit of fun with the birds," he suggested, "okay head over there," he pointed into his two o'clock and I advanced the throttle. Noise increased, stick back, found the sweet spot and we lifted. There was a large gathering of birds sitting on the water, as we approached they all took off, he told me to keep it low and just fly with them. Wow it was fantastic, just like 'Out of Africa' there were birds all around me. I could hear their wings beating the air, I could see their outstretched necks and heads perfectly steady, looking forward as they flew inches from me. I was living the song: "She flies like a bird in the sky – eye eye eye!" There is a real eccentric, on the airshow circuit. He flies in his micro light with cranes, they follow him like their mother duck, I saw him at the Middle Wallop air show and I thought of him at that moment, with a great deal of emotion and empathy.

The last item on the syllabus really got the 'fun meter' into the hard over. The 'take-off in a confined space', for example from a small lake where there is not the long stretch of water necessary to act as a runway. You start going round in tight circles with full power on, using the controls, you lift one float out of the water, the opposite wing tip is almost skimming the surface and you buzz around on one float in this rather unusual attitude until you reach take-off speed. This was undoubtedly the 'Sweeney' manoeuvre. You take off in a curve which is strange, when both floats are out you straighten up and off you go, unless you have to clear some tall pine trees harbouring grizzlies in which case you can keep the circles going until you have 'comfortable' altitude.

Back in the UK, well, there's not much opportunity for float planes, but one quiet Sunday afternoon having lunch at Frensham Ponds in Hampshire I was staring out over the still water and I let my mind meander off back to those sun drenched lakes and those swirly take-offs. What would people make of a 'confined space take-off' here? I wondered. I saw myself in the cub on the water tearing round in circles and lifting up up and away over the trees whilst Mrs Cholmondsley Struthers complained of the frightful din and called the police!

So I can't say I have used my float plane licence much living in Berkshire, but I certainly enjoyed learning about it. I sure did envy the two float plane pilots I met in Bahamas while they were filming Bond. They would park up in the islands, get the spear gun, go and catch lobster and conch and eat them while sat on the big floats in the sun then swim to the beach. They flew around in colourful shirts and baseball hats – yes life was generally a party. It is another world.

The Hunting Lodge in South Africa

Raindrops ploughed their way down the grimy window on the catering bus. It was a dismal day at North Weald, we were having lunch during a film shoot. In walked a South African, looking for Mike Woodley. He was a professional hunter working for an American, who was Mike's friend and a fellow gun on the pheasant shoot. The South African – Campbell Dashwood-Smith had been sent up by his boss to look at a Cessna 337 with which they wanted to expand their area of operation into Botswana and Zimbabwe – the perfect aircraft for that environment.

A few hours later, having continued this meeting in town, where he treated us to some fine South African wine, I ascertained that Campbell was a reluctant pilot so I thought it a brilliant idea to ask if I could help out on his hunting concession in Northern Transvaal. I *wanted* to fly, *his* passion was hunting. I was between jobs, and had just lost my father to cancer, I needed something new – an adventure to lift my spirits and offer direction. I had just finished a stint on Citations and although very scant on twin prop hours I thought *this* would be a great experience (plus I rather liked him!). So, it came to pass I talked my way into a summer down on a hunting farm, flying clients up from Johannesburg to a private strip near the border of Botswana.

The Cessna 337, bless its pugnacious little soul, is not the prettiest of aeroplanes but what it lacks in pulchritude it makes up for in outstanding short field performance. I was told while doing a walkround at Lanseria in Johannesburg, that the pilots jokingly call *that* plane the 'kaffir tart' because it will do anything for you but you don't want to be seen with it. They're not known for their political correctness!

Those months gave me a unique insight into how things run on a hunting concession, and I shall just 'tell it as it was' no sparing the gory details. Although not an activity I would embrace, I did learn the 'positive side' of hunting. I appreciated the dedication of the professional hunters and their commitment to conservation. The owner of *these* twenty-four thousand acres spent a great deal of money on feed for the animals and general maintenance. The hunters must make sure they only kill a certain number of grown males and on top of this they tackle the poaching problem thereby ensuring the animal population remains buoyant.

Sitting in the Cessna 337 for the first time made me journey back to flight school and reacquaint myself with the wonders of 'Manifold Pressure', 'Boost' and RPM, having become used to N1s and N2s (jet readings). The 337 is a 'push pull', so, it has one propeller at the back – the pusher and one at the front – the puller. On the plus side – there is no asymmetric imbalance in the event of an engine failure, the thrust remains 'in line'. It was used widely in the Rhodesian war and was perfectly suited to this environment. Rugged and strong, it was fitted with STOL (short take-off and landing), which are modifications enabling it to perform safely on short unpaved bush strips.

We'd fly the passengers, normally only two, from Johannesburg to the farm near Potgeitesrus in Northern Transvaal. Thank God for the small GPS – 'Apollo fly buddy' because after the beacon at Lanseria there was precious little in the way of navigation aids so it was vital for providing track and distance information as we headed out into the baked thorny African veldt – a landscape utterly unfamiliar to me. I read the manual on the GPS the night before and off we went.

Africa. A magical word for me since I was born and raised there. The name conjures up a variety of different images – fiery sunsets, warm soupy air filled with the sound of cicadas, red hibiscus the size of plates, mosquitoes, the beating of drums, and dancing women wrapped in bright cloth. No one can dance like an African!

One hour north of Johannesburg, Campbell pointed out the strip so I'd recognise it again. The landmark was the red roof of the lodge. There was a waterhole nearby where animals sipped furtively. I banked round onto a base leg and he told me to do a low fly past to clear the kudu and impala from the strip – that was a first. Oh deep joy at being allowed to do a low fly past without Mrs Fortesque Holmes in Barbour and headscarf ringing up the flight center and screaming in her best 'Surr-eh accent:

"Would you please stop these wretched planes flying over my farm. I have brood mare in the paddock and I'll never get anything out of her with this darned racket going on!" (She unfortunately lived on the threshold of runway 06).

The animals darted off the runway with that elegant spring and I pulled round downwind and turned in short to land. These planes can certainly approach steeply. I bumped along the uneven orangey sand surface towards the small hangar which was like a carport. As I closed the mixtures to shut her down I saw two women walking through the corridor of red dust which hovered over the strip and heard their chattering and high pitched laughter. These were the two housemaids / cooks who'd come to greet their boss. They spoke broken Afrikaans, Campbell was joking with them, I understood nothing but I picked up plenty from their gestures and expressions:

"Aa Aa" and "tch tch" as they sucked in through their teeth, raised their eyebrows and then doubled up with laughter and pulled their hands down the length of their faces, all very familiar.

The senior one, Emma was a large woman, dressed in a woolly cap, socks and slippers and a blue nylon overall which stretched over acreage of bosom.

She greeted me warmly clasping my hand in both of her huge fat warm hands and beamed, she looked like Scarlet's nanny in *Gone With the Wind.* "Goeidag" they both said. Campbell introduced us and they both unloaded bags from the aircraft. Annie, dressed the same, was as thin as a rake, and shy. Emma took a huge piece of luggage, balanced it on her shoulder, head on one side, bent the knees and did a mini jump to secure it in position and walked off slowly but steadily with the ambling sway of a female elephant. Her toes poked out of her slippers and the backs, trodden down, flapped up against her heels which were like great semi circles of hard cheese. To my amazement, Annie took an even bigger piece and followed suit. She might have been skinny but she was strong.

The lodge was luxurious with high vaulted ceilings and plenty of beautiful stone and wood. Animal skins were scattered over the stone floors, gemsbok, kudu, wildebeest and impala heads were mounted on the walls and glass sliding doors gave on to a veranda fringed with tumbling bougainvillea overlooking a swimming pool and then a waterhole which was frequented at dusk by various animals. Yes this was definitely going to be an interesting experience and quite a change from the flying I was used to – Heathrow to Paris Le Bourget with ministers and chairmen.

Next to the pool there was a bonfire pit, which every evening was our oven, the fillets of which ever animal had been shot were wrapped in foil and cooked slowly in the embers. Each night we'd sit in the 'director' style chairs round the fire with a chest full of fine South African wine under the Southern Cross and countless other twinkling stars and eat *thee* most delicious meat I'd ever tasted. Emma – in her woolly hat would be 'chief stoker' carefully turning the pieces of meat in foil with her tongs and giving a little muffled "Ah-yeee" when a cinder popped out and burnt her foot, then she'd kill herself laughing when she saw me chuckling. Peter the chef and Annie the maid would join in from the side lines pointing at the meat and offering suggestions, they were always tut tutting and shaking their heads with laughter as they gibbered away to one another in their dialect of 'sutu'. Some were from Zimbabwe, they spoke Shona or Matabele but they all communicated.

Forget billions, we are talking 'gazillions' when it came to the stars which filled the black velvety sky every night. It was just staggering, I had a permanent crick in my neck with the upward gazing which had me utterly overawed.

It was during these moments when I listened to the 'Wilbur Smith' type tales of courage, danger and marksmanship; of Winchesters, Rigbys and Purdies (all super-duper guns).

"I swear to God hey," the hunter would start with his strong South African accent, glass of red in one hand and index finger of the other pointing and waving determinedly.

"The bloody lioness came out of nowhere hey, Jeeesus I nearly died, if it hadn't been for my 500 I'd be a dead man hey."

With that the index finger would snap against the third finger and he'd shake his head. Highly seasoned tales of charging buffalo, solitary leopards and other gung-ho homilies filled our evenings.

"Shit I loved that Winchester hey, I could shoot the eyebrow off a bloody baboon at 600 hundred yards."

I learnt all about grains and nozzlers and barrels and different kinds of guns. A story which made him chuckle the most was the one about the wildebeest or 'vilderbeerst' as he pronounced it, turning on the African tracker and head butting him. Nobody was hurt but he positively exploded with laughter when he described the shock and panic when the 'vildie' turned on the African and tossed him in the air before beating a retreat.

"Croist you should have seen him run hey, it was hysterical..."

Each night the only sound, apart from the crackling fire, was that of the hyenas and jackals howling in the distance and the ubiquitous buzzing of the cicadas as they grated the air. On a couple of occasions when it was late, Campbell and I jumped in the land cruiser and drove round to see the nocturnal animals, like the bat eared fox and the night jar. It was exciting chewing on a chunk of biltong and bumping over the uneven tracks watching creatures in the headlights or seeing their big dark eyes staring up from the bottom of a hole. At times we just cut the engine and listened to the sounds of the bush. The little Cessna 337 looked great parked up under her protective roof, the moon shining down.

Guns were just a way of life out there. Wandering round the lodge one day, I went into a study to admire some paintings. A few moments later I heard."What are you doing in here, you shouldn't be in here."

I'd come a bit too close to his gun cupboard. Eventually, before I left South Africa, he did show me the contents of the padlocked trunk. There was a row of different guns in clasps. He outlined the size and application of each one.

"This one is a twenty-two with a silencer, this one is an over and under shotgun for the birds, that one is a Winchester rifle, this is a Purdie, this is a five hundred elephant gun" ... and so on.

"And what the hell is *that* one?" I asked staring at a rather evil looking black 'machine gunny' type one.

"*Thit* one, ma dear is for the poachers."

The aircraft was off to Maun in the Okavango. I had to drive on my own from Jo'berg to the farm to bring more supplies. Campbell briefed me on the Toyota Landcruiser, then put a handgun in the glove box slammed it shut with the words "*Just* in case hey ... don't take any shit from anybody."

"Right!" I said punchily like the new Corporal barking back at his regimental sergeant major, as I had a sudden thought of juju dancers jigging round a black cauldron swinging over a fire with nothing but my shins and trainers sticking out of it.

Some of the roads I journeyed down were so long and straight they would converge into a dot on the horizon. Glancing in my rear view mirror I would see the clouds of red dust churned up by the heavy tyres on the truck. If I saw another vehicle coming towards me, it was up with the window quick smart – the dust was asphyxiating. My eyelashes and hair were orange at the journey's end.

Small groups of African children walked barefoot down these hot dusty roads for what seemed like hundreds of miles. Diversions were obviously scant because they stopped to stare at me coming and hung on to me until I was out of sight. About ten minutes later I would pass a little school which I presumed was their destination. Some of them would be tapping a big hoop along the road beside them with a stick. I jostled along, just me and my gun through breathtaking scenery – dramatic escarpments and valleys. The land was so expansive, so open. The sky was bigger than it had ever been and was dazzling lapis blue, benignly dotted with puffy little flat bottomed cumulus. I was *in* the actual picture of 'fair weather cu' from my met book.

I stopped in a small Afrikaner town. I needed to buy some nails and hooks for the lodge. Looking around at some of the townsfolk I could certainly see how the gruelling hardships of the Great Trek of 1835 would have been all in a day's work for this lot. Here was a town of tough and hardy Boers. The store I entered had that charming 1950s feel when stores had wooden floorboards, packets of Omo, boxes of hard toilet paper and smelled of Vapona and mothballs, where small waisted housewives in flared skirts sat at the old-fashioned cash tills and things cost 1/6 (one shilling and six).

As I approached the counter, instead of seeing June Allison with a hairband and dimples, I recoiled in shock. In amongst the trekker ancestors there must have been oxen because here was a descendant. I asked for some picture hooks and there followed a lively exchange between 2 or 3 who didn't speak English, each trying to be the first to understand me. Finally the redhead with the tree trunk legs and the tufted mole bustled outside and returned triumphantly dragging a young reluctant woman behind her; she plonked her in front of me like an exhibit.

"Can ah help you?" muttered the town's English speaker. I accepted her help, made my purchases and went on my way concluding that visitors were not common here. The two burly farmers (of Gary Larson cartoon fame) sat in chairs outside the store and were unfazed by the enveloping dust storm unintentionally created by my disappearing wheels. They stared granite faced straight through it to make sure I was well and truly gone. I flipped the glove box open to glimpse my gun, it was strangely reassuring and off I went towards the Botswana border.

The hunting was done at dawn and again at about four p.m. after the midday sun had had its say. The easier targets were shot first i.e. Blesbok, Wildebeest and Warthog, the faster more elusive ones such as Steenbok, Gemsbok and kudu took a little longer. I went along on a few hunts for the experience and sometimes to video on behalf of the client. A role I offered a bit more frequently after we sat through toe curlingly painful footage shot by Connie the Californian wife who had 'all the gear and no idea'. After three minutes of her bunions crunching over gravel as she inadvertently filmed, we were subjected to total darkness as we heard him firing his winning shot, followed by her saying inanely over and over "The great white hunner, the great white hunner".

It was enough to curdle yoghurt, and I could see the shoulder slumping disappointment in her husband's face after coming half way round the world to have the crucial moment of glory banished to oblivion because his wife forget the lens cap.

"Maybe we should let Aneeda have a go," chirped the exasperated husband the next day, eager not to offend as he subtly but surely put the video in my hands. I am *certainly* no whiz kid with cameras but just by holding it the right way up I was already ahead. And what timing …*that* was the day of the kudu hunt which will be engrained in my memory for ever.

The tracker would always stand at the back of the truck so he could survey the area. If he spotted something he would shout excitedly so the hunter would stop the vehicle and lift his binoculars. The magic words from the tracker were "manetjie" pronounced manneki (male), then "groot groot" (big). The hunter would decide whether it would make a good trophy, if yes, he'd tell the client to take aim, if they were a bit far, they would alight silently and tread quietly through the bush to get nearer. That morning the tracker shouted "manetjie, groot" and pointed excitedly into the distance. The client took aim with his 370 Winchester rifle from the front of the truck. The ear shattering noise ripped through the landscape, the volume, just brutal. The kudu started off into the bush, he had been hit. The hunter, followed closely by his tracker, with lightning speed, took off after it, his sole aim now to finish it off as quickly as possible. The client followed, hoping for another shot at it, but his age precluded him from the rigours of a chase like this, he struggled to keep up. We ran through the scorched thorny bush, the kudu would pause then on hearing us again he would take off. We followed a blood trail and its spore.

The pace quickened into a frenzy, the client remained, and I instinctively ran full speed following the hunter, we ran down then up dry riverbed walls, through a good mile of thorny bush. I struggled to keep up with Campbell and his tracker who were now a tight unit shouting urgent information to one another. I ran in an awkward stoop ducking and diving under the spiky branches which could rip your clothes and skin. The only sounds were my feet thudding on the sandy ground, my heavy rapid panting, the snapping of twigs and the odd rip of my shirt as I snagged the thorns.

The poor beast ran and eluded us for a few minutes. Campbell was desperate to find it and kill it. Sweat was pouring from me. We finally caught up with the kudu. He had collapsed with exhaustion, his front legs buckled under him, his rear in the air and his hind quarters strangely elevated resting up against a tree. "For Christ's sake put him out of this misery," I muttered breathlessly to myself. But before I finished that thought I heard the shattering sound of Campbell's Rigby going off. With lightning speed he had positioned himself and put a bullet straight through the animal's vitals. It was over. I actually saw two streams of air exhaust from the kudu's nostrils like two little clouds of smoke punched out of a cylinder by a piston. In silence and with wide staring eyes he slumped as his spirit left him and a thick doughnut of red dust rose then floated down around him. I filmed all of this and recorded the celebratory chatter in Afrikaans between hunter and tracker as they shook hands and discussed the chase. Although I didn't have a word of their language, I could tell they were disparaging the client for having missed the target.

Then the elderly San Franciscan emerged from the bush, red faced and panting, his gun over his shoulder.

"Wow that's a nice seta horns there huh," and he paced around his future fireside mount. After photos were taken the hunter jogged off into the bush to retrieve the truck – God knows how he located it but he obviously had his methods.

While he was gone the tracker sat astride the animals back much like a surfer waiting for the next wave. Then, much as we doodle with pens while on the phone he had a sort of fiddle with the kudu. I saw him push the eyeball right into the socket with his index finger. I suppose when you look death in the face every day a carcass is a carcass. Having winched the animal on to the truck we drove back to the lodge where the next phase was the skinning.

Wilson was the skinner, a right character, he was a deep, matte black, with wild bushy hair sticking out of his backward baseball cap. His eyes were bloodshot and a soggy roll up was wedged permanently on the side of his mouth. He was amusing with his odd Americanism "Yeah man" or "Dat's cool man". He rolled his own cigarettes in newspaper but his 'party piece' was the way he would, mid stroll across the garden, just suddenly do Michael Jackson's moonwalk.

Once I saw him put another roll up between his teeth, totally unaware that he had the tiniest remnant of the previous one cemented in the corner of his mouth – it never fell out! But credit where credit is due he was an undeniably proficient skinner. I had only come here to help ferry persons and luggage in a little twin prop, but I was getting a real education to boot. This was a whole new environment.

Big pots on the boil surrounded the skinning shed. Emma would put the heads in the boiling water to remove the meat from the skull and the horns from the rest of the head. It was like a scene from primeval times. I'd been invited to dinner by the Palaeolithic ancestors.

"Do you fancy coming over to our cave tonight? Nooma and Hwll speared some nice Bison locally."

The fillet and liver was kept for us at the lodge, the rest of the meat went for biltong, the skin for mats and the horns and facial skin for the taxidermist. Mighty hooks hung from the ceiling in the shed. Winston winched the animal up by the back legs on a motorised chain. The day I saw him do a fully grown eland I was impressed by his precision and skill. The kill attracted all the Africans, they would shuffle around excited by the 'chop' to come. Honestly *nothing* was wasted. After he had slit the belly open, all the entrails would be lying on the concrete in the sun, this was like a clarion call "à table" to every fly in the Transvaal.

Winston would squat, his body was so long his knees nearly reached his ears. He inserted the hose into the opening of the intestine and turned the water on full chat. It was like a gigantic snake coming alive. About fifteen meters of slippery entrails would jump and twitch into life. It was an immodest serving of faecal matter which sprayed out the other end under a healthy PSI. Blood and crap were flying everywhere showering the Africans who didn't seem to mind in the least. Winston was getting serious splash back but he carried on just blinking and grinning with his days old roll up – still there, grasping the intestine as though he had a dragon by the tail. Once the guts were cleaned, they would provide a delicious meal for any interested party on the compound.

Dusk on the farm was bird shooting hour. We'd climb on the Land cruiser and bump off into the bush, Tuppy swinging on the back whistling his usual tunes and chattering away in Shona. It was not only the stars in their billions, which will lodge in my memory for all time but the *colours* as well. Early evening had a magic which made you thank God you'd been born. The light was somehow different from any I had seen, it was syrupy and warm. The ground was red and sandy, which added to the special hue, the whole bush, now bathed in golds and ambers, glowed with a radiance which a New England autumn would struggle to match. Even our skin looked different – like Butterscotch.

As we rounded a corner we startled some giraffes, they took off with that slow motion lope. There was a lag as their legs started a slow gallop and their heads needed time to turn from the trees and swing round to catch up with the rest of their body, absolutely beautiful! They ran gracefully alongside the truck, then, when too close for comfort, one would suddenly dart off at right angles, once at safe distance they would stop and stare at us with that benign sideways chew. They were at one with the bush, their dappled hides the same tones as the earth.

Campbell arrived at the waterhole where he would shoot some birds. A gorgeous female Nyala (antelope family) sipped quietly with her young from the thick green pond. It was quite a sight, their beauty and innocence somehow enhanced by the damped 'oboesque' tones of the dusk. Quiet as I was, she looked straight at me, chewing and then she shepherded her young off into the bush. We waited, guns ready for the birds to arrive, the landscape now was like a leathery saddle, tanned and worn, the insects and frogs were audible. But it was the sand grouse we awaited. One fluttered in, POW, Campbell had it, the shot echoed round the bush shattering the silence. The sand grouse swooped and glided in, landing sometimes a tad unceremoniously on the red sand. The hunter was a marksman (years in the military fighting in Namibia and Angola) and picked them off one after the other.

Tuppy walked around retrieving, gathering them by the feet and tossing them into the back of the Land Cruiser. Empty shells sprung out all over the place littering the ground. The light slipped away, we picked up the empty shells, opened a couple of cold beers, Tuppy lit a cigarette and we climbed on the truck, and drove back, the headlights shining through the bush. Campbell stopped and showed me the head of a little creature crouched down a hole, (he was good at spotting things!) it had huge bat like ears and big eyes. We bounced and keeled over the terrain, going slowly down the steep sides of the empty river. The truck, with traction like a tank went almost vertical, then drove along the parched riverbed and climbed steeply up the opposite incline.

As we popped up over the far bank of the dried river I saw the spectacular sight of the five resident rhinos, their thick hides glowing in the last rays of light. They all jerked their heads up from the peanut hay to look at us. As we moved closer they grunted and tossed their heads and trotted off snorting and farting. Despite their bulk, their trot was remarkably springy and rhythmic. Their big hooves sent up clouds of dust which fell slowly back to the ground in the still and breezeless air. As we passed them they watched us intently then returned to their grazing as we moved off. They were just magnificent and it was a thrill to get within ten feet of such an animal.

Nothing was quite as humorous as the resident ostriches – they were the ones from Walt Disney's Fantasia. What a combination: huge clumsy hoofs, spindly little shins, knobbly knees and great strapping rugby player thighs with the texture of a plucked chicken. Next the ballerina's tutu of feathers around the hips, and then sitting on top of that freakishly long neck, the face of the old lady without her teeth in. God was certainly feeling creative when he made this one! They lived in a spacious pen on the farm and I became quite friendly with them. The other creature I took to my heart was a tiny baby Gemsbok that had been abandoned by its mother because of the drought. It was still covered with afterbirth on it when we took it into our care. I fed it milk, he would actually come to me and huddle around the boiler outside, staggering around on its tiny legs. It made great progress and happily, it survived.

Often, we would take an evening stroll down to a river pool (a small part of the river which had not dried up). It was the time of evening when you could stare straight at the sun, it had frayed edges, much of its power dissipated in the low suspended dust. Animals proliferated here because water was so scarce. Crocodiles slithered into the pond, white egrets stood statuesquely on the banks. Swarms of mosquitoes hovered over the stagnant water. The thick warm smell of Africa hung in the air. It was a scene of mesmerising serenity but danger lurked on the edges and I was *always* aware of that.

One night to my absolute delight I saw two fat hippos in the water, their ears twitching madly just above the surface. They checked me out staring intently, snorting and flaring those nostrils. I'm told they are extremely vicious. Baboons swung and shrieked in the treetops above us. Campbell had his 22 rifle.

"They are running bloody riot at the lodge and eating all the birds eggs."

He lifted the butt of his gun into his shoulder, closed one eye, put his cheek firmly by the side and curled his finger round the trigger. When he fired, the flat glassy pond of our silence, erupted as though some monster from 'something lies below' just surfaced. Frenzied shrieking came from the trees, leaves and branches shook violently as colonies of baboons vacated the area. The crocodiles flipped their tails and took a nosedive and the egrets spread their wings and took off for a more conducive spot.

There were many unforgettable moments such as these during my stay. Hunting is a controversial issue and it is not everybody's cup of tea. I personally don't enjoy killing but I'm sure most abattoirs are grim. I eat meat and fresh game is exquisite. I'm grateful for the chance to have seen all sides. It will always be an incendiary topic.

Every few days, new clients (mostly American) would come, they'd be picked up from Johannesburg and flown up to the lodge. Flying to bush strips on game reserves in South Africa, Vic Falls or Lake Kariba, is a far cry from jet charter flying out of Heathrow to European capitals. I knew I couldn't stay forever, and at the end of the summer the career move was calling so I left, feeling enriched by the experience and taking home with me indelible memories of a spectacular and a very special land.

You Make Flying Fun
The wonderful United States of America!

American flying clubs and schools, are terrific places.

Amongst the popcorn, ice machines, and sunny patios you'll also find instructors in shorts, and commercial pilots in a casual ensemble of jeans and flying jackets saying things like:

"Hey Gene howzit goin', where y'all headed?"

"Oh just taking the Lear down to drop the boss off in Fort Myers."

"Alright ... you have good one."

"You bet."

There is a wonderful sense of ease and 'anything is doable' feeling about the Americans with their aircraft, planes are tools and they enjoy them.

The differences in style and general learning techniques are marked and anyone who has taken flying lessons in America will, I'm sure have been touched by just what a great attitude our American friends have.

At 'American Flyers' in Fort Lauderdale where I trained, there was a pool outside, and the students would be 'hanging out' there waiting for their lesson. There'd sometimes be a little barbecue going at lunchtime and people of many different nationalities would be sitting in the sun in shorts and flip-flops – the attire they would go flying in!

"Okay Ramon you're up!" the instructor would shout coming out to the pool with a spare headset, and pick up his pupil.

"That's okay bring your soda if you haven't finished it," and off they would go to climb into the Cessna. This is of course very different from hanging around in the English airfield café eating your bacon sarnie in the drizzle!

The day we all dread is the flight test day. Student pilots do their test with CAAFU which is the examining wing of the CAA, (they are very important – the SS of aviation). When you're ready, the uniformed instructor briefs you with the solemn tone of a pall bearer.

We are talking gold braid and lots of it! I can't speak for all, but mine was frightful. His introduction was stiff, formal and devoid of smiles. He watches in stony silence as you twitch and fumble your way through the 'walk round' and things don't improve once inside. He slid his chair back, said nothing and let me get on with it. You just see them making the odd note in their notepad ... you dread to think what...!

His brief went something like:

"After take off you'll put the instrument hood on (so you can't see out). I will simulate instrument conditions, I will expect you to fly with reference solely to those instruments, *you* will talk to Brize, *you* will be in control unless *I* say I have control. All checks are *your* responsibility." And so it goes on. I felt that Jesus had a better day schlepping up the via Doloroso with a cross on his back! When you land back, a nervous wreck after a gruelling test, the briefing is formal and the humour scant, and then he charges you like an injured bull for the privilege of all this. Yes the cost is prodigious.

In the States my examiner was casually dressed, wore a baseball hat, had a big smile, he chatted interestedly about life in England and offered me endless cinnamon tic-tac's. *His* brief went something like:

"Okay Aneeda let's have some fun with this; I'm sure everything will be cool. We'll put the old 'party hat' on you when we get airborne (*their* name for the hood) and you just get comfortable and we'll do the holds and ILS and VOR approaches juuuust like normal okay. I'll help you out on the radio if it gets real busy ..." And so it goes on, you are instantly at ease even though the flight test itself is very difficult and the standard high. In fact they throw little unknowns at you such as changing the holding pattern.

"Enter the hold on the two four zero radial left turns," he might say. So you have to quickly gather all your spatial awareness and fly a racetrack pattern on a radial other than the published one. So they **do** really test your skills but somehow it's more enjoyable. When I had finished my test the instructor took the controls from me and said, "Good job, now it's Miller time, let's have some fun." That means happy hour and he flew me low level all down the beaches from West Palm, Pompano and back to Ft Lauderdale.

"You take the party hat off now Aneeta"

Because my training was on a twin (Cessna 310) there was a fair bit of single engine work after simulated engine failure. The instructor's style was punchy, in a 'US Marines' kind of way.

"You gotta move on those levers girl, get on it I wanna see 'em firewalled."

Another favourite:

"Get that mother feathered" I couldn't really hear Wing Commander Smithers with his pukka accent coming out with

"Get that mother feathered" ... No ...

Sometimes if I was too low he'd chirp

"We're sicklin' through the grass here!"

They were firm and thorough but friendly and light-hearted, nothing was too much trouble and they had a candour and approachability which was so refreshing. At the end of the day a relaxed pilot is a good pilot.

The other *really* noticeable difference is the chit chat or RT as we call it. Americans have mastered economy. When enjoying the remarkable experience of flying right over the top of LAX – Los Angeles (you'd never get a clearance here to fly smack over Heathrow), you'd hear these wonderfully clipped and condensed transmissions.

"Los Angeles radar howdy, twin beech four south of Van Nuys for Carmel, three thousand checking in."

A more typical British transmission would be:

340

"Good Afternoon Luton radar, this is Golf Bravo Mike Kilo Yankee, a PA28 cross-country from Southampton to Turweston, presently five miles to the south of you at three thousand feet on a QNH of one zero two five, squawking three one zero six, requesting radar advisory ..." And a partridge in a pear tree. Sometimes we *can* be a bit long-winded. Having said that I think our pilots are clear and comprehensible and our controllers certainly amongst the best in the world. Plus we have many different nationalities of diverse languages flying in the skies over here so we *have* to be clear.

It is still quite a 'big deal' and rather prestigious to have your own plane in the UK but in the States loads of people seem to be climbing aboard their Bonanzas, throwing the dog in and cruising up to Santa Monica for a weekend. Yes we do have the 'Le Touquet for lunch crowd' but generally light aviation is much more patronised in the US and I do believe they make it easier and cheaper to run and maintain aircraft.

I passed, (phew) and after three weeks of training in Florida, I headed off to Miami airport to catch the flight home. What is it about bars in American airports? A melting pot of humanity, you always end up meeting someone with a story. I went to the 'Cheers' bar with the tiffany lampshades, lots of beer on tap, an urn of clam chowder and smiley happy bar staff practicing their bottle tossing. There was a bar stool free between large biker type and stressed out corporate blonde frantically jabbing her laptop, it looked safe, I moved in.

"Michelob please and some clam chowder."

"No problem," as little square serviettes are rotated at high speed in front of me to clean the area.

I took grateful glugs of the ice cold beer feeling elated at the acquisition of an American Airline Transport Pilots' licence. It was a big achievement and a very useful ticket to have in the world of corporate aviation, because so many of the private jets (which were *my* goal) are on the Cayman register (Victor Papa), or Bermuda and Aruba, all of which recognise the FAA licence.

I glanced at the girl to my left with a nod, but she was far too busy working on her reports for any sort of jollity. The deadline whip was cracking over her head. Then, just as I was thinking I'd get nothing more than Harley Davison speak about the 'Fat Boy' and 'braided hoses man', I got a surprising and rather intuitive "Cheers" from the chap on my right.

"Where you headed out to?"

"England."

"Ok cool, you've been on vacation?"

"No, actually just done some flying training over here."

"Alright – you a pilot?"

"Trying to be!"

On the TV screen at that point was something about Cuba, and I asked a casual question about Castro, the strange history of that country and its displacement in the world. Well hey presto, this guy was an unlikely expert in shady politics. I didn't know if he was one of these conspiracy theorists or actually involved somehow but, my God he told me some intriguing stuff that night in Miami as I waited for my BA flight back to London. I enquired spiritedly about Cuba because I've always fancied sipping a Cuba libre in a straw hat on a colonnaded balcony overlooking dancing couples, and old 1950s cars, with salsa music and cigar smoke in the air. Here's what he told me.

"The Maarfia (as all Americans pronounce it) had been running everything. When Batista left, Castro came in and turned against prostitution and all that kinda stuff, so the CIA teamed up with Batista and tried to get Castro out. Ya know there were over thirty attempts on his life."

He fiddled with some toothpicks, snapping them occasionally. But where *you all* come into this story ... you Bridish people," he said with a wry grin, "is that *your* Hawkers (or Haahkers, as he pronounced them) they were shooting down the CIA planes."

"How come?" I asked genuinely confused as to why Hawkers should be over there. He explained that the British had supplied them to Batista before Castro took over.

"And then the Goddamn CIA disguised their planes as rebel planes, *you* all were on the side of law and order but you didn't know – how could ya? ... that those planes were *actually* CIA planes in disguise, you see they wanted to make it look like they were rebel planes, so they'd have an excuse to go in there and kick some butt! Yea some say Kennedy caused the failure of the Bay of Pigs by not allowing the CIA to have air cover." He looked up at the barman.

"Can we get another pitcher of margaritas here please?"

He could see I was fascinated by this medley of intrigue, politics, aeroplanes and secret missions! There was I having enjoyed the States so much and now this guy was telling me about the CIA's failures in Mao's China, with the Mujahideen in Afghanistan and how they ran teams of assassins, economic hit men and had endless association with criminal rackets. It made me glad not to be in politics!

"Remember Noriega in Panama? He was imprisoned by the CIA even though they'd been working together, he was supposed to be stopping the drugs coming in but he was in *league* with the drug barons, so he went to prison. Yea stoopid I know. So there's this Lear jet on the ramp in Panama City and we put a team of seals in there, all they had to do was disable the Lear – you wouldn't think too much for a team of navy seals right? When the seals arrive they find drug runners loading coke so they abandon their mission and try to arrest the druggies. Someone had tipped off the guards at the airfield that the Americans were going to attack so the guards started shooting at them and they got caught on the ramp. The guards in the hangar were protected behind oil drums, they had armour piercing bullets and slaughtered some of those seals."

"God how awful," I said genuinely imagining an opening scene from a Tom Clancy novel.

"Yea real awful when you consider that we called in the C130 spectre gun ship, which was awesome and could blow the shit outta anything – even take out armoured tanks. The guy on the ground couldn't contact the C130 and

342

scream for help but he *did* manage to contact headquarters to say for Christ sake help us! But the goddamn thing would **only** fire if it got orders from the guys on the ground, well too f****** late – the commander had been killed! It was a total humiliation, I don't suppose you guys heard about it but boy it was a screw up! Still I think The Seals managed to blow out a couple of tyres on the Lear jet – great result huh?"

"What happened to Noriega?"

"Oh he got sanctuary, apparently he went into a catholic church in Panama, I reckon he paid them a lot of money! But what the CIA *did* to get him out was to play *really* loud music day and night, pop music blaring out of all these speakers that surrounded the place – they knew that would drive 'em **nuts!** I guess in the end the old Catholic padres couldn't stand the goddamn music any longer and they threw him out.

"Blimey *then* what happened to him?" I asked

"Oh he went to the yellow submarine in Miami and was never heard of again."

"Would all passengers on British Airways flight to London please proceed …" came the voice over the tannoy announcing my departure. I pulled my bag over my shoulder and said goodbye to this stranger with a firm handshake.

God knows if was all true but it was an eye opening encounter – amazing what you can learn at bars in airports!! I was just glad to have my US license done, I'd soon be pootling around hopefully on my private jets in 'civi' street without incident. Still, amazing what's going on out there!

Spitfires lined up
during film shoot

De Havillard Repide of set of 'piece of
cake', Charlton Park

Spitfires during filming. View from my
seat in cockpit.

Learning to shoot at the
hunting lodge South Africa

ME109 and Spitfire in dog fight.

Diving on the wrecked DC3. Bahamas.

Rather unsettling notice in the plane - Bahamas

On location for Bond, Bahamas. Daniel Craig on right

Just about to take off for 'bone shaking'

With the Russians at their space
station. Mike Woodley on far right.

CHAPTER SIX: Tales from the Slipstream

THIS IS A COLLECTION OF OTHER PEOPLE'S STORIES. Some funny and silly, some quite dramatic and moving but they are stories told to me by friends in aviation... We have many hours to while away in the cruise or in various hotels and airports around the world – therefore much reminiscing and tale-telling has been enjoyed and I felt some of their memories were too good to go unrecorded!

A Crash into the Sea off Corfu

This is the story from Mike Woodley who crashed after a bird strike shortly after taking off from Corfu on a delivery flight in a Beagle 206 in November 1978. The intended route was: Alice Springs, Darwin, Broon Den Pasar, Jakarta, Singapore, Bangkok, Calcutta, Delhi, Karachi, Dubai, Bahrain, Jeddah, Cairo, Heraklion then Corfu which is sadly as far as he got. He is the only person I know to have lived through such a crash ...

I interviewed and recorded him. In his own words:

The three Beagle 206s were going to Jim Hill in Fort Lauderdale, we'd bought them and he'd agreed to buy them on once we got them from Australia to England, then *he'd* have ferry pilots to take them on from there. So there was myself and Sniffer in one plane, Rick Collerby and Slim in another and Rex Parker and Bill Webb in the third.

There were so many funny moments, one was Rex – he was supposed to be *the* HF operator (that's long range radio communications and requires a different transmit and receive technique). He'd been banging on how he'd been an HF operator on Sunderlands so we put him on the plane with HF and that would be *his* department. So his big moment came to work the radios as we approached Burma in loose formation. I called him, telling him to contact Burma on the HF because we were thirty minutes from their airspace – otherwise they might shoot us down with their Mig. It was a dangerous place.

So anyway off he goes, but he'd forgotten to switch from VHF to HF. So he transmits:

"Burma Radio Burma Radio, this is Victor Hotel Echo Foxtrot Golf, do you read?"

But the silly sod isn't going out on the HF, so I pick up the mike and in my best 1940s English voice I say. "This is Croydon airport say again Croydon airport, hello aeroplane hello aeroplane, come in."

Then there's a big silence and Rex tries again.

"Burma Radio Burma Radio ..."

So I come back and say, "Croydon Airport Croydon Airport, we understand you have forgotten to change to HF, over."

So realising his mistake, he looks like a right twit, goes into a sulk and won't speak to us, so we don't know if he contacted Burma or if we were going to be shot down. Oh dear we had all *that* kind of nonsense.

I suggested to Mike at this point in his story that it must be a 'bloke thing' that no adventure is possible without a bit of chest thumping competition. I was convinced that this **was** indeed the case when he told me the 'hot chilli' story:

We were all in this restaurant down in the Far East, bragging about how we could eat any kind of hot chilli. I knew this particular one was unbearably hot so when one of the lads said he could nibble them raw I said well *you* have *that* one and I'll bite *this* one. So he bit it ... and ... (at this point he went into a shoulder lifting chuckles).

"What happened?" I asked.

"Well he sort of went scarlet and broke into a sweat, his eyes went bloodshot and he pushed himself away from the table and seemed to double in size. When he went to draw breath it was so deep he created a vacuum which nearly emptied the aquarium next to us! Then for the next twenty minutes he went deaf, poured with sweat and was seeing double, so that shut him up for a bit!"

"Any other memorable moments before the dreaded Corfu episode?" I asked.

"Yes one horrid moment was in Calcutta when I went to have a pee in some latrine shed outside and I saw this dark shape in the corner, it looked like some old sacks that had been dumped. Out of curiosity I approached to have a close look and as I did so I disturbed what must have been a hundred billion flies 'cause the whole thing exploded and I saw quickly that it was a rotting corpse of some sort, so I ran out of there like a scalded cat being chased by a huge cloud of horrible flies. Christ I ran fast!"

So the Corfu bit, ... well, we got stuck there because of bad weather, we didn't have any de-icing, the DMEs were Aussie and didn't work on any other channels other than 'Butterworth' in Malaysia or wherever it was. We had one VHF and one VOR so we were *not* airways equipped. We waited for days, it was December. On the third day the cloud base lifted to about 600 feet so we decided to have a go, since the weather at Nice, where we were headed, was reasonable. We decided to go at the same level at twenty minute intervals. We were very heavy 'cause we were carrying a drum of fuel and lots of spares so we were overloaded but on a ferry flight you can be 10% over gross.

Rex took off first with Bill, they disappeared. So twenty minutes later Sniffer and I line up on the southerly runway. I took off, I kept the aircraft level below cloud, got the gear up, and tried to pick up some speed before I went into cloud. As I went passed the Hilton Hotel millions of seagulls appeared. The noise of the first aircraft had disturbed them, so they'd flown off. Now they were all returning to their spot and next thing I knew there were seagulls bashing into the plane, all over the place, it was like a Hitchcock movie, they were going in one side of the wing and out the other, banging against the fuselage, bloody feathers everywhere, the windscreen shattered. I was hitting them at about 120 knots and they were huge, apparently there were over thirty found on the airfield.

Then it all went quiet and we were through the flock of birds. I was still at about 400 feet with take-off flap. The plane was rattling and shaking, I decided to do a 180 degrees turn and land, there was not much wind so I would go straight in. There was so much vibration coming from the left engine, I made sure the emergency boost pump was on, firewalled everything and we were still losing height round the turn. I told Sniffer to put out a mayday and get to the back of the aircraft to get the dinghy and life jacket in case we ditched. Then my left engine quit, we must have been below the VMCA (minimum single engine speed) and the bloody thing just rolled over onto its back, there was no way I could control it, it rolled over and just dived into the sea – wing first which was lucky cause it just sliced in like a knife through butter. Then I hit the windscreen and the control column went straight through my ribs, and I thought this is it, I am going to die now. I didn't feel a thing as my head went through the windscreen I said … Oh shit so that's what it's like to die, fairly painless, there's so much adrenalin!

Then, like a boxer when he's been knocked out and someone pours water all over him, I came round many seconds later when tons and tons of freezing cold water came rushing in on top of me. The fuel tank had burst open and was mixing with the cold water all around me, my eardrums burst, and I was aware of the plane sinking, it was upside down. I was trapped, so then I thought I'm going to drown. Bugger, so that was *two deaths* now. That bit was really frightening 'cause it was like a submarine crew trying to escape up a ladder or something. I knew I was about to drown so I fiddled for my harness and managed to undo it. Fortunately it was the only thing keeping me in, no trapped legs or anything otherwise I wouldn't have been able to escape. So as the plane fell I went out through the windscreen. It wasn't diving down but it was sinking, if we hadn't been so heavy maybe the thing would have floated, I don't know.

So then I come up to the surface, plomp – like a champagne cork. I took a huge gulp of air and swallowed loads of gasoline which made me instantly sick. I couldn't see anything 'cause my glasses had gone. Everything was going round and round 'cause my eardrums had burst and I was totally disorientated and confused I even started swimming *down* at one point. I started to grab at any bits of wreckage and stuff them under my jerkin. I hadn't put my life jacket on. Never ever laugh at people who put their life jackets on before take-off – *they* are the sensible ones.

Then I realised that I had a chance of survival and I felt keen to carry on and fight, though being in the sea at this time of year I didn't have too long! I could just make out the mountains of Albania through the misty drizzle. I thought God if I'd landed in their territory I probably would have staggered up to the beach and been shot. I found a map, a headrest, a VOR aerial and other things. The salty water kept me afloat, I got rid of coins and shoes and the contents of my pockets and took a leak, anything to lighten the load! I hoped and prayed that Rick and Slim in the third aircraft would find me, someone must have heard my mayday. I was wondering what the hell happened to

Sniffer who'd gone to the back of the plane as we hit. I'm not going to last too long before hypothermia gets me.

Suddenly I felt *really really* cold and started to shiver uncontrollably. Then the pain just swept over me and I was in bloody agony. Then I thought here comes the *third death,* I've done the impact death, the drowning death, now the hypothermia death. The pain was bad. (Mike paused here and was blinking back the tears as he obviously revisited that moment – I let him regain his composure.) Then suddenly I heard the noise of distant propellers –we-ow we-ow. They got louder and louder and then shot straight over my head at about thirty feet. Had they seen me? What had happened is that a *gardener* from a local hotel had seen me go down, had called the airport, who told Rick and Slim that they lost radio contact with me so the two of them took off.

I thought why don't they slow down and throw me something instead of beating me up and going back and forth. What they were *actually* trying to do was fly across the front of a boat – the international sign for 'follow me', they were trying to lead him to me. At first the fisherman in the boat waved his fists, he was annoyed. They had spotted the huge oil slick in the water and *that's* what they flew to, when they saw me waving, they naturally got very excited and opened up a special hatch which flying doctors' planes had and started throwing me life jackets, but they weren't opened so they went bouncing along like Wallace's bouncing bomb and landed miles away from me. So that was useless to me but I got a new spurt of energy believing that I would be rescued. My teeth were chattering out of control now.

The government patrol boat couldn't come out apparently because it was on maintenance, so these two police guys had gone down to the harbour and commandeered a fishing boat. "Who's paying" said the fisherman but police just got out their guns and said they were *taking* it. But this boat didn't go off 'whoosh' it went 'put put put' at five knots. They finally got to me and there were big tyres hanging over the side. I grabbed one and they dragged me in and put me in a hold full of stinking fish boxes, it stunk and it was freezing but at least I was on it. I wasn't doing too well on this concrete floor and they were trying to ask me in broken Greek and English if there were any other people. I said yes, so then they thought a VC10 or something big full of passengers, had crashed. I managed to explain but still they spent the next hour going around looking for Sniffer.

I found out later he'd been picked up by another boat, the door at the back had flung open on impact and he got thrown out. He was very fit, and about ten years younger than me, and had struck out to the shore. The boat which Rick was trying to buzz had actually come across Sniffer and picked him up. So *his* boat was looking for me and *my* boat was looking for him, no one had any radios – it was chaos. Several other boats had joined in now, meanwhile I am in this bloody freezing hold, dying. If I had to describe the pain … it was like someone plunging you into a frozen river, dragging you out getting a hammer and breaking your ribs, hitting you in the eye then pouring neat petrol down your throat. Then tipping you on your head. All of this with no warning so you've got shock to contend with as well.

Eventually we get to shore, it's two hours since the crash so there's police and the press and TV crews all over the place. They take me to hospital and put me on a trolley and someone wheels me straight into a wall and bangs my head. I remember lots of screaming and shouting and a policeman hitting a guy who falls down, a small fight breaks out and I lay there thinking 'Mmmmm I'm having one of those days'. There are needles and drips going into me, I'm being sick – probably dead fish, seaweed and gasoline coming up all over. No one has given me any morphine or anything. Then they X-ray me which I thought a bit stupid 'cause there were about five of me at this stage all shivering and jumping – I couldn't keep still. They put me in a room like a prison. I think the thing with Greek hospitals, there are like three tiers. You can lay in the corridor and hope someone finds you, or you can go into the sort of place I was, **or** if you've got money you can go into a private ward which is like our national health wards. I've got no money 'cause my briefcase is at the bottom of the sea along with my favourite gold pen given to me by Alerado Hess of Hess oil. My log books, licenses everything – gone.

Suddenly I hear Rick and Slim, they try to comfort me and they tell the hospital people they've got money and I *must* have a private ward. So I get wheeled into a less grubby area. I lie there bleeding and there's a bloke sewing up my eye and more needles going into me. I woke up at eleven the next morning. I am deaf and aching and can't breathe properly. My left eye is closed and black. A woman comes in looks at some charts and tells me I have pneumonia and leaves. 'Crikey' I think, all those famous racing drivers who crash, *they all die of pneumonia*. They have the best hospitals in the world. It's always pneumonia that gets everyone in the end isn't it? There's no cure for it, shit I've come this far and I'm going to die of pneumonia.

Then a Bishop Macarios type figure comes in with a huge hat and great big crucifix. He kneels down and holds my hand and starts crying. Christ it's the last rites, this is it! I thought of all my friends, my life, my plans, it's all over, I tell you it hits you like a block of ice. If you think you are going to die, it's horrible, it brings you to your knees, it's very chilling. I'm crying, he's crying, I can hear the bloomin' church bells going outside, he puts a Virgin Mary statue there near me and I'm thinking at least I'm getting a decent send off and I'm not being eaten by a bunch of lobsters on the seabed.

Meanwhile, back in Surrey, *Rick's* girlfriend was staying with Caroline – *my* girlfriend, in our house. News broke that *Rick* had crashed so Caroline was comforting *his* girlfriend, then the real story arrived; – sorry chaps it's actually Mike *Woodley* who had crashed and was in intensive care so then Rick's girlfriend started comforting *Caroline*. I was not going to make it through the night, so there was drama back in the kitchen in Surrey. Meanwhile, Rex had pushed on, made it to Nice and finally Gatwick. He rang Caroline and he arranged her flight down to me.

The next day I woke up and thought 'hang on *this* isn't heaven'. I'm alive I'm alive and what's more I am starving. There was some soup, it had gone cold, been there for hours probably. I drank it. Then I remember these rusks, I bit one and it exploded into tiny bits, crumbs went all over the bed. It was then that I looked down into the bed and saw that my skin was coming off where the fuel had burnt my skin. I couldn't tell the difference between the rusk bits and my skin, so I didn't eat the crumbs! (It reminded me of my first time in Florida as a penniless student pilot. 'I'd never been in the sun and I got burnt to a bloody crisp gawping at all the girls on Fort Lauderdale beach, I was skinny and white and went like a lobster, all my skin fell off a few days later and I remember the ants in my trailer where I was living carrying off great pieces of skin the size of crisps to go and build their houses with.) I didn't much care for these rusks and they piled up next to my bed like the leaning tower, but still the nurse kept bringing more. I thought it must be a special diet, but actually not, if I'd had money I could have been eating steak.

Then I realised something quite amazing. The reason for the priest, his tears and the tolling bells, was because **that** day was the patron saint of Fishermen day. They have a day to celebrate people being saved from the sea and it was THAT day. So all the newspapers covered it – I'd been saved you see. If it had been St Christopher's Day or some other saint I probably would have died.

We both looked at each other as he told this detail in the story and admitted that this was quite uncanny and really rather wonderful.

Fortunately I improved and left the hospital, then all the political nonsense started like 'Well you can't leave you don't have a passport'.

'I know it's at the bottom of the sea'.

There was lots of arguing and toing and froing The Hilton Hotel was great, they gave Caroline and I a free room, I finally got some good grub, a delicious steak and recovered. We jumped on an Olympic 737 to come home. They gave me a nice seat but after take-off I was holding a hankie to ear 'cause it was so painful. Then I realised that the hankie was soaking wet – all my brain juice was leaking out!

When I got home I went to see Doc Perry, he told me one ear drum was perforated and one completely gone, he said he had to pull my medical, and my ears would have to be rebuilt using skin from elsewhere.

I got straight on to my insurers where I had loss of license insurance and this was the beginning of my realisation of what a bunch of thieving crooks insurers are. I got through, and this was the conversation:

"Hello yes, I've lost my medical."

"Accident or illness?"

"Accident."

"What sort of accident?"

"I crashed in a plane."

"You did what?!"

"I crashed in a twin engine plane on a delivery flight from Australia, it happened off Corfu."

It was as if she was wondering what the *bloody hell* I was doing in a plane.

"Oh ... um ..."

"Well I'm a pilot, you know, so I was in a plane ..."

"How long ago?"

"About three weeks."

"Right give us a ring in three hundred and sixty-five days' time and we might consider it."

"*WHAT?*"

"Read the small print, no claims considered for a year, if it had been illness we would have considered it within three months."

"Hang on a sec …"

It was useless they were not going to help.

"Well that's the last subscription you ever get from me!"

"No, we'll sue you if you don't carry on, you're under contract to pay for ten years," or however bloody long it was.

Shortly after this, the head of this company was seen leaving the country in a 125 jet, he was a complete crook apparently I didn't get a penny from them. I claimed for my Rolex watch and they said: "Now you have an *all risk* policy, I suppose you thought, (sinister smile like that of a ventriloquists dummy comes over his face) that actually meant *all risks*."

"Well yes I did actually."

"Oh no you've been out of the country for more than three months, it's invalid, goodbye."

It was rather like a Monty Python sketch, I have never trusted insurance companies ever since, and they were caught up very soon after by lawyers who I realised were also there to mess your life up, cause you maximum agro and get as much money out of you as possible.

"Still," I concluded to Mike, "better to be alive and fighting the insurers and dealing with the hassle, than say …"being a meal for the crustacean on the seabed."

"Yes," he said pensively, his fingertips touching, the two index fingers against his lips. "Yes I suppose you could say I'm still dealing with bottom feeders but in a slightly different capacity!"

Well done Mr Woodley for surviving *that* one!

Memories of a VIP Hostie

Her name was Jo, she was a scream. She had flown just about every celebrity and VIP in the book on an executive airbus. We found ourselves marooned in Tanzania together having taken a small party of titled Europeans big game hunting in Serengeti. We shared a two hour boat ride to Zanzibar during which time I learnt much about the shenanigans taking place in the back! I might have seen some damned good sunsets and electrical storms, but she sees the whole caboodle, and was able to bring quite a new dimension to executive flying. So over to you … Jo.

The Vodka and the Russian

Jo: *"We were flying on an executive airbus from Russia to New Zealand. The passenger was a Russian, an ex-Olympic cyclist, he must have been about, say forty. He had a girlfriend with him who was about fourteen, well she looked it anyway (a bit of exaggeration never hurt!). The other hostie on board was inexperienced and a bit stroppy. There were some other passengers all friends, but this guy was sort of head honcho. I don't know exactly what was going on but there was lots of tin-foil and small gadgets, some sniffing and the odd bit of smoke. (I think we don't need an A level in chemistry here!)*

"The girlfriend kept giving him naked massages in the bedroom. I was taking canapés down to the back and generally looking after them and they were getting absolutely out of it. Suddenly this guy collapsed, he went straight down and his eyes literally rolled to the back of his head. I was ringing the bell frantically to get my colleague to bring the oxygen and she was hysterical and panicking, so I ran passed her to get it myself, brought it back, held this guy's head in my arms and put him on oxygen. He was completely out!

"I rushed forward to tell the Captain and he said that we were over Mongolia and China border so their next stop would be the Philippines, therefore if it was really serious we would have to turn back now for Russia. It would be about another five hours before they could land anywhere halfway civilised, if they pushed on. When I got back to him, his girlfriend had taken the oxygen off and was bathing his head in vodka. She'd stripped him naked and started to bathe his whole body in vodka with small towels. I swear to God she just rubbed him gently as though she was anointing him in some ritual, and I couldn't believe it but he started to come round. This was a man whose eyes had rolled round the back of his head, who was cold and clammy and limp. She obviously knew what she was doing so I let her get on with it. He made such a full on recovery they were locked in the horizontal lambada by the time we were over Nanjing!

"And they say Heineken refreshes the parts most beers cannot reach ... I think we ought to hear it for the Vodka!"

The Rock Star

Jo: *"We were doing the tour for 'xxxx' (one of the most famous heavy metal bands of all time). The lead singer, as expected was a wild crazy, druggie. His team had to get him off the aircraft and to the venue before he got too drunk, otherwise god only knows what would have happened. Still ...* **BAD** *and* **NASTY** *are two of the many requisites for being a true heavy metal star.*

"We were in Lisbon for the evening concert, it was a huge do. I noticed in his drunken state he'd left his jacket on the seat, I knew his 'stash' would be in there so I was standing by for the phone call. His long suffering right hand man/ tour organiser was very green and I think a bit out of his depth with this

guy. He called shortly after and said kind of sheepishly, 'Um we've left something on the plane'.

"They kept referring to it much to my amusement as 'an item'.

"So I said, 'Oh right … would you like the jacket?' trying to help him out, knowing full well what it was."

Savvy Jo had already noticed the tin in the pocket as she hung the jacket up – so she had a hunch someone would be back! It was the manager a young South American who proved to be on the ball and arranged a suitable place to meet with Jo and hand over the jacket.

"We said something like: 'I'm sure this will help to keep him going! We don't want him catching cold' and gave a little nod".

Jo told me the concert was momentarily suspended while the star 'changed outfits'.

The crew, forever tied by slots, night closures and jet bans were anxious to take-off on time.

Jo: "It was so funny because they'd call and ask how long before they had to be back at the plane, because **he** had to get completely trashed after the show. I'm sure someone was, working out how many 'lines, spliffs and swigs' and party paraphernalia they could manage before departure!

"Once we called the manager for an update and they tried to fob us off with 'Oh, he's just in the shower' and we could hear him singing and partying in the background. They were always late and he was always wasted. I think in a way he was a bit insecure … this made him bad tempered. Do you know so many band members got fed up with his addictions and subsequent unreliability they left and formed their own band!"

'The Dancers'

Jo: "We had a client who we always called the 'Fat Prince' because that's what he was. We flew him down in the Airbus to the Seychelles. He took over the same hotel every year during Christmas and New Year for this massive party. He was **very** rich like most Saudi princes so he could afford anything he wanted. There were tons and tons of booze and food, it was quite a bash. What we used to do was pick up the 'dancers' from Milan, who all had their own male 'managers'(she made the inverted commas gesture twice!) and they spent their lives going round the world as guests at different parties. I remember distinctly they would hardly eat a crumb on the way down there (presumably to keep the tummies flat and the bums pert) but coming back to Milan … in the New Year, holy cow they literally ate every last morsel of food on the aircraft. The starvation was over and it was drinks and food round, they finished every scrap – I remember giving out broken biscuits – that is **all** that was left.

354

"They would have a few days off during which time they would eat anything they pleased, then they would prepare for the next 'party'. They spent their lives being the invited 'totty' at numerous glamorous functions. They told me they were off to Los Angeles shortly after the Seychelles."

(Sound exciting? I used to think so until I saw one young girl who had been dancing all night on a boat in Monte Carlo probably thinking 'Wow this is a good deal, champagne, cool vibes, millionaires, musicians, great party' slowly being marched off and handed over to a hirsute and rather repulsive, corpulent, chap in a white suit with a piratical leer, and earrings. I was overcome with delirium to be alone in my Novotel room drinking tea, fiddling with nothing more than the remote whilst the familiar CNN theme tune played in the background and I was almost trampolining on the duvets celebrating my impecunious though solitary status.)

Enquiring about 'dancers' again, Jo told me of her work on a private MD83 at around about the same time.

Jo: *"There was this group of Russian girls, all being carted around together with one guy looking after them. I took them down from Italy to St Maarten in the Caribbean. Sometimes I would see their true colours, and they were really no more than frightened children. They were all huddled together like little lambs, they'd all had the 'cricket ball' boob jobs, and the necessary cosmetic procedures. About a year later I met that guy who'd accompanied them and I asked after them. He just said that the Arab guy had got fed up with them and just sort of passed them on to someone else."*

Idle Gossip

Jo indulged me with a veritable smorgasbord of bite size pieces of gossip. She had me shaking my head with disbelief sometimes. It struck me just how pretentious, demanding and unreasonable some of these stars can be. Well-known actresses and singers making outrageous demands involving décor, hotel, food and perks for the entourage. The prize goes to the one who made his staff pick out all the brown M&M's because he did not like the colour! Would someone please punch him then send him to the army.

Another world famous and hugely successful American pop star who had been going through a rocky patch was the subject of Jo's next tale. (We'll just call her Miss Case.)

Jo: *"When I was flying her tour, she had so much to drink that she had to be poured off the plane sometimes.*

"I'd give her a bottle of wine and a to go cup when she got off the plane that was for the journey home. Consequently her weight ballooned up and down – something which kept the seamstress busy, who was constantly letting out or taking in dresses when the Diva chose to wear them. I could just imagine:

355

" 'I wanna wear the little black dress tonight.'

" 'Okay Miss Case.'

"Then in a silent frenzy the challenged and overworked seamstress ran for the sewing box, grabbed the unpicker and made hasty work of the darts, then re stitched in super quick time.

"The funniest thing was that when she came on board I had to clap."

This comment just had me covering my nose and mouth in my hands, eyes tight shut in disbelief. It was so well … so ridiculous. And of course Jo who is a natural giggler went into fits remembering *that* bit.

"Yes I had to stand at the top of the stairs and applaud when she walked on board!

"Once she was asleep they wouldn't wake her. The manager would say, 'Don't wake her up! Don't wake her up! You can't put the light on it might disturb her.'

"You see she had to wake up with natural light. The manager, to wake her gently would start rubbing her temples and whispering in that saccharine LA 'therapy class' voice.

"It's okay xxxx (her name) we can work this together ... it's okay, try and wake up."

(I had to chuckle as I remembered being woken up at school by a grimacing matron with large bell!)

"I'd have to cater all three meals," continued Jo. *"Because she never knew what time of day it was, so it could be breakfast, lunch or dinner. She was so often exhausted and she liked me to cut up her grapes for her."*

"No?"

"Yes ... absolutely always into four.

"She liked cheese and biscuits as well, I'd have to keep it in the fridge so it was really cold and I'd have to prepare it meticulously for her.

"She would never appear without make-up and once we landed at Luton in the middle of the night. She insisted on make up going on **just** *in case there were some fans or someone would see her. It was quite sad because she stood on the top of the air stair and the place was deserted, just the ground crew man in the fluorescent jacket, who shouted up 'Do you need a toilet service?'*

"She was very professional and dedicated and would exercise her voice on board with her backup singers. Also she really picked up shortly after that, changed her manager or something and came out of the depression. But my God what a prima Donna."

Don't forget to clap!

'Mummies'

Things happen when women give birth. Thank God nature and instinct have all the necessary tools (hormones and synapses) to suddenly produce lorry loads of love and patience along with the ability to do a job, which would normally be thankless and tiring, with unquestioning gusto and unflagging enthusiasm. Jo told me of her flight with one of the film world's global mega stars, she was without doubt a beautiful Hollywood 'A' list girl with a string of big block busting movies behind her. She had recently given birth. She had become the embodiment of all that was motherly and yielding. Her willowy svelte body, changed into a 'Rubenesque' child bearing unit. Jo took her, her hubby and baby on a trip in Europe.

"Being a very tall girl anyway, she had turned into this huge woman – all boobs and HIPS, wow I couldn't believe it ... really big bum, made us all feel a lot better!" joked Jo actually with affection!

*"Everything now in the whole wide world revolved round the little creature, which of course was already showing talent and insight **way** beyond his two months!"*

"Yes I have seen on a couple on my travels, the 'mega star' turned 'earth mother', they are very happy but they don't so much *talk* to you as *lactate* at you".

Jaylo's Fruitcake

Jo: *"Although she (Ms Lopez) was sometimes undecided what she wanted to eat, one thing she was sure of getting was a beautiful huge fruitcake at the end of the tour. The manager would order a cake on the last day, this cake was enormous and it had her large and impressive logo on the top, it was quite stunning.*

"We'd done about ten concerts, she was fantastic, and the next one was Manchester, the manager said to me 'please get a cake for tomorrow Jo, it's for thirty people and I need the logo on it ...you know like before.

*"We left Milan I had phoned ahead to Manchester asking the handling agent, begging him to sort something out with a **good** baker, this was very important. He said he'd sort it:*

"'Cake with her logo on it, right-oh love leave it wi' me.' This was seven o'clock in the morning and the cake was for that evening. They got back to me and said everything was 'tickety boo', the cake was on order.

"When they delivered the cake it was really light and in a normal sized box. I thought oh my God this is not going to be like the sumptuous expensive luxury fruitcake. I opened it hesitatingly expecting the worst and there it was ... a small cheap sponge cake the sort you have at a kids' birthday party, but they had put a picture of her on the icing. God I was so embarrassed, I was

just dreading presenting this thing. Ben the manager was gay and very intuitive, he asked me if I had the cake, I just said yes, but he knew I was not happy.

"Anyway we took off, the champagne was poured, she took the mike and thanked her dancers and everybody for a successful tour. She was great – a real pro. A few speeches were made. Then lastly they said 'And Jo ... the cake'.

"God, here goes this is going to be embarrassing.

"Then ... Ta deeerr ... I presented her with the cake.

"She looked at the cake and then at me. I was expecting the worst!

"She said words to the effect of: 'Oh my Gaaad, it's got a picture of me on it. That's my face.'

"I was just about to launch into a series of apologies when she whisked it off down the cabin to show everyone this thing of beauty, this work of art – her face on a cake. All I remember was trotting along behind her with the bread knife saying 'I'm so sorry, I'm so sorry'.

"She was delighted. I didn't know whether she was just being kind or if she really liked it – it seemed she loved it".

So, I said to Jo "it doesn't matter what you serve up. As long as it's flattering and massages the ego a bit, you're home and dry".

Mr Mugabe

Robert Mugabe (whose name backwards by the way says 'E ba gum' a famous Yorkshire expression!) yes dear Robert would sleep with his eyes open.

Jo: "We took him, his wife and son on the airbus to Tripoli. I'm sure they thought they were going on holiday. But it was the Africa to Africa conference hosted by Gadaffi. Every year he would send business jets all over Africa collecting presidents and heads of State at colossal expense.

"I accidentally tripped up while he was lying on the bed at the back, I didn't think he was asleep because his eyes were open, but suddenly he jumped, which really surprised me. Then his bodyguard said to me that he sleeps with his eyes open. Very strange I thought. Little Robert junior was busy with the biro all over the beautiful leather upholstery; he was an absolute terror and went totally unchecked."

(Funnily enough another hostess I flew with told me Gadaffi's son was a horror as well – used to buy his way into football teams, and made his bodyguard shoot into the crowd once when he was booed.)

"On arrival in Tripoli we were ordered very aggressively 'OFF' the plane. We had really tried to go to Malta to layover as we had done in 1996 the year before but it was full and they couldn't take us so we got stuck in this god forsaken place. There were all these female military personnel and they were in high heels and sunglasses marching up and down in their uniforms. We were literally held at gun point."

I chuckled with appreciation having been bought up in Africa and being quite familiar with the 'kleptocrats', their predilection for power, that uniformed pomp that self-congratulating swagger. Not forgetting the mirror shades!

"They hadn't sorted out any facilities or rooms for us so we ended up crammed in these hotel rooms together, I remember I was with a crew from a Russian Antanov and an East German crew, one of their hosties went insane and almost leapfrogged over the reception ready to strangle someone. God it was so awful. She was nobly assisted by the formidable Russian purser who was a lesbian. This Russian Captain suggested going back to the aircraft and waiting on board – it would be more comfortable. But there were armed guards with guns who wouldn't let us go anywhere. There were fourteen men in one suite and ten girls in another. Some had been dumped in a government building, they told me later they'd had to sleep in some chairs.

"The poor female soldiers, I saw a few of them flagging with feet tired, but the high heels had to stay on. They had to keep up the bravado.

"In these situations when you're all suffering together you start to make silly jokes to entertain yourself. The big Russian lesbian purser was a good source of entertainment. Angie and I got accosted by two black guys in military uniform in the foyer. But I spun them a yarn when they asked for our room number – I told them the room of the big burley and somewhat fed up racist Russian guys who were at the end of their tether with these Africans. God knows what happened there.

"Our crew had to fly a dignitary back to Benin – he was second in Command (the president himself couldn't come he was busy with an election – wise move eh getting out of this assignment). Then I took the Sierra Leone leader back. We dropped off several dignitaries who all seemed relieved it was over. I vowed to try and avoid Mugabe and to never be rostered for any more of Gadaffi's African gatherings or magical mystery tours! **What** *egos they have!"*

A Plane Full of Bird Poop

Jo: *"The client was from the United Arab Emirates we were on the airbus going from Algeria to Abu Dhabi. They were into falconry in a big way. We had boxes of pigeons (these were for the falcons to chase) then we had these other birds which looked like pheasants. They were beautiful – called flou flous or something like that, they were in string bags so they couldn't move.*

"We put plastic all over the floor but it didn't stop the bird shit going absolutely everywhere. It was like a zoo, I'd never seen anything like it. We had falcons with hoods on flapping their wings, they were perched on stands or on peoples arms. They were fluttering all over the place.

"One of the princes in his white dish dash had a hubbly bubbly with live coals!"

(Some of the little details Jo remembered sure made me chuckle.)

"So it was like a cross between being in Alfred Hitchcock's 'The Birds' and one of those Bedouin tents?" I suggested.

"*Yes yes that's it!*" Jo chirped screwing her eyes up and pursing her lips as she giggled looking not unlike a little budgie herself!

"*People in robes were just wandering around the cabin with birds on their arms. Some were perched on the seat backs and when the plane took off, they all leaned forward in unison with their little tasselled hoods on, and similarly on landing they all leaned back to counteract the forces they were experiencing.*" I found that rather a lovely image.

"*I swear I have never seen that much crap in my life! There was bird shit absolutely everywhere, it was up the walls, all over the seats. It got under the plastic somehow and all over the upholstery, and it absolutely stank.*"

"*Plus they wanted to be entertained, so because the system was down I jokingly suggested to the flight engineer and the other hostess that they should do a dance. Not missing an opportunity to show off a bit, he agreed! It was just hilarious, because he was short and fat with glasses and just started jigging around the cabin, pushing his specs up as they slid down his nose. They turned the volume up on the ghetto blaster and you know what the Arabs are like they love a knees up and a belly dance with all their clapping! So they were cheering and hollering which egged him on. I assured him he'd get tipped but he never did. Meanwhile Dave in the galley was running around giving out meals but because they all kept swapping seats he kept presenting the meal to the wrong person.*

"'*God they all look the bloody same in those outfits', he exclaimed, harassed! To make things worse he had to duck and dive round all the flapping wings of these damn birds.*

"*The birds continued to crap everywhere, we had to get the whole interior industrially cleaned.*

"*That was definitely one of the most bizarre flights of my life!*"

The Russian Porn Star

Jo: "*We picked up a wedding party from St Petersburg and Moscow and flew them down to the Seychelles for the reception. There was a mixture of men and women, when these girls got on board they were already legless, they wore ripped jeans and long fur coats, we'd been told they were movie stars*" (Squawks of laughter from Jo).

"*Well it was my first brush with the mile high club because shortly after take-off they drank a bottle of Chivas Regal (they didn't want glasses ... just the bottle!) then she promptly marched her new hubby off to cavort in the toilets. She described this as the christening of the vows. The funny thing was when she came out she described to all her friends how they'd done it! Everyone cheered.*"

I had to admit I found this a fine example of wedding party team spirit.

Jo: "*I remember empty bottles of Chivas being tossed into the galley. We stopped in Dubai to shop and they bought two suitcases specifically to put all the Chivas Regal in!*
"*They didn't stop partying the whole way down to the Seychelles, there were fourteen of them and boy could they drink! The music boomed out for the entire journey and they were doing their sexy dancing. A couple of them were bonking down the back!*"

I had to admit to Jo they sounded decidedly more animated than some of the poker faced 'stuffed shirts' and villains, we'd both ferried about the place over the years.

"*Oh yes,*" agreed Jo, "*they were certainly out for a wild time, but the bride did get very stroppy and obnoxious towards the end when she was hammered, and was rude to the flight engineer who didn't take kindly to that!*"

"What happened?" I asked.

"*Oh I can't really remember but I did have to stop him using her full length sable as a set of chocks when we got to Seychelles!*"

Fast and Naked!

This little ditty was told to me by a free-lance Scandinavian flight attendant over a drink in the Irish Village Dubai. We'd flown in from Helsinki via Kiev.

We were taking a phenomenally rich businessman and his mistress (one of many)to a New Year's party so when we arrived we unloaded expensive garment bags full of black tie garb ready for the big bash, which would feature celebrities, racing drivers, models and the usual glam entourage.

Anyway we had one evening there – just long enough for this hostie (my new-found friend) to have a drink together. She told me something so funny, I was crinkled.

"*I was flying xxxx (a world champion formula one driver) to some Islands off Africa, when he decided it would be a great idea to take **all** his clothes off.*"

"What d'you mean he stripped off … what everything*?*"

"*Everything!*" she returned with a grin.

"Why?"

"*Don't know he just thought it would be funny since he was so drunk to take all his clothes off.*

"There sure are some lively characters out there; was he with friends?"

"*Yeah he had mates with him.*"

"Did they take their clothes off?"

"*No no just him. Then he asked the Captain to get out of his seat so he could have a picture of himself sitting in the cockpit.*"

My God it puts a whole new meaning on the word!

Roger and the Maid

This story came from Peter an ex-BA Captain. A friend, and man of excellent wit and faculty. He told me of his friend and co-pilot Roger who flew many years ago with him on an Argosy in the Air Force. They had just had a spell in the Elizabeth Hotel in Teheran during which time Roger the co-pilot had enjoyed some horizontal refreshment with the beautiful maid in the hotel. There was a long standing playful feud between Roger and the flight engineer who had been the victim of several of Roger's pranks.

Another crew on the wonderful Vulcan bomber had also been on operations alongside Peter and his Argosy crew. Roger had apparently boasted about his conquests to the Vulcan crew and they sneakily had let the engineer know. In the cruise between Cyprus and Malta everything was going swimmingly and Roger was feeling very pleased with himself, when the engineer chirped up.

"By the way, we need to replace the first aid kit because I gave it to the Vulcan crew before we left."

Peter, being in on the prank, enquired why and the engineer said casually, *"Oh because the boys were telling me they'd enjoyed dalliances with the second floor maid, yes trouble is now they've all come down with something rather nasty."*

"Oh God," said Peter being the master of the practical joke, *"nothing serious I hope."*

"Well apparently, they are calling it the 'Black Syph'! ... and from the sounds of it, it's pretty bloody awful."

Poor Roger just stared straight ahead and was reduced to a loose assembly of slumping limbs. The odd whimper came from him, the colour completely fled from his face and he asked sheepishly if he could be excused his flying duties, he didn't feel up to making this approach and landing.

They can be buggers can't they?

Too Many Drinks Kills the Fish

This tale (of good harmless fun category) comes from my friend Tony, Captain on the Embraer 145 and ex-British European and British Airways. This was told to me late one night in the 'Downtown Hotel' Sophia, Bulgaria in front of, surprisingly one of the finest whisky collections I have ever seen ... In his own words:

I was working for Flybe or British European as it was, in April 2000. I was Captain on the 146 and we were under contract for Air France, so we were a

British European crew doing their flights. We always used to stay in the Copthorne Hotel in Charles de Gaulle (it's the Millennium now). The hosties used to take all the booze off the plane after the last flight and we used to have these room parties.

Well this one night everybody got completely larruped, but especially the first officer who was French, yes I thought with their wine drinking tradition he would have been able to handle it but anyway he was smashed. He then loses his room key – those card things, they are easy to lose, so he decides to go down to the foyer and get another one from reception because he's realised it's time to go to bed. So off he goes downstairs, gets to reception and they issue him with another one. As he turned to try and make it back to the lift (that can be a long five meters when you're seeing four lifts going round and round) he starts feeling very ill and wretches a bit and then realises he's going to have an almighty chunder. He looks round desperately for somewhere to throw up, and sees the mosaic tiled fish pond which is in the middle of the foyer. So he's as sick as a dog into this pond full of very expensive koi. The fish instantly think it's feeding time and all start munching away.

Well guess what? One hour later all the sodding fish are dead. They are floating in the pond … Ah Merde! The management were furious and expelled us from the hotel, two whole crews out on the street at two in the bloody morning. They were *not* happy I can tell you. After a bit of negotiating they let us stay just that night. When I came down later in the morning there were these guys in white coats fishing the dead bodies out and putting them in plastic bags. Oops.

We were never allowed to stay there ever again. Are we surprised?

Too Much $$$$$

These tales came from a couple of friends, both of whom had worked extensively in the Middle East on private jets.

"Wally Bin Tail Chaser as we called him, a very senior Saudi was just SOO rich used to get on board his jumbo, often with a group of Bedouins dressed in their desert robes and he'd make them sit on the floor then he would literally just throw money in the air – lots of it and then he'd watch them scramble for it! It was either the Boeing 777 or the 747 he had both. He would only have female flight attendants and he'd order photos of all of them in three different uniform 'outfits', then he would choose which ones he wanted on the flight".

I interrupted with a "You mean like Miss World and the swimsuit/evening dress/casual …?"

"Yea, a bit like that!"

But something I had *never* heard before even amongst the most advanced stages of ego maniacal brain warp was this: He would demand that **both** aircraft get ready to go – that means fully crewed, fuelled and catered (the cost of this is, believe me prodigious). He would turn up at the airport and stand, looking at both of them and at the last minute decide which one to take.

"Er ..." finger on lip looking from one to the other. *"I'll take the 777 today."*

I asked what happened to the other aircraft – the poor unchosen one!

"Oh the crew had a party and tucked into the catering and then went home laden with goodies."

"If you think that's excessive listen to this:

"I crewed a flight from Dubai to Kuala Lumpar, this particular sheik was an open tap when it came to money. He ordered eighteen of each dish, so I personally unwrapped eighteen beef Wellingtons and eighteen canon of Lamb. When I queried this he explained that he wanted enough in case everyone wanted an 'end' part of the lamb, or the pink 'middle' part – they could all have it. If everyone wanted beef they could have that too. So with eighteen of everything including mezes (two or three of which are sufficient) off we went. Four of them slept the whole way the others picked, it was practically all untouched. He used to like everything cleaned with Evian as well. The jumbo would often take one wife with a friend to New York to buy shoes!

"Once he asked us to 'fly over the boat' so he could take pictures of his flying palace from the deck of his floating palace".

Canine Cruiser

*"Our problem was ... the dog! We were flying the boss's daughter, her boyfriend and her dog. The route was Cyprus to London, but you have to be an approved carrier to take a dog into the UK – we were not one! So she decided to get as near to the UK as possible which was Le Touquet in northern France then ... wait for it ... she ordered a Net Jets plane to take the dog to Biggin Hill. Net jets are approved to carry dogs! But (and this was the bit which had my hands over my mouth) she insisted on a Hawker not a Citation – the latter being too small for precious poochie. **And** she wouldn't lower herself to actually go with the dog on the HS 125 that was too small for her – she sent the chef with the dog, she would stay on the nice big Challenger.*

"So there we are practically in formation going to Biggin Hill, her on my plane and the dog with the personal chef on the other!"

"Did he make little fois gras canapes for the doggie on his journey?" I asked jokingly.

"No it liked Aberdeen Angus."

Well … that told me!

"*This little terrier was indeed, blessed because his owner – aforementioned daughter of big boss, despatched us with the jet to London one day empty to buy five bags of 'IAMS' which is a dog food, and which now, in my mind stands for 'International Airfreight for Mutts which are Spoilt'.*

"*Yes this dog really did get spoilt, not only did it fart all the time (bad ones!) but it used to stand at the bottom of the air stair and if I hadn't put the carpet down (we had a roll-up carpet which we put on the stairs for the passengers) it would stand at the bottom and not budge, in fact he actually shook his head!, he would have to be picked up and carried up the stairs.*"

"Did she look after it properly I mean did she exercise it?" I asked.

"*No not personally she hired a dog walker.*"

As my friend 'P' continued with this catalogue of canine 'carry ons', I entertained amusing images of this dog (I pictured a bull dog) with a diamond collar and bib, sitting, Churchill like, on a big leather chair, tucking into Tournedos Rossini – medium rare, off a Royal Worcester dish on his private jet while the personal chef, in long white apron and large hat raised the St Emillion in one hand then the Chablis premier Cru in the other, enquiring with a raise of his eyebrows as to the hound's choice.

"Wrruff" would go the dog raising his nose towards the St Emillion which would then duly be poured into the lapis lazuli dog bowl. Ah dear me, you have to laugh don't you?

"My God," I said, "was she just allowed willy nilly to use the jet?"

"*Oh God yes,*" said P, "*she said to me once, 'Can you pick us up from Samos?' I said no problem and asked where she was going.*

"*'Kos'.*

"Oh But that's only twenty-five miles away wouldn't it be better to stay on the yacht and go on that?

"'Yea but the seas a bit rough today, I'd rather fly.'

"'Nooh, surely?' I said in disbelief.

"'Swear to God'.

"So we flew bloody miles to pick her up from Samos and fly four minutes over the water to Kos, and she was already on the family yacht which was going there!"

I can just see Ellen Macarthur binning the round the world sail and calling 'coastguard' to fire up the Sea King and come and get her, because there is a bit of 'chop' in the Solent.

So good people of the earth ... when you are nagged about not filling your kettle every time you have a brew, or unplugging your telly at night to help global warming, just remember, there are people out there who don't care one iota if the hole in the ozone gapes like a wizard's sleeve.

A Heavyweight in a Helicopter

(And finally, we are back in the UK for this 'last but not least' little snippet).

This was told to me by my friends at the helicopter charter centre in Surrey where I was a flying instructor. I felt it fitted in rather snugly with the 'too much money' theme.

A very rich media mogul chartered a helicopter for a trip which terminated at Fairoaks. At the end of the days flying a colleague of mine (who worked there) went out to greet the returning passenger and go through the niceties of, "Welcome back, how was your day sir? I hope everything was ok for you ..."

The Captain saw her emerging from the flight centre and as he was shutting down the engines, he drew his fingers across his throat which meant (she found out later) "Don't even think about ever, and I mean EVER, rostering me to fly with this man again in my life because I will NOT".

She put her head in the cabin of the Augusta 109 helicopter and (to quote her) it absolutely stank, the smell almost knocked her sideways. Not feted for his attention to cardio vascular health, he was, shall we say a ... *large* man. She said she'd simply never seen anything like it before. Every single miniature had been opened and emptied, poured into the bar and into the drip tray. All the food had been opened and what hadn't been eaten was squashed and was messed all over the cabin.

"But why?" I asked her incredulously.

"God knows, but that bar and all that catering had been paid for by him 'cause it's included in the price of the charter."

"So what's the …?"

"I guess he must have thought well **I've** paid for it so **no one** else is going to have it."

I couldn't believe it, but she described the mess and the smell and her astonishment at every miniature on board being opened and emptied out! And this guy was in the absolute top league of wealth – he was one of the world's richest men.

God such self-loathing must make you want to kill yourself sometimes.

Bribery with the Bottle

Faroes to Moscow

This story came from a friend, a colleague Shane whilst sipping Limoncello in a piazza in Florence. Quick outline of Shane – he came up flying single crew propeller aircraft such as Navajos. He has won the 'most laid back person ever' prize for twenty years running, all he cares about is being able to smoke his stogie and avoid hassle. He's the sort of guy who would say "Oh was she?" with raised eyebrows if you were to inform him that Joan Collins had been on board for the last two hours. He is a 'fuss free zone' – cares not a jot for celebrity.

*"Well I commonly used to do bloody five sector days out of Humberside and ended up in Northern Norway or something but on this particular occasion I ended up in the Faroe Islands halfway between Scotland and Iceland. It was damn cold and the weather was shite. I flew up three trawler men who were going to court after being busted for fishing with the wrong nets. I ended up being stranded there for blumin days. It was completely fogged out at one end of the runway and the tower wouldn't let me take-off in case of engine failure and you had to come back in – it was just their rules – both ends **had** to be clear. Well the fog hung around for days.*

*"There's of course not much to do up there – I remember the only entertainment being a movie in the town hall or someplace like that – it was a Swedish film (and they're not exactly cheery!) dubbed in Finnish with Danish subtitles or something ridiculous! In the end I got so desperate to leave that I came up with a cunning plan – to bribe the guys in the tower with all the miniatures I had on the plane. Booze is **so** expensive up there you can't afford to have a drink. So when I went up to the tower with this lot, whisky, gin and all the rest, and told them I had to get going, they were over the moon and released me."*

We both agreed that booze on the plane has come in very useful at times. I then told him about the time we'd been grounded in Russia on an exec 727 because the American Captain had forgotten his passport. There was the gimlet eyed Russian autocrat who told us **no way** we were going anywhere (he had the nose for a juicy bribe). However, the Syrian boss instructed me to get the red box – a request which prompted from me: "What... *Thee* red box?" It was the 'imperial' box – large, formal, leather with inlaid fleur-de-lys, and ...**locked**. It housed a priceless bottle of brandy nestling in crimson satin. It had sat in the rear cupboard and never been opened. We handed it over – hands were shaken and we were soon retracting the gear heading west.

Chit Chat in Aerodrome Cafés

We spend vast amounts of time waiting for the weather to clear up, for some part to arrive, or, if we are filming, for *our* next 'bit' to happen. During this time we sit in canteens drinking cups of tea and telling stories. Because of the mix of 'characters', aficionados of war birds, etc., I have listened intently to many a yarn as we've sat in catering buses folding up sugar wrappers into little wands and shepherding the lose grains into tiny piles, chewing on plastic stirrers and laughing really hard while the raindrops plough jaggedly down the window panes.

On a rainy autumn day at North Weald airfield in Essex, I was helping the Aces High team, their Heinkle bomber was involved in some ground shots. We were having lunch on a double Decker bus indulging in colourful conversations – fascinating aviation facts such as the typhoon owner who mysteriously disappeared, they found his blood but not his body.

"What?" I said in disbelief.

"Yep," continued the man in overalls telling the story. "So and so bought the plane from the executors of the will. The guy disappeared about ten years ago, his business partner was suspected of murder, he had a history of foul play and fingers in the till. But they couldn't convict him because there was no body just loads of blood." Gosh, you don't expect such villainy amongst 'Biggles' types.

Then came the story of the Sea Fury that crashed, the Fockewolfe 190 D that was found in perma frost, *this* was a nice story – it landed in a forest, the pilot took some trees out but survived – he got out and walked away having shut the canopy. Fifty years later it was found in the frost, the Russians salvaged it and it went first to a wealthy English owner then to the States – to Paul Allen – the guy with the boat the size of the QE2.

One very feisty Brenden O'Brian was there one day during a shoot and he entertained us with stories of his ferry flights down to the Antarctic as well as his famous truck top landings – his 'party piece' where he would land his tail dragger on top of a moving truck! A likeable rogue with a taste for adrenalin, he had long hair and a swagger, and often appeared with his Harris Hawk on his shoulder! He was a radio ham – often disappearing off to odd places like the Gambia to indulge his passion. He told me about his white knuckle rides in small biplanes over the channel, delivery trips to Antarctica and flying inverted, not forgetting his trips to remote scary super high altitude strips in deepest Africa with fellow nutty chums to practice take-offs in 100 metres in mountainous terrain and get that rush of the near death experience. I've seen him often on television presenting flight programmes. Great pilot and a real card!

Funnily enough, (a quick deviation here) after fifteen years or more I ran into him at White Waltham when I was off with two friends flying to St Mawgan, Cornwall, and he was doing a display check ride for someone. After all the 'long time no see' exchanges, we swapped numbers and he said "If you ever want to come flying give us a bell..."

My birthday came round in December as they do! Should I have a drinks/dinner party only to be let down by those last minute phone calls. "Oh I'm sorry but not feeling well/ just can't shake the cold off/ Lucy is in a netball tournament/ Jeff's in-laws are coming/ Tarquin is a shepherd in the nativity play..." OR... should I go flying? No brainer!

"Hi Brenden, you know you said if I ever wanted to go flying? Well it's my birthday, any chance?"

"Yea great no problem be at North Weald at two o'clock.".

Well on a crisp cold December afternoon he treated me in his little Cessna to a treasure of a flight along the Thames estuary. We discovered we were both avid bird lovers and he flew very low level all along the shore line through flocks of Knots, Curlews, Red shanks and Oyster Catchers. We flew right amongst them banking over steeply, sending hundreds of them into the air, they were right on our wing then they'd settle down further up the river and we'd repeat the process – we were making silly attack sounds ..."ee-OW". Such kids! The winter sun was low over Canary Wharf in the distance, and there was Southend pier – downstream. The light reflected the shallows of low tide where old abandoned barges lay in the muddy waters. Brenden, being only 5% sensible and 95% loony gave me a fun flight, full of 'G' and a lot of whizz! It was absolutely fantastic.

Back to the chit chat...Someone recalled the crash he witnessed at Binbrook in Lincolnshire during the filming of Memphis Belle. It was a B17, part of the first unit, (the second unit was filming at Duxford). There were five B17s up there, two from the States, a couple from France and the 'Sally B' from the UK, what a glorious sight! Americans are used to certain standards while on film sets, vis-à-vis restaurants and a few of them were finding the Grimsby experience a bit, well, 'Grim', especially when the one and only decent French restaurant burnt down.

It was the French plane. A brake had locked during the take-off roll, it swerved off to the right getting airborne momentarily, then number four engine hit a pile of gravel then the left wing hit a tree. It cart wheeled and broke up. The tail flew off, the engines were torn off and it broke in half. Mike Woodley chased after it in his four wheel drive and pulled people out of the wreck.

"Yea I was wading around in what I thought was mud, then suddenly realised it was bloody **fuel!** As we dragged the last person out of the plane, it blew up and exploded. The rescue helicopters an RAF Sea king and a Bristows S76 arrived and ferried the injured to Grimsby hospital. They all survived with various degrees of injury."

My God it really shocked me to think how dangerous some of these shoots can be. Fortunately there were no deaths apart from that of the magnificent ill-fated Flying Fortress.

Visiting the new museum at Duxford, one day I chatted to a guy in the canteen there who told me about the L39 crash. The plane landed too far down and too fast so went on to the M11. The guy in the front panicked and ejected to avoid the trucks but didn't realise they were not zero zero seats, (the ones you can eject from on the ground) apparently you need over sixty knots or two hundred feet to eject. The parachute opened on impact and floated down over his corpse. The guy in the back, the instructor, did not eject and he survived. Very sad incident.

I heard a story about a man in the aviation world who was fantastically mean and horrid – very charming and believable (format for most crooks!) but hugely disliked. How true it was I'll never know, but there *were* allegedly contracts out on him – he'd done dodgy deals in Kosovo, made a movie and snaffled all the money, he had enemies everywhere (no surprise) and had even faked his own death! This was a good 'starter' to the 'main course'– a gritty little tale of people hiring heavies to go and 'cause a bit of agro' after expensive things went missing! Apparently, *this* particular 'heavy' felt maddeningly underutilised and broke out into an anxious sweat if he couldn't pummel someone. If it was just a bit of shouting, and no dislodging of the patellas, he got most upset.

Still all these stories were good preparation for some of the 'teak hard' lotharios I would encounter on the big executive jets later down the road. All very educational.

It's Just 'Plane' Funny
(Gone Crazy – back soon!)

This is a tale from my airline days of the disappearing Flight engineer who fell under the charms of Dublin's fair city where the girls are so pretty. We flew the 727 to Dublin and night stopped. The next day we were to position back as *passengers* on Aer Lingus. "Great", thought everybody, pressure is off. Drinks flowed in the bar that night and many different crews mingled. I chatted to a Danish pilot who put away lots of Carlsberg and told me fascinating tales of his recent stint for the Antarctic survey down at the research station on the ice. I saw our fight engineer Mark (cracking guy and great pal) disappear off with a feisty and slightly mad Irish blonde who was also airline crew - based Dublin. In brief here's what happened.

Next morning no sign of Mark. Our operations call from Gatwick:

"Er, slight change of plan, you guys DO have to fly after all, you must operate back to Manchester"

I knocked on Mark's door, no answer, informed front desk and the receptionist, considering this a piece of gossip **way** too juicy not to get stuck into, giggled, went "Oooo", grabbed the master key and trail blazed over to the lift. The bed was untouched, the case open on the floor....yep, he's done an all nighter! I call his mobile - voice mail, 'oh dear' or words to that effect. I call ops.

"Right, er, one small problem"

"What?"

"No flight engineer"

"What do you mean where has he gone?"

"Downtown Dublin I think with a local lass, cabin crew, he met in the bar last night"

"Well when will he be back, d'you know?"

"Tried him, but not answering his mobile"

"Well what the hell's he doing?"

"Er, ..recovering from an all night Hooley in Dogherty's, snogging Molly Malone, swimming naked in the Liffey, gawd knows - anyone's guess mate but I think Guinness was involved"

"Right I see, I'll have to try and get hold of the standby flight Engineer"

"Yup I think thats a good plan"

Meanwhile Mark had turned his phone on, seen a thousand missed calls and checked in. He 'fessed up' to ops and said in his cheeky northern accent "I don't think there's much chance of me flying back as operating crew!"

I was waiting for him with loaded toothbrush, asprin, a bottle of water and knowing smile when he arrived in a cab looking a bit 'creased'

"Neets, luv, how much **shite** am I actually IN?" he asked with a massive grin in that pure Scouser accent - which he always did for me cos he knew I loved it.

"Well to use turbulence terms, moderate to severe" I chuckled as I helped him get his stuff together. The girls on reception were loving it.

"Good night?"

"Flamin' blinder luv, absolutely brilliant" he said lifting his hand to shield his eyes, and looked skyward with a big exhalation.

A Fresh Engineer flew out, and, and Mark thought a couple of Bloody Mary's down the back would be just the ticket for the 'hair of the dog' and subsequently was quite the hero with his engineer mates - the 'blokes' not the 'stick in the muds' . After a small 'Coffee, no biscuits' tick off from management, all was forgiven, we *had* after all been told to 'stand down' (be off duty) the next day.

Well he certainly had the James Joyce 'Ulysees' experience, and as they say in Ireland for Cheers..... *"Slainte!"*

The Glasses Half Smashed!

This was told to me by my Irish friend who was the flight engineer on the executive 727. He was on board a 727 during a ferry flight back from USA to England. He was not acquainted with any of the crew and in such a situation there has to be a certain amount of trust – you want to rely on each other for high standards of airmanship and professionalism. The aircraft's resident engineer was short-sighted and wore glasses. There was an unfortunate accident during which his specs fell from his pocket and were smashed. There followed a very comical scene which left John with the bewildered expression of a 'You've been framed' victim.

The engineer, now more or less blind, nose scrunched, eyes like slits, fumbled around, for some spare glasses which he did not have. So he found two of those magnifying reading glasses which fold away in their own little plastic sheath. My mum used to have one for reading really small maps in the car. They are about an inch and a half across and the lens is so powerful that you must get very near the print to read it, say an inch or so off – as soon as you move away it's all a blur. Anyway this man proceeds to rip them from their housing, grab the heavy duty grey masking tape and, …yes you've guessed it – stick them to his head! He had to stand most of the time to get his eyes near enough to the panel to read the gauges. You've got to love those engineers, so resourceful; they really can solve any problem! Good job there were no cockpit visits on *that* flight!

Lift is Better than Drag

Some people ask me:

"Have you encountered any prejudice or hard times being a female in aviation?" I have to admit I've had mostly nothing but encouragement, fair play and good friendship. Having said that I admit one of the nicest trips I did was yonks ago with my friend Sally who was flying a twin prop out of Gatwick. We were both in our twenties, newly qualified and she asked me to join her in taking Jason Donovan (famous Ozzie actor and singer) to Amsterdam. The aircraft was very basic, with just flasks of coffee and tea. We told him it was a short flight and we wouldn't be able to offer him any catering service. Well what a tip top chap, he poured the tea himself – and one for us and handed it to us in the cockpit. We had a lot of fun that day and it was good flying with another girlie!

It has been an in interesting journey. Like any walk of life you will get the rather unpleasant scratchy types, the tumescent egos who enjoy that morbid feeling of power as they put you down, score points, or make fellow colleagues struggle unnecessarily. Invariable it is a 'power thing'.

One, in the airline, actually threw the performance manual across the cockpit at me and snarled, "It's your bloody leg, *YOU* do it!" This is after politely asking him if he could fill the take-off card out (his only responsibility as non-handling pilot) because I was busy loading both Inertial navigation systems, doing a load sheet, in fact I never left my seat during this turn around in Sarajevo because I was so busy, *he* meanwhile was outside chatting up the attractive handling agent! He never really got over Pierce Brosnan pipping him at the post as 007.

But when all is said and done the majority of pilots are adventurous and good natured, but one thing is for sure … if it's a gaggle of geese or a flock of birds or a shoal of fish the collective term for pilots should be a 'whinge'! Their theme tune would be symphony in B moaner.

One poor soul I got teamed up with was just so miserable I actually ended up feeling very sorry for him, he moved around under a dark cloud all the time – I hardly needed the weather reports because I knew when he showed up it would be overcast and drizzling. Laughter was a 'long ago' dream and the muscles for smiling had long since atrophied. He was gruesomely dull and unnervingly uncommunicative and when he did speak it was invariably to criticise or moan. We actually ended up friends – I realised it wasn't me he disliked it was just life itself. When he told me he ironed his socks and thought this a worthwhile activity a lot of things fell into place.

Another was actually Buzz Lightyear – I wanted to sing "The universe and Beyond"!! He was the chest thumping egomaniac who looked like he belonged in Robin Hood's band of merry men. He just couldn't hold himself back from telling you all he knew – and that was *a lot!* An ex-fighter pilot – so obviously quite brilliant and *far* better than anyone else, he made sure you knew how many millions of pounds the government had spent on his training – *and rightly so!* With an ego like Andromeda, he was the Adam of Aviation. He was very short and, as we all know, that makes things quite a bit worse. Although really quite fun and chatty and I have no doubt extremely capable, he couldn't help being absolutely wrapped up in his own exceptional aptitude and reminding everyone else how – well, inferior they were. The sort of guy who, even when you were actually tying your noose round an obligingly handy hook to hang yourself, he'd be oblivious, and continue to bang on about flying inverted at mach 3, five feet off the water through a field of icebergs. He suggested in a roundabout way that I should perhaps try tractor driving.

There has only really been one who manifested an unpleasantness of quite a more sinister nature. This was 'small man syndrome' in its most advanced stages. A pusillanimous and peevish little man, disliked by absolutely everyone. Being short and bald made him try to behave in an 'alpha male' manner which of course caused great hilarity amongst us. I read a quote once which said 'no dog barks like the underdog who finds himself on top'. Here we had it. He was sneaky, duplicitous and calculating and his fierce competitive nature made him sly and manipulative. Completely lacking in *real* courage he hid his self-centred intentions behind a false smile.

"I think it's wrong that women are discriminated against in this industry – it must be *so* hard," he once said with palpable insincerity.

A self-proclaimed champion of political correctness, he told someone once who was moaning about fundamentalists in UK that they should go on a diversity course – you rabid Tory! He was cloyingly sycophantic to the point of actually disappearing up the fundaments of rich passengers or anyone in power, while at the same time talking very condescendingly to anyone his junior. He mistook his own obsequiousness for diplomacy and his obvious exploitation as popularity.

When passengers were friendly he saw it as affection, when *really* they *used* him because he would never say 'no'– thereby would exhaust himself by flogging round the world **on** his days off, have minimum rest then fly back … repeatedly!

"Jump!"

"How high sir?"

He didn't mind getting pissed on as long as it was from someone rich and therefore from a great height, because if *they* liked him he *must* be ok. (Obviously hadn't stopped to think that most of those rich 'get there' because they don't care whether you live or die).

I think, we have here a Dickens's Uriah Heep. *But* in fact, he made "ever so umble" Uriah Heep look like a prop forward for England. I used to wonder what he was *all about,* then, one night:

'… Ta Daaa!'– I watched Lord of the Rings and realised one of the illustrators **must** have met him too, because he had been, without doubt the inspiration for Golom.

Born just a bit too late to join Goebbels, Himmler and the boys, I met a bit of a … no … let me rephrase that, a screaming full on Nazi. I'll call him Captain 'N'. Despite being highly intelligent he was spectacularly nasty, although, he *was* the perfect man to deal with difficult or obnoxious passengers. He feared nobody and took no nonsense.(He actually said once on air "I hate the Jews" when puzzled co-pilot looked sideways, he explained that just in case he screwed up the landing he wanted those to be his last recorded words.) He watched me and flight attendants struggle with doors and bags:

"I am surrounded by idiots!" he would sneer sarcastically, feet up on the crew bus, yabbering away on his mobile in German without offering help. Some said he was a touch schizophrenic. He said to me once in the foyer of a hotel.

"If I had a gun now, who would I shoot first?" then he'd sniff the air if there were foreigners about and gleefully go through all the different nations – he could never decide who would be second … the Pakistanis or the French. I of course being female would be high on the exterminate list. He certainly had a dark side. I started to wonder why I always ended up flying with him then I found out that *all* the other pilots had refused to.

He would disappear once we checked in to a hotel; I could never find him. Operations would call me.

"Have you seen Captain XX we can't get through to him?"

I had to say no, so they asked me to push messages under his door. He would then turn up just before check-out telling me about the hookers he'd gone with and how revolting some of them were. I know … odd.

I was kneeling on the cockpit floor once looking through some paperwork

"I love a woman on her knees in front of me," he said. Lucky for him I save my reactions for things which *really* matter in life, and not being one to go crying to the diversity and discrimination board I just turned him into a reliable source of entertainment. Strange feller. I saw him put full power on just as one Captain under training was about to flare, he shouted "Go around" for no apparent reason just to frighten him. He enjoyed that. I wondered how on EARTH someone like that gets into this position of authority. Then I found out, and guess what? It was that old chestnut... MONEY! In brief there was a tax break at the time, for rich owners to register their jets on the Austrian register OE (Oscar Echo), but certain criteria had to be met – an address in Vienna, an Austrian training captain etc. So... realising the lever of his role and his utter indispensability, on came the jack boots and I had a crash course in über weirdness.

"Where did you do your training?" he asked me on day one.

"Paris," I said.

"They are obviously shit."

Lots of little touches of warmth to make you feel *really good.*

"Go and do the walk round and the preflight, he said with a shooing gesture on day one. *This* is supposed to be part of the training, *he* is meant to show me! It was intimidating but of course that's what he wanted.

Some of his ex-colleagues threw a company party in Vienna once to celebrate his departure. He found out and decided to turn up to embarrass them. He smiled sinisterly as he told me; I do believe he was fiercely proud of being hated.

He liked nobody, so I dare say his Christmas card list was not too extensive. I did coax out of him some very interesting and alternative conversations though – he was no slouch (medically and legally trained) *and* I have to say his lack of political correctness was at times bracingly invigorating. *He was certainly* the man to deal with the bastards! But around him, you certainly had to turn down the gain switch on your sensitivity radar.

It happened that the infamous Captain N was assigned to an aircraft belonging to a very famous, high profile, multimillionaire Jewish businessman. Let's call him Mr A. That *was* an interesting dynamic!

This Captain wasn't scared or intimidated by **anybody.**

So ... can you *imagine* the fireworks when two **big male** stags locked horns – the quintessential Jewish business man Mr A and self-confessed Jewish hating bigot. It was gladiatorial. My fellow pilot and colleague K who also worked in the company was sent out on this particular trip as third pilot. The trip was to collect Mr A from Florida.

This is what he told me. Firstly, Captain N booked himself into **thee** most expensive country club where Mr A had his house! – not a good move. K arrived at the airport, and noticed that the £1,800 worth of crockery and glasses etc., which *belongs* to the aircraft had been left (after being cleaned) in Fort Lauderdale! He asked Captain N how he was going to get it all up to the aircraft, answer: he had no intention of doing so. K hurriedly made arrangements for it to be delivered up from Lauderdale.

In the middle of all this kafuffle Mr A turns up with his son having been informed that all the aircraft crockery was 'lost' at the moment. At the bottom of the stairs he said something like

"Which idiot has left all the equipment in Lauderdale" deliberately loud enough for the Captain N to hear. K explained that the stuff was on its way at which point Mr A's son advised K to stay out of it in case it got nasty and come to the back of the aircraft. Then …**show time**… the two male lions on the same hill.

They had a seismic row and the insults were flying. (In fact Captain N told me a few weeks later – never missing an opportunity to relay a bit of agro that Mr A had called him and the rest of the bloody Austrians a pain in the a***.(And the rest!) Then Captain N roared up out of his seat.

"What did you call me?" When Mr A repeated it Captain N reminded him that *he* was in command of this aircraft, and of course *then* Mr A reminded him that *he* was the bloody owner!

Then Captain N declared he'd had enough and growled words to the effect of – Ok if it's *your* aircraft *you* fly it back to London! (If there had been keys to throw *that* would have been the moment.) With that he grabbed his bag, got off and started walking back to the terminal … Oh Dear! Then the 'sue' word was mentioned, Mr A shouted after him – if he dared do this he would never fly another aircraft again. *This* was definitely the sort of fracas which a bear baiting crowed would have paid good money to watch. Mr A then spoke to the co-pilot urging him to explain to Captain N the consequences of his action and he meant business. He duly went after him, ten minutes later Captain N arrived back and mutinously agreed do the flight to London, but then *that* would be **it**!

The flight took place under – should we say a bit of an atmosphere. At Stansted as soon as Captain N shut down the engines he deliberately walked off the plane *before* Mr A disembarked (for maximum insult) and he disappeared! I think a tip was out of the question! Male egos eh?

The Day a Helicopter did an Emergency Landing in my Garden!

There have been so many 'you've gotta be kidding me' stories from people I've met, but you just cannot include them all. For example the story told to me by the flamboyant and utterly crazy Simon Oliphant Hope who flew around the world solo in a luminous orange Hughes 500 E helicopter. I interviewed him with a little tape recorder and was frankly blown away with his descriptions of crossing vast swathes of hostile Siberia and the Baring Straights. His story deserves a book to itself. Anyway…the point is, that he picked me up in his helicopter from my garden, when I interviewed him, and obviously remembered where I lived.

Years later…

It was the snowy blizzard of Christmas 2009. I was sitting in my front room watching telly, the snow was falling – it was FREEZING. England had come to its customary halt with this inclement weather. It was the afternoon and I was settled on the sofa for a night in. I heard the sound of a helicopter overhead and thought 'Oh it's Sheik Maktoum of Dubai' who lives about 3 miles away on the other side of the main road. We hear his helicopter all the time. He has to live near Ascot because of his love of horse racing. I thought he must be off to Newmarket or somewhere for a Christmas race meet. But the sound got louder and louder. The snow was coming down like huge crazed white moths in the swirling chill wind. The grey cloud was menacingly low and the mist was rolling in – it was a grim day. Then I realised this was NOT an overfly, someone was hovering very low and VERY near, in fact it sounded like overhead my lounge. Then the thrashing blades got so loud I couldn't hear the telly and I thought bloody hell someone is crashing into my house! I instantly thought of that phrase, 'if helis are safe – why are there no vintage helicopter fly-ins?'

I ran to the door to see a huge burgundy coloured and strikingly beautiful helicopter hovering inches above my lawn sending the snowflakes into a frenzy! It was an Augusta 109, a seriously flashy, all leather, big cabin, top-notch, well-equipped, super sophisticated, machine worth millions.

Once the blades had stopped rotating and the 'cool down' was over. The door popped open – out jumped Simon.

"Hey Ho sweetie, so sorry about this, tried to get through at Biggin, tried to get across the zone, just can't get through anywhere too much icing, too dangerous. I'll have to leave it with you– couldn't call us a cab could you – got a meeting to get to."

It WAS nearly Christmas Eve so I couldn't resist a little Christmas cheer:

"Oh Simon – that is such a gorgeous gesture – but *YOU COULD HAVE PUT A BOW ON IT FOR ME* !"

Helicopter in my garden after emergency landing in blizzard.

Mike Woodley's crash in Beagle 206 off Corfu

**Goodwood –
Always a great day
out!**

Vickers Vimy – First plane to
cross the Atlantic.

Those 'Catch me if you can' Pan Am days.

The rare and elegant Spartan Executive.

Final Reflection: Our Beautiful Planet

Let's celebrate this sphere of strange beauty and wonder which we all call our home – planet earth.

There could so easily have been nothing … but there is all this… and IT'S GOOD! During whatever crazy cosmic games were played back in time, the truth is we threw a double six. So here's why:

1. The other great 'rock' which collided with us also had liquid iron core – so, we got magnetism, bird migration, navigation, protection from solar wind, Northern Lights.
2. Our moon was created – stability, tides, climate regulation (without it we'd tilt chaotically under the gravity of Jupiter or the sun).
3. The 23 degree tilt – seasons, migration, diversity.
4. Our crust was the right 'thinness'– shifting plates, mountains, rift valley, new habitats. Volcanoes formed because molten rock burst through this thin crust, this was accompanied by nitrogen and carbon dioxide – the basis of our atmosphere. With that came the glorious WATER VAPOUR, which condensed to form oceans where life began 4 billion years ago.
5. We are just the right distance from the sun which along with the abundance of water sustains life here for us lucky inhabitants!.. And so it goes on. We are the living, breathing, joyously celebrating, consequence of good and I mean REALLY *good* luck.

When people ask me what life is like as a 'jobbing pilot' there *is* genuine curiosity, particularly about the training but more so about the passengers. Folks like to know what the PM ate for breakfast, how Joan Collins looked, why Hugh Grant had a tantrum! When all is said and done we are just delivering these people from A to B safely in a fast airborne taxi and have fairly limited interaction. Without doubt the biggest 'gift' for me has been the privileged glimpse this job has afforded me into the treasures of our world. I am grateful for the financial success of my passengers because it means I have seen this world from a special place … from 'a Bird's-eye view'.

Yes the private jets are beautiful and often filled with stars and millionaires from all over the world. When all is said and done, if Posh has a few pimples or someone is 'much shorter' than we thought – it's all very 'so-whatish'. Notwithstanding the gloss and the froth, the cherry on the cake, is what I actually *see* out there, the unique exposure I have to the workings of our atmosphere. There are sights of just such staggering beauty it makes the soul sing. When I stare in awe at the splendour and magnificence of the planet I think –wow I'm glad I made it here! Aren't I lucky? That hard earned seat is a window onto the inexhaustible energy and ever changing face of our small spinning Earth. It never ceases to amaze me just what a show can be put on when photons, water particles, magnetic fields, electrons, dust, celestial bodies, winds and a bit of interesting meteorology come together and you fly through it all at five hundred miles an hour. We get that rare glimpse of just how magical and curious things can be.

Here are a just a few 'good moments'.

Coming out of Seville early one evening I saw a low moon that was of the deepest red; a soft red, like a gigantic cherry. It was below me in the sky rising behind a craggy, dusty mountain range and I looked *down* on it. In the same moment I had the disappearing sun sinking away in the west. Slowly the moon rose to become the familiar opalescent orb gazing down on us, but its nascent stages were indeed lovely – a frayed edged ball emerging from below and glowing through the dust.

Staying with moon, and all her protean guises. I've seen it as a barely visible fingernail then as a shiny, painted dinner plate with beaming smile. Sometimes it is the pointy chinned jester sideways on. Sometimes it is strangely yellow like a big crumbly Wensleydale cheese. We are fortunate indeed to have a moon. She lights our dark wintry evenings and, for millennia helped our distant ancestors while they trod quietly, spear raised, hunting for food. She is a friend to the moping owl on cloudless nights and a guardian of secrets for the baying wolf. She endows our oceans with endless productivity, her silent but inexorable powers have turtles scuttling up beaches to lay eggs on a *particular* night and reproductive cycles ticking away like metronomes in all corners of the world. She is the great maestro conducting the symphony of ebb and flow around our magnificent shores.

Another striking sight was the top half of a 'slice' of moon. It was silvery, only the top was visible, nudging out from some low cloud. Again it was well below me so the picture it created was of a shark's fin protruding from what looked like the sea. The *giant 'silver finned'* shark. It also looked like a luminous, billowing sail on a yacht, cruising across a vast silvery ocean. It's fun to *use* the imagination, it creates another reality which somehow engages our higher self with unimpeded energy. Where would we be without a sprinkling of imagination? it is the stardust which stirs and invigorates us, connecting us to the magic. All these sights whether it is the moon, or the dawn at forty thousand feet or a strange cloud; they are, some might say, just the 'common face' of nature – but add a little imagination and suddenly we have a world of infinite possibility which can transport us, put us in an exalted mood! With a bit of vision we can pass beyond the ordinary into the transcendental thanks to that capacity to fashion our own world and engage with the mysteries of life. Looking out from that cockpit window has given me infinite possibility on the interpretation of our natural phenomena (and has made me realise how small we are out there!).

I have seen the rise of a star (maybe a planet) which, when still on the horizon glowed and wobbled like a jelly. The two of us have stared and been unable to identify exactly what it was – this throbbing dot sort of deliquescing in front of us which actually changed colour from green to rose to white then back again. At first it resembled an aircraft because of the flashing light but when we saw that it wasn't moving relative to us, we realised it was some celestial body, but so unusual in its ascent. Eventually it rose high in the sky to become a stable white dot but its early minutes near the horizon were truly a fascination. It was like a multicoloured jellyfish.

Dawn at forty thousand feet is always a feast for the eyes. It is that thin, straight and very defined line of tangerine and indigo that stretches across the horizon and a couple of brilliant white stars still twinkle like diamonds in a navy blue night sky. It's quite a spectacle and it gets me every time! In exactly the same way the departing sun can be an equal show stopper. I love to watch it disappear over the horizon like an elegant liner bound for the 'Americas' leaving flecks of gold in her wake. Sometimes you get that incredible glow for a few moments afterwards – when the world seems to turn into a great ripe cantaloupe melon.

Clouds... where do I start? They are intimate friends and a never ending part of any pilot's life. Their variety is infinite, their motion, the ultimate celestial dance. Sometimes choppy, rebellious and violent, sometimes silent drifting and meditative. Clouds pass over nations, oceans and continents, unaware of boundaries, owned by no one, billowing, detached and free. They have inspired poetry throughout the ages, like these lines from Shelley:

I am the daughter of Earth and Water,
And the nursling of the sky
I pass through the pores, of the ocean and shores
I change but I cannot die.

Electrical storms are an old favourite; no log book is complete without those! Italy in the summer is normally a good time to catch them, or anywhere the cumulonimbus is rising as high as forty-five thousand feet. You can see the clouds bubbling up like exploding cauliflowers, and if you are flying at night, the light show is tremendous. Every so often the whole sky will become completely lit up for a split second, so from seeing very little, suddenly you see the entire outline of the gigantic, riotous clouds. Powerful coruscations come from deep within them so that they become gargantuan light bulbs flashing on and off. It is quite surreal. In these circumstances, pilots request changes of heading, to take avoiding action. The controllers naturally do what they can to accommodate you but if you do venture too near one, the turbulence is monstrous and sometimes quite frightening, the power can blow the flaps off the trailing edge of a wing! We must stay well away.

Taking off from Moscow one night in a Boeing 727-100 en route to Kuwait, the whole of the outer pane of my windshield fractured into tiny veins. It resembled the lattice work on a dried leaf – the window consists of a vinyl layer sandwiched between an outer and inner pane. It is the inner which is the primary load carrying member. Fortunately it was my outer pane which cracked (the inner has much more cabin pressure bearing outward on it, therefore it is more critical and the cabin differential would need to be reduced). It was extremely unnerving though, flying along with a smashed window in front of you – it had been caused by a short in the heating filaments. Then came St Elmo's fire, which really turned it into something very eerie and other worldly. Threads of indigo and deepest violet were snaking all over the windshield. Little fires, like those on top of your Christmas pudding were dancing and exploding all over the glass. It was quite bewitching.

The next time I experienced St Elmo's fire (which can happen any time – not just with a shattered windscreen) was decidedly more shocking. The usual blue light was snaking and dancing all over the screens but suddenly a fireball shot straight through the window down the aisle and out of the rear of the aircraft. Now *that* was indeed spooky. It is a strange phenomenon occurring when the atmosphere becomes charged and an electrical potential becomes strong enough to cause a discharge between the object (in our case, our aircraft) and the air around. Ship's masts have been known to experience this on their tops. The amount of electricity involved is not considered dangerous; however, this is why we have static wicks on the trailing edges of our wings – for discharge. It's the sort of visitor we don't want hanging around in the cabin, no matter how fascinating! A colleague, Peter Shaw told me of a lightning strike that came through the window along the central consul, down the metal rails of the flight engineer's seat, up his desk and through his pencil, which split in half and flew out of his hand!

I feel my life is richer for having seen the 'Grande Dame' of all light shows – the aurora borealis or Northern Lights. Although I saw them en route to western Ireland one winter by far the most dramatic sighting happened whilst working in the airlines, en route from Gatwick to Keflavik (Iceland) in winter. That night was a 'ten', it was utterly unreal, quite amazing, and the image will stay with me forever. I saw actual wavy curtains of shimmering fuzzy light, it was as though the atmosphere was folded and was swaying in the wind. Shafts of silver and green came down like celestial rods. The thing which really astounded me was that you never got any nearer, I felt we were flying towards it and eventually would penetrate it as you would a cloud, but despite it being just **'there'** … it is illusory like the rainbow, it was never *really* **there**, quite mysterious, so distant and intangible. It is a fascinating phenomenon when electrons and protons from the sun get trapped high above the earth's atmosphere then get channelled to the polar regions by the earth's magnetic field. The charged particles enter our atmosphere and collide with air molecules thus exciting them into luminosity. It often happens during sunspot activity or magnetic storms. God does give us a generous sprinkling of magic doesn't He? *That* trick is called 'fun with photons'. When things get you down it's worth remembering the magic and – it's all free!

If there was ever an interplanetary beauty contest, like a Miss Universe for locations, Earth's entry would have to be Iguazu Falls on the border of Argentina and Brazil. I was lucky enough to walk round and fly over it. Nowhere encapsulates the magic and abundance of this world with such style. Billions of gallons of water tumble every second, thunder roars, cool mist enshrouds the vivid colours of ancient rock and rainforest which is teeming with bright toucans. Gigantic dragon flies hover in the mist, and giant condors soar lazily overhead in a brilliant blue sky, then... the whole scene is framed with multiple rainbows.

Early morning over the Alps is a winner. After 'ridiculous o'clock' starts from Gatwick, we were often over the Alps just before 7 a.m.. We flew south across France toward Geneva and into the mountains and were met with a scene of indescribable beauty. Just the tips of the peaks were lit by the pinks and reds of the rising sun. The mountains look like giant mango ice cream cones. The Matterhorn stood like a mighty monument gesturing into the cloudless, baby-blue sky, and the surrounding mountain tops were covered with creamy apricot snow gleaming in the sun. The light of dawn is a special light – clean and citrus. We regularly cruised over the vast awesome landscape of basins and peaks, which are our treasured Alps. Because of their great height, we are nearer to the land. There is a feeling of closeness and the sight of these ancient grandees of the earth has my forehead pressed against the window every time.

Shooting stars, roaming satellites, cities at night which look like huge bejewelled cobwebs, delicate cirrus – ice crystals high in the troposphere, looking like angels wings and the weird luminosity of the aurora Borealis; it is all out there. Now that the vertical separation has reduced to one thousand feet between aircraft in opposite directions, it is quite a sight when a massive jumbo jet or airbus 340 goes straight over your head at what looks like a thousand miles an hour, then you fly along underneath the contrails like four mighty tunnels lit in the bright sunlight. They are strong and thick at first then peter out into swirling circles of misty, rotating vapour. Some are perfectly formed circles like a smoke ring.

Flying over the North Sea at night is always enchanting because of the flickering fires of oil rigs. They stand like beacons in the watery darkness. Sometimes the moon pours a silvery light over the dark black sea. From my seat the rigs are little spots of light but I am cognizant of the amount of industry and hightech activity going on aboard those platforms. What a strange thought, all those men on that tiny space, beavering away in the middle of the ocean. I imagine the unrelenting noise of the great clanking drills and heavy machinery. I spare a thought for the divers; poor guys having to plunge into that heaving freezing water and troubleshoot problems below the surface. Of course when *they* look up at *us* they also see no more than a small cluster of lights, red green and white, moving across the night sky. Funny though, both little spots of light are harbouring millions of pounds worth of 'state of the art' equipment, specialised instruments, avionics, and outstandingly clever gadgetry invented by *very* brainy people in lofty, well-funded technical institutes round the globe. Folks who have more mental acuity and vision in a thimble full of brain than I could ever have. Let's be grateful for their assiduous work and invention. We just operate it – *somebody* actually thought of and created it.

England on a calm summer morning has a special grace. Whilst based at Gatwick, early departures were common. The morning sun is such a purifier, rinsing everything out into a brand new shiny day. I recall the Westerly departures where the route takes you straight ahead and then turns you south after a few miles towards Southampton or SAM, as it is fondly known. The gear comes up and the power is reduced for noise abatement and then we cruise at about five thousand feet until Air Traffic give us a further climb. This is a wonderful opportunity to see the splendour of the English countryside on a summer's morning. We fly over the top of Dunsfold (where the Harrier jump jet was assembled and tested); to the right is the elegant ridge of high land, with lovely houses perched on the south-facing slopes. The towns of Dorking and Reigate nestle at the foot of the ridge. To the left the sea gleams like molten silver. Ahead, in one big expansive picture (and it only happened once!) I saw three cathedrals; Chichester, Winchester *and* way in the distance, Salisbury cathedral with its unmistakable spire towering into the sky. The M3 motorway snakes its way down to the south coast and the M4 continues straight ahead towards the Cotswolds and Bristol. To the north I could, sometimes *just* make out the large cluster of cooling towers at Didcot in Oxfordshire; a special place for me, since that's where I went to Flight School. When the visibility is this good, you know a bliss which is rationed and *must* be savoured. You can spot the runways of Farnborough, Lasham and Middle Wallop and the big round golf balls of Oakhangar. Soon the rippling and intricate coastline around Hayling Island and Portsmouth is beneath us and I'd always try and spot HMS Victory in its berth. Thank you Nelson!

The scene is peaceful and serene; sometimes you'd glimpse an early riser walking the dog on the sands of West Wittering near the meandering inland waters around Chichester. The little boats – people's dreams come true, would all swing round together in the ebb tide – their sterns to the sea. They'd be scattered along the glimmering estuary. Small white sails dot the water around the Isle of Wight; the first ferry ploughs along towards Cowes. The impressive round forts stand immutable in the Solent, our defences against Napoleon, one of them has a helicopter pad on it. We'd turn south towards the Isle of Wight clocking the long sandy beach at Bournemouth and lovely harbour of Poole off the right wing. The white chalk of Harry's Rocks in Dorset lead off into the Purbeck hills, the start of our famous Jurassic coast. We get cleared direct to *Ortac* – our navigational point out at sea, this takes us towards the Channel Islands where we change frequency to Brest control in France. I find myself looking forward to seeing the whole scene again that night when we would return and the lights will be twinkling in the dusk.

Ah England, I love her with all my heart. I feel blessed to be from this land – a special country. Shakespeare was spot on when he enthused: "this sceptered isle … this precious stone set in a silver sea". Each time I fly home and cross our coast at Hastings, Southampton or the Thames Estuary, I think of all things English – Mini Coopers with union jack paint, comedy programmes on the Radio full of incisive verbal quip and laughter, village fetes, fish 'n' chips; our many satiric wits like Ian Hislop and Monty Python. Costume dramas on BBC, country pubs, Big Ben, James Bond, Blenheim Palace, Steve Wright in the afternoon, cider by the cricket green. I think of country houses with the odd mad folly, elegant topiary and backlit butterflies on herbaceous borders, fat bumble bees crawling like little babies into roomy pink foxglove hoods, tea rooms with homemade cake. Gnats hovering over the river, canal boats, Sunday lunch, Fools and Horses, outdoor concerts with brollies going up (but no grumbling!),frosty winter mornings … and so much more. Each return into our airspace after a few days away, is like coming back to a good friend (and of course – to a decent cuppa!).

We are treated on most of our 'home legs' to a glimpse of the famous White Cliffs, I thank those boys who, in their spitfires and Hurricanes endured tense and furious battle. God, the fear in their hearts; max rate turns, heat, noise, white knuckles, flying for your life, hacking around in cloud and bad weather, not knowing if a bullet would send you plummeting to your death any minute! Pilots of undaunted pluck and verve, who defended us and died for us. I think of all those brave girls (and they were no more than girls) who worked tirelessly and courageously for the Air Transport Auxiliary based at White Waltham during the war. They would literally be handed a manual on a Spitfire or a Lancaster bomber "Here, make sure you read this" and off they'd go. These women definitely came from the 'Getonwithit' era. I read the obituary of one such woman in the paper, she was caught above cloud and had no instrument experience so couldn't let down. She considered bailing but felt uncomfortable because of her skirt! She ended up picking up a signal from a beacon, made contact with the ground and was highly praised for a brave and daring descent and cloud break. There are many inspirational stories of inexperienced girls delivering high performance planes for the war effort. I like the one about the girl who used to take the scenic route in her Spitfire via Cornwall to see her lover. They were extraordinary women and exemplify the achievements that can be made when fuss is kept to a minimum and gritty, determined people are allowed to just get on with it. Good on them!

The privilege of seeing other cultures and other countries is no less important. There have been countless **'special'** moments while wearing this uniform. Tramping through a moonlit Siberian wood, racing along through the busy streets of Delhi in a taxi, swerving to avoid cows, watching the June sun flood into my bedroom at midnight in northern Finland, sitting in a big old tractor being driven to the airport in Ireland, bouncing across the lagoon at sunup in a Venetian water taxi, stopping the cab en route to the hotel in Phuket, to give away trays of delicious surplus catering to some roadside vendors, they smiled, put their hands together … "Kop koon kaa!"

The aeroplane is a marvellous thing, enabling us to make deep reaching shifts in our lives, to displace us albeit momentarily to an entirely new landscape and boundless possibility. It can help us overcome feelings of isolation and inertness, free us from the commonplace. The sheer bulk and size of an aeroplane always had me nagging my parents. "But **how** does it stay up in the air … how…? Why?" Even after the study of aerodynamics, it has not divested any of the astounding magic from this machine, its unlikely nimbleness and never-ending 'motion'. How can such a massive, weighty, seemingly earthbound object become an exemplary symbol of escape, and moreover overcome gravity so successfully. It has been a long assiduous journey by many great brains! I love to visualise brothers Orville and Wilbur lying on their backs in the grass for hours staring at the wheeling gulls soaring in the sun – what inspiration they found there and how they acted upon it.

The book *Jonathan Livingston Seagull* was a great read for me while I was learning. I couldn't put it down – it affected me profoundly, I loved it. Here's one last quote from it:

"How much more there is now to living! Instead of our drab slogging forth and back to the fishing boats, there's a reason to life! We can lift ourselves out of ignorance, we can find ourselves as creatures of excellence and intelligence and skill. We can be Free! We can learn to *fly*."[4]

---

[4] Bach, p. 27.